An Open Design for Computer-Aided Algorithmic Music Composition: athenaCL

by

Christopher Ariza

ISBN: 1-58112- 292-6

DISSERTATION.COM

Boca Raton, Florida
USA • 2005

An Open Design for Computer-Aided Algorithmic Music Composition: athenaCL

Dissertation.com
Boca Raton, Florida
USA • 2005

ISBN: 1-58112- 292-6

An Open Design for Computer-Aided Algorithmic Music Composition: athenaCL

by

Christopher Ariza

A dissertation submitted in partial fulfillment

of the requirements for the degree of

Doctor of Philosophy

Department of Music

New York University

September, 2005

Advisor: Elizabeth Hoffman

Acknowledgments

Thanks foremost to my parents, Deborah and Augusto Ariza, for their boundless faith, encouragement, and support over the many years of my studies. Thanks also to my brother, Philip, and the rest of my family for their support. Much gratitude to Shruti Mahindrakar for her encouragement, solace, and patience over many years.

My work in computer music, and the existence of athenaCL, are directly the result of the teaching and encouragement of my advisor, Elizabeth Hoffman. Had she not given me access to new tools, today I would likely have only graphite and paper. Had she not encouraged the development and presentation of athenaCL, today I would have a bundle of incomprehensible code fragments. Her comments on my compositions, papers, and this text have been invaluable. For these reasons and more, I am particularly grateful for her dedication and support over the duration of my graduate education.

It is difficult to imagine how I could have completed this document had it not been for the teaching and experience of Paul Berg. His seminar in algorithmic composition, as well as our many conversations, helped me to refine many of my ideas, to lead me in better directions, and to ask better questions. His assistance with the literature, the history of the Institute of Sonology, and this text were a great benefit. His AC Toolbox provided numerous valuable ideas for refinements of athenaCL. I am very grateful for the time he devoted to helping me with this project.

Thanks to Robert Rowe for his assistance and advice with my previous research and this text. Additional thanks to Jairo Moreno, David Burrows, and Louis Karchin for serving as committee readers. Thanks to Ruth and Gottfried Michael Koenig for their hospitality, time, and conversations. Thanks to the following people for discussing their research: R. Lundbeck, Max Mathews, and John F. Sowa. Thanks to Nicole Falque (Shell Coordination

Centre S.A., Monnet Centre International Laboratory, Louvain-La-Neuve, Belgium), Lida van der Horst and Anneke Schelvis (Shell Global Solutions International B.V., Shell Research and Technology Centre, Amsterdam, the Netherlands), and Nicole Simpson (The New York Public Library, New York) for research assistance. I am also grateful to the anonymous reviewers of the 2005 International Computer Music Conference (ICMC) for comments on an article derived from components of Chapter 3 (Ariza 2005b).

Thanks to my composition teachers for wisdom and guidance over the course of my education: Mario Davidovsky, Michael Gandolfi, Elizabeth Hoffman, David Horne, Louis Karchin, and Jeff Nichols. Thanks to Joseph N. Straus for inspiring many of the theoretical components of athenaCL, as well as many valuable discussions concerning nomenclature, post-tonal theory, and his voice leading model. Much gratitude as well to Jacob T. Schwartz for suggesting, many years ago, that I work in Python rather than C. Thanks to the faculty and administration of the New York University Graduate School of Arts and Sciences Music Department for their flexibility in letting me pursue my academic interests. Particular thanks to Rena Mueller and Pauline Lum, as well as former and current department chairs Gage Averill and Michael Beckerman. Also, I am grateful for the department's support of the Washington Square Computer Music Studio, graduate course offerings in Computer Music, and the Electro-Acoustic Music concert series; all were essential for promoting my research and music.

Thanks to the United States Fulbright program, the Institute for International Education (IIE), and the Netherlands-America Foundation (NAF) for providing funds and support for my work at the Institute of Sonology in Den Haag, the Netherlands. My work and research at the Institute, as well as its students, faculty, and technical resources, were of great importance for this text, my software, and my work as a composer.

Thanks to the following people for reading early versions of this document and providing comments: Augusto Ariza, Rachel Coupe, Paula Matthusen, and Red Wierenga. Thanks to my colleagues at New York University, particularly those that took the trouble to, early on, investigate, learn, and provide comments on athenaCL: Sean Carson, Ryan Dorin, Paula Mattheson, Jonathan Saggau, Jesse Sklar, and Juliana Trivers. Special thanks to the numerous unnamed persons who have supported athenaCL over the course of its development, through downloads, links, and comments. Additional thanks to my friends around the world for putting up with my ramblings about algorithmic composition for so many years, and often offering valuable advice or respite.

I am grateful to the following libraries for providing research materials and quiet spaces necessary for the composition of this text: the Library of the Courant Institute of Math and Sciences and the Elmer Holmes Bobst Library, New York University, New York; the Langson Library and the Science Library, University of California Irvine, California; the Music Division of the New York Public Library for the Performing Arts, New York; the Centraal Bibliotheek Den Haag; the Openbare Bibliotheek Amsterdam; the Universiteit Leiden Bibliotheek; and the Koninklijk Conservatorium (Instituut voor Sonologie) Bibliotheek, Den Haag. Finally, I am grateful to the authors of the open-source software tools that were used in the production and typesetting of this text: DocBook, OpenJade, Python, and ImageMagick.

Abstract

This dissertation introduces a new design for a computer-aided algorithmic music composition system. Rather than exploring specific algorithms, this study focuses on system and component design. The design introduced here is demonstrated through its implementation in athenaCL, a modular, polyphonic, poly-paradigm algorithmic music composition system in a cross-platform interactive command-line environment. The athenaCL system offers an open-source, object-oriented composition tool written in Python. The system can be scripted and embedded, and includes integrated instrument libraries, post-tonal and microtonal pitch modeling tools, multiple-format graphical outputs, and musical output in Csound, MIDI, audio file, XML, and text formats.

Software design analysis is framed within a broad historical and intertextual study of the themes, approaches, and systems of computer-aided algorithmic composition (CAAC). A detailed history of the earliest experiments, as well as analysis of the foundational CAAC systems, is provided. Common problems and interpretations of CAAC are then presented in a historical and intertextual context, drawn from the writings and systems of numerous composers and developers. Toward the goal of developing techniques of comparative software analysis, a survey of system design archetypes, based on seven descriptors of CAAC systems, is presented. With this foundation, athenaCL system components are analyzed in detail. System components are divided into abstractions of musical materials, abstractions of musical procedures, and system architecture. For each component, object models, Python examples, and diagrams are provided. Further, each component is given context in terms of its compositional implications and relation to alternative and related models from the history of CAAC.

Table of Contents

List of Examples

Chapter 1. Principles and Methods

1.1. Introduction

The object of the present volume is to point out the effects and the advantages which arise from the use of tools and machines;—to endeavour to classify their modes of action;—and to trace both the causes and the consequences of applying machinery to supersede the skill and power of the human arm.

—Charles Babbage (1832)

1.1.1. An Open Design

Techniques of algorithmic composition have been applied in European concert music for centuries. Implemented in computer software, however, these techniques have expanded into systems of music representation and production. Unlike software for sequencing, mixing, or notation, these systems are often diverse and innovative, breaking with traditional musical paradigms of meter, part, or score. These systems expand compositional resources, and offer diverse models of compositional design. Computer-Aided Algorithmic Composition (CAAC) refers to the use of these systems. The design of a new CAAC system, athenaCL, is the focus of this dissertation.

Software systems for CAAC emerged in the late 1950s and early 1960s, notably with the first experiments of Robert Baker, Lejaren Hiller, Leonard Isaacson, Max Mathews, and James Tenney in the United States, Pierre Barbaud and Iannis Xenakis in France, Gottfried Michael Koenig in Germany and the Netherlands, and Rudolf Zaripov in the Soviet Union. Since then numerous CAAC systems, employing a variety of algorithms, interfaces, and designs, have been created. Often such systems, though employing common models and architectures, are individual and creative.

It is an error to think of algorithmic composition as the replacement of humans with music-writing machines. The techniques of algorithmic composition are employed at a great variety of compositional levels, often in a complex mixture of algorithmic procedure and human choice, and always bound by the musical interpretation of a human composer. The levels and mixture may be so intermingled as to make crisp distinctions impossible. Often, a composer's original materials are modified by composer-designed processes. Often, the composer is expanded, not removed. Fixed materials, algorithms, and the tuning of algorithms all become compositional materials.

This dissertation introduces a new design for a computer-aided algorithmic composition system. Where much research has focused on the application of particular algorithms, this study is concerned primarily with system design. The design introduced here is demonstrated through its implementation in athenaCL, a complete software system for computer-aided algorithmic composition. This software is compared to historical precursors and is shown to offer advantages in design, user experience, and development model. Design of software components will be analyzed in detail, exposing object models and interaction, system organization, and compositional implications.

The design of athenaCL is based on the premise that any musical structure (imagined or found), taken at a small enough temporal window, may be algorithmically generated by a highly specialized procedure. If a musical structure of a given duration eludes algorithmic implementation, a shorter duration will succeed. This claim is difficult to refute. At the extreme of the smallest temporal window possible, a single complex musical moment, algorithmic implementation is always obtainable.

This claim asserts that given a musical structure within a sufficiently short temporal window, a specialized procedure can produce a similar structure that, even with algorithmic variation, will maintain the musical identity of the source. For any found or imagined musical moment, an infinite number of variants is available. These variants may offer subtle alterations of musical parameters such as timbre, amplitude, pitch, or timing, or more drastic alterations of event configuration. These variants, each unique, form a family of alternatives that may retain both the identity and the local or global musical significance of the source. A highly specialized procedure may be developed to produce one or more of these variants.

The design theory presented here advocates incremental, bottom-up tool development within a common environment. Bottom-up algorithmic composition, as defined by Eduardo Reck Miranda (2000a), is the algorithmic generation of small musical materials that are then composed into larger musical structures: "higher level musical sections are composed (with or without the aid of the computer) by extending these smaller segments to form the entire piece" (2000a, p. 10). Top-down algorithmic composition begins with a large-scale compositional plan, and then uses algorithms to create the lower-level details. This should not be confused with the use of the same terms in cognitive science and artificial intelligence, where "top-down" refers to symbolic, goal-driven tools, and "bottom-up" refers to sub-symbolic, data-driven tools (Bel 1992, p. 67). A bottom-up tool, as used here, relates more to the position of the tool in the production of a work, where the bottom is the generation of low-level materials. These bottom-up tools could employ symbolic or sub-symbolic methods.

Algorithmic composition attempts to solve the problem of music generation. Rather than solving any single large problem, athenaCL solves many small problems and provides a common repository for solutions. Large problems, leveraging these small solutions, may become solvable in the future. This is a practical theory based on practical needs, designed to give composers incremental tools without waiting for, or even requiring, a complete solution. This design admits that many problems may never be solved. This design rejects the goal of a single solution and embraces multiplicity.

Descriptive and comparative CAAC software analysis is employed in this dissertation. Since 1955 over ninety systems for computer-aided composition have been developed; over thirty systems can today be found in use and development (Ariza 2004a). There has been no systematic comparison of these systems, nor is there a standard method of description or analysis. A thorough comparison of every system is beyond the scope of this study. Selected systems are used to demonstrate the design of athenaCL. Components of related systems are analyzed and compared to corresponding components of athenaCL.

This study does not offer a proof of the aesthetic success or musicality of algorithmic composition. The "pure" algorithmic component of a composition cannot be extracted and held to independent critique; the mixture of composed music and composed algorithm cannot be untangled. This study presents an argument for a design, and relies upon detailed, code-level analysis of object models and interaction. The focus is the compositional implication of this design.

Labels such as algorithmic composition, automatic (or automated) composition, composition pre-processing, computer-aided (or -assisted) composition (CAC), computer composing, computer music, procedural composition, programmed music, and score synthesis have all been used to describe overlapping, or sometimes identical, projects in this field. No attempt will be made to distinguish these terms, though some have tried (Spiegel 1989; Cope 1991, p. 220; Burns 1994, p. 195; Truax 1999, p. 25; Miranda 2000a, pp. 9-10; Taube 2004; Gerhard and Hepting 2004, p. 505). In order to provide greater specificity, a hybrid label, introduced above, is used here: CAAC (pronounced "sea-ack"), or computer-aided algorithmic composition. (This term is used in passing by Martin Supper (2001, p. 48).)

This label is derived from the combination of two labels, each too vague for continued use. The label "computer-aided composition" lacks the specificity of using generative algorithms. Music produced with notation or sequencing software could easily be considered computer-aided composition. The label "algorithmic composition" is likewise too broad, particularly in that it does not specify the use of a computer. Although Mary Simoni has suggested that "because of the increased role of the computer in the compositional process, algorithmic composition has come to mean the use of computers…" (2003), there remain many historical and contemporary compositional techniques that, while not employing the computer, are properly described as algorithmic. David Cope supports this view, stating that "… the term 'computer' is not requisite to a definition of algorithmic composition…" (1993, p. 24).

The field of CAAC provides a core collection of models and techniques employed in all generative music systems. Interactive music systems (Rowe 1993), for example, must include some sort of a CAAC sub-system: if an interactive music system takes part in both machine listening and machine composing, it must contain sub-systems for both music analysis and music generation. The relevance of CAAC research is independent of particular applications.

The production of music with automatic instruments and algorithms has a long tradition. The history of automatic instruments, with the earliest examples provided by third century BCE Greek water organs (Ord-Hume 1987), has been well documented (Buchner 1978; Ord-Hume 1983). As Ord-Hume describes, research in machine music has not always been accepted: "until a few decades ago, no serious student of music would have dared to risk arousing the vehemence of [her/his] professor by talking about music played by machinery" (1983, p. 167).

Distinct from automatic instruments, algorithms and procedural rules for music generation have been used in European music since the earliest forms of notation. In *Micrologus* Guido of Arezzo (c991-c1033) describes a method of generating melody from text by mapping vowels to pitch, or how "anything that is spoken can be made into music" (1978, pp. 74-77). This technique is frequently cited as the first documented method of algorithmic composition (Roads 1985, p. 166). The system of *tala* and *color* in isorhythmic motets (Hiller and Isaacson 1959, p. 49), the fifteenth century vowel-to-pitch mapping of *soggetto cavato* (Loy 1989, p. 300), the "arca musarithmica," a theoretical composing machine proposed by Athanasius Kircher (*Musurgia universalis* (1650)) (Gardner 1974, p. 132; Luening 1975, p. 3; Toop 2002, p. 118), the technique of spraying ink on manuscript paper proposed by William Hayes (*The Art of Composing Musick by a Method Entirely New, Suited to the Meanest Capacity* (1751)) (Hiller 1959, p. 112; Zaripov 1969, p. 120), the compositional dice games of Johann Philipp Kirnberger (*Der allezeit fertige Polonoisen- und Menuettencomponist* (1757)) (Loy 1989, p. 303), the compositional dice games attributed to Wolfgang Amadeus Mozart (*Musikalisches Würfelspiel* (1787)) (Hiller and Isaacson 1959, p. 54), Arnold Schönberg's twelve-tone system (Hiller and Isaacson 1959, p. 49), Joseph Schillinger's composition system (1941; Myhill 1978, p. 312), and John Cage's aleatoric techniques demonstrated in the *Music of Changes* (1958) (Hiller and Isaacson 1959, p. 53) are all frequently described as pre-computer algorithmic composition.

Enthusiastic connections between these generative music systems and CAAC are often overstated: the computer offers a significant change in the way compositional procedures can be specified, stored, scaled, and deployed. This study focuses only on computer-implemented procedures for creative generative music production.

1.1.2. Overview of the athenaCL System

The athenaCL system is a software tool for creating musical structures. Music is rendered as a polyphonic event list, or an EventSequence object. This EventSequence can be converted into diverse forms, or OutputFormats, including scores for the Csound synthesis language, Musical Instrument Digital Interface (MIDI) files, and other specialized formats. Within athenaCL, Orchestra and Instrument models provide control of and integration with diverse OutputFormats. Orchestra models may include complete specification, at the code level, of external sound sources that are created in the process of OutputFormat generation.

The athenaCL system features specialized objects for creating and manipulating pitch structures, including the Pitch, the Multiset (a collection of Pitches), and the Path (a collection of Multisets). Paths define reusable pitch groups. When used as a compositional resource, a Path is interpreted by a Texture object (described below). In addition to tools for storing and editing Paths, athenaCL provides resources for analyzing Paths as static sets (set classes) and as transformations (map classes or voice leadings). These analysis tools borrow nomenclature and metrics from post-tonal music theory.

The athenaCL system features three levels of algorithmic design. The first two levels are provided by the ParameterObject and the Texture. The ParameterObject is a model of a low-level one-dimensional parameter generator and transformer. The Texture is a model of a multi-dimensional generative musical part. A Texture is controlled and configured by numerous embedded ParameterObjects. Each ParameterObject is assigned to either event parameters, such as amplitude and rhythm, or Texture configuration parameters. The Texture interprets ParameterObject values to create EventSequences. The number of ParameterObjects in a Texture, as well as their function and interaction, is determined by the Texture's parent type (TextureModule) and Instrument model. Each Texture is an instance of a TextureModule. TextureModules encode diverse approaches to multi-dimensional algorithmic generation. The TextureModule manages the deployment and interaction of lower level ParameterObjects, as well as linear or non-linear event generation. Specialized TextureModules may be designed to create a wide variety of musical structures.

The third layer of algorithmic design is provided by the Clone, a model of the multi-dimensional transformative part. The Clone transforms EventSequences generated by a Texture. Similar to Textures, Clones are controlled and configured by numerous embedded ParameterObjects.

Each Texture and Clone creates a collection of Events. Each Event is a rich data representation that includes detailed timing, pitch, rhythm, and parameter data. Events are stored in EventSequence objects. The collection all Texture and Clone EventSequences is the complete output of athenaCL. These EventSequences are transformed into various OutputFormats for compositional deployment.

The athenaCL system has been under development by this author since June 2000. The software is cross platform, developed under an open-source license, and programmed in the Python language. An interactive command-line interface is the primary user environment of athenaCL, though the complete functionality of the system is alternatively available as a scriptable batch processor or as a programmable Python extension library.

1.1.3. Design Principles of the athenaCL System

The first design principle of athenaCL is ease of use. This tool is designed to be light weight, portable, and easy enough to learn such that users with no programming experience can quickly become proficient with the system. The cross-platform design, the text-based interface, and the data storage format (eXtensible Markup Language (XML)) provide complete compatibility between diverse systems and platforms. Further, the interactive command line is flexible and inviting: it provides interactive prompts, automatic acronym expansion, user syntax correction, and help.

The second design principle is the use of flexible string processing and intuitive string notations. Flexible string processing means that user-provided data is parsed to allow for abbreviations and error-correction. Intuitive string notations means that musical symbols such as pitch, rhythm, and specialized structures such as Markov transition strings or Xenakis sieves (Ariza 2005c) are readable, compact, and when possible, approach notations familiar to musicians. Though the user at times provides code-like text fragments, notations are not bound by the underlying programming language.

The third design principle is uniform levels of abstraction. This means that rather than offering numerous different object types, a limited number of object types are offered, each capable of internal specialization and external interpretation. The ParameterObject, for example, may contain any level of internal subsystem complexity, including procedures for value generation, selection, and mapping, all within a single object that operates within a fixed system hierarchy. All Textures have a uniform external interface, are independent of Instrument model and OutputFormat, and may be used to abstract a wide variety of musical models. The Clone offers a single, uniform hierarchical relationship to the Texture.

The fourth design principle is context-dependent interpretation of objects. For example, the Path may be used as a sequence of chord changes, or as a harmonic distribution: the interpretation of the Path is completely Texture-dependent. The interpretation of ParameterObject values by a Texture, in a similar manner, is completely Texture-dependent: one TextureModule may apply each generated amplitude value to each Event, whereas another TextureModule may use the amplitude value to specify a mean for a bundle of related Events.

The fifth design principle is representational redundancy. This means that, in carefully chosen ways, components offer redundant configuration and notation. This provides multiple methods of achieving similar results, and occurs at many design levels. Low level notations, such as those used for Pitches, Multisets, and Pulses, accommodate diverse representations. Within a Texture, adjustments to event timing may be made with the rhythm parameter, or by use of a dynamic tempo parameter. Pitch variation may come from a Path, or from dynamic transpositions from a Texture's local field or local octave parameters. Microtonal pitch fluctuations may come from a Temperament, or from the Texture's local field parameter. Two different TextureModules may offer similar results for some parameter settings, but offer different parametric interfaces. Finally, the complete system can be used through the interactive interpreter one Command at a time, as a batch process of multiple automated or scripted Commands, or as a Python CAAC Application Programing Interface (API) extension library. This flexibility allows the same code-base to function, for example, as an application, as a Common Gateway Interface (CGI) script, or as an embedded system within a Graphical User Interface (GUI) application.

The sixth design principle is support for diverse sub-system models and designs within a single integrated environment. This is achieved primarily through collections of ParameterObjects, TextureModules, Orchestras, and OutputFormats, but is also available in lower level musical, numeric, and symbolic representations. In addition to the development of new models, the system supports the incorporation of diverse historical models within a common and compatible framework.

The seventh design principle is support for system expansion and collaborative development. This is achieved in many ways. The complete source code is distributed under an open-source license (the General Public License (GPL)). A SourceForge-based development environment is used to provide tools for collaborative development and version control. Additionally, the system is a browsable, modular environment designed to encourage the accumulation of user-contributed modules. Future developers may contribute components to the system at many different design-levels. Within the system, these components can then be easily explored by other users. The ultimate goal of this design is a library of compatible contributions from numerous composers, each representing unique, modular, and reusable approaches to algorithmic composition.

1.1.4. Design Principles in Practice

It is worthwhile to consider briefly how the design principles stated above might affect the needs of an average user. Such a user, although desiring to make interesting musical structures, may have little concern for the nature of musical abstractions or representational redundancy. The following narrative provides practical examples of how athenaCL design principles improve user experience. A related use of narrative can be found in Schottstaedt (1989b). This discussion, necessarily limited, provides only a small sample of athenaCL functionality. When relevant, design principles introduced above will be identified by name and number.

Imagine that a user named Guido desires to explore polyrhythmic constructions with athenaCL. After skimming the *athenaCL Tutorial Manual* (Ariza 2005a), Guido decides to give the system a try. Since the software is cross-platform, free, and widely available on the internet, Guido does not have to worry about buying a license or if the software will work on his computer. Guido knows that athenaCL, in order to function, requires Python to be installed on his computer. But as a MacOS X user, Guido is not troubled by this: his operating system includes Python as a standard feature. Guido downloads athenaCL, uncompresses the software, and with a Terminal application enters at the command line `python athenacl.py` to start the program.

Guido is interested in working with percussive sounds. Since he desires to work with a MIDI sound source, he needs to set the EventMode to "midiPercussion." Guido enters the command emo (or EMo for EventMode select), and is prompted for the name of the desired EventMode. Guido is lazy and does not want to type the complete name; knowing something about a feature called "automatic acronym expansion," Guido simply enters mp and the Interpreter confirms his selection of EventMode "midiPercussion." This is an example of (1) ease of use and (2) flexible string processing.

Guido knows that he needs to create a Texture to make music. Guido enters the command tin (or TIn for TextureInstance new) to create a new Texture. Guido is prompted for a Texture name (he chooses "x") and is then presented with a list of available Instrument numbers. Guido does not know what these numbers mean, but sees a question mark offering help. Entering a question mark, Guido is presented with a list of General MIDI percussion instrument names. Guido selects number 70, maracas. The Interpreter confirms the creation of his Texture. Wanting to see what he made, Guido enters tiv (or TIv for TextureInstance view) to examine the Texture. Not really understanding what the display means, Guido decides to listen to the Texture. He enters eln (or ELn for EventList new) to create a new EventList. After being prompted for a file name and an appropriate directory, Guido confirms the creation of the EventList. The Interpreter returns the name of the generated file. Guido enters elh (or ELh for EventList hear) to listen to the file. The Interpreter, through the operating system, opens the MIDI file: Apple's QuickTime launches and presents a controller with Guido's new MIDI file. Guido hears his maraca babbling away with a precise, but rather uninteresting rhythm.

The Texture is the single, primary generative structure of athenaCL and provides (3) a uniform level of abstraction of the musical part. Guido need not concern himself with different abstractions for different part structures, OutputFormats, Instrument models, or basic parameter functionality. Textures can come in different varieties, providing different options and processing models; to the system, however, all Textures are uniform.

Seeing some potential, Guido decides that some amplitude variation would improve his solo maraca. Assuming there are some random generators available within the system, Guido enters tpv (or TPv for TextureParameter view) and, after being prompted for a search string, enters random. The Interpreter returns a list of Generator ParameterObjects. Guido decides to use "randomUniform." After entering tie (or TIe for TextureInstance edit), Guido is prompted to select a parameter to edit. He enters a for amplitude, and is then prompted for the ParameterObject arguments. Comfortable now with acronym expansion, Guido enters ru, .5, 1. The Interpreter accepts his arguments. Viewing the Texture again, Guido sees that the amplitude parameter, in expanded form, is now set to randomUniform, (constant, 0.5), (constant, 1). Guido wants to create a new MIDI file to hear his edited Texture. Remembering that, if separated by a semicolon, multiple commands may be given at once, Guido enters eln ~/ao.xml; elh; this single string creates a new EventList in Guido's user directory named "ao" (eln ~/ao.xml) and then immediately opens the MIDI file in QuickTime (elh). Now that his maraca has some amplitude variation, Guido is pleased.

Desiring to alter his Texture further, Guido looks for ways to control rhythm. Searching the rhythm ParameterObjects with TPv, Guido finds a Rhythm Generator called "loop." Seeing that this Generator can do more than loop, Guido examines the provided documentation and learns that he must provide arguments for a Pulse list and a selection method. Guido wants to experiment with the following pattern: 3+3+1+4. Recalling athenaCL Pulse notation from the documentation, Guido knows that he can enter this rhythm in a variety of ways, such as (4,3,1), (4,3,1), (4,1,1), (4,4,1) or as (1,3,1), (1,3,1), (1,1,1), (1,4,1). As Guido likes to think in terms of sixteenth-note values, the former is preferable to him. Further, rather than looping this rhythm, Guido wants to produce equal measure-length permutations. Guido sees that the "randomPermutate" selection method will produce random permutations of his four element rhythm. With this information, Guido enters `TIe` to edit the Texture and selects the rhythm parameter. Guido provides the following argument string: `1, ((1,3,1), (1,3,1), (1,1,1), (1,4,1))`, `rp`. The interpreter accepts his arguments. Examining the Texture, Guido sees that the rhythm parameter, in expanded form, is now set to `loop, ((1,3,+), (1,3,+), (1,1,+), (1,4,+))`, `randomPermutate`. Repeating the `ELn` and `ELh` commands and hearing his solo maraca perform numerous permutations of his favorite 11/16 rhythm, Guido is satisfied.

The two rhythm notations Guido considers are an example of (5) representational redundancy. The rhythm selection method Guido uses is one of the two selection methods implemented in the early 1960s by Koenig in Project 1 (1970a); this is an example of (6) support for diverse and historical algorithmic models.

Guido, now more comfortable with athenaCL, realizes he would like to hear four Textures that simultaneously vary this rhythm. Guido realizes he can quickly make three copies of his Texture by providing command-line arguments to the `TIcp` (TextureInstance copy) command; he enters `ticp x p q r` to make three copies of Texture x named p, q, and r. Guido knows that, with the ParameterObjects he has chosen, each Texture will produce a different sequence of algorithmically generated amplitudes and rhythms. Guido repeats the `ELn` and `ELh` commands to audition the results.

Guido is disappointed. The Textures, each using the same MIDI instrument, are not properly isolated within the polyphony. Guido is curious, and investigates using his collection of Textures with Csound. After properly installing Csound, Guido changes the athenaCL EventMode to CsoundNative, and then examines the available instruments by entering `emi` (or `EMi` for EventMode instrument). Guido finds instrument 80, pluckTamHats, intriguing. Rather than editing each Texture one at a time, Guido uses the TEe (TextureEnsemble edit) command with command-line arguments to quickly edit all of his Textures. Guido enters tee i 80. The Interpreter reports that each Texture's instrument has been edited. Creating a new EventList, Guido notices that more files are now created: a Csound score and orchestra are automatically generated, as well as a MIDI file. Entering elr (or ELr for EventList render), Csound is automatically called and his audio file is rendered. Entering ELh again, both the MIDI file and the rendered audio file are opened in QuickTime. Listening to the Csound version of his maraca quartet, Guido is pleased.

The ability of a Texture's EventSequence to be simultaneously transformed into a Csound score and a MIDI file, as well as the use of the ELn, ELr, and ELh commands, are examples of (4) context dependent interpretations of Textures and Commands. Texture amplitude values, for example, are automatically mapped to the necessary ranges for Csound and MIDI output; Instrument numbers and MIDI channel settings are automatically configured without conflict; and, depending on active EventMode, the EventList commands perform the appropriate operations.

With a collection of MIDI and audio files, Guido saves his work and exits athenaCL. Taking these materials to a digital audio workstation, Guido continues composing, layering, shaping, and modifying these materials into interesting structures. Thinking about his experience with athenaCL, he wishes there were a way to generate rhythms with cellular automata (CA). Examining the athenaCL source code, Guido decides that it would not be too much trouble to implement such a Rhythm Generator. After a few weeks of learning Python and testing some code, Guido completes a CA Rhythm Generator. By joining the athenaCL project on SourceForge.net, he is able to submit his code over the Internet via the Concurrent Versioning System (CVS), and add it to the standard athenaCL distribution. This is an example of (7), support for collaborative development.

1.1.5. Chapter Overview

The remainder of Chapter 1 details the methods of software comparison and analysis to be used in this dissertation. Chapter 2, rather than a complete history, introduces selected topic-based themes from the history of CAAC. These themes are introduced and framed by the first experiments of Hiller (with Isaacson and Baker), Xenakis, and Koenig. Chapter 3, while providing techniques to distinguish and describe CAAC systems, localizes athenaCL in the landscape of contemporary and historical systems.

The second group of three chapters analyzes athenaCL system components. Because of the nature of their interactions, the object components of athenaCL cannot be explained in a linear or strictly hierarchical fashion. Chapter 4, "Abstractions of Musical Materials," demonstrates models of musical objects such as Pitch, Multiset, Path, Pulse, Rhythm, Event, EventSequence, Instrument, and Orchestra. Chapter 5, "Abstractions of Musical Procedures," demonstrates object models of generative and transformative procedures. The ParameterObject, Temperament, Texture, and Clone objects are discussed. Chapter 6, "System Architecture," discusses large-scale system design. The AthenaObject, Performer, OutputFormat, OutputEngine, and EventMode objects are explained. Details of system interface components, such as the Command and Interpreter objects, are also provided.

For each software component object models are discussed and object design is defined. Diagrams and interactive Python examples are additionally provided as needed. After analyzing structural design, compositional implications are discussed and components of related systems are compared. Each athenaCL component will be shown, at least in part, to support the design principles articulated above.

1.2. Methods of Software Comparison and Analysis

1.2.1. Structures to be Compared and Analyzed

The focus of this study is software design. A user-level instruction manual, such as the approach provided within the *athenaCL Tutorial Manual* (Ariza 2005a), will not be provided. Prose descriptions, comparisons to related systems, diagrams, and Python Interpreter examples will offer an analysis of essential design features and their compositional implications. This treatment, however, will not exhaustively demonstrate the utility of athenaCL components. As the complete source code of athenaCL is well commented and publicly available, direct code examples will not be provided.

The utility of CAAC software is not easily measured. Software for optimizing shipping routes, for example, would be deemed better or worse depending on the quality of its results, that is, how economically a package might be shipped. Software for music making, or for any generative aesthetic output, cannot be judged simply by its output, as the results are highly contingent on the users, their skill and creativity with the system, and their interpretation and deployment of the results. In this way CAAC systems are more like any creative tool, such as an airbrush or a saxophone: the qualities of the tool cannot be completely measured by examining singular, or even multiple, output instances. Gustav Ciamaga, describing hardware rather than software, supports this claim: "… no machine or system has been proven superior to any other despite the claims and conterclaims of designers, manufacturers, or composers … ideally, the composer chooses among the available electronic music systems for their creative potential and not because of any claims for efficiency…" (1975, p. 117). Software for aesthetic production must be analyzed toward determining limits and potential; utility and efficiency provide only vague metrics.

Analysis begins by dividing system components into groups. As shown above, CAAC system components may be divided into three groups: abstractions of musical materials, abstractions of musical procedures, and large-scale system architecture. This approach relates to the traditional division of software into data structures, algorithms, and system configuration (Winograd 1979, p. 396).

The abstraction of musical materials refers to how software objects model music structures and entities. In some cases, these design choices may be very relevant to the user's experience, directly affecting what features are made available. In all cases, these design choices determine the interaction of software components and the nature of internal system processing. The abstraction of musical procedures is the encapsulation of generative or transformative processes within musically useful objects. Musical procedures determine the nature of compositional operations. How procedures are modeled and organized, what parameters are exposed to the user, and the scale at which procedures operate are important considerations. System architecture specifies how component objects interact and are presented to the user at the highest level. The choice of interface, graphical or otherwise, is an aspect of system architecture.

Using these divisions, it is possible to compare the athenaCL system to related software systems developed over the past fifty years. It will be shown that component design, perhaps more than particular algorithms or technologies, has significant implications for creative utility. As Daniel Oppenheim states, "the problems which have to be solved in order that computers may better support creative musical activity … are conceptual problems: design, rather than advances in technology" (1991, p. 387).

The diversity of CAAC software, however, makes comparison difficult, as a given software system may relate in one way but otherwise provide completely different functionality. In describing the diversity of computer-user communication in music systems, Bruce Pennycook supports this claim, stating that it is "... impossible to devise evaluation schemes that can be generally applied to all music interface specifications" (1985, p. 270). The task of analyzing and comparing software is further complicated by other issues: target platform obsolescence (in the case of historical systems), platform dependent or closed-source development, expensive commercial licenses, or the lack of any extant source code. For this reason it is impossible to compare all software systems with the same degree of specificity.

Comparative software analysis in general is an ill defined problem constrained by many difficulties. As Françoise Détienne points out, in software design "there exist several acceptable solutions for the same problem, which cannot be evaluated according to any single criterion" (2001, p. 22). Unfortunately, some solutions, for various political, social, or economic reasons, are elevated over equally viable alternative solutions. Michael Hamman, embracing the need to scrutinize these assumptions, likewise affirms that with technology, and software for creative production in particular, "... any given problem will usually yield a surplus of possible solutions" (2002, p. 95).

Unique features of any particular system often cannot be isolated, as design is frequently based on reuse: "the design of a computing system is a task that rarely results in an original solution ... it can be said to involve as much the reuse of solutions already known as creation of new ones" (Détienne 2001, p. 43). These challenges may account for the scarcity of comparative analysis of CAAC systems. Many presentations simply offer new designs without any consideration of historical precursors. As Jeff Pressing observes, "... articles about compositional procedures often fail to cite previous work, or do so in ... a perfunctory way ..." (1994, p. 29). Though comprehensive system evaluation and comparison may be impossible, component analysis offers a practical approach. At a minimum, this analysis demonstrates, for any particular component, a landscape of options and approaches. This perspective is valuable to users as well as to developers.

Software design for aesthetic production manifests particular problems. Pennycook, commenting on the nature of such systems, states that unlike conventional software, "… in which measures of productivity can be gathered empirically, in most musical settings productivity and aesthetic value become hopelessly confused" (1985, p. 270). Composition software, as a special case of music software, is even more difficult to evaluate. As Simon Holland states, "in open-ended domains such as music composition, there are in general no clear goals, no criteria for testing correct answers, and no comprehensive set of well-defined methods" (2000, p. 240). Quoting Rittel and Webber (1984), Holland calls these "wicked problems": "in such domains, there cannot be, in general, definitive formulations of problems, let alone answers … learners must not just solve problems, but also seek problems" (2000, p. 240). Holland uses the term "problem seeking" to describe this situation, noting that problem seeking refers to a reflective approach where "problems are treated as ill-defined and open ended, there is a continual intertwining of problem specification and solution, there are few clear criteria for completion, context greatly affects the interpretation of the problem, [and] problems are always open to re-interpretations and re-conceptualizations" (2000, p. 240). Stephen Travis Pope, discussing CAAC systems, echoes these concerns: "composers need software support for the refinement of incompletely specified ideas …" (1995). In designing software for creative music generation, there are then few clear goals, and even fewer measurements of success.

1.2.2. Object Modeling and Analysis

The athenaCL system is thoroughly based on object-oriented design principles. Object-oriented software design, originating in the 1960s, is one of many programming paradigms.

Simula 67 (1967) is often cited as the first full-featured object-oriented language, although the concepts of objects, classes, and inheritance were introduced as early as 1960 as an extension of ALGOL 60 (Kim 2002, p. 104). Today, use of object-oriented software design is widespread, and many have claimed its superiority over alternative design paradigms. Studies have even provided some empirical evidence of its advantages (Boehm-Davis et al. 1992, p. 27).

Although the principles of object-oriented design are well documented (Gamma et al. 1994, Pope 1996), a brief summary is necessary to establish vocabulary used throughout this study. An object is a software component that, within a single entity, brings together both data and operations to be performed on that data. A class is the abstract definition of an object and acts as an archetype from which separate object instances are created. The data storage units of an object are called attributes; the processing functions of an object are called methods. Methods and attributes can either be public or private. Private attributes and methods are used only within the object, for internal processing by the object itself. Public attributes and methods allow other objects to communicate with and operate upon the object. A public method, for example, may perform an internal operation, calling on any number of private methods or internal objects in the process, and then return a useful result. The design of an object's public methods is an interface (Gamma et al. 1994, p. 13). The object interface determines the opportunities for communication and transaction between objects.

Object-oriented design has affirmed a number of design principles. Encapsulation refers to hiding an object's attributes behind public methods (Pope 1996, p. 56). Polymorphism refers to using the same method name with different objects such that, irrespective of the object type, the appropriate behavior results. Different objects can then be used interchangeably (Pope 1996, p. 57). Polymorphism is used throughout athenaCL:

many groups of components, such as ParameterObjects, Textures, Clones, Orchestras, OutputEngines, and Commands, though individually specialized, are polymorphic and interchangeable.

Inheritance is the process by which one class is defined as a specialization of one or more other classes. This specialized class, or sub-class, may be referred to as a "child" of a "parent" super-class. Single inheritance refers to the specialization of a single parent class; multiple inheritance refers to the specialization, within a single child, of two or more parent classes. A collection of classes can then form a "tree-like specialization of inheritance hierarchy" (Pope 1996, p. 56). Sub-classes, though sharing a common interface, may override operations of the parent class to provide specialization (Gamma et al. 1994, p. 19). As an alternative to inheritance, object composition is the specialization of objects by assembling or composing other objects into a single interface. Gamma et al. have promoted this model, suggesting that developers should "favor object composition over class inheritance" because, in some ways, "inheritance breaks encapsulation" (1994, pp. 19-20). Most components of athenaCL, such as Orchestras, ParameterObjects, OutputEngines, and Commands, are specialized through inheritance. Textures make use of both inheritance and, through the embedding of ParameterObjects, object composition. The Clone and the EventMode exclusively employ object composition.

Throughout this text, frequent reference will be made to "user objects" and "utility objects." User objects refer to system components that are directly configured and manipulated by the user. Paths and Textures, for instance, are created and manipulated by the user, and are thus user objects. Utility objects are used for internal system processing and are not directly manipulated by the user. Factory objects, such as the MultisetFactory, are utility objects used for creating and configuring other objects.

Hamman has defined the steps necessary to create musical representations in software: "… implementing a representation means first producing a logically correct algorithm and a correct though efficient set of data structures, and then implementing these correctly as program code…" (2002, p. 103). In the context of object-oriented software design, this definition is incorrect. System components and their interactions can be designed without logically correct algorithms or efficient data structures. Object-oriented design permits system architecture and component interactions to be created separately from solving problems of logical correctness and efficiency. This opportunity is particularly important in the case of software for creative production, and has been essential to the design of athenaCL.

1.2.3. The Unified Modeling Language and Object Diagrams

Diagrams and graphical models will be provided to supplement prose descriptions and Python demonstrations of object design. Unified Modeling Language (UML) class diagrams and inheritance hierarchies will be used. The UML is a graphical language for "… specifying, visualizing, constructing, and documenting the artifacts of a software-intensive systems" (2003, p. 1). The UML was developed by Rational Software in 1994 and is currently distributed by the Object Management Group (OMG). The use of UML-style diagrams in the description of CAAC systems has been demonstrated by Pope (1996) and Paul A. Fishwick (2002). A small subset of UML tools will be used in this study.

The class diagram provides a simple layout for illustrating the methods and attributes of an object. Traditionally, only public attributes and methods are listed; here, private attributes and methods will occasionally be included to support object description. The class diagram features the name of the Class followed by a list of attributes and a list of methods. For example, given a Rectangle object, attributes for `length` and `width` could be defined. A method called `area()` could provide the product of the `length` and the `width` attributes. The following example presents this Rectangle object in a class diagram.

Example 1-1. Sample Class Diagram

```
Class Rectangle
Attributes:
    length
    width
Methods:
    area()
```

The inheritance diagram demonstrates a hierarchy of class specialization through inheritance. Any class named below another class and connected to it by a line is a subclass. A class definition may go through numerous layers of specialization. The Rectangle class described above, for example, could be a specialization of a Quadrilateral class. This Quadrilateral, in turn, could be a specialization of a generic Shape class. The following example illustrates this specialization in an inheritance diagram.

Example 1-2. Sample Inheritance Diagram

```
Shape
|
Quadrilateral
|
Rectangle
```

UML, though widely used, is neither suitable nor idiomatic for all modeling needs (Ambler 2002). For this reason a minimal modeling language is used here. Based loosely in UML archetypes, this language will provide object component diagrams and activity diagrams.

Component diagrams illustrate the configuration and organization of objects. Of primary concern is the type, number, and arrangement of lower-level objects embedded in higher-level objects. In most cases, no more than one level of embedding is illustrated. The visual orientation of component objects does not imply internal hierarchical or procedural relationships. If significant, illustrated components may be object references rather than object instances. In all cases, component diagrams name objects only by their parent class; particular subclasses are not named. The following example provides a key for understanding component diagrams.

Example 1-3. Component Diagram Key

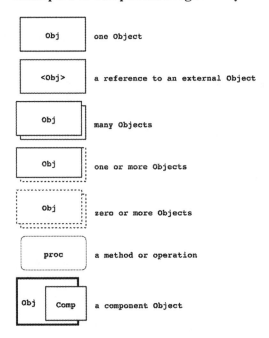

Activity diagrams illustrate the procedural activity of an object or collection of objects. Of primary concern is the sequence of object creation, transformation, or reference passing. Object representation follows the format of component diagrams; activity diagrams add arrows to illustrate procedural or object-based interactions and transformations. Activity diagrams present one sequence of operations from a single perspective; some relevant information, including the influence of related objects and processes, is necessarily excluded. The following example provides a key for understanding activity diagrams.

Example 1-4. Activity Diagram Key

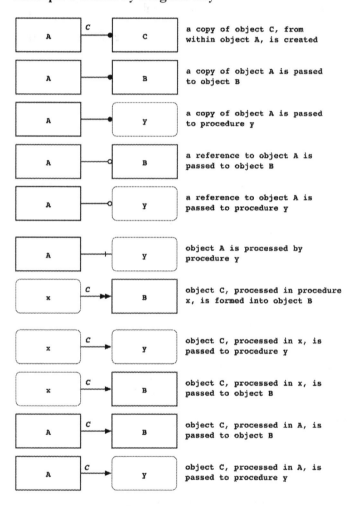

1.2.4. Python and the Interactive Session

The athenaCL system is implemented in the Python programming language. Python will be used throughout this dissertation to demonstrate athenaCL functionality. After discussing the history of Python and its influence on athenaCL design, basic features of the Python language and the interactive session will be described.

Guido van Rossum, creator of Python, released the first version in 1991. Python is a young language compared to languages such as Fortran and Lisp, developed in the 1950s, or C, developed in the 1970s. The design of Python was the result of features inspired by Modula 3 (1988), ABC (1987), and C. ABC was influenced by SETL, a language created by Jacob T. Schwartz and developed by researchers at New York University's Courant Institute of Math and Sciences (Schwartz et al. 1986).

Python emphasizes readability and reusability: "as an object-oriented language, Python aims to encourage the creation of reusable code" (van Rossum 1996). John Rahn, expressing the importance of these features in general, notes that in order to "fulfill the potential" of CAAC systems, "… it will be necessary to write large, readable, portable, maintainable, and easily modifiable and easily extendible software systems…" (1990b, p. 181). As a very high-level interpreted language, Python's primary weakness is speed. Rossum has argued that sacrificing speed for readability and reuse, however, is acceptable: "with ever-increasing hardware speed, the accumulated running time of a program during its lifetime is often negligible compared to the programmer time needed to write and debug it" (1996).

Lisp was invented by James McCarthy (1959, 1960) as a tool for symbolic list processing and, ultimately, research in artificial intelligence (AI). Stephen Smoliar's Euterpe system demonstrates an early use of Lisp for music representation and generation (Smoliar 1967a, 1967b). Interest in the use of Lisp for CAAC systems grew in the 1980s, first with a general introduction to the computer music community (Kornfeld 1980), and then through the development of Lisp-based systems including Formes (Cointe and Rodet 1984; Rodet and Cointe 1984) and Flavors Band (Fry 1983, 1984a). At least since the late 1980s, Lisp has been the most widely used language for CAAC.

Some have claimed that Lisp, more than other languages, is particularly suited for CAAC. Arguments generally focus on Lisp's facility for symbolic processing and recursion. Rahn, defining symbolic processing as "the processing of abstractions" (1990b, p. 181), suggests that for music "… a symbolic processing language such as LISP is idiomatic" (1990b, p. 181). Although Lisp does provide great flexibility for defining symbols, the manipulation and processing of abstractions is just as well facilitated by many other data types of modern languages, and more generally, by object oriented programming. The interest in recursion is motivated by the assumption that, as Peter Desain states, "… hierarchical structures are common in music"; since "recursion is the natural control structure for hierarchical data …" (1990, p. 201), Lisp's use of recursion becomes attractive. Recursion is certainly useful for processing hierarchical structures, and some music, under analysis, does exhibit such hierarchical structures. Desain's claim, however, is perhaps too broad. Although Lisp offers performance benefits for some types of recursive operations (Abelson and Sussman 1985), recursion is nevertheless available in many modern languages.

Lisp, like Python, is a very high-level language. Lisp and Python share features like automatic memory management, garbage collection, and dynamic binding. Both languages have concise syntaxes. Python's syntax, however, closely resembles pseudo-code and is often praised for its clarity, even for novice programmers. An important difference is that where Python is only interpreted, Lisp can be interpreted and compiled, providing significant speed advantages. Python, however, has the advantage of being from its initiation an object-oriented, cross-platform, open source, and portable language with one primary implementation. Lisp has had many implementations, some platform specific, some closed-source. Object orientation, further, came to Lisp well after language design. With careful use, however, Lisp can offer true platform neutrality: Heinrich Taube, for example, describes his move to Common Lisp and the Common Lisp Object System (CLOS) from the Stanford Artificial Intelligence Language (SAIL) so that his system would have broad platform compatibility (1991, p. 21).

The development and design of athenaCL have been influenced by Python. Python is an open-source software project, distributed for free, and designed to work seamlessly on all platforms. This has been a model for athenaCL: the system is open, free, and has no platform bias. Python strives for clear, concise, consistent, and intuitive notations. In athenaCL, notations likewise follow a consistent, intuitive organization and are accepted in a range of formats, the system often correcting for human error. The Python interactive interpreter lets users execute program code one line at a time; this facilitates learning and testing the language. The Python interactive interpreter, as well as the UNIX command-line shell, directly inspired the text-based interface of athenaCL.

Object functionality is demonstrated throughout this study with the Python interactive interpreter. Interactive sessions concisely demonstrate small software components, while also illustrating how procedures, at the code level, use an object. Further, readers at a computer with a Python interpreter may test the demonstrated code. Most UNIX-based operating systems, such as GNU/Linux and MacOS X, are distributed with Python. Examples will provide complete, executable Python interactive sessions. The Python prompt is the ">>>" string. Comments will be used to provide additional commentary; comments in Python are preceded by the "#" string. Examples will provide minimal syntax formatting: user input is given in bold text, comments are given in italics, and interpreter output is given in plain text.

Example 1-5. Starting Python from the Shell

```
% python
Python 2.3 (#1, Sep 13 2003, 00:49:11)
[GCC 3.3 20030304 (Apple Computer, Inc. build 1495)] on darwin
Type "help", "copyright", "credits" or "license" for more information.
>>> print 'yo' # printing hello world to standard output
yo
```

Elementary features of the Python language will be briefly discussed. In Python, everything is an object, including numeric types, strings, functions, and modules. Every object has an identity, a type, and a value. An object's identity never changes once the object is created, and is analogous to a memory address. The value is the data abstracted by the object. if an object's value can change, it is a mutable object; if an object's value cannot change, it is an immutable object. Objects may be assigned one or more identifiers, or names. Names are said to be "bound" to objects. Each name is a reference to an object. More than one name can refer to the same object. If no names refer to an object, it cannot be reached, and will be removed from memory automatically by the garbage collector. There are no "pointers" in Python: there are only objects in memory and names associated with those objects. At times it is necessary to pass, from one object to another, an autonomous copy of an object. In these cases a copy must be explicitly created. At other times it is sufficient to pass only a name as a reference. Access to the original object is then shared by multiple names.

Python features a small collection of powerful built-in data objects. Of importance here are the string, tuple, list, and dictionary. Use of these words in Chapters 4, 5, and 6, unless specifically noted, will always refer to Python data structures. With knowledge of the syntax of Python's basic object types, Python code is nearly transparent. Python strings are immutable character sequences; all strings must be quoted, and either single or double quotes may be used. Strings contain numerous methods to perform common string operations. The list and the tuple, like the string, are sequence types. The list and the tuple store ordered collections of objects that can be retrieved by a numerical index, where zero is the index of the first object. Where tuples, notated with parentheses, are immutable objects, lists, notated with brackets, are mutable and contain numerous methods to provide in-place manipulations such as sorting and appending. There is an important syntax difference between tuples and lists. A one-element tuple must have a comma: (None,). Without a comma, a one-element tuple will be evaluated as a parenthesized expression, and simply yield the object in the parentheses. A one element list need not have a comma: [None]. A Python dictionary is represented with braces: {}. Dictionaries are a mapping type, and store objects in unordered key and value pairs.

Objects stored in sequence or mapping types can be obtained by supplying the index or key in brackets following the name of the container. Sequence type index values count position starting from zero: the third item in a list named x, for example, can be obtained with the syntax x[2]; a value stored under the key 'time' in a dictionary named y can be obtained with the syntax y['time'].

Python names are case sensitive. Throughout this text simple object names like x and y will be used. The following Python session demonstrates basic features of the string, tuple, list, and dictionary objects.

Example 1-6. The String, Tuple, List, and Dictionary in Python

```
>>> x = "athenaCL" # a string named x consisting of eight characters
>>> x[0] # return the first character in the string
'a'
>>> x[6:8] # return a slice of two characters starting at index six
'CL'
```

```
>>> print x.replace('a', '*') # replacing all "a" characters with "*"
*then*CL
>>> print x.lower() # convert all characters to lower case
athenacl
>>> print (None) # without a comma, an expression, not a tuple
None
>>> print (None,) # with a comma, a tuple
(None,)
>>> print [None] # without a comma, a list
[None]
>>> print [None,] # with a comma, a list
[None]
>>> y = (9,1,7) # creating a tuple
>>> y[2] # returning index 2, or the third position
7
>>> z = [9,1,7] # creating a list
>>> z[2] # returning index 2, or the third position
7
>>> z.sort() # the sort() method sorts a list in place
>>> print z
[1, 7, 9]
>>> z.append(x) # the append method adds an object to the list
>>> z.append(y)
>>> print z
[1, 7, 9, 'athenaCL', (9, 1, 7)]
>>> a = {} # creating a dictionary
>>> a['z'] = z # assigning name z to the string "z"
>>> a['q'] = 'python' # assigning "python" to "q"
>>> a.keys() # return a list of keys
['q', 'z']
>>> a.values() # return a list of values
['python', [1, 7, 9, (9, 1, 7), 'athenaCL']]
>>> a['q'] # return a value for a key
'python'
```

The following Python session demonstrates the difference between assigning a name to one or more objects (passing a reference), and creating a copy of an object.

Example 1-7. Assigning a Name and Copying and Object in Python

```
>>> x = [9,1,7] # the name x is assigned a three element list
>>> y = x # the name y is assigned the same object as x
>>> y.append(3) # altering y is the same as altering x
>>> print x
[9, 1, 7, 3]
>>> # copies of Python objects can be made with the copy module
>>> import copy
>>> z = copy.copy(x) # assigning a copy of x's object to z
>>> z.sort() # altering z has no effect on x and y
>>> print z
[1, 3, 7, 9]
>>> print x, y # the objects named by x and y remain unchanged
[9, 1, 7, 3] [9, 1, 7, 3]
```

Python provides the facility to implement object operations that are invoked with the same syntax as Python's built-in object types. Syntax elements, such as the use of brackets following the name of sequence types to obtain values (x[2]), can be implemented for user-defined classes. Operations for built-in functions such as print and len() can also be defined. This form of operator overloading is achieved by designing classes with specially named methods. These methods are always named with leading and trailing double underscores, such as __call__(), __str__(), or __getitem__(). By defining such methods, classes can be designed to model built-in Python objects.

Although neither Python's built-in functions nor control structures will be described here, a few features, used in interactive session examples, require explanation. The built-in Python range() function provides a list of integers: range(0, 4), for example, produces the list [0, 1, 2, 3]. Python list comprehensions, after a similar feature in the Haskell language, provide a unique syntax to produce lists from a single line of code. List comprehension expressions combine a finite loop with an evaluated expression. For example, the expression [pow(x, 2) for x in range(0, 4)] will return the list [0, 1, 4, 9]. The new list is created by taking each value from the list following "in" ([0, 1, 2, 3], or the result of range(0, 4)), assigning this value to the variable following "for" (x), then using this value in the leading expression (pow(x, 2)). List comprehension will be used to concisely demonstrate repeated operation of a method with a range of argument values. The following Python session demonstrates the range() function, the construction of a list with a loop, and a list comprehension.

Example 1-8. Building a List in Python

```
>>> range(0, 4) # returning a list of integers
[0, 1, 2, 3]
>>> # using a "for" loop to create a list of squared integers
>>> q = []
>>> for x in range(0, 4):
...      q.append(pow(x, 2))
...
>>> print q
[0, 1, 4, 9]
>>> # using a list comprehension to create the same list
>>> [pow(x, 2) for x in range(0, 4)]
[0, 1, 4, 9]
```

1.2.5. Conventions Used in this Text

Following common object-oriented programming style conventions, classes will always be named with leading capitals, such as the TextureModule class. An exception is made for Python objects such as the string, tuple, list, and dictionary. Methods and attributes of objects will always be named with a leading lower-case character and typeset with an equal-spaced font. If a name has more than one word, names will be joined with mixed case. Object methods will always be given with parentheses following their name: for example, the `get()` method of the Pitch object. Private object methods and attributes are named with a leading underscore, such as `_data`.

Pitch references will use C4 to represent middle C. Time signatures will be expressed with a slash (4/4), accepting, of course, that meters are not fractions.

Chapter 2. Historical and Theoretical Foundations

2.1. Introduction

… I don't have anything whatsoever against computers, but rather against the false confidence which they endow upon a whole generation of young musicians, fascinated by the window-display; I feel that one should beware of introducing these young musicians to corridors that will soon afterwards be barred by Markoff chains, with the necessity of giving passwords in FORTRAN or ALGOL.

—Pierre Schaeffer (1970, p. 67)

2.1.1. History of the First Experiments

The earliest electronic digital computers began operation between 1942 and 1946, and include the Atanasoff-Berry Computer, the Colossus, the Harvard Mark I, and the Electrical Numerical Integrator And Calculator (ENIAC). Around 1955, within a decade of the ENIAC, the first research in computer-aided algorithmic composition (CAAC) was initiated.

The earliest documented use of an electronic digital computer to produce music was in 1951 (Doornbusch 2004, p. 15). The Australian Council for Scientific Industrial Research (CSIR) Mk 1 computer (later the CSIRAC), developed in Sydney in the late 1940s, was programmed by Geoff Hill to play simple melodies through its integrated loudspeaker (Doornbusch 2004, p. 10). The research of Doornbusch (2004) refutes the claim of Dodge and Jerse that "… composition with the computer predates the use of the computer as a medium to synthesize sound" (1997, p. 341): Hill, and later Thomas Cherry, programmed the computer to synthesize pre-composed, fixed musical structures.

The first documented, complete musical work composed with the assistance of a computer was premiered on television. On 15 July 1956, the science show "Adventure

Tomorrow" featured a tune composed with the assistance of a Datatron computer, a product of the ElectroData division of the Burroughs Corporation. The tune, titled "Push Button Bertha," was the result of programming by Dougles Bolitho and Martin L. Klein, and lyrics provided by Jack Owens (Anonymous 1956a, p. 51, 1956b, 1956c; Darreg 1957; Klein 1957; Pierce 1961, p. 259; Hiller 1970, p. 46; Ames 1987, p. 169). The *New York Times*, on 3 July 1956, reported that this music was generated by substituting "… numbers for notes and equations for tempo…" and that "the formula is a mathematical expression of melody-writing laws that date to Bach and Mozart" (1956a, p. 51). The system required the user to enter a ten digit random number. This value was then used to generate 1000 digits, each representing one of ten possible pitch values. Pitches were selected randomly from this collection and then filtered with musical constraints (Hiller and Isaacson 1959, p. 55; Ames 1987, p. 170). As Curtis Roads notes, the resulting tune "… failed to storm the hit parade" and was "… the trio's only foray into the computer arts" (1996, p. 831).

Less than one month later, on 9 August 1956, the first three movements of an incomplete string quartet titled the *Illiac Suite* was premiered at the University of Illinois (Hiller and Isaacson 1959, p. 6). This piece was composed by Hiller and Isaacson with the aid of the Illiac computer, and, having started work in September 1955, represented nearly a year of programming and experimentation (Hiller and Isaacson 1959, p. 5). With the addition of a new coda for the third movement and the complete fourth movement, the piece was completed by November 1956 (Hiller and Isaacson 1959, p. 7). This project was mentioned in the *Wall Street Journal* on 19 September 1956 (Cony 1956). Hiller and Isaacson note that "… the technique developed by Klein and Bolitho was similar…" to their technique (1959, p. 56).

The work of H. J. Krajenbrink, D. A. Caplin, and D. G. Prinz at the Koninklijke/Shell-Laboratorium Amsterdam (KSLA) (now called the Shell Research and Technology Centre), dating from 1955 or earlier, potentially provides the earliest research in CAAC. As a side activity of their primary research, these studies were poorly documented: the only written information is known through letters sent to Hiller by R. J. Lundbeck prior to 1959 (Hiller and Isaacson 1959) and by Caplin in 1960 (Hiller 1970, p. 47). Hiller notes that this research "… dates back to 1955…" and "… ranks among the earliest attempts at computer composition" (1970, p. 47).

The installation of a Ferranti Mark 1 at the KSLA began in 1953. By January of 1955 installation was complete (Schweppe 1989, p. 150). The computer was given the name MIRACLE: Mokum's Industrial Research Advanced Computer for Laboratory and Engineering (Lundbeck 2005b). As early as 1954, Krajenbrink began developing what were called "visitors' programs": software demonstrations for computer room visitors. These programs included random number generators, calendar programs, prime number analyzers, and a basic implementation of the Mozart *Musikalisches Würfelspiel*. Complete, measure-length segments of music were stored and recombined into new compositions with the use of a random number generator. Output was provided by an attached sound generator capable of producing simple pitched tones (Lundbeck 2005a): the Ferranti Mark 1, as the CSIRAC and other first-generation computers, had a built-in loudspeaker (Doornbusch 2004, p. 12).

Hiller, based his correspondence with Caplin, reports that additional experiments were later conducted by Caplin and Prinz at least until 1960, using first the Ferranti Mark 1, and later a Ferranti Mercury computer. These later experiments employed a generative model based on melodic motion rules and algorithmically generated rhythms, and produced printed alpha-numeric output. Depending on metric position, pitches were chosen from fixed chord sequences based on transitional probabilities (Hiller 1970, p. 48). Hiller quotes Caplin's comments on these experiments: even though the results were "… rather dull tunes of the sort which one used to hear in Victorian hotel lounges," an output from the system, taken by

Prinz to a computer conference in Darmstadt, was "… hotted up by the dance band in the hotel where he was staying and was given a warm reception at its first performance" (Hiller 1970, p. 48). The year of this performance and conference is not known.

After these initial experiments, numerous diverse CAAC projects were conducted around the world. Experiments up to 1965, excluding those of Hiller, Koenig, and Xenakis, include the research of Brooks et al. (1957; Cohen 1962, p. 144), Barbaud with Roger Blanchard (Barbaud 1960, 1966), D. G. Papworth (1960), W. R. Reitman (1960; Cohen 1962, p. 161), D. J. Champernowne in 1961 (Hiller 1970, p. 82), Stanly Gill (1963), Tenney (Mathews 1963; Tenney 1969), Zaripov (1963), Knut Wiggen in 1963 (Hiller 1970, pp. 87-88), Mother Harriet Padberg (1964; Hiller 1970, p. 71), Jacob T. Evanson in 1964 (Hiller 1970, pp. 73-74), M. Havass (1964; Hiller 1970, pp. 91-92), A. Sychra (1964; Hiller 1970, p. 94), Herbert Brün in 1964 (1970; Hiller 1970, p. 56; Ames 1987, p. 172), E. N. Ferentzy (1965; Hiller 1970, pp. 92-93), Zdenek Fencl in 1965 (1966; Hiller 1970, p. 93), John Myhill in 1965 (Hiller 1970, p. 57), and Max Mathews and J. E. Miller (1965). The abundance and diversity of research, within a decade of the first experiments, demonstrates a broad interest in CAAC.

Although, as stated in Chapter 1, computer implementation properly divides CAAC from non-computer and mechanical algorithmic composition, a handful of pre-computer models strongly influenced the first CAAC experiments. Claude E. Shannon and Warren Weaver's 1949 text *A Mathematical Theory of Communication*, based on an earlier text by Shannon (1948) and influenced by the work of Norbert Wiener and his *Cybernetics* (1948), became the foundation of information (or communication) theory. This theory sought to quantify and measure information in terms of choice or uncertainty, to discover methods of encoding, transmitting, and receiving messages as symbols, to measure information entropy, and to filter noise accumulated in message transfer. Shannon and Weaver are careful to distinguish their use of the word "information" from meaning and semantics. The authors state that "… information must not be confused with meaning" (1949, p. 8) and that the "… semantic aspects of communication are irrelevant to the engineering problem" (1949, p. 31). Further, the authors explicitly limit the application of their theory to ergodic systems, or systems that produce messages with statistical homogeneity: "ergodic systems … exhibit a particularly safe and comforting sort of statistical regularity" (1949, p. 12). Types of communication systems that the authors consider ergodic and applicable to their study include "… written and oral speech, … music, the pictorial arts, the theatre, the ballet, and in fact all human behavior" (1949, p. 3). Music is frequently offered as an example of an ergodic system of discrete symbols that can be described with information theory (Shannon 1948; Shannon and Weaver 1949).

In the generation of messages, information theory investigates the probabilities of possible message formations: "… information is a measure of one's freedom of choice when one selects a message" (Shannon and Weaver 1949, p. 9). This led the authors to explore the use of Markov chains to model the probabilities of message formations as collections of symbols. Markov processes, named after mathematician Andrei Markov (1856-1922), provide probabilistic methods for selecting from a finite collection of symbols based on zero or more previous states. Shannon and Weaver call such probabilistic symbol generators stochastic processes: "a system which produces a sequence of symbols (which may, of course, be letters or musical notes, say, rather than words) according to certain probabilities is called a stochastic process, and the special case of a stochastic process in which the probabilities depend on the previous events, is called a Markoff process …" (1949, p. 11). Shannon and Weaver demonstrate the use of Markov chains to generate new sentences from English letter and word transition probabilities (1949, p. 43). Making clear the need for automated computation methods to continue these techniques, the authors state that "it would be interesting if further approximations could be constructed, but the labor involved becomes enormous at the next stage" (1949, p. 44).

Shannon and Weaver's frequent mention of music, as well as their examples of algorithmic text generation, provided a point of departure for numerous pre-computer algorithmic systems and early CAAC implementations. The earliest example is reported by John Pierce (1956; 1961), who states that "… in 1949 M. E. Shannon (Claude Shannon's wife) and I undertook the composition of some very primitive statistical or stochastic music" (1961, p. 255). Their method involved throwing three dice and the use of a table of random numbers to select pre-composed measure-length musical fragments. With the addition of a fixed repetition scheme and imposed harmonic patterns, numerous short "primitive rondos" were produced (1961, p. 256). Similar experiments, called "stochastic composition of music" were described in Pierce's fictional short story "Science for Art's Sake" (1950), written under the pen name J. J. Coupling (Hiller and Isaacson 1959, p. 32; Hiller 1970, p. 45).

The influence of Shannon and Weaver is found in many other analytical and generative music systems employing Markov chain probabilities without computer implementation. Calculations for some of these experiments were done by hand. In 1955 Fred and Carolyn Attneave, after analyzing Western Cowboy songs to obtain first order Markov transition probabilities, produced two new, "perfectly convincing" cowboy songs (Cohen 1962, p. 143; Quastler 1955). Richard C. Pinkerton proposed a "Banal Tune-Maker": a procedural method for generating melodies based on first-order Markovian analysis of thirty nine nursery tunes (1956). Though he suggested computer implementation, Pinkerton selected pitches by choosing a card from one of many appropriately weighted and shuffled stacks (1956, p. 84). Joseph E. Youngblood (1958) and Baker (1963b) demonstrated additional Markov-based analysis techniques. Other models employed mechanical, quasi-computer devices. In 1956 John F. Sowa, using the Geniac "Electronic Brain Kit," developed a simple program after

Pinkerton (1956) that, combined with a number of steps and coin tosses, indicated the pitches of a melody (Sowa 1957, 2005; Cohen 1962, p. 143). Rather than the nursery tunes used by Pinkerton, Sowa derived Markov transition probabilities from "… exercises in several piano books for beginners" (Sowa 1957). An advertisement for the Geniac from 1956, in addition to reproducing one of Sowa's notated melodies, states that "using a statistical analysis of simple tones plus the special circuitry of GENIAC … you can compose original tunes automatically" (1956). Instructions for recreating Sowa's system were distributed with the 1957 edition of the Geniac (Sowa 2005), and later advertisements claimed that the kit included everything necessary to build computers that "… reason, calculate, solve codes and puzzles, forecast the weather, compose music, etc." (1958). Harry Olson and Herbert Belar built a significantly more sophisticated electronic machine that, based on Markovian pitch and rhythm analysis of eleven Stephen Foster songs, produced and synthesized new melodies (1961). Olson and Belar consider their device "… a species of computer developed for a particular application" (1961, p. 1166).

A fundamental flaw in the application of information theory to music, however, is that it necessarily assumes that music is an ergodic source: that any small sample of a musical fragment is statistically representative of the whole. Although some music may satisfy this condition, for much music, arbitrary segments are not statistically representative of the whole. In considering written language as an ergodic source, Pierce states that "all writers writing English text together constitute an approximately ergodic source of text" (1961, p. 63). For written language to be ergodic then, it would require the aggregation of all texts, and even then, this would provide only an approximately ergodic source. Music, having no fixed grammar nor semantics, cannot be seen as ergodic, even if all music texts could be aggregated. Pierce, questioning the utility of information theory in the arts, responds that "… it has very little of serious value to offer except a point of view…" (1961, p. 253). J. E.

Cohen, after a broad examination of applications of information theory to music, is likewise critical, stating that "it may well be that information theory is essentially incapable of providing a model of the compositional process" (1962, p. 154).

Though this initial work is valuable, the early work of Hiller (with Isaacson and Baker), Xenakis, and Koenig provides a superior historical foundation for CAAC research. Their work stands out for two reasons: their publications provide extensive documentation of their endeavors, and their work has had a considerable influence on subsequent systems. As early as 1978 William Buxton isolated their work as foundational examples of "composing programs" (1978, p. 11). Though these systems have frequently been discussed in later literature (Hiller 1981; Loy 1989; Cope 1991; Burns 1994; Chadabe 1997), most descriptions fail to provide sufficient specificity to illustrate important parallels in system design. For example, no single discussion has properly isolated the event parameters produced by each system. Applying a uniform level of description, a brief history and analysis of these systems is presented below. Using this research as a point of departure, common themes in CAAC software are then examined.

In the article "Music Composition with a High-Speed Digital Computer" (1958) and the book *Experimental Music* (1959), Hiller and Isaacson systematically investigate the use of a computer to write music. The authors state that their research began in 1955 (1959, p. 5). *Experimental Music* provides the first complete, multivalent investigation into the techniques of CAAC, and Hiller and Isaacson even regard it as "the first serious study in this field" (1959, p. 46), despite related experiments concerning "the production of music by means of high-speed electronic digital computers" (1959, p. 55). The study is organized around the creation of a four-movement composition for string quartet titled the *Illiac Suite* (1957). Hiller and Isaacson's approach is strongly influenced by the information theory of Shannon and Weaver. Each movement, or Experiment, employs different approaches to algorithmic composition and is constrained within a single historical idiom, such as modal counterpoint or serial music. Hiller, possibly from his composition studies with Milton Babbitt (Hiller 1981, p. 78), was familiar with serial techniques and explored their algorithmic implementation. Hiller and Isaacson are careful to excuse the *Illiac Suite* from aesthetic scrutiny: "our primary aim was not the presentation of an aesthetic unity — a work of art" but rather music as a "research record — a laboratory notebook" (1959, p. 5). Elsewhere Hiller describes the *Illiac Suite* as a "… presentation of sample results … in the form of a four-movement transcription for string quartet" (1956, p. 248).

Hiller and Baker, expanding the techniques used in the last two movements of the *Illiac Suite*, continued this research with the MUsic SImulator-Interpreter for COMpositional Procedures (MUSICOMP) system (Baker 1963a; Hiller 1967, 1969). Development of MUSICOMP began in the late 1950s, and is considered by Loy as "the granddaddy of all programming systems for automatic music generation" (1989, p. 368) and by Roads as the "first composition language" (1996, p. 815). This system was used to create the *Computer Cantata* (1963), a composition for chamber ensemble, voice, and tape originally titled the *Second Illiac Suite* (Hiller and Baker 1964, p. 63; Hiller 1959, p. 120, 1970, p. 52). The reason for the title change was practical: the original namesake, the Illiac computer on which the authors began their research, had been replaced by an IBM 7090. Hiller and Baker, in a similar manner to that of Hiller and Isaacson (1959), excuse the *Computer Cantata* from aesthetic scrutiny, stating that "these studies were designed to test the efficiency and ease of use of MUSICOMP…"; that some techniques "… proved of greater aesthetic value than others…" (1964, p. 62); and that the composition was "the first and admittedly not particularly refined exploitation…" of MUSICOMP (1969, p. 71). Working with Cage, Hiller later expanded the MUSICOMP system with subroutines for *I Ching*-based number selection (ICHING) and *Musikalisches Würfelspiel*-inspired selection procedures (DICEGAME) (Hiller

1981, p. 79). From 1967 to 1969 these tools were used in the production of *HPSCHD* (1969), an extended composition employing seven harpsichords, fifty-one computer generated tapes, eight slide projectors, and seven film projectors (Chadabe 1997, p. 277). *HPSCHD* was never defended as an experiment or a test.

As early as 1954 (1992, p. 8), prior to having access to a computer, Xenakis began development of a computationally intensive method of algorithmic composition based on probability and statistics. He composed *Pithoprakta* (1955-56) and *Achorripsis* (1956-57) with these techniques of "stochastic music." His article "La crise de la musique sèrielle," published in 1955, criticizes twelve-tone techniques and, at the same time, justifies the techniques of stochastic music: "… linear polyphony is destroyed by its own present complexity. One hears in reality only aggregations of notes at various registers. The enormous complexity makes it impossible for the ear to follow the tangled lines, and its macroscopic effect is that of an unreasoned and fortuitous dispersion of sounds throughout the entire frequency spectrum" (1966, p. 11). Xenakis offered his stochastic method, distinct from that suggested by Shannon and Weaver, as a way of breaking free from the "impasse of serial music" (1966, p. 12). His 1960 article "Elements of Stochastic Music" discusses these techniques in depth; though direct computer implementation is suggested, Xenakis used only manual mathematical calculations and graphs.

In 1961 Xenakis contacted IBM France to gain access to a computer capable of realizing the techniques of stochastic music. François Génuys permitted Xenakis limited access to an IBM 7090. As Nouritza Matossian states, Xenakis was aware of the work by Hiller and Isaacson, "but Xenakis was critical of its failure to confront the real musical problems of the present" (1986, p. 158); Xenakis saw the work of Hiller and Isaacson more as "musicological research" (1992, p. 133) than as the development of tools for creative composition. Xenakis designed a flow chart of the *Achorripsis* process and programmed an implementation in Fortran, commonly called the Stochastic Music Program (SMP). The first composition Xenakis completed with this system, *ST/10-1, 080262* (1956-1962) was premiered at IBM France in 1962. Additional pieces composed with this system include *ST/48-1, 240162* (1956-1962), *Atrées (ST/10-3, 060962)* (1956-1962), and *Morsima-Amorsima (ST/4, 2-030762)* (1956-1962). Xenakis published the complete source-code for the SMP (a mere 448 lines of code) in an article titled "Free Stochastic Music from the Computer: Programme of Stochastic Music in Fortran" (1965).

After nearly ten years of extensive work in electronic music at Cologne's West German Radio studio (WDR), Koenig studied programming from 1963 to 1964. During these studies he conceived of a "program for the calculation of musical structures" called Project One (PR1). In 1964, at the University of Bonn, he tested the first version of this system (Koenig 1970a, p. 32). Like Xenakis's SMP, PR1 was written in Fortran II for use on an IBM 7090. It was later rewritten in ALGOL 60 for use on the Electrologica X8 (Koenig 1970a, p. 32), and then, in 1974, in Fortran IV for use on a PDP-15 (Koenig 1980b, p. 9). In 1978 a version called PR1X, and later PR1XM, was made to support direct output to VOice SIMulation (VOSIM) oscillators (Koenig 1980b, p. 9). Koenig's explicit point of departure was serial music. In a statement remarkably similar to that of Xenakis (1955), Koenig writes, "it appears that the trouble taken by the composer with series and their permutations has been in vain; in the end it is the statistic distribution that determines the features of a composition … serial technique appears as a special case of aleatoric compositional technique" (Koenig 1970a, p. 33). Where Xenakis sought alternatives to serialism in continuous distributions from mathematics, Koenig sought to evolve serialism and aleatoricism into discrete selection methods. In its earliest versions, PR1 was primarily designed for personal use: as Koenig states, "it cannot have much interest for other composers as they can exert hardly any influence on the rules and the individual data" (1971b, p. 100). Koenig used PR1 in the production of numerous compositions, including *Projekt 1 - Version 1* (1965/1966) and *Projekt 1 - Version 3* (1967), both for small orchestra; *Output* (1979), *Segmente 1-7* (1982) for piano, *Segmente 99-105* (1982) for violin and piano, *3 Asko Stücke* (1982) for small orchestra, *Segmente 92-98* (1983) for violin and violoncello, *Segmente 85-91* (1984) for flute, bass clarinet, and, violoncello, and *Beitrag* (1985/1986) for orchestra.

Koenig quickly followed work on PR1 with Project Two (PR2), developed from 1965 to 1969 (Koenig 1983, p. 27). PR2 was designed as a tool for a broader audience: "there ought … to be programmes which any composer can use just as [s/he] uses manuscript paper, a piano or a tape-recorder, without any knowledge of computers or mathematics" (1970b, p. 4). PR2 was programmed in ALGOL 60, and later ported to Fortran for use on the PDP-15 (Koenig 1980a). Koenig employed PR2 in the production of *Übung* for piano (1969) (Koenig 1971b, p. 112) and *60 Blätter* for string trio (1992) (Koenig 2005b). As of 2005, Koenig maintains updated versions of PR1 and PR2 written in Visual Basic for Microsoft Windows (Koenig 1999, 2005a).

The initial experiments of these three composers, taken as a whole, cover many of the impulses and themes that have guided development of CAAC systems over the last fifty years. After detailed discussion of each of their projects, an examination of common themes is provided. These themes are derived from their work and reinforced with research from throughout the history of the field. These themes will help to clarify design issues that are treated throughout this dissertation.

2.1.2. The Early Systems of Hiller, Isaacson, and Baker

With the four Experiments of the *Illiac Suite*, Hiller and Isaacson demonstrate diverse approaches to CAAC. The order and nature of each Experiment documents a process of exploration, rather than the creation of an integrated multi-movement composition. As a process of exploration, these experiments demonstrate an interesting trajectory. Their point of departure was from compositional pedagogy: they attempted to create a system based on the way a composer might be taught, with rules and simple musical forms. In the end, such methods were abandoned, at least in part, for techniques more idiomatic to the computer. With MUSICOMP and the *Computer Cantata*, Hiller and Baker continued to explore these more idiomatic techniques.

The goal of Experiments One and Two was to produce strict counterpoint. In order to achieve this, the rules of Johann Joseph Fux's 1725 treatise *Gradus ad Parnassum* (1965), encoded as computational heuristics, were used to filter randomly generated diatonic pitches. If a candidate pitch passed the tests, it was retained, and the process was repeated. If a candidate pitch failed, the pitch was discarded and the process repeated. If, after numerous attempts, a solution was not found, the accumulated sequence of pitches was abandoned and started again; this was called the "try-again process" (Hiller and Isaacson 1959, p. 76). Hiller describes these techniques as extracting order from chaos: "this act of composition is therefore thought of as the extraction of order out of a chaotic environment" (1956, p. 248). In general, the process of randomly generating values to find candidate solutions is called the Monte Carlo method, and was first suggested by John von Neuman and Stanislas Ulam as a method of solving neutron diffusion problems (McCracken 1955, p. 90). As employed in all of Hiller and Isaacson's Experiments, the Monte Carlo technique can be seen as a special case of the broader category of "generate and test (GAT)" techniques (Roads 1996, p. 893). As Hiller and Isaacson note, the Monte Carlo method is only useful with the speed of a computer: "the method is obviously hopelessly inefficient without a device such as an automatic computer" (1959, p. 3). The authors report that they had used the Monte Carlo method prior to their Experiments, and that "… a sizable portion of the basic programming techniques … was adapted from this earlier research" (1959, pp. 5-6).

Hiller and Isaacson outline sixteen rules for pitch selection. Seven rules govern melodic production, including limits on melodic range (within an octave), starting and ending pitches, forbidden intervals for melodic skips, constraints on motion following leaps, restrictions on repeated notes, and rules disallowing the repetition of high notes. Five rules govern vertical intervals, including limits on the first, last, and penultimate verticalities. The four remaining "combined rules" restrict types of parallel motion and voice movement (Hiller and Isaacson 1959, pp. 82-88). The analysis methods tested randomly generated note sequences at lengths of one, two and four notes. A special routine was applied for cadential formulae (1959, p. 93).

For Experiment One, some 500 monophonic melodies were created (1959, p. 91). For Experiment Two, the Fux model was expanded to generate four-part counterpoint. In both cases, pitch was the only musical parameter generated. Though Fux's rules were borrowed, Fux's pedagogical procedure was not: rather than writing counterpoint based on a supplied cantus firmus, the system created sequences of verticalities. Again, special cadence routines were required (1959, p. 108). Experiments One and Two, when presented in the *Illiac Suite*, were constructed from numerous outputs randomly screened and combined. Rhythm was assigned equal-duration values, and tempo and dynamics were added without algorithmic aid.

After encoding models of 18th century music theory, Hiller and Isaacson turned to 20th century music theory, or "experiments more related to contemporary music" (Hiller 1981, p. 78). Experiment Three was designed to produce constrained chromatic music. In this experiment the number of algorithmically generated event parameters was expanded from one (pitch) to four: pitch, rhythm, amplitude, and performance articulation. Measure-length units of rhythm types, pre-determined, were selected and randomly repeated or sustained (1959, p. 111). Rhythms for multiple voices were selected together (1959, p. 113).

The amplitude parameter was encoded with two attributes: a static value (a symbolic marking from *pp* through *ff*), and a dynamic value (either diminuendo, no change, or crescendo) (1959, p. 114). Performance articulations were selected from a list of sixteen possibilities. Articulations were assigned to each part independently, although multi-part assignments to link voices were occasionally performed (1959, p. 117).

Pitch selection in Experiment Three is similar to Experiments One and Two: random pitches, selected here from the chromatic scale, are generated and filtered through heuristics (1959, p. 118). Rules specify the size of melodic skips, register limits, tritone resolutions, and special octave interval handling (1959, p. 119). Additionally, tools for the generation of twelve-tone and interval-sequence rows were developed. These rows, built from randomly selected pitches (1959, p. 129), were varied with the serial operations inversion, retrograde, and retrograde-inversion (1959, p. 130).

The goal of Experiment Four was to discover a more idiomatic technique, "… a style of composition peculiarly appropriate to a computer" (Hiller 1959, p. 119). Hiller and Isaacson sought "to generate samples of music based upon certain more abstract formulations which we believed might eventually be related to structural devices in musical composition such as tonality and melodic profile" (1959, p. 131). Realizing that rule collections would only grow in complexity, they sought simpler, more fundamental methods of musical construction (1959, p. 132). The Markov chain offered such a method, and was used for the selection of adjacent intervals and harmonies. The use of theoretical musical models, however, was not completely abandoned: a hierarchical structure, based on Heinrich Schenker's analysis methods, was used to shape melodic trajectories (1959, pp. 134-135). Tables of weighted probabilities were constructed for zero, first, and higher order Markov chains (1959, pp. 141-148). This Experiment, in its final presentation in the *Illiac Suite*, is the only movement not produced from a combination of numerous separate outputs (1959, p.

153). Tempo, meter, and dynamic indications were inserted during transcription without algorithmic aid (1959, p. 162).

Commentary concerning the *Illiac Suite* has frequently misrepresented the role of the computer. James Moorer, for instance, states that the Illiac "produced a string quartet that was composed entirely by computer" (1972, p. 104); Loy states that Hiller and Isaacson "… applied no retroactive valuation or editing of the results obtained from running their computer model save the choice of one complete output of the program over another" (1989, p. 313); Simoni states that "the output of their software created the *Illiac Suite…*" (2003). Not only was the alpha-numeric output transcribed by hand into Western notation (allowing for casual interpretation as needed), it has been shown above that significant additional parametric musical data was added in all cases except, perhaps, Experiment Three. Further, all movements were based on a selection and combination of multiple outputs except, the authors state, Experiment Four.

Where Experiments One, Two, and Three attempted to encode musical formalisms derived from historical music theory and pedagogy, Hiller and Baker sought to create a modular, reusable system "that is not bound to specific style parameters, historical or otherwise" (1964, p. 62). They did not completely succeed, but instead expanded the techniques of Experiments Three and Four. The *Computer Cantata* contains five movements, each divided into smaller strophes, prologs, preludes, and epilogs. As with the *Illiac Suite*, each sub-section employs a different configuration of algorithmic techniques. Two basic approaches were used.

The first approach, called nth order "stochastic approximation," was used in the majority of sub-sections and employs Markov transition tables to generate four parameters: pitch, rhythm, dynamic value, and performance articulation. A portion of the second movement of Charles Ives's *Three Places in New England* was analyzed and used as the basis for some of the deployed probabilities (Hiller and Baker 1964, p. 68; Hiller 1970, p. 54). The sung text was generated in a similar manner, though in this case Markov analysis was applied to the arrangement of phonemes rather than to musical parameter values. The analysis of "a corpus of English text drawn at random from publications…" was used as the source of transition probabilities (1964, p. 68). The large-scale form of the entire work was demarcated, in part, by using texts generated with different orders of Markov transition tables. These texts, resulting from zeroth order through fourth order Markov chains, were presented in series (1964, p. 68).

The second approach, called "totally organized instrumental music," was used in two sub-sections and employs a twelve element serial method applied to pitch, rhythm, dynamic value, and performance articulation. Hiller and Baker state that this approach "… was taken almost *in toto* from György Ligeti's account of the compositional procedures which Pierre Boulez used for his *Structure Ia*, from *Structures, for Two Pianos, Four Hands*" (1964, p. 78; Hiller 1970, p. 54). The authors note that they use a different twelve-tone row, instrumentation, and sectional arrangement than Boulez. The twelve-tone row, created by random selection without replacement, was processed to produce the forty-eight standard row permutations (1964, p. 79).

As with the *Illiac Suite*, numerous significant musical features of the *Computer Cantata* were chosen without computer aide: the instrumentation (1964, p. 65), the size and arrangement of the large-scale form (1964, p. 64), bundles of values from which selections are made (1964, p. 76), and the combination of particular serial row forms for various parameters (1964, p. 84). In the last case, Hiller and Baker state that the function of the computer is "… more that of a 'compiler' rather than a 'composer'" (1964, p. 84), although such a distinction is of questionable utility.

An important aspect of MUSICOMP was that it was a portable, modular system designed for general use. The system, in addition to some Fortran components (Hiller 1969, p. 71), was programmed in the IBM 7090 machine language Share Compiler Assembly Translator (SCAT). Such a machine language was, at the time, considered portable because the IBM 7090 was popular: "… because it is a standard computer that is widely used … MUSICOMP becomes immediately available to many potential users…" (1964, p. 63). The system was described by its authors as "a completely generalized programming scheme" (1964, p. 62). Musically intuitive notations were used in the hope of increasing accessibility: composers could learn the system quickly "… since it employs much ordinary music terminology as part of its programming vocabulary" (1964, p. 63). Further, the system was modular and reusable, consisting of a number of independent compositional subroutines: the system "… accepts subroutines for various compositional problems and thus serves as a foundation for extended investigations into computer music compositional processes" (Hiller 1970, p. 53). By 1969 the system had accumulated over thirty compositional subroutines, including tools for selection by probability (ML.nDST), selection by Zipf's law (ML.ZPF), pitch selection within dynamic boundaries (ML.PCH), selection of rhythmic modes (ML.MOD), pitch selection and transposition from standard twelve-tone row forms (ML.ROW), random reordering of a series (SHUFFL), Markov chain generation (ORD.n), measures of consonance and dissonance (ML.CDC), pitch sequence generation and melodic resolution rules (ML.RLn), tools for phrase generation and phrase imitation, and a program, after Papworth (1960), to model the practice of change ringing (Hiller 1969, pp. 72-73).

2.1.3. The Early System of Xenakis

Xenakis sought the creation of original music based on new principles of musical production. In his 1966 article "The Origins of Stochastic Music" (1966), Xenakis states that "our first task is to make an abstraction of all inherited conventions and to apply a fundamental critique of acts of intelligence and their realization" (1966, p. 10). Xenakis's critique of serial music (1955) has already been mentioned. His abstraction of musical conventions led to the use of probabilities: instead of specifying particulars, he specified continuous distributions, means, and ranges.

Xenakis's SMP builds musical structures based on a series of steps. (1) Durations of sequences (sections or movements) are calculated based on a mean duration provided by the user. (2) The density of sounds in each sequence is defined in terms of events per second. (3) The instruments for each sequence are chosen from a table of instruments organized by timbre class (which includes non-uniform classes such as "percussion" or "glissando" or "vibraphone"). (4) Within each sequence, the start time of each event is calculated based on the density value determined in step 2 and the previous event's start time. (5) With the use of weighted probabilities, each event is assigned an instrument number from the ensemble calculated in step 3. (6) Each event is given a pitch within a defined range particular to each instrument, and influenced by the instrument's previous pitch. (7) For instrument classes that allow glissandi, a glissando speed is calculated based, in part, on performance-speed constraints. (8) Each event is given a duration based on a maximum, the sequence density, and the probabilities used in the selection of timbre class and instrument number. (9) Each event is assigned a performance dynamic selected from forty-four possibilities. Some dynamic configurations, within a symbolic range from *ppp* to *ff*, are static, while others employ variable amplitude contours with two or three points (Xenakis 1992, pp. 134-142).

The SMP divides an event into nine parameters. These parameters are (1) start time; (2) timbre class; (3) instrument number; (4) pitch; (5-7) glissando values; (8) duration; and (9) dynamic value. Of particular interest is that Xenakis devoted three parameters to glissando, an instrument-dependent technique that was likely used for only a minority of events

(Xenakis 1992, p. 153). The calculation of events and sequences is linear: event start times are produced in sequential order (Myhill 1978, p. 273). The output of the system, an alpha-numeric table of values, required manual transcription into notation.

2.1.4. The Early Systems of G. M. Koenig

Koenig's PR1 was a closed system designed primarily for personal use: the user had minimal control of the system's output. Stylistic issues influenced Koenig's design. As he states, "faithful to the fundamentals of the nineteen-fifties, all the parameters involved were supposed to have at least one common characteristic" (1980a). The common characteristic that Koenig used was the distinction between "regular" and "irregular." Regular means that a parameter value is frequently repeated; irregular means that a parameter value is not repeated until a number of alternative values have been used. A parameter's behavior, between regular or irregular, was randomly selected by the system. A user was permitted to specify six tempo values, twenty-eight entry delays (rhythmic values), a random generator seed value, and the length of the composition. As is clear, "all details are generated by the automatism of the program" (1980a). Koenig frequently used the term "variants" to describe the multiple, unique outputs produced from a single set of input data.

Rather than the continuous distributions favored by Xenakis, Koenig explored discrete selection methods. PR1 employs two selection procedures: "series" and "alea." Higher-level generative procedures are programmed using these two tools. Series provides random selection without replacement. Given a list of elements, permutations are created, each a randomly selected ordering of every element in the source list. Koenig saw this technique as a progressive abstraction of twelve-tone procedures: "the need for variation is satisfied without there having to be the pretense that somewhere deep inside the work the twenty-fifth permutation is still being systematically derived from an original series" (1970a, p. 34).

Alea provides random selection with replacement: values were simply selected from a list at random.

PR1 contains tools for creating periodic and aperiodic sequences, grouping tones and chords, and generating twelve-tone rows based on ordered interval cycles (1970a, p. 39) and transposed and inverted three-note pitch groups (1970a, p. 42). These trichords are deployed to produce complete twelve-tone aggregates (1980b, p. 19). On the largest scale, each parameter in PR1 is controlled by a unique seven-section formal structure. Each section is assigned a value from one to seven. Each value represents a step within a spectrum from aperiodic to periodic, with value four representing a balance between these extremes (1970a, p. 36). This opposition between regular and irregular (or periodic and aperiodic) is called the RI principle. The "branching table" assigns each parameter a sequence of these seven values, each sequence generated with the "series" selection method.

Events in PR1 are divided into six parameters: (1) timbre (instrument or instrument group), (2) rhythm, (3) pitch, (4) sequence, (5) octave register, and (6) dynamic. The application of the "sequence" parameter is not directly specified: Koenig considers it a "spare parameter," capable of referring to the tones in a chord when the octave parameter was not used, or to the timbre of an event when the dedicated timbre parameter designated a group of instruments rather than a single instrument (1970a, p. 35). All parameters are independent, except that entry delay constrains chord-size (1970a, p. 35).

The aim of Koenig's PR2 is a more general, user-configurable system. PR2 divides events into eight parameters: (1) instrument, (2) harmony, (3) register, (4) entry delay, (5) duration, (6) rest, (7) dynamics, and (8) mode of performance. Koenig devised a unique mechanism that allowed parameters to have user-defined precedence. Parameters are interdependent, and the user may configure their order of calculation: "once a parameter has been composed ... the following parameters must adapt to those already composed" (1970b, p. 9). Parameter values are chosen with user-configured selection procedures. Koenig, expanding the repertory of selection methods from PR1, offers six algorithms in PR2: (1) series (random selection without replacement), (2) alea (random selection with replacement), (3) ratio (weighted random selection), (4) group (series with element repetition), (5) sequence (ordered selection), and (6) tendency (random selection within dynamic boundaries). These selection procedures are used to select discrete index values from lists of either user-specified numeric or symbolic values (lists, stockpiles, or tables), or new, algorithmically generated expansions of user-specified numeric or symbolic values (ensembles).

Koenig offers two types of rests in PR2. A "pseudo rest" is one that results from spaces between the end of one event and the start of the next event, and is a side-effect of entry delay. An "autonomous rest," based on the dedicated "rest" parameter value, is "inserted independently of all other parameters" (1970b, p. 51). An autonomous rest, calculated after event entry delays, may then temporally shift other events: "this means that the actual structure duration is increased by the sum of all inserted rests" (1970b, p. 112).

In PR1 a parameter's behavior, as discussed above, is controlled by a series of seven values representing discrete steps within a spectrum from irregular (aperiodic) to regular (periodic). This design, encoded in the branching table, may be seen as a sensitivity to musical repetition. By deploying gradients between aperiodic and periodic, Koenig sought to formally control repetition and variation at the broadest musical level. Although promoting a different approach to specifying and generating musical materials, PR2, with what Koenig calls the "lists-table-ensemble principle," maintains this sensitivity by different means. In PR2, the user provides lists, or "stockpiles" of data for each parameter, and may organize values from these lists into tables. Rather than simply drawing event parameter values from a single list or table with a selection method, the selection methods are used to transform these values into numerous intermediary groups. Otto Laske calls this process a "procedural enlargement" of the input data (1981, p. 121). Values from these groups, collected into an ensemble (a stockpile of stockpiles, or a collection of generated groups all derived from the same source list), are then selected to obtain the actual values applied to event parameters (1970b, p. 33).

By creating intermediary groups from a single source list, each resultant group has a different ordering and distribution of a single collection of elements. The difference between these groups depends on how they were selected. Because the selection methods will produce varying degrees of regularity, the resultant groups will provide a spectrum of source list interpretations which, in some cases, may produce value sequences that range from aperiodic to periodic. By selecting values from these groups, and using only this repertory of generated groups, final parameter values are more tightly constrained than possible with direct selection from the source list. The "lists-table-ensemble principle" is a method of meta-selection.

PR2, compared to PR1, is a more open and configurable system. To produce a variant, the user provides the computer 63 data entries, including parameter value-ranges, parameter controls, parameter hierarchies, and settings for global system configuration (Koenig 1970b, p. 130). PR2, in some ways similar to MUSICOMP, is a modular system: reusable components could be applied for different purposes at different levels of abstraction.

2.2. The Problem of Music

2.2.1. The Unique Position of Music

Composers and system designers frequently claim that music, as a medium, is uniquely suited for algorithmic generation. Most arguments for this view claim that mechanical generation is possible because music is both abstract and is frequently shaped by abstract procedures.

Hiller and Isaacson state that "because music has fewer tangible models in nature … meaning and coherence in music are achieved by more purely formal procedures than are usually applied in either the graphic or literary arts" (1959, p. 10). The authors suggests that meaning in music, more than in other arts, is encoded in formal procedures. Koenig, while not commenting on meaning, offers that "more than any other art form, music tends to have rules for its composition" (1971b, p. 93). Xenakis, while not suggesting that musical meaning is derived from form, asserts the importance of music as an abstract medium: "music, by its very abstract nature, is the first of the arts to have attempted the conciliation of artistic creation with scientific thought … its industrialization is inevitable …" (1992, p. 133). In describing "…one very important specific peculiarity which distinguishes music from all other forms of art," Zaripov states that music "…expresses, not a concrete thought, not an exact description of some phenomenon, object, or process, but a mood, a certain emotional orientation, abstracted from a precise concrete sense" (1969, p. 120). Zaripov justifies the use of automated composition techniques, both by hand and by computer, with this assessment.

More recent authors have also emphasized the unique position of music for mechanical production. The symbolic representation provided by a score is a frequent justification. John Rothgeb states that score-based music, because "it is normally set down in the form of a notated score that can be represented almost completely in a code consisting of discrete symbols" is "… accessible to analytic probing in a depth not approachable in many other art forms" (1980, p. 657). Some have made a historical and formalist claim. Though they offer no evidence, Gareth Loy and Curtis Abbott state that "historically, algorithmic procedures have always been fundamental to the creation of music" (1985, p. 236). Invoking the writings of Cassiodorus (c485-c580) and the assignment of music to the mathematical disciplines, Loy states that, "of all the arts, music is considered to be open to the purest expression of order and proportion, unencumbered as it is by material media" (1989, p. 292). Others have asserted that music is simply unique: Miranda writes, "perhaps more in music than in any other application, the computer can be programmed to be creative…" (Miranda 2000a, p. 9).

The famous prediction of the Countess of Lovelace, Augusta Ada (Byron) King (1815-1852), is made upon similar claims. Published in 1843 in editor Richard Taylor's *Scientific Memoirs*, Lovelace describes the difference between Charles Babbage's Analytical Engine (1837), the proposed (and never built) mechanical predecessor of the computer, and other machines such as the Jacquard Loom. She states that, where the Jacquard Loom weaves flowers and leaves, the Analytical Engine weaves algebraic patterns. She posits that the Analytical Engine might act on things other than numbers, if the object's "mutual fundamental relations could be expressed by those of the abstract science of operations" while at the same time accommodating the "operating notation and mechanism of the engine" (1842). She offers music as an example, and suggests that if "the fundamental relations of pitched sounds in the science of harmony and of musical composition" could accommodate these adaptations, "the engine might compose elaborate and scientific pieces of music of any degree of complexity or extent" (1842). Although often quoted, few have commented on the meaning of Lovelace's statement. Lovelace does not claim that a machine will have composer-like intelligence, or that music will be created with mathematics (Green

2001). Rather, she claims that if music can be symbolically represented, a machine, using the "abstract science of operations," might create a new music.

Music, however, is not that unique: computer-based algorithmic techniques have been used in many arts. Algorithmic design and architecture perhaps exhibit the greatest relation to CAAC. Research in this field is conducted under a variety of names, including computer-aided design and drafting (CADD), computer-aided architectural design (CAAD), and Architectural CADD. An early example, dating from 1968, is provided by John Week's design for a hospital building in North London, in which "… the visible structure has its appearance determined wholly as a result of a computer-orientated programme" (1968, p. 69). Nicholas Negroponte's *The Architecture Machine* (1970) provides an early model of the use of computers as architectural design assistants. Numerous related models of highly specialized, "intelligent, knowledge-based systems…" (Day and Powell 1993, p. 167) for CAAD have been researched and programmed. The exploration of shape grammars by Stiny and Gips (1972) provides a foundation for a wide variety of related work in generative design. Stiny and Gips demonstrate the application of shape grammars to painting, and suggest their application to sculpture, music, and other mediums (1972, p. 131). Shape grammars were subsequently used to model and explore diverse architecture and design styles, including designs as varied as the Prairie Houses and windows of Frank Lloyd Wright (Koning and Eizenburg 1981; Rollo 1995), chair backs of George Hepplewhite (Knight 1989), and Chinese lattices (Stiny 1977). The early incorporation of scripting languages such as Lisp in computer-aided design (CAD) software has facilitated such explorations, and Lisp continues to be an important resource in CAD software (Bousfield 1998). Contemporary work in this field employs many of the same algorithmic techniques used by composers (such as heuristics, cellular automata, and genetic algorithms) to generate structures, textures, and interior spaces (Kalay 2004).

The 1968 exhibition *Cybernetic Serendipity*, held at the Institute of Contemporary Arts in London and organized by Jasia Reichardt, provides a valuable point of departure for work in generative art in many mediums (Reichardt 1968; MacGregor 2002). Although many non-computer exhibits were included (some were analogue machines), the event and accompanying text demonstrated generative techniques in dance, poetry, visual media, film, and music. Composers whose work and writings were included in the book that accompanied the exhibit (Reichardt 1968) include Schillinger, Pierce, Karlheinz Stockhausen, Brün (1968), Tenney, Hiller, Cage, Gerald Strang, Peter Zinovieff, and T. H. O'Beirne (1968). Reichardt describes the event as "… an international exhibition exploring and demonstrating some of the relationships between technology and creativity," but notes that the exhibit "… deals with possibilities rather than achievements, and in this sense it is prematurely optimistic … there are no heroic claims to be made…" (1968, p. 5).

Applications of generative procedures in visual media, animation, and virtual environments are now common. Benoit Mandelbrot's influential research in fractals (1982) inspired many to explore computer-based techniques for generative visual art. Fractals are, however, one of many techniques. The earliest experiments in computer-generated visual art began in 1960 (Reichardt 1968, p. 70). The work of Kurd Alsleben, employing an electronic analogue computer in 1960 (Reichardt 1968, p. 94), and F. Nake in 1963 (1968) offer early examples. Providing impetus to further experimentation, the journal *Computers and Automation*, as early as 1963, began an annual competition in computer-generated visual art (Reichardt 1968, p. 70). K. C. Knowlton, working at Bell Labs between 1963 and 1967, developed techniques for computer-generated animation on film with the use of an IBM 7094 (1968). The artists Peter Struycken and Harold Cohen, early innovators in generative computer art, began their work in the early 1970s on computers such as the PDP-15. Struycken, working at the Institute of Sonology in 1969, developed techniques for generative abstract graphics based in part on the selection procedures of Koenig's PR2 (Struycken et al. 1970; Struycken 1975). Cohen developed a system for computer-controlled drawing and painting called AARON (Cohen 1986). Steven Holtzman, reflecting on twenty years of development, states that "... AARON is probably the most sophisticated rule-governed creative system developed to date" (1994, p. 187). Numerous studies have employed shape grammars and related techniques to generate new works in the style of various painters. Works of Piet Mondrian (Noll 1968), Wassily Kandinsky (Lauzanna and Pocock-Williams 1988), Joan Miró, Richard Diebenkorn (Kirsch and Kirsch 1988), and Juan Gris (König 1992) have all been the subject of generative computer models.

Regardless of how abstract music may be, it is the lack of explicit semantic structures and the ease of diverse symbolic representations that provide an opportunity for generative production. Aural, visual, and spatial arts have these features in common. Natural-language-based mediums such as poetry, drama, or literature more often have explicit semantic structures. Such explicit semantic structures often elude algorithmic generation. Jonathan Swift's well known depiction of the Academy of Lagado, within *Gulliver's Travels* (1726), details a mechanical writing machine by which "the most ignorant person ... might write books in philosophy, poetry, politics, laws, mathematics, and theology, without the least assistance from genius or study" (Swift 2003). The machine randomly combined a fixed vocabulary of words into new phrases that were then evaluated and recorded. Swift's aim was to satirize impractical scientific pursuits; similar techniques, however, have been employed in the production of natural language, both with and without the aid of a computer (Bailey 1974, pp. 283-284).

The writings of Dadaist poet Tristan Tzara in the 1920s (Tzara 1981) and André Breton's 1924 *Manifesto of Surrealism* (1969) provide early examples of algorithmic text-generation. As discussed above, the use of Markov chains to algorithmically generate English text is demonstrated in Shannon and Weaver (1949), though creative application is not suggested. Additionally, the generative grammars of Noam Chomsky (1957), while seemingly ignored by creative writers, have frequently been used as a point of departure for computer-based generative work in other mediums (Rader 1973; Laske 1973a; Roads 1977; Holtzman 1980, 1994). Some of the earliest computer-based techniques for generating poetry date from 1961: N. Balestrini, using an IBM 7070 in Milan, generated an Italian poem made from recombined, juxtaposed, and permuted fragments of three documents (1968). R. M. Worthy produced poetry by filling a grammatical template with randomly selected words and phrases (1962). In 1964 J. A. Baudot, employing a program based on a mathematical model of simplified French grammar and a fixed dictionary of grammatically categorized words, published a complete, computer-generated text (1964, 1968, p. 58). Despite these early examples, there appears to be little contemporary research by poets, playwrights, or novelists in this field. Meanwhile, generative algorithmic tools are now common in both CAD and 3D rendering software, as well as notation, sequencing, and digital audio software. A word processor equipped with tools for natural language text generation would not only be surprising, but potentially amusing.

2.2.2. The Constraint of Idiom

Hiller, Xenakis, and Koenig all approach their systems within the context of producing a particular musical form. System design is first constrained within the bounds of musical style or idiom. This constraint is demonstrated throughout the history of algorithmic music software: at certain levels, the tools for generating one idiom are often incompatible with the tools for another idiom.

Each movement of the *Illiac Suite* reflects a particular stylistic constraint. Though Hiller suggests that a "complete departure from traditional compositional practice" (1959, p. 4) is possible, his experiments produce historically recognizable styles for performance by a classical string quartet. Xenakis and Koenig, more concerned about musical production than scientific experiment, designed software to extend their personal compositional style, styles within the frame of European concert music. Despite different motivations and approaches, the work of all three composers can be seen at least in part as a response to serialism, the reigning idiom-constraint of the 1950s.

As Koenig states concerning PR1, "… a particular compositional principle is concealed behind the rules for selection and combination of the elements, a principle that can be derived from the serial method of composition" (1970a, p. 32). Serial procedures, though in a more constrained model, were programmed by Hiller and Isaacson (1958), Gill (1963), and many others. Where these other researchers implemented common twelve-tone techniques, Koenig generalized serial procedures into flexible tools. Concerning the selection procedures of PR2 Koenig states, "the connection is thus made between serial music, in which particular orders and permutations play an important part, and aleatoric music, in which it is merely the presence of particular elements, the relative frequency at which they occur and the manner in which they are scattered that is important. The selection programmes … attempt to mediate between these two extremes" (1970b, p. 25).

The constraint of idiom may result from practicality: it is easier for both human and machine to follow an existing model than to invent a new model. Hiller and Isaacson (1959) speculate on the potential of training a computer system with the analysis of existing music (1959, p. 31). Hiller and Baker, as already mentioned, implement such a system based on the music of Charles Ives (1964, p. 68). The use of statistical analysis for algorithmic generation is found in the earliest CAAC experiments, such as those of Brooks et al. (1957). Zaripov spoke optimistically of the potential for computer-based music analysis, stating that "machine analysis is an objective analysis, without any subjective premises…" (1969, p. 144).

Zaripov discusses the potential to train a system based on the analysis of existing works, and calls this procedure "analysis-synthesis" (1969, p. 144). This style-based replication is similar to the approach taken in much of the research of Cope. In Cope's EMI, SARA, Alice, and CUE systems the style of extant works, represented in MIDI files, are analyzed and then used to create new works. Of one such system Cope writes, "ultimately programs like CUE are not very creative. The basic CUE program is designed to imitate, not to create anew" (1997, p. 34). Hiller and Isaacson, discussing the possibility of a system designed to emulate the work of other composers, claim that "this type of study is, in the final analysis, a logical tautology since it produces no information not present initially" (1959, p. 176). Though offering some insight, their criticism relies on the questionable premises of information theory; analysis synthesis techniques may produce musical structures that, no matter the amount of resulting "information," sound like unique formations.

Systems with strong idiom constraints are often considered "intelligent," primarily because the results can be verified empirically in terms of how closely they match a model. Cope's *Experiments in Musical Intelligence* provides an example (1996). The desire for system verification has led some to attempt to develop complete theories of the compositional process. Laske claims that CAAC systems, described as "structured task environments," benefit from coherent, complete musical models. He contends that "while it is not a prerequisite for building intelligent music systems to have a full-fledged theory of the activity one wants to support, it is certainly more effective to design such systems on as much theory as one can harness" (1992a, p. 6). Although implementations based on full-fledged theories of composition may be more "effective," and certainly more verifiable, a gap remains between the theory and the human composer. Cope has suggested that there is no gap, that "… most composers can describe methods which, when followed in a step by step manner, would produce music in their style or … music which fits their aesthetic" (1993, p. 24). This is a very optimistic assessment of the ability of composers to completely articulate their methods: the methods of human composers, though successful, are often ineffective, unverifiable, and based on partial, inchoate theories.

Some CAAC systems, intelligent or otherwise, have explicitly focused on narrow stylistic production. The problem, as Cope states, that "empirical definitions of style seem not to exist" (1991, p. 27), has not deterred such attempts. In some cases the style is that of the system designer (Ames 1983; Jacob 1996, p. 159). In other cases well-known styles are modeled. Rothgeb states that common-practice era tonal music, due primarily to its structural organization and "highly constrained syntax embodying many known regularities …" is "… especially suitable as an object for rigorous (and therefore computational) study …" (1980, p. 657).

A popular idiom for algorithmic modeling has been jazz (Ulrich 1977; Fry 1980, 1984b; Levitt 1981; Steedman 1984; Giomi and Ligabue 1991; Johnson-Laird 1991; Penneycook et al. 1993; Biles 1994; Ramalho and Ganascia 1994; Toiviainen 1995; Papadopoulos and Wiggins 1998). Some systems have attempted to model a collection of discrete idioms, often including jazz. Peter Langston's IMG/1, for example, is a CAAC system designed for producing incidental music "… devoid of semantic content" (1991, p. 28); the system uses specialized algorithms to produce styles such as "bebop," "bluegrass," "boogie," "classical," "march," "Mozart," "samba," "sequence," "swing," and "tone-row" (1991, p. 30). Charles Ames and Michael Domino, with their Cybernetic Composer software (1992), offer a poly-genera system that, in addition to "be-bop style jazz" offers "standard jazz," "Latin jazz," "rock," and "ragtime" genre emulation. Style operates as a constraint because it is verifiable and relates to the authors' experience: in selecting which "… practices should be incorporated into the program, we were guided primarily by our own background tastes, and sense of what would be practical" (1992, p. 194).

The Bol-Processor (BP1 and BP2), developed by Bernard Bel and James Kippen, is a system designed with an idiom constraint outside the Western concert tradition (Bel 1989, 1992, 1996, 1998; Kippen and Bel 1989, 1992, 1994). Initially Bel and Kippen sought to model the performance of North Indian (Hindustani) tabla musicians, particularly the improvisation of *qa'ida*, by use of generative grammars (1992, p. 368). This research was style specific because, the authors argue, musical thinking is style specific: "our problem is not so much finding a universal abstract representation of music but identifying certain forms of musical 'thinking' that may be rendered operative in the design of tools for computer-aided music creation …" (Bel and Kippen 1992, p. 397). Though their research later "migrated" (Bel 1998, p. 57) to include Western and South Indian (Carnatic) music, their work is still designed to model one approach to musical thinking.

An emphasis on using CAAC systems for generating Western notation can be seen as an idiom-constraint. This is the approach taken by many systems developed at the Institut de Recherche et Coordination Acoustique/Musique (IRCAM), including OpenMusic. As Gérard Assayag states, "notation acts ideally in a CAC environment not only as a materialization of information going around in the system but also as a medium where formal inventiveness lives … notation should in the long term constitute the natural environment of experimentation" (1998). Such an emphasis constrains a CAAC system within the language of Western notation. This influence is felt in other systems not directly concerned with notation. Miller Puckette relates the window of a new Max patch to an empty sheet of manuscript paper. Considering that "the whole idea of incorporating paper in the music-making endeavor is central to Western art music," Puckette describes an empty Max window as carrying "… stylistic and cultural freight …" (2002, p. 39).

All composition systems, in employing musical abstractions, make genre- and style-based choices. The constraint of idiom can be mitigated by designing open systems, but it cannot be completely avoided. Christopher Fry, seeing this as an aspect of compositional problems in general, states that "completely general composition programs are impossible to design because the problem space of composition is unbounded" (1984b, p. 295). Loy, discussing the use of musical formalisms in general and algorithms in particular, suggests that "the analysis of formalisms can ... reveal important values of an individual or culture" (1989, p. 293). Software cannot escape such formalisms. Puckette, supporting this claim, sees this as an unavoidable situation: "perhaps we will eventually conclude that no matter how hard one tries to make a software program culturally neutral, one will always be able to find ever more glaringly obvious built-in assumptions" (2002, p. 39). This should not be a surprise: Hamman, in considering software in general, states that "... software tools carry huge ideological and epistemological payloads that the human user must accept, silently or otherwise" (2002, p. 96).

There have been, however, frequent claims for style neutrality in composition systems. For example, after describing the flexibility of MUSPEC's musical structures, Jack Citron states that "... the program may be used to produce results which conform to any style the user is capable of defining" (1970, p. 97), suggesting, unfairly, that unobtainable styles are do to insufficient user definition, not the constraints of the system. Carla Scaletti and Ralph Johnson state that "one of the goals of Kyma is to provide a uniform and flexible structure which does not impose stylistic assumptions upon the composer" (1988, p. 232). After describing the difficulty of anticipating the needs of composers, Schottstaedt states that "only a system that is completely open-ended is even a satisfactory beginning" (1989b, p. 223). He implies that his Pla system offers such freedom. Oppenheim, responding to this trend, states that "many systems try to offer an 'ultimate' environment having 'no limitations.' This in itself is not a significant musical goal. ... A more worthy aim should be to provide the composer with an improved interface, even though the system were to remain relatively limited. After all, composers of conventional music have dealt very well with limitations" (1986, p. 445). Oppenheim, acknowledging that all systems are limited, offers instead attention to usability and interface.

The aesthetic predilections of composers affect the software models they deploy. Koenig, in describing the development of PR2, states that the system is based on his own personal models, "… based on experience acquired in musical composition … and was consequently conceived against a background of a compositional theory which is influenced by the writer's personality" (1970a, p. 34). Koenig here describes his personal collection of techniques and aesthetic choices as a compositional theory. In a chapter titled "Remarks on Compositional Theory," part of a larger collection of writings (1971a), Koenig explores the steps involved in the production of electronic music in the voltage-controlled studio and the relationship between serial and aleatoric techniques. In a similar speculative fashion, Koenig describes additional applications of PR2 besides the production of musical structure variants, such as "… research into compositional theory" (1970b, p. 4). This includes investigating "… what in music can be programmed, to what extent rules of serial or aleatoric music … are valid," and to find, within the framework of the software system, "… the extent to which the composer is ready and able to formulate … structural principles … to plan the course of a piece of music in advance and to translate this plan into constellations of individual parameter values" (1970b, p. 4).

Some have redefined composition theory as an aspect of empirical cognitive musicology. This is a significant deviation from the usage demonstrated by Koenig. Laske states that a theory can be developed around "… the use of explicit rule systems" that underlie "… the design and realization of musical compositions…" (Laske 1981, p. 119). These rule systems are not simply musical formalisms or individual aesthetic choices, but mental processes. Balaban et al. state that composition theory is "… a new discipline of

music research oriented toward an empirical theory of compositional processes in music …
by empirical theory we mean a theory formulated on the basis of empirical data regarding the
mental process of composition…" (1992, p. 182). The first step for such a study is
developing tools for gathering this empirical data, or details of "… how composers actually
think when developing musical ideas" (1992, p. 184). The totality of mental processes,
creative or otherwise, has consistently eluded scientific capture. The use of CAAC systems
has, unfortunately, led some to believe that through such systems compositional processes
can be completely observed. Laske states that with CAAC systems, and technology in
general, "composition becomes a traceable, interactive process whose structure can be
documented, researched and understood…" (1993, p. 28). Balaban et al. state that CAAC
systems "constitute a unique task environment for empirical research, since they only do
what they are told to do, and since they are capable of retaining information about the
compositional process of their user that ordinarily gets lost" (1992, p. 183). Although a
CAAC system may retain information that "ordinarily" is lost, this is not the same as the
totality of mental processes that are used to produce a composition. Laske, who has written
frequently on composition theory (1981, 1988, 1989, 1991), developed a CAAC system
called Observer dedicated to obtaining this information (Laske 1973b, 1992b).

As will be demonstrated below, music produced with a CAAC system, no matter the
sophistication of the system, is always subject to human interpretation. A CAAC system thus
fails to capture the sum of all compositional choices and processes. Further, although CAAC
systems may use rules, and many composers during certain historical periods have shared
similar rule systems, it is not clear how "compositional theory" differs from constraints more
commonly called style or technique, all entities equally hard to define, observe, and contain.

In attempting to define composition theory, Laske divides musicological research into
two paradigms, listening and composition. Laske states that listening, "… is a mysterious

process that is little understood, since it leaves no traces and encompasses perception as only one of many ingredients"; further, listening is "massively based on imagination, that is, massively interpretive" (1993, p. 29). Laske claims that "all of present musicology and music theory (so-called) is based on the Listening paradigm" (1993, p. 29). Composition, in contrast to listening, provides "… firmer ground as to the structure of the activity one is researching" and that "one is less prone to speculation when looking at musical activities empirically through the lens of Composition … rather than Listening…" (1993, p. 29). Composition, as used by Laske, is assumed to refer to the rule systems found in the mental processes of composers. However, contradicting his binary division, Laske states that his notion of composition does not "… deny the fact that composition as an activity encompasses listening as an ingredient" (1993, p. 29). Laske does not address the manifest contradiction: if listening is "mysterious" and "massively interpretive," and if listening is held within (encompassed by) composition, then listening must shake composition from its purported firm ground; if listening "leaves no traces," and if listening is a component of composition, then composition cannot be a "traceable" activity.

Peter Kugel offers an argument, based on the work of John Myhill (1952), that further challenges the claims of composition theory. Kugel, framing what he calls Myhill's Thesis as the aesthetic analogue of Gödel's Incompleteness Theorem (1990, p. 24), states that "musical thinking cannot be wholly accounted for in computational terms" (1990, p. 12). Myhill's Thesis makes two claims: a positive claim "… that all musical thinking can be characterized scientifically" and a negative claim "… that certain aspects of musical thinking cannot be precisely characterized in terms of computations alone" (1990, p. 12). Myhill and Kugel make this argument not because art or creativity have mystical properties, but because certain types of processes, trial-and-error processes (Putnam 1965) or limiting computations (Kugel 1992, pp. 34-35), are relevant to musical thinking and are not accounted for by computational processes. The halting problem, a well known example of a problem that is undecidable for a computing machine, is closely related to these trial-and-error processes (Kugel 1990, p. 13).

Kugel does not claim that such trial-and-error processes cannot be run with a digital, deterministic, and finite program (1990, p. 14). Rather, Kugel states that a machine running such processes, what he calls a Putnam-Gold machine (2002), can never announce it has found a final result; it has to "keep an open mind" (1990, p. 15). As an example of such a process, Kugel offers the problem of determining whether a piece of music is beautiful, and states, after Myhill, that such an evaluation can never be found by computation. Further, "if we find that 'beautiful' cannot be characterized computationally," though humans "can recognize it by listening … then the process of listening must involve more than computing" (1990, p. 23). The process of composing, like listening, involves more than computing. As asserted by Laske (1993, p. 29) and shown above, composition essentially contains some aspect of listening, and listening is always, at some level, an interpretive act. Myhill's thesis, in part, is an argument for the necessity of interpretation in the use of CAAC systems: no computing system can perform all the tasks of composition.

2.2.3. Nature and Musical Complexity

The imitation of nature, throughout history, has been a frequent artistic goal. Ferruccio Busoni, in the 1911 translation of *Sketch of a New Esthetic of Music*, provides an example. Busoni states that "… all arts, resources and forms ever aim at the one end, namely, the imitation of nature…" (1962, p. 76). One rationale for this goal is that since nature is beautiful (taken *a priori*), then by copying nature, beauty can be captured. In the field of CAAC, it is frequently suggested that (1) music follows nature and (2) certain equations, number systems, or procedures are natural, or represent nature, and when applied to music, are more likely than others to produce aesthetically pleasing music. In many cases these systems are those used by mathematicians and scientists to model natural phenomena: non-linear dynamic systems (chaos theory), recursive self-similar objects (fractals), genetic algorithms, cellular automata, or neural nets. Many of these systems have been made possible only with the speed of computer computation.

The application of information theory to music, Hiller and Isaacson state, "… is yet another attempt to codify musical aesthetics in terms of natural law" (1959, p. 33). In their discussion of musical form and the principles of composition, the authors affirm the use of models derived from nature: "considerable interest has been shown by composers in structural principles superficially more nearly extra-musical … one of the most obvious of these … is the 'imitation of nature,' a musical tradition with a respectable history" (1959, p. 46). Xenakis's attraction to certain mathematical distributions can, in part, be seen in this context. Xenakis describes influences that led to the "stochastic crossroads": "natural events such as the collision of hail or rain with hard surfaces, or the sound of cicadas in a summer field" (1992, p. 9). These events, to Xenakis, follow "aleatory and stochastic laws" encoded in mathematics. Xenakis sees even complex human social interactions, like the "sonic phenomena of a political crowd of dozens or hundreds of thousands of people," exchanging chants or dispersed by gun fire, as governed by stochastic laws (1992, p. 9). Xenakis uses these distributions (what he calls laws, such as Poisson's and Gauss's) to expand musical resources. Though he is aware that "they are not an end in themselves, but marvelous tools of construction…" (1992, p. 16), his justification for their use in music is that they purportedly describe natural phenomena.

Jeremy Leach and John Fitch make a direct claim for the association of music and nature, proposing the existence of an "axiom that music mimics the way nature behaves…" (1995, p. 30). It is not clear if this "axiom" is indeed self-evident or is simply the impression of the authors. Rather than mimicry of nature or science, Brün suggests that CAAC systems, and artistic systems in general, embody desires and projections of future states: "while the sciences observe or stipulate systems which are *to be analogous* to an existent truth or reality, and while technology stipulates and creates systems that are *to function* in an existent truth or reality, the arts stipulate and create systems which are analogous to an existence *desired to become* true or real" (1971, p. 189).

The relationship between models derived from nature and CAAC is often overstated: Kristine H. Burns claims that "in every instance of algorithmic-computer music applications, the scientific community's work on specific algorithmic procedures … preceded that of the composition community" (1994, p. 28). Though this is obvious for cellular automata, neural nets, and other models of natural systems, this ignores many of the most common techniques of parameter selection and generation. As Koenig demonstrates through the use of tendency masks and selection principles, or as Xenakis demonstrates through the sieve (Ariza 2005c), musical procedures can be found in a wide variety of algorithms that do not model nature and are of no interest to the scientific community. That many musical procedures can be symbolically represented and mathematically described does not make them the work, or even the concern, of the scientific community. Further, composers have frequently rejected scientific, "natural" models of sound-description: the non-standard algorithmic synthesis systems of Koenig (Sound Synthesis Program (SSP)) (Berg et al. 1980) and Paul Berg (PILE) (1979) employ methods of creating sound without scientific acoustic models, "… based on no known acoustic principle or parameter, but rather on basic microlevel data manipulations" (Truax 1999, p. 24).

Warren Burt describes the initial appeal of "chaos and fractal theory" for some as "… a hope that somehow this new theory would provide us with a 'golden key' to find finally a truly beautiful 'natural music' lying hidden behind the veil of mathematics" (1996, p. 170). In a related passage, Martin Supper, after summarizing algorithmic composition techniques that simulate natural phenomena asks "whether composers secretly see algorithmic composition as a way of generating natural forms naturally — forms which are taken to justify themselves by their naturalness alone" (2001, p. 53). This quest for a golden key, this secret justification, is made explicit in some scholarship. Rick Bidlack, in his discussion of the use of chaotic systems for compositional algorithms, states that, "chaos is of potential interest to composers ... because it offers a means of endowing computer generated music with certain natural qualities not attainable by other means" (1992, p. 33). Further, "rather than viewing the output of chaotic systems as music in its own right ... it is probably best to consider such output as raw material of a certain inherent and potentially useful musicality" (1992, p. 33). It is not clear how any musical material, devoid of context, could be inherently musical. David Little, after his survey of applications of chaotic processes, asks, "does a strange attractor underlie a piece which gives us a feeling of anticipation and resolution, of simplicity within complexity? Do its patterns show resemblance to the patterns revealed in nature by fractal geometry?" (1993, p. 50). Little does not provide an answer, but nonetheless states a frequent, optimistic speculation.

And yet there is no golden key to a beautiful music. Burt states that "like Pythagorean harmonic methods, or the Fibonacci series, chaos was simply another tool, with no more (and no less!) magic in it than any other" (1996, p. 170). Such techniques bring to the fore the greater problem of translating numerical values to musical values, or as Burt describes, "the same old eternal problems of mappings" (1996, p. 170). This process of mapping is a compositional process, requiring compositional choices. As James Harley states, "the output of a chaotic system tends to be unusable without the strong reliance on the selective judgment of 'the composer's ear' ..." (1994, p. 209).

Horacio Vaggione has emphasized that scientific models, when used for composition, are necessarily transformed. He states that such musical processes "… cannot be considered properly as modeling activities, even if they use — and deeply absorb — models, knowledge, and tools coming from scientific domains…." Further, "… music transforms this knowledge and these tools into its own ontological concern: to create specific musical situations …" (2001, p. 54). Even if a scientific model describes nature, when deployed in music, what it describes is fundamentally changed. Kevin Jones, failing to recognize the transformation Vaggione describes, argues that, regardless of source or application, "… any algorithm derived from or related to prevailing scientific models and theories should have valid musical potential" (1995, p. 19), in part because use of the algorithm will "… inevitably reflect the composer's perceptions of broader cultural and scientific priorities" (1995, p. 22). Scientific models, transformed into a musical context, are unlikely to reflect much of either the algorithm's or the composer's cultural ideologies.

In the development of CAAC systems, some have declared opposition to natural models as an explicit point of departure. Giuseppe Englert has framed the attraction of natural models as one side of "the debate that once engaged Baudelaire (poet of the artificial) and the disciples of Rousseau (who yearned to return to nature)…" (1981, pp. 135-136). Acknowledging that among musicians who use computers "… Rousseau's ideals have more supporters than ever," Englert affirms the position of Baudelaire: "my approach … leads me to avoid all that derives from what is called nature…" (1981, p. 136).

The research of Richard Voss and John Clarke contributed greatly to the assumed connections between mathematical models of nature and music (1975, 1978). The $1/f$ noise equation has been of interest to researchers in modeling natural phenomena for decades (West and Schlesinger 1990). Inspired by these connections, Voss and Clarke analyzed recordings of Western music in terms of amplitude and frequency variation, and then used an analogue $1/f$ voltage source to generate new melodies. Based on the results of these experiments, Voss and Clarke make three claims. The first is that "... the audio power and frequency fluctuations in common types of music ... have spectral densities that vary as $1/f$" (1978, p. 258). The second is that $1/f$ noise is superior to other types of noise for generating musical structures: based on empirical surveys of several hundred people, they state that "the music obtained by this method was judged by most listeners to be much more pleasing than that obtained using either a white noise source ... or a $1/f^2$ noise source..." (1975, p. 318). The third is that not only does their research have "... implications for music composition procedures" (1978, p. 258) but that "... a '$1/f$ noise' ... may have an essential role in the creative process" (1975, p. 318).

Under the influence of this research, Leach and Fitch state that "it has been shown statistically that most widely acclaimed music has a very similar distribution to ... a $1/f$ or 'inverse frequency' distribution" (1995, p. 24). Such a broad statement is made without acknowledgment that this "widely acclaimed music" of Voss and Clarke's study, in addition to samples of Bach, Scott Joplin, and five twentieth century Western composers, consisted of continuous, twelve-hour segments of AM classical, jazz and blues, rock, and talk radio broadcasts. Music, speech, advertisements, and other sounds were intermingled in the radio samples analyzed (1978, p. 260). Further, melodic frequency variation was determined solely by counting waveform zero-crossings (Voss and Clarke 1975, p. 318, 1978, p. 260; Nettheim 1992), a measure that Voss and Clarke naively suggest "roughly follows melody" (1975, p. 318). Broad statements concerning the relationship of $1/f$ noise to music, similar to those of Leach and Fitch (1995), have been made by numerous other writers based on the claims of Voss and Clarke (Gardner 1978, p. 24; Dodge 1988, p. 11; Roads 1996, p. 881; Dodge and Jerse 1997, p. 369; Simoni 2003).

Though a preference for melodies generated with $1/f$ noise, compared to white $(1/f^0)$ or brown $(1/f^2)$ noise, may be supported in empirical studies, much of the methodology of the original Voss and Clarke experiments has been rejected (Nettheim 1992; Pressing 1994, p. 30). As Nettheim states, "the claim of Voss and Clarke that $1/f$ processes well represent pitch in music has been found … to have only slender support, and the claim for duration must evidently be rejected" (1992). The $1/f$ equation, as many equations from the natural and physical sciences, may model natural systems. An equation to model creative process or aesthetic preference, however, is a different and significantly more challenging problem.

Natural systems, not just their models, are complex and produce dynamic, noisy data. In some cases authors of CAAC systems appeal to complexity itself as a means of approximating natural phenomena. Kevin Jones suggests countering criticisms of computer music as "fastidiously sterile, too regular, and hence too artificial" by using stochastic procedures "to produce fuzzy edges and to 'humanize' computer-generated sounds" (1981, p. 382). Stephen Travis Pope, in a similar statement, suggests that by "adding some amount of random variation to its parameters…" a structure can be made to "… seem more 'life-like'" (1995). Often it is the ability of a system to exclude exact repetition, through the application of noise or other variation, that is used to suggest naturalness. Miranda, describing a system based on cellular automata, states, "the most important CAMUS characteristic concerning musical form is that there is no exact repetition" (1993, p. 14). A similar sentiment is expressed by Laske concerning his experience with PR1. Laske claims that the system's generative procedures are comparable to the process of through composition, where exact repetition is never employed: "… the system processes implement a radical notion of *Durchkomponieren* (through-composing)" (1981, p. 126). Laske assumes, however, that algorithmic variation is equal to musical variation. Algorithmic variation can also be confused with thematic development: Jacob, in describing his Variations system, states that "… by ensuring that all of the notes used in the resultant piece belong to phrases related to each other through transformation, a certain amount of thematic development is inherent, almost inevitable…" (Jacob 1996, p. 159). Through composition and thematic development, as the terms are commonly used, involve much more than arbitrary combinations of generative or transformative procedures: they assume ordering, timing, and design.

2.3. The Parameterization of Events

2.3.1. Music as Discrete Information

Hiller and Isaacson, as others in many of the early experiments, interpret music through a model of information theory: they describe composing as "the extraction of order out of the chaotic multitude of available possibilities" (1959, p. 1) and cite numerous suggestions, from Shannon and Weaver and others, of the application of information theory to music (1959, p. 29). Though, as shown above, the description of music with information theory is flawed, a useful outcome of this approach is the explicit parameterization of musical events. This is done by defining music as discrete information, and then by expanding that discrete information with parametric values. The first step of this process is analogous to digitization, by which continuous values are approximated with discrete values. The second step, rather than treating each discrete slice as a single value, encodes each slice as an n-dimensional parameter array.

Hiller and Isaacson, using the terms of information theory, ask whether music is a discrete, continuous, or mixed communication system. They answer: "we should like to propose that it is effectively a discrete system" (1959, p. 30). In claiming that music consists only of discrete information, the viability of modeling music as events is asserted. While suggesting that music is like language (1959, p. 30) and reminding the reader of Shannon and

Weaver's use of Markov chains to generate new English sentences (1959, p. 23), the authors distinguish music from other discrete communication systems. Where in language only one symbol is considered at a time, they note that in music "… a number of elements are normally in operation simultaneously" (1959, p. 30). A sound-entity, or sound-entity component, is then interpreted as a discrete event consisting of parametric data. This event may be complex. Its complexity can be encoded through parameters, each parameter adding more discrete information into the event. Parameters may provide data for static or dynamic phenomena, and events may scale to moments so small as to seem continuous.

Western notation, which defines sounds as singular, discrete elements (notes), is perhaps the origin of this concept, and Hiller and Isaacson acknowledge this connection (1959, p. 31). The history of Western music notation can be seen as the accumulation of parameters. Where first only pitch contour was specified, additional parameters accumulated: discrete pitch, meter, rhythm, dynamics, phrasing, and articulations were progressively added until, in some late 20th century idioms, vast collections of parametric instructions became common (Stone 1980).

Sources other than Western notation contributed to the parameterization of the musical event. Miranda states that "parametrical thinking in general is a natural consequence of the increasing trend towards computer-oriented systematizations of our time…" (2000a, p. 12) and suggests, as others have, Wiener's *Cybernetics* (1948) as the source of this trend. The term cybernetics has come to mean many things; in Wiener's usage, it refers to the study of communication and control in machines and animals. For some time after Wiener's work the term was often used as a synonym for research in artificial intelligence. In the preface to the translation of Zaripov's study *Kibernetika i muzyka* (1963), translator Michael Kassler notes that Zaripov's research was conducted under the Cybernetics Council of the USSR Academy of Sciences (Zaripov 1969, p. 115). Zaripov describes one of the tasks of cybernetics as "the simulation of various forms of intellectual activity, in particular of those which are called creative…" (1969, p. 118). The association of cybernetics with CAAC is found as early as 1960: Pierre Barbaud, qualifying this association, states "le terme de cybernétique, qu'on applique souvent à notre activité, est inexact" (1960, p. 92). Pierce, while describing cybernetics as including information theory, detection and prediction theory, and applications of negative feedback (1961, p. 219), states that "cybernetics is a very useful word, for it can help to add a little glamor to a person, to a subject, or even to a book" (1961, p. 228).

Koenig and Xenakis, while employing parametric models, have both acknowledged the limits of this formulation. Koenig writes, "the manifold combinatorial possibilities of several parameters can never do justice to all the requirements of a composer" (1970b, p. 4). Xenakis, in referring to the parameterization of a sound event as a "multidimensionality," states that "music goes beyond multidimensionality — it is even more complex" (1996, p. 146). Xenakis describes parametric values as occupying the lowest of three levels. The next level represents aggregates of parametric values, like a phrase or a theme; at the highest level are "interrelationships of a more complex character" (1996, p. 146).

In some CAAC systems event parameters are coupled: parameters have an interdependent relationship. In other systems parameters are decoupled, each parameter value the result of independent processes. For example, in Hiller and Isaacson's Experiment Three, rhythm, amplitude, and pitch parameters are each calculated independently (1959, p. 115). Hiller and Isaacson suggest linking parameter generation for future improvement (1959, p. 170). Xenakis's SMP has numerous interdependent parameters. Parameter 3, instrument number, is dependent upon parameter 2, timbre class. Parameter 4, pitch, is restricted by the pitch range specified by the selected timbre class and instrument number. The three parameters specified for glissando data (parameters 5 through 7) are calculated together. Koenig's PR2, as already mentioned, permits the user to control parameter dependence by defining parameter evaluation order, attempting to avoid potential parameter conflicts (Laske 1981, pp. 125-126).

Though limited use of linked parameters is found in these early systems, use of this model is not widespread: many systems effectively employ independent parameter generation. Koenig, having used both interdependent and independent parameters, states that unlinked parameters can promote more diverse event combinations: "specific parameter-combinations can only ensue if the parameters can be produced individually. As in the serial compositional system, they are only isolated in the studio in order to be put together again at will" (1971a, p. 13).

2.3.2. The Division of Musical Instruction and Production

The division between information for musical instruction (like a score), and information for musical production (like an orchestra) has its origins, like parameterization, in Western notation. As used here, musical instruction refers to event and parameter information; musical production refers to the information contained in the design of sound producing entities. The early systems of Hiller, Xenakis, and Koenig all separate event instructions from event sound production. As each composer produced tables of alpha-numeric data for score transcription and performance by acoustic instruments, this division was assumed. Newer technologies have minimized this division and, in some cases, have allowed it to be nearly removed.

Hiller and Isaacson, at the end of their text, suggest that "perhaps the most significant application of computers would be the combination of computers with synthetic electronic and tape music" (1959, p. 174), suggesting the direct connection between instruction and production. Hiller and Baker approached this goal with MUSICOMP and the CSX-1 synthesis system (Divilbiss 1964). The connection was, however, far from direct: punched cards from the IBM 7090 had to be converted to paper tape for the CSX-1 (Hiller and Baker 1964, p. 84). Xenakis, from the time of his initial experiments, likewise looked toward the combination of instruction with production. In his early, pre-computer descriptions of stochastic music he speculates on how computers might complete the final three phases of a musical work: (1) implementation and calculation, (2) final symbolic result, (3) and sonic realization. Xenakis notes that, with the aid of computers, the symbolic result might be realized by "an elaborate mechanization which would omit orchestral or tape interpreters, and which would assume the computerized fabrication of the sonic entities and of their transformations" (1992, p. 22).

The notions of event parameterization and the instruction-production division are intertwined. The Music N family of synthesis languages, from Mathews' Music III (1960) to Barry Vercoe's Csound (1985), have relied on the division between score (event information) and orchestra (signal processing information). In such languages, instrument definitions contain few details about what behavior or events they might perform; score definitions contain only parameter values, implicitly controlling the nature of sound production but having no means of dynamically changing the design of the instrument itself (unless such features are exposed as parameters). Careful design of instruments can mitigate some of these problems, but critics have desired more control over the instrument than parameter definition alone. As Bel states, "the orchestra/score dichotomy is often resented as a limitation of Csound" (1998, p. 62).

Mathews argues for the separation of score and orchestra on claims of software reuse and division of labor. Mathews, describing Music V, writes, "the program represents a compromise between a general procedure, through which any sound could be produced but which would require an inordinate amount of work on the part of the composer, and a very simple procedure, which would too greatly limit the range of musical sounds obtainable. In order to give the composer flexibility between these two extremes, the program is divided into two parts" (1963). In this context, the terms score and orchestra are perhaps poor metaphors: they imply a historical production model when, more accurately, they represent a particular response to the demands of software production.

These metaphors have been influential: Agostino Di Scipio describes the use of score and orchestra files in Music N languages as a "dualistic paradigm" that "... reflects the clear-cut cognitive separation typical to instrumental music writing..." (1995, p. 368, 1994, p. 203). As Scaletti states, however, "composers have developed Music N instruments which strain the instrument/score analogy..." and that this demonstrates that "composers do not view the composition of timbre and the composition of event lists as completely separate activities" (1989a, p. 44). The division used in Music N is neither clear-cut nor typical of instrumental music: a Music N score might use a very simple instrument to produce complex timbres with numerous parametric events (via granular techniques or otherwise); alternatively, a Music N orchestra might define an instrument that has multi-event or gestural behavior (via large-scale dynamic envelopes or otherwise). John Rogers, commenting on the flexibility of these extremes, describes these as "... two radically different philosophical approaches to computer instrument design" (1975, p. 259).

The design of Music N languages opposes a direct, hierarchical relationship between score and orchestra. This is a source of compositional flexibility. Barry Truax, concerned for the maintenance of hierarchical structures, has criticized the "simplistic notion of the score as 'recipe' or algorithm," or as "simply a representation of the organization of acoustic structure..." (1976, p. 250). Such concerns are not necessary: when used within higher-level systems, the relationship between score and orchestra can be abstracted into any variety of interfaces, hierarchical or otherwise.

The design of instruments in Music N languages asserts the musical importance of software interface design. In the case of a Music N instrument, the interface is the number and nature of the parameters exposed to the score. This interface represents a layer of abstraction, and directly influences a user's musical experience with a software component. Tenney, recognizing the importance of these choices in designing Music N instruments, describes this process as involving "… a number of compositional decisions that are not necessary in any other medium" (1963, p. 27). In the case of CAAC systems, the interface design of higher-level software components has the same compositional importance. Truax has related the importance of these choices to the design of acoustic musical instruments: "just as the design of a musical instrument has a constraining influence on the performer, so the design of various tools used today by composers influences the type and nature of the compositional process…" (1976, p. 228).

In the case of Xenakis, Koenig, and Brün, the division between instruction and production was reduced by developing systems without external instrument definitions. Rather than instructing an instrument model, events instruct the direct movement of a waveform. Xenakis, through the software systems GENDYN and the Unité Polyagogique Informatique du CEMAMu (UPIC), generated waveforms algorithmically. GENDYN employs a technique called Dynamic Stochastic Synthesis: numerous bi-layered continuous random-walks generate separate time and amplitude points (Hoffman 2000). These values, as break-points, are interpolated to produce waveforms (Xenakis 1992, p. 289). UPIC, developed at the Centre d'Etudes de Mathématiques et Automatiques Musicales (CEMAMu) in the mid 1970s (Marino et al. 1993, p. 260), provides a powerful indirect representation of sound production through the mapping of nested graphical notations to parameter values and waveforms. Koenig, through the SSP system (Koenig 1971b, pp. 113-114; Berg 1978; Banks et al. 1979; Berg et al. 1980), achieved similar results through different means. Using techniques derived from PR2 (the selection methods and a modified form of the lists-table-ensemble principle), SSP generates waveform amplitude and time values directly, without any reference to "frequencies, spectral components, pulse widths, modulation indices, [or] unit generators…" (Berg et al. 1980, p. 25). Brün's Sawdust system offers a related model: waveforms are generated from collections of amplitude points that are ordered, concatenated, cycled, interleaved, interpolated, and mutated with numerous flexible procedures (Blum 1979; Brün 1980). Brün, describing the use of such tools as a process of exploration, states that "it is one thing to aim for a particular timbre of sound and then to search for the means of making such sound and timbre audible … it is another thing to provide for a series of events to happen and then to discover the timbre of the sounds so generated" (1969, p. 117). Where event generation was initially conceived only as the creation of musical instructions, it has been shown that, at small scales, the same techniques can be applied to direct waveform specification and sound production.

More recent systems have overtly attempted to avoid the division between instruction and production. As Scalletti says of Kyma, "timbre and event lists are part of a continuum which is organized through the use of sound objects … there is no fixed line between 'instrument design' and 'score composition'" (1989a, p. 66).

2.4. Formalism and Algorithms

2.4.1. Empirical Music Theory

Hiller and Isaacson, in implementing models derived from Fux and Schenker, provide the first example of a CAAC system based on principles of music theory. Their use of Markov chains happened only after the accumulation of Fux-derived style rules became overwhelming. Despite this, Hiller and Isaacson remained optimistic on the utility of such models: "the application of ideas such as Schenker's concept of chord prolongation and of

Meyer's concept of purposeful musical motion would undoubtedly be useful in these studies" (1959, p. 170). Xenakis and Koenig, in contrast to this approach, never attempted to employ models from music theory and analysis.

Koenig was skeptical of attempts to apply the tools of music theory to music generation: "... rules, or at least the regularities in a composer's output or in a stylistic period can be discovered ... the question remains as to whether it supplies the required indications for the synthesis of music. Analysis and synthesis do not cover each other perfectly enough for the results of analysis, if used productively, to lead back to significant music; analysis proceeds from questions which are not necessarily those of the composer..." (Koenig 1980a). Berg, calling such CAAC systems explorations in "empirical music theory" (1996, p. 25), states that "these example-based systems may increase our knowledge of certain styles or make other music theory contributions. ... Fundamentally, however, the domains of music theory and composition are different ... music theory is inherently normative and reflects a codification of past achievements. Composition is creative and expands the theory" (1996, p. 25).

Others have reinforced this criticism. Brian Smith, in considering musical representations for the LASSO project, states that "music theory texts are good starting points, but there is evidence that textbook heuristics are inadequate, and often incomplete, specifications of expert musicianship" (2000, p. 229). Loy, in arguing for the use of connectionist models, states that "... even modern versions of these music theories are not complete: they are a necessary, but not sufficient, guide for a composer who wants to learn to write music in a well-known style..." (1991, p. 364). Leach and Fitch, in considering analysis methods of Schenker, Roudolph Reti, and Hans Keller, state that although potentially useful, "the analysis techniques lack generality, objectivity, and the ability to account for all the constructs that occur in music" (1995, p. 23).

Despite these criticisms, many systems have been designed to reverse engineer music production from music-theory models. Perhaps the most commonly employed theories have been those of Schenker, found, as discussed above, in the earliest experiments of Hiller and Isaacson, and in later systems developed by Stephen Smoliar (1979, 1980), Hiller (1981), Kemal Ebcioglu (1984, 1988), and Bruno Degazio (1997, p. 31, 2004). Schenker's theories have led some to draw conclusions about the way composers work. Cope goes as far as to suggest that the "composing process" itself implements the reductive analysis of Schenker in reverse: "the order in which analysis strips away during its attempt to reveal a work's *Ursatz* can be seen as a retrograde of the order of the composing process" (1991, p. 38).

Theoretical models from particular Western musical practices, particularly those with abundant textual descriptions, have been modeled in great detail. Often the results of these studies are not substantial. Rothgeb developed a system, based on the treatises of Michel de Saint-Lambert (1707) and Johann David Heinichen (1728), to interpret seventeenth and eighteenth century *basso continuo* figured bass notations (1968). The provided theory proved insufficient for mechanical implementation: "it gradually became clear that general solutions to the unfigured-bass problem were probably inaccessible to procedures of the type represented by those of Heinichen and Saint-Lambert" (1980, p. 661). Rothgeb, neglecting the utility of such treatises for humans, concluded that the computer succeeded in "… exposing deficiencies in the theories under investigation…" (1980, p. 661).

The four-part harmonization of a chorale melody in the style of Johann Sebastian Bach, a common exercise of the student of tonal harmony, has received particular attention. The earliest related experiments were conducted by John Seirup in Fortran (1973). Further studies, using a variety of methods, were conducted by M. Baroni and R. Jacoboni (1975), Marilyn Taft Thomas (1985), Hild et al. (1992), and R. A. McIntyre (1994). The work of Ebcioglu and his CHORAL system, however, provide the most widely known research in this area (1984, 1987, 1988). Ebcioglu's study, employing a first-order predicate calculus language called the Backtracking Specification Language (BSL) (1988, p. 44), included from 150 (Roads 1985, p. 175) to 350 (Cope 1991, p. 16; Laurson 1996, p. 212) prioritized heuristics. Though the system employed a large knowledge base, backtracking, and multiple views of the chorale, the system's competence, at best, "… approaches that of a talented student of music who has studied the Bach chorales" (Ebcioglu 1988, p. 49). Ebcioglu, commenting on the difficulty of the task, writes "… the algorithmic representation of the knowledge underlying the seemingly simple Bach chorale style is a task that already borders the intractable" (1988, p. 43).

Much attention has been given to the *Generative Theory of Tonal Music* of Fred Lerdahl and Ray Jackendoff (1983). While pointing out that their model "is not intended to enumerate what pieces are possible, but to specify a structural description for any tonal piece" (1983, p. 6) the authors leave open the possibility "… that a sophisticated alternative approach of constructing computational rules to 'compose' pieces might not also be valuable. … such an enterprise could dovetail with our theoretical paradigm" (1983, p. 112). Attempts at implementing variations of this model have been pursued by many, including Pope's "TR-Trees" (1991) and "extended generative theory system" (1995), Leach and Fitch's "event tree" (1995, p. 23), and Degazio's MIDIFORTH and MOE systems (1997, p. 31).

2.4.2. The Myth of Algorithmic Integrity

Algorithmic integrity is the idea that, by properly representing and maintaining the "pure" expression of an algorithmic process, integrity (aesthetic, compositional, or musical) is gained. This is nothing more than a strict formalism. Such claims overstate the purity of a computer system and disregard numerous aspects of non-computer agency. Variable effects due to non-algorithmic elements of system design, errors in computation or programming, choices of parameters, mapping, transcription and encoding, and final musical context are all ignored. All algorithmic systems are based, at some level, on ad-hoc choices made by a system designer; all algorithmic output must be interpreted, at some level, by a system user. Non-algorithmic intervention cannot be avoided. The term "algorithmic integrity" is borrowed from Laske who, in his use of PR1, is reluctant to correct manually "errors" generated by the system. Laske states that "… if the composer wishes to maintain the algorithmic integrity of the output, a consistent strategy for resolving such conflicts should be developed" (1981, p. 124). It is not clear what formal, aesthetic, or perceptual qualities might be gained by such a strategy.

Some analysts attempt to separate algorithmic processes from a composer's choice of input parameters, system design, or selection and deployment of generated materials. Although this relates to the role of interpretation, discussed below, this is often based on the idea that the algorithmically "pure" can be isolated. Peter Hoffman has introduced the term "rigorous algorithmic composition (RAC)" to attempt to distinguish systems where "the program is responsible for 100% of the final music output" (2004, p. 138). The idea of a RAC system relates to what Sever Tipei calls a "comprehensive program" (1989, p. 324; 1994, p. 5). Hoffman claims that Xenakis's *GENDY3* (1991), "is entirely the output of the program; it does not depend on any other information than that coded into the program lines" (2000, p. 31), and further, "… we have two times 100% original output, because Xenakis combined the mono output of two separate program runs into a stereo file, with an 80ms delay between the channels" (2004, p. 138). Hoffman frequently contradicts this claim, however, by pointing out the many ways Xenakis, in the production of *GENDY3*, did exert non-algorithmic influence. There is the choice of time delay between these two channels. There is the choice of parameter settings which, illustrated in a hand-drawn manuscript bearing Xenakis's revisions, "… gives evidence to the fact that he thoroughly investigated the interdependencies between parameter settings and resulting fixed pitch" (2004, p. 139). There is the selection and ordering of a subset of the sixteen "sequences" or "tracks" Xenakis generated, which Hoffman describes as an "arbitrary succession" (2000, p. 34). And finally, there is the choice, in some cases, to completely alter the algorithmic procedure, Xenakis "… forcing his program to bypass the random walks altogether, directly specifying the length of waveform segments" (Hoffman 2004, p. 142). Xenakis, in controlling the creation of his music, "… sacrificed the stochastic 'purity' of his program…" (Hoffman 2004, p. 142). The claim of algorithmic purity, at 200% or otherwise, is a myopic interpretation of compositional procedures.

The suggestion that some algorithmic processes can be "pure," while others, presumably, corrupt, can be found elsewhere. Burns suggests that a "pure form of algorithmic music" is the production of a complete piece without human intervention (1994, p. 13). But such a suggestion, as stated above, ignores the many levels, either in system design or system use, that non-algorithmic human intervention always plays a role. Di Scipio has demonstrated a more nuanced approach, extending Laske's notion of compositional task environment (Laske 1990) to include "the totality of tools and communications that form an artist's habitat and includes a variety of [human]-machine interfaces, programs, and interfaced digital devices" and that "… as a whole, these tools must be considered deliberately chosen means…" (1995, p. 361). Such task environments assume choices and interpretations that Di Scipio considers essential parts of the compositional process.

Some composers have insisted that the use of algorithmic techniques mandates allegiance to algorithmic integrity. Tipei has gone so far as to say that altering the output of an algorithmic system is both "foolish, because it cancels the most important gain offered by this kind of endeavor, that of a qualitatively different approach to composition," and "dishonest, because it interferes with the experiment by altering the outcome to make it fit a preconceived image of the piece" (Tipei 1987, p. 49). Further, if such "experiments" are taken as a game, "changing the rules in the middle of the game — or after the game is over — amounts to simpleminded cheating" (Tipei 1987, p. 49). Tipei does not seem to consider performance and interpretation by human musicians dishonest or simple minded: many of his works, algorithmically generated, are encoded in notation for acoustic performance.

Roads, questioning the utility of algorithmic integrity, states that "simply because certain parameters of a piece … conform to an arbitrary set of axioms is no guarantee that the listener will hear consistency or originality in the final product … musical consistency and originality are cognitive categories for which little theory yet exists" (1996, p. 846). Vaggione has likewise challenged the myth of algorithmic integrity, stating that such integrity ensures nothing in the final musical result: "composers, especially those using computers, have learned … that the formal rigor of a generative function does not guarantee by itself the musical coherence of a result" (2001, p. 54). Vaggione expands this argument to challenge all musical formalism and reductionism, stating that music "cannot be confused with (or reduced to) a formalized discipline: even if music actually uses knowledge and tools coming from formalized disciplines, formalization does not play a foundational role in regard to musical processes" (2001, p. 54). Vaggione does not state that algorithmic processes are not useful; rather, he qualifies their use by affirming the necessity of music-creation's "irreducible" activities: "concrete actions and perceptions" are necessary "to qualify results and choices according to a given musical project … formalization is not foundational, but operational, local, and tactical" (2001, p. 56).

2.5. Problems of Mechanized Composition

2.5.1. Interpretation and Abundance

CAAC systems are capable of quickly producing large quantities of musical material. In many cases, the output of such systems is filtered, selected, or manipulated before final deployment, either by a human or by an algorithm. Where some have overtly criticized filtering algorithmic output (as shown above), the musical interpretation and deployment of generated materials is an enduring and necessary tradition. This tradition is as old as documented algorithmic technique itself: when using his system of vowel-to-pitch mapping, Guido of Arezzo recommends only taking the best results from several attempts: "… after practice … select from the numerous possibilities only the more effective and those that fit together better" (1978, p. 76). After selection, additional non-algorithmic editing is recommended: "if you then fill in gaps, space out the constricted places, draw together the overextended, and broaden the overcondensed, you will make a unified polished work" (1978, p. 76).

The early systems of Hiller, Xenakis, and Koenig all required manual transcription of computer output into Western notation. The computer output of these early systems was in the form of alpha-numeric data tables: each row represents an event, each column represents an event parameter value. In spite of the likely errors that might occur, there is ample evidence of willful and perhaps necessary elaboration of these materials in transcription. Xenakis, separating the mechanical procedures of stochastic music from their musical deployment, writes, "the theory and the calculation define the tendencies of the sonic entity, but they do not constitute slavery. Mathematical formulae are thus tamed and subjugated by musical thought" (1992, p. 34).

The foundational importance of interpretation in the deployment of algorithmically generated materials is demonstrated in Koenig's annotated transcripts from his lectures during the 1974-1975 course at the Institute of Sonology. Koenig provided his students with the raw, tabular output of a PR1 variant. As an assignment, the students were instructed to use this event data to write new pieces in Western notation (1979, p. 33). From this example it is clear that, to Koenig, computer generation is but one step in the production of a composition. Koenig refers to this process of interpretation, "by which the data of the computer printout are transformed into the 'aesthetic object' we hear as a performed piece of music," as "aesthetic integration" (1983, p. 31), and elsewhere provides details to his approach (1999). What Koenig suggests for the interpretation of PR1 score tables can be generalized to apply to the use musical materials from any CAAC system.

The term interpretation, in early electronic music, was used to refer to an activity assigned only to performers of scores (Western concert musicians). Many composers eagerly embraced electronic music as a means of circumventing this type of interpretation: Edgard Varèse, in 1939, wrote that with the electronic medium "… whatever I write, whatever my message, it will reach the listener unadulterated by 'interpretation'" (2004, p. 19). Without the interpretation of a score by a performer, the composer, as Varèse claims, may communicate without an intermediary. Nonetheless, the completion of a musical work still requires multiple phases of production. In the case of electronic and computer music, where musical materials are often first generated by procedures (whether algorithmic, electronic, or mechanical), interpretation (or aesthetic integration) may then be included as an additional compositional process applied to these materials. This process may have an aesthetic influence analogous to the performance of a score.

Tenney, whose work at Bell labs between 1961 and 1964 resulted in the development of numerous specialized CAAC PLF subroutines for Mathews' Music IV (Tenney 1966), provides an early example of the role of interpretation with computer-generated analog materials, rather than with alpha-numeric score tables. Tenney's *Noise Study* (1961) for tape was produced with instrument definitions that embedded basic CAAC functionality: parameter values supplied means and ranges for synthesis parameters such as center frequency and bandwidth. Despite a specific pre-compositional plan, after musical realization Tenney was disappointed with the results, and was forced to further manipulate system output: "though it introduced some new conditions that deviated from the original formal outline … the original analog tape was re-recorded at half speed and at double speed, and these mixed with the original" (1969, p. 30).

Though Tenney designed mores sophisticated CAAC instruments where amplitude, duration, and frequency were all specified by means and ranges, "it became clear that programming facilities were needed that would make it possible to derive a computer 'score' from another 'composing' program, maintaining a separation between the compositional procedures and the actual sample-generation" (1969, p. 40). Following this model, and with assistance from Mathews, Tenney wrote his first "stochastic music" program in 1962 as a Music IV subroutine called PLF-2. In addition to the number of events and event density, input parameters to the PLF subroutine specified means and ranges for numerous event and synthesis parameters. With PLF-3, Tenney desired "… to vary the large-scale mean-values in each parameter so that some sense of 'direction' could be given to longer sequences, while still allowing the smaller details to vary randomly" (1969, p. 44). Tenney's implementation is related to the tendency mask selection method used by Koenig in PR2: for each parameter, initial and final values, mean, and two ranges were specified. PLF-3 additionally provided CAAC tools for selecting stored functions used for envelopes and waveforms (1969, p. 44). Even with this more sophisticated model, Tenney describes how *Dialogue* (1963), composed with PLF-3, required addition mixing and interpretation after computer synthesis (1969, p.

46). It is clear that Tenney, as Koenig, saw computer generation, and even computer synthesis, as only one step in the production of a composition.

Loy points out that, even though composers of Western music have used formalisms for centuries, "… all formal ordering methods are usually held by composers to be as plastic as the material they order" (1989, p. 298). Loy then concludes that, since these methods are subject to "arbitrary aesthetic tempering" and lack sufficient rigor, "… few compositional ordering practices are strictly algorithmic," and are in fact closer to the terms procedure or method (1989, p. 298). Although there is no demand to emulate historical practice, this arbitrary aesthetic tempering is similar to the interpretation and manipulation of CAAC system input and output. Strang, in a related passage, describes the process of selection as having a similar arbitrary aesthetic condition: "this semirational, disorderly 'stewing over' the material appears to be an essentially human characteristic" and that, at some levels, "the evaluation of the products of random processes seems to be a responsibility which the composer cannot avoid" (1970, p. 40).

Further, not only the products of CAAC systems, but the systems themselves, their inputs and interfaces, are selected and interpreted. What Di Scipio has suggested for a particular case is applicable to many cases: "the user interface becomes a true compositional control structure only if interpreted and internalized by the user, that is: after the user makes sense of it with some particular compositional task in his/her mind, not beforehand" (1995, p. 396).

Analysts have, in some cases, considered evidence of such interpretations to be either errors or abnormal deviations. Linda M. Arsenault, in her analysis of the algorithmic procedures used in *Achorripsis* (1957), describes how Xenakis varied both the system and its results to accommodate his needs. Though Xenakis constructed a tightly specified system,

"Xenakis adjusted the mathematics, albeit only slightly, to make the numbers suit his purpose and scheme" (Arsenault 2002, p. 62). Even though Xenakis stated that *Achorripsis* was the result of strict application of the Poisson distribution, "Xenakis did, indeed, alter the mathematics to suit his scheme as individual situations arose" (Arsenault 2002, p. 70). Hoffman, defining algorithmic music exclusively as music that "can be generated by a Turing Machine," states that "this designation does not apply to most of Xenakis' composition procedures, where formal models are often employed in an informal way, and/or mixed with others" (Hoffman 2002, p. 123). As shown above, all formal models, at some level, are mixed with non-formal procedures. The designation "algorithmic music" is essentially broad.

The abundance of material produced by CAAC systems has inspired diverse techniques of filtering system output. One method employs algorithms in autonomous meta-systems that observe and possibly analyze the output of a lower-level system, and then select from these outputs based on specific criteria. Hiller and Isaacson provide an example. Rather than manually selecting computer output for inclusion in the *Illiac Suite*, they desired "some sort of unbiased screening procedure to select representative musical output" (1959, p. 153). They use various methods of selection, taking at times every tenth output, arbitrarily from the beginning or end, or purely at random. Perhaps more sophisticated than blind selection, a meta-system might employ algorithmic analysis and evaluation of lower-level musical output. An early approach to quantitative aesthetic measurement, including the evaluation of musical structures, is found in George D. Birkhoff's *Aesthetic Measure* (1933). The search for computational methods specialized for musical evaluation can be seen in Schillinger's *The Mathematical Basis of the Arts* (1948), where the author attempts to develop mathematical techniques of aesthetic analysis. Stiny and Gips, in their *Algorithmic Aesthetics* (1978), suggest computer-based models of aesthetic generation and evaluation. While asserting that they "consider any approach to art to be legitimate" and that "none of these aesthetic systems is taken to be definitive" (1978, p. 15), the authors propose integrated criticism and design algorithms applicable to music and a wide variety of other mediums.

Modeling a computer aesthete is a difficult problem. Computer listening, though also difficult, is a less challenging problem. Analysis of musical contour and parameter distributions may be used to initiate alterations in the generative mechanism or filter the output of a generative system. Moorer suggests such a model in evaluating Markov and grammar-based algorithmic techniques, stating that what is needed is "… a selection mechanism that filters out things that can be represented too simply" (1972, p. 107). Moorer draws further evidence for the necessity of such filters from the experiments of Brooks et al. (1957), where he concludes that "the Markov method produces some reasonable pieces, but it took human judgment to select the final examples" (1972, p. 111). Roads describes a CAAC system that, upon analysis and evaluation of its output, adjusts the generative system to avoid stasis or excessive repetition (1996, p. 906). An approach to filtering has been explored by Robert Rowe with the "critic" component of his Cypher system (1992): "the critic analyzes the material Cypher is about to play just before it is performed. A set of rules is keyed to the result of this analysis, such that the nature of the program's output can be changed according to what are essentially aesthetic preferences" (2000, p. 154). Similar models have been used elsewhere: J. P. Lewis proposes a creation by refinement (CBR) model that trains a neural net to function as a "music critic": "preferentially judging musical examples according to various criteria" (1989, p. 181, 1991); Jacob proposes a software component called an "ear" to evaluate algorithmically generated thematic variations (1996, p. 159).

The need for such a "critic," whether human or algorithmic, is common. Though CAAC systems are capable of producing an abundance of material, composers often only select a small portion of this total output. CAAC systems are often inefficient: in some cases desirable output from such systems is rare. Cope, in a statement concerning his EMI system, supports this claim: "even its best efforts often achieve less than satisfactory results. The majority of its works — fall much further from acceptability" (1997, p. 20).

2.5.2. The Liberation of a Means of Compositional Production

The practice of Western composition has traditionally been limited to those literate in Western notation. Software tools for music generation are among the many technological changes that have altered this barrier. CAAC tools have frequently been seen as enabling the production of music by people not trained in Western music composition. The ability of these tools to be easily distributed and transported, further, has promoted new conceptions of sharing musical knowledge, experience, and resources.

Reichardt, in the introduction to *Cybernetic Serendipity*, comments on the potential of technology to decrease barriers to artistic production. While acknowledging that, in general, "new possibilities extend the range of expression…" in the arts, she notes that "it is very rare, however, that new media and new systems should bring in their wake new people to become involved in creative activity, be it composing music, drawing, constructing or writing" (1968, p. 5). Reichardt sees this new access to creative tools provided by computers as "the most import single revelation…" of the *Cybernetic Serendipity* exhibition (1968, p. 5).

Xenakis considered the SMP portable and of potential use to other composers, stating that the program may "be dispatched to any point on the earth … and may be exploited by any composer pilot" (Xenakis 1992, p. 144). Well before the concept of open-source software, Xenakis was eager to share his source code, publishing not only the program listing (Xenakis 1965, 1992), but some of the parameter data used in an actual composition (*Atrées* (1956-62)) (Xenakis 1992, pp. 151-152). Throughout his life, Xenakis expressed hope for spreading and extending musical creativity with software tools. Lamenting the educational, technical, and social barriers to Western composition, Xenakis states that within traditional practice "… the individual and the society are deprived of the formidable power of free imagination that musical composition offers them." Yet, through computers and technology, "we are able to tear down this iron curtain…" (1985, p. 186). For example, Xenakis saw his UPIC system, in addition to being a creative tool for innovative work, as a powerful pedagogical aid for teaching children compositional knowledge "without being tormented by solfège…" (1985, p. 186).

Mathews describes the potential for broadly empowering musical self-expression through software tools for musical production: "… compositional algorithms can be used to supplement technical knowledge, thus allowing music to be composed by people without formal training … if the day comes when each house has its own computer terminal, these techniques may make music as a means of self-expression accessible to everyone" (1968, p. 114).

Composers and developers are still optimistic that CAAC systems encourage diverse musical production. Joel Chadabe defines "interactivity at home" as the use of generative systems by amateurs "perhaps without talent or skill" (1997, p. 332). Interactive music systems encourage musical creation because "… the aspect of musical performance which requires skill, namely playing the notes, can be eliminated from the performer's tasks" (1997, p. 332). Chadabe affirms the value of this opportunity: "it allows people to participate in musical processes in a meaningful artistic level whether or not they have previously studied a musical instrument" (1997, p. 332). Cope, concerning the use of CAAC tools, writes that "… this use of technology is a positive development, not the negative one so many fear. This use will free creative artists to think on increasingly higher planes. What many fear — that computer programs will eliminate living composers — is, in fact, contrary to reality. Such programs will assist many more individuals to compose…" (1997, p. 34).

2.5.3. Fear and Distributed Authorship

The Romantic notion of the composer as genius and producer of works (Goehr 1992) is challenged by the use of machines and automation in the creation of Western concert music. Historically, this challenge has led some to raise questions about authorship and the merit of using such tools. Certainly, these concerns are historically localized: since the 1960s, the role of computers in compositional processes has become, to some extent, commonly known and accepted. Nonetheless, the application of computers to music composition has consistently raised common questions. These questions continue to exert influence.

Hiller, framing CAAC as the automation of composition, states that "we are also aware of the problem of misinformation concerning computers and automation" (1959, p. 8). The misinformation Hiller refers to is the idea that automation, in the form of computers, will replace humans. Hiller later recalls that, during his 1956 presentation at the Association of Computing Machinery (ACM), "attitudes toward this early work ranged from curious to skeptical to overtly hostile … computer scientists were more open minded than musicians, and musicians were more open minded than scholars in the humanities, many of whom seemed to regard me as monstrous" (1981, p. 79). Brock Brower, writing in the *New York Times* in 1961, attempts to quell speculation that the "electronic brains" will replace human brains: "it is best to view the electronic brains as instruments of human calculation, which achieve results that lie beyond human time and precision, but not beyond human intelligence" (1961). Brower describes Hiller and Isaacson's *Illiac Suite* as a "… rather ludicrous extension of the machine-brain equation to artistic creativity…" (1961). Zaripov, suggesting the presence of similar popular sentiments, writes, "the opinion is still widespread that if music is composed by an electronic machine, than it is bound to be cacophonic, unusual to our ear" (1969, p. 142). Herbert Russcol, separating attitudes toward mechanical sound production and mechanical composition, states: "antipathy toward the 'machine music' of the electronic synthesizer is mild compared with the shuddering hostility aroused by discussion of the use of computers as a tool to aid composition and musical exploration" (1972, p. 181). As Hiller implies by discussing the fear of automation, Russcol likewise states that "probably much of this fierce opposition to computer research in music is due to our dread that these 'supermachines' ultimately will make [humans] obsolete" (1972, p. 181). Roads, as recently as 1996, states that for these and additional reasons "… use of composition programs remains controversial" (1996, pp. 844-845).

Xenakis describes possible reactions of "the general public" to the "alliance of the machine with artistic creation" as ranging from rejection to over-enthusiasm (1992, p. 131). He in turn argues the necessity of community-defined rules of construction in all of the arts: "there have always been rules in every epoch because of the necessity of making oneself understood" (1992, p. 132). Xenakis suggests that, "if people's minds are in general ready to recognize the usefulness of geometry in the plastic arts … they have only one more stream to cross to be able to conceive of using more abstract, non-visual mathematics and machines as aids to musical composition…" (1992, p. 132).

Positive encounters with computer-produced musical structures, though less common in the early experiments, were recorded. Papworth modeled the traditional practice of bell change-ringing with a computer, and built a system to play sequences of changes on a loudspeaker. Papworth reports that "it is amusing to note that a party of change-ringers who heard this program were extremely impressed by what they called the 'perfect striking' of the machine" (1960, p. 50). If Papworth's system could have actually controlled real bells, these change ringers, perhaps fearing the loss of their employment, may have been less enthusiastic.

Composer George Rochberg reported in the *New York Times* that he "… didn't think the computer is capable of producing music … it creates something else … music comes out of human beings, not computers" (Severo 1982). Rochberg, assuming the computer itself is somehow responsible for its output, raises an important and common question of authorship. Authorship, though potentially distributed, is a designation that requires intention. In the choice of models, algorithms, and interface, the design of a CAAC system is a creative constraint. The system designer has an intention, and is an author. At the same time, the composer using the system has varying degrees of control over what is produced. The selection of algorithms, parameters, and component arrangements strongly determines the output. What is then done with this output is an additional compositional procedure. The composer, using the system, has an intention, and is an author. Music made with a CAAC system may have a distributed authorship, existing, to varying and perhaps indecipherable degrees, somewhere between the system designer and the composer. The computer itself, lacking intention, is simply a medium. Ian Cross has used intention to define music rather than authorship (1993), an argument not affirmed here.

Many authors, without considering intentionality, have simply asserted that the computer bears no authorship. Strang states that "the computer does not compose; it carries out instructions … the computer as composer must be considered a mirage" (1970, p. 41). In a similar statement, Gary Nelson asserts that "the computer does not compose … the computer is a musical medium in direct proportion to the musicality, technical skill, and imagination of those who use it" (1978, p. 330).

Distributed authorship is not a problem, though some have thought it so. Bruce Jacob, paraphrasing a common criticism, describes algorithmic composition as "… a cheat, a way out when the composer needs material and/or inspiration" (1996). Jacob suggest that this criticism results from a question of authorship: "music produced by algorithmic composition is considered somehow inferior not because it was produced by an algorithm, but because it is someone else's music — it belongs to the designer of the algorithm, and not to the user of the algorithm" (1996, p. 157). Jacob expands this view by stating that the goal of an algorithmic composition system should be to "reproduce the composer's creative methodology" (1996, p. 158) and that "the more closely an algorithm reflects a composer's methodology, the less question there is that the work is authentic" (1996, p. 158). Thus, if another person were then to use this system, they would be composing the system-author's music and "not their own" (1996, p. 158). This claim has many faults, and betrays a facile conception of algorithms and authorship. This claim assumes that all composition is "pure" algorithmic composition devoid of interpretation, a concept rejected above. By similar argument, compositions that employ specific synthesis algorithms, such as frequency modulation (FM) (Chowning 1973) or Karplus Strong (1983), are of dubious authorial integrity.

Any single output of a CAAC system is often one of many possible output variants. CAAC systems can be considered open works, works that "reject the definitive, concluded message and multiply the formal possibilities of the distribution of their elements" (Eco 1989, p. 3). The raw output of a CAAC system, in some contexts, may be an open work. An interactive, real-time sound installation, for instance, provides an example of a CAAC system functioning as an open work: the work itself is the accumulation of numerous variants. In many applications, however, CAAC tools are used to create closed works: the musical materials of a system are interpreted, filtered, recast, and arranged into fixed music by a composer. This process of interpretation may combine CAAC materials with more conventional, directly-specified materials. In such cases it is difficult, if not impossible, to isolate contributions from the system versus contributions from the human.

Some have distinguished between author and "meta-author" (Miranda 2000b, p. 8) or artist and "meta-artist" (Holtzman 1994, p. 221). In considering the authorship of an algorithmically-enabled composition, Miranda writes, "… the ultimate authorship of the composition here should be to the person who designed and/or operated the system"; further, "even in the case of a program that has the ability to program itself, someone is ultimately behind the design and/or the operation of the system" (Miranda 2000b, p. 8). Holtzman, going much further, imagines autonomous computer agents with their own creative objectives. These computers will "prodigiously compose, paint, write, and sculpt all day every day" while "oblivious to the debates surrounding origination, authorship, intentionality, and meaning" (1994, p. 221). It is likely that, even if such systems are built, the human designers, maintainers, and funders of such agents will be seen as possessing authorship, be it "meta" or otherwise.

Hamman has argued that the work itself subsumes the tools from which it originated, negating the idea that a musical work is autonomous from its technical methods. As Hamman states, with generative composition tools "composition becomes a form of 'system design' and musical artifacts become traces of that design … the musical work, per se, includes the acoustical trace (the acoustical 'artifact') plus the technical means by which that artifact is imagined, realized, and conceived" (2002, p. 110). Such a conception is appealing in that it captures many aspects of a work. Hamman does not address, however, how to delimit the boundaries of any particular technical means. For example, a composition composed with athenaCL may include materials from unrelated software tools, such as SuperCollider or Max/MSP. Further, athenaCL is built in Python. Perhaps the composer used athenaCL's Csound instruments. Csound and Python are built in the C language. All these tools, further, can only function on a general purpose computer that in turn relies on a host of additional technologies. Technical means are rarely discrete, and in the case of software, often rely on a long chain of dependencies. It is difficult to conceive of a work as including its technical means when technical means in turn include all the technology at ones disposal.

Some writers reject the dilution of authorship, and offer instead that the human motivator is always, essentially, the author. Varèse states that "the computing machine is a marvelous invention and seems almost superhuman … but in reality it is as limited as the mind of the individual who feeds it material" (1962, 2004, p. 20). Zaripov, in a related passage, emphasizes the essential role of humans in any musical production process: "the character of machine music, its orientation — all this depends wholly on the [person] setting up the program, on the programmer, on what [s/he] gets out of the machine, and finally, on [her/his] own concern for music" (1969, p. 142). Koenig, commenting on this problem, states "how difficult it is to separate the actual composition of a piece of music from auxiliary actions which are partly predominant or subordinate in the composition…" (1980a). What is considered subordinate in the composition, further, is often a matter of interpretation. Despite these complications, a composer, in some fashion, will always be responsible for a piece, either at the level of system user or system designer. Strang states that, no matter the degree of computer participation, "the main esthetic judgments are made by the composer, either in setting the conditions, or in evaluating the result … [s/he] formulates the criteria, and [s/he] retains the power of rejection"; in all cases, at a minimum, "acceptance or rejection must remain the responsibility of the composer" (1970, p. 41).

Chapter 3. The Landscape of Composition Systems

3.1. Introduction

A parade of computer music workstations has provided composers with the promise of brute strength, but most of these advances seem to be primarily technological in nature. Often the hardware technology of the 1990s uses the software technology of the 1970s and the 1980s to realize the musical concepts of the 1960s. That is the rub.

—Paul Berg (1996, p. 24)

3.1.1. A Definition of a Computer-Aided Algorithmic Composition System

Since 1955 a wide variety of CAAC systems have been created. In order to provide context for athenaCL system design, this chapter surveys the landscape of composition systems. This survey focuses on systems that relate to the design of athenaCL, and does not attempt a comprehensive examination. Despite Hiller's well-known claim that "computer-assisted composition is difficult to define, difficult to limit, and difficult to systematize" (Hiller 1981, p. 75), a definition is proposed.

A CAAC system is software that facilitates the generation of new music by means other than the manipulation of a direct music representation. Here, "new music" does not designate style or genre; rather, the output of a CAAC system must be, in some manner, a unique musical variant. An output, compared to the user's representation or related outputs, must not be a "copy," accepting that the distinction between a copy and a unique variant may be vague or contextually determined. This output may be in the form of any sound or sound parameter data, from a sequence of samples to the notation of a complete composition. A "direct music representation" refers to a linear, literal, or symbolic representation of complete musical events, such as an event list (a score in Western notation or a MIDI file) or an ordered list of amplitude values (a digital audio file or stream). Though all representations of aural entities are necessarily indirect to some degree, the distinction made here is not between these representations and aural entities. Rather, a distinction is made between the representation of musical entities provided to the user and the system output. If the representation provided to the user is the same as the output, that representation may reasonably be considered direct.

A CAAC system permits the user to manipulate indirect musical representations: this may take the form of incomplete musical materials (a list of pitches or rhythms), an equation, non-music data, an image, or meta-musical descriptions. Such representations are indirect in that they are not in the form of complete, ordered musical structures. In the process of algorithmic generation these indirect representations are mapped or transformed into a direct music representation for output. When working with CAAC software, the composer arranges and edits these indirect representations. The software interprets these indirect representations to produce musical structures.

This definition does not provide an empirical measure by which a software system, removed from use, can be identified as a CAAC system. Rather, a contextual delineation of scope is provided, based in part on use case. Consideration must be given to software design, functionality, and classes of user interaction.

This definition is admittedly broad, and is perhaps better suited to delineate what is not, rather than what is, a CAAC system. This definition includes all of the systems described in Chapter 2: the Experiments of Hiller and Isaacson (1959), Xenakis's SMP (1965), and Koenig's PR1 (1970a) and PR2 (1970b). In these cases the user provides initial musical and non-musical data (parameter settings, value ranges, stockpile collections), and these indirect representations are mapped into alpha-numeric score tables. This definition likewise encompasses Xenakis's GENDYN (1992) and Koenig's SSP (Berg et al. 1980). This definition includes any system that converts images (indirect representations) to sound, such as Mathews and Rosler's Graphic 1 system (1968) or Xenakis's UPIC (1992; Marino 1990; Marino et al. 1993). It does not matter how the images are made; they might be from a cellular automaton, a digital photograph, or hand-drawn. What matters is that the primary user-interface is an indirect representation. Some systems may offer the user both direct and indirect music representations. If one representation is primary, that representation may define the system; if both representations are presented equally to the user, a clear distinction may not be discernible.

This definition excludes, in most use cases, notation software. Such software is used primarily for manipulating and editing a direct music representation, namely Western notation. New music is not created by notation software: the output, the score, is the user-defined representation. Recently, systems such as the popular notation applications Sibelius (Sibelius Software Limited) and Finale (MakeMusic! Inc.) have added user-level interfaces for music data processing in the form of specialized scripting languages or plug-ins. These tools allow the user to manipulate and generate music data as notation. In this case, the script and its parameters are an indirect music representation and can be said to have attributes of a CAAC system. This is not, however, the primary user-level interface.

This definition excludes, in most use cases, digital audio workstations, sequencers, and digital mixing and recording environments. These tools, similar to notation software, are designed to manipulate and output a direct music representation. The representation, in this case, is MIDI note data, digital audio files, or sequences of event data. Again, new music is not created. The output is the direct representation that has been stored, edited, and processed by the user. Such systems often have modular processors (plug-ins or effects) for both MIDI and digital audio data. Some of these processors allow the user to control music data with indirect music representations. For example, a MIDI processor might implement an arpeggiator, letting the user, for a given base note, determine the scale, size, and movement of the arpeggio. In this case the configuration of the arpeggio is an indirect representation, and can be said to have attributes of a CAAC system. This is not, however, the primary user-level interface.

The notion of indirect and direct music representations relate, in some ways, to distinctions offered by other authors. Chadabe, discussing voltage-controlled systems, proposes a division between memory automation, where "… an automation system is used to realize what a composer has previously detailed" and process automation, where "… the composer decides the 'rules of the game' … and an automation system supplies … the details of the composition" (1975b, pp. 172-173, 1975a, p. 8). In the context presented above, direct representations relate to memory automation and indirect representations relate to process automation. Loy (1989) proposes two classes of music representations: symbolic, where tokens "… bear no overt resemblance to the sonic event" and iconic, where tokens "… resemble the sound being represented" (1989, pp. 321-322). Loy, referring to both programming languages and Western notation, states that "both symbolic and iconic elements seem necessary in music notational systems and languages" (1989, p. 322). Loy implies that symbolic and iconic representations are distinct, and does not address the interrelationships between these two terms. In the context presented above, indirect representations are related to Loy's symbols; direct representations are related to Loy's icons. The correspondence, however, is incomplete. Where Western notation is considered here to be a direct representation, Loy considers it to be a mixture of both symbols and icons.

Although categories for software systems are necessarily fluid and require overlapping, fuzzy boundaries, limited categorization is possible. Within the field of software systems, two categories of sound- and music-related systems may be isolated: synthesis systems and generative music systems. These categories partially overlap: some systems may have attributes of both synthesis systems and generative music systems. Though the category of generative music systems may include a wide range of software systems, two subcategories may be isolated: interactive music systems and CAAC systems. These two subcategories may overlap, and both may also overlap with the category of synthesis systems. Such a multi-layered delineation provides a context for considering the position of CAAC systems. The following diagram, combining aspects of Venn and Euler diagrams, illustrates this arrangement.

Example 3-1. The Position of CAAC Systems

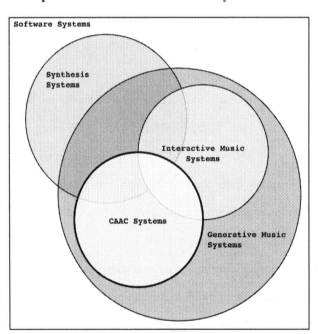

3.1.2. Research in Categorizing Composition Systems

The number and diversity of CAAC systems, and the diversity of interfaces, platforms, and licenses, have made categorization elusive. Significant general overviews of computer music systems have been provided by Roads (1984, 1985), Loy and Curtis Abbott (1985), Pennycook (1985), Loy (1989), and Pope (1993). These surveys, however, have not focused on generative or transformative systems.

Pennycook (1985) describes five types of computer music interfaces: (1) composition and synthesis languages, (2) graphics and score editing environments, (3) performance instruments, (4) digital audio processing tools, and (5) computer-aided instruction systems. This division does not attempt to isolate CAAC systems from tools used for modifying direct representations, such as score editing and digital audio processing. Loy (1989, p. 323) considers four types of languages: (1) languages used for music data input, (2) languages for editing music, (3) languages for specification of compositional algorithms, and (4) generative languages. This division likewise intermingles tools for direct representations (music data input and editing) with tools for indirect representations (compositional algorithms and generative languages). Pope's "behavioral taxonomy" (1993, p. 29), in focusing on how composers interact with software, is near to the goals of this study, but is likewise concerned with a much broader collection of systems, including "... software- and hardware-based systems for music description, processing, and composition ..." (1993, p. 26). Roads's survey of "algorithmic composition systems" divides software systems into four categories: (1) self-contained automated composition programs, (2) command languages, (3) extensions to traditional programming languages, (4) and graphical or textual environments including music programming languages (1996, p. 821). This division also relates to the perspective taken here, though neither degrees of "self-containment" nor distinctions between music languages and language extensions are considered.

Texts that have attempted to provide an overview of CAAC systems in particular have generally used one of three modes of classification: (1) chronological (Hiller 1981; Burns 1994), (2) division by algorithm type (Ames 1987, pp. 179-182; Dodge and Jerse 1997, p.

341; Miranda 2000a), or (3) division by output format or output scale (Buxton 1978, p. 10; Laske 1981, p. 120). All of these methods, however, fail to isolate important attributes from the perspective of the user and developer. A chronological approach offers little information on similarities between historically disparate systems, and suggests, incorrectly, that designs have developed along a linear trajectory. Many contemporary systems support numerous types of algorithms and numerous types of output formats. Taking the user as the primary perspective, this study classifies systems by their user-level interface. This categorization will be shown to be one of seven possible, and equally valid, descriptors of CAAC systems.

3.2. Primary Descriptors

3.2.1. The Difficulty of Distinctions

As discussed in Chapter 1, comparative software analysis is a difficult task, even if the software systems to be compared share a common purpose. Despite these challenges, such a comparison offers a useful vantage. Not only does a comparative framework demonstrate the diversity of systems available, it exposes similarities and relationships that might not otherwise be perceived.

In order to describe the landscape of software systems, it is necessary to establish distinctions. Rather than focusing on chronology, algorithms, or output types, seven descriptors of CAAC system design are proposed. These descriptors are scale, process time, idiom affinity, extensibility, event production, sound source, and user environment. All systems can, in some fashion, be defined by these descriptors. For each descriptor, a range of specifications is given. All CAAC systems have at least one specification for each descriptor. These specifications, in some cases, represent a gradient. In all cases these specifications are non-exclusive: for a single descriptor, some systems may have aspects of more than one specification. The use of multiple descriptors to describe a diverse field of systems is demonstrated by Pope in his "taxonomy of composer's software" (1993), where eighteen different "dimensions" are proposed and accompanied by fifteen two-dimensional system graphs. Unlike the presentation here, however, some of Pope's dimensions are only applicable to certain systems. John Biles, in his "tentative taxonomy" of evolutionary music systems (2003), likewise calls such descriptors "dimensions."

It is unlikely that an objective method for deriving and applying a complete set of software descriptors is possible in any application domain, let alone in one that integrates with the creative process of music composition. Consideration of use case, technological change, and the nature of creative production requires broad categories with specifications that are neither mutually exclusive nor quantifiable. The assignment of specifications, further, is an interpretation open to alternatives. Though this framework is broad, its imprecision permits greater flexibility than previous attempts. At the same time, this framework clearly isolates essential aspects of systems from the entire history of the field.

3.2.2. Scale: Micro and Macro Structures

The scale of a CAAC system refers to the level of musical structures the system produces. Two extremes of a gradient are defined: micro and macro. Micro structures are musical event sequences commonly referred to as sound objects, gestures, textures, or phrases: small musical materials that require musical deployment in larger structures. Micro structures scale from the level of samples and grains to collections of note events. In contrast, macro structures are musical event sequences that approach complete musical works. Macro structures often articulate a musical form, such as a sonata or a chorale, and may be considered complete compositions. The concept of micro and macro structures closely relates to what Miranda (2000a) calls bottom-up and top-down organizations, where bottom-up composition begins with micro structures, and top-down composition begins with macro structures.

Alternative time-scale labels for musical structures have been proposed. Vaggione has defined the lower limit of the macro-time domain as the note, while the micro-time domain is defined as sub-note durations on the order of milliseconds (2001, p. 60). Roads, in *Microsound* (2002, pp. 3-4), expands time into nine scales: infinite, supra, macro, meso, sound object, micro, sample, subsample, and infinitesimal. Macro, in the usage proposed here, refers to what Roads calls both macro and meso, while micro refers to what Roads calls meso, sound object, micro, and sample. Unlike the boundaries defined by Roads and Vaggione, the distinctions here are more fluid and highly dependent on context and musical deployment. Musical structure and temporal scales are, in part, a matter of interpretation. A composer may choose to create a piece from a single gesture, or to string together numerous large-scale forms.

Such a coarse distinction is useful for classifying the spectrum of possible outputs of CAAC systems. A few examples demonstrate the context-dependent nature of this descriptor. Xenakis's GENDYN, for instance, is a system specialized toward the generation of micro structures: direct waveform break-points at the level of the sample. Although Xenakis used this system to compose entire pieces (*GENDY3* (1991), *S709* (1994)), the design of the software is specialized for micro structures. Though the system is used to generate music over a large time-span, there is little control over large-scale form (Hoffman 2000). Kemal Ebcioglu's CHORAL system (1987, 1988), at the other extreme, is a system designed to create a complete musical form: the Bach chorale. Though the system is used to generate music over a relatively short time-span, concepts of large-scale form are encoded in the system.

3.2.3. Process Model: Real-Time and Non-Real-Time

The process model of a CAAC system refers to the relationship between the computation of musical structures and their output. A real-time (RT) system outputs each event after generation along a scheduled time line. A non-real-time (NRT) system generates all events first, then provides output. In the context of an RT CAAC system, the calculation of an event must be completed before its scheduled output. Some systems offer a single process model while others offer both.

Whether a system is RT or NRT determines, to a certain extent, the types of operations that can be completed. RT processes are a subset of NRT processes: some processes that can be done in NRT cannot be done in RT. For example, a sequence of events cannot be reversed or rotated in RT (this would require knowledge of future events). Mikael Laurson, addressing the limitations of RT compositional processes, points out that an RT process model "can be problematic, or even harmful": "composition is an activity that is typically 'out-of-time'" and further, "there are many musical problems that cannot be solved in real time ... if we insist on real-time performance, we may have to simplify the musical result" (1996, p. 19). Though a CAAC system need not model traditional cognitive compositional activities (whether out-of-time or otherwise), an RT process model does enforce computational limits.

In general, an RT system is limited to linear processes: only one event, or a small segment of events (a buffer, a window, or a frame), can be processed at once. An NRT system is not limited to linear processes: both linear and nonlinear processing are available. A nonlinear process might create events in a sequential order that is different than their eventual output order. For example, event start times might be determined by a Gaussian distribution mapped within a fixed time range; events in this case will not be created in the order of their ultimate output. An RT system, however, has the obvious advantage of immediate interaction. This interaction may be in response to the composer or, in the case of an interactive music system, in response to other musicians or physical environments.

As with other distinctions, these boundaries are not rigid. An RT system might, instead of generating one event at a time, generate events within a temporal frame, thus gaining some of the opportunities of NRT processing. Similarly, an NRT system, instead of calculating all events at once, might likewise calculate events in frames and then output these frames in RT, incurring a small delay but simulating RT performance.

Leland Smith's SCORE system (1972), for example, has an NRT process model: music, motives, and probabilities are specified in a text file for each parameter, and this file is processed to produce a score. James McCartney's SuperCollider language (1996) has an RT process model: with SuperCollider3 (SC3), instrument definitions (SynthDefs) are instantiated as nodes on a server and respond to RT messages (McCartney 2002).

3.2.4. Idiom Affinity: Singular and Plural

Idiom affinity refers to the proximity of a system to a particular musical idiom, style, genre, or form. Idiom, an admittedly broad term, is used here to refer collectively to many associated terms. As demonstrated in Chapter 2 as the "Constraint of Idiom," all CAAC systems, by incorporating some minimum of music-representation constructs, have an idiom affinity. A system with a singular idiom affinity specializes in the production of one idiom (or a small collection of related idioms), providing tools designed for the production of music in a certain form, from a specific time or region, or by a specific person or group. A system with a plural idiom affinity allows the production of multiple musical styles, genres, or forms.

The idea of idiom affinity is general. If a system offers only one procedural method of generating event lists, the system has a singular idiom affinity. Idiom affinity therefore relates not only to the design of low-level representations, but also to the flexibility of the large-scale music generators. The claim that all CAAC systems have an idiom affinity has been affirmed by many researchers. Truax states that, regardless of a system designer's claims, "all computer music systems explicitly and implicitly embody a model of the musical process that may be inferred from the program and data structure of the system…" (1976, p. 230). The claim that all systems have an idiom affinity challenges the goal of "musical neutrality," a term used by Laurson to suggest that "the hands of the user should not be tied to some predefined way of thinking about music or to a certain musical style" (1996, p. 18). Laurson claims, contrary to the view stated here, that by creating primitives that have broad applicability and allowing for the creation of new primitives, a system can maintain musical neutrality despite the incorporation of "powerful tools for representing musical phenomena" (1996, p. 18). Musical neutrality can be approached, but it can never be fully realized.

Koenig's PR1 (1970a), for example, is a system with a singular idiom affinity: the system exposes few configurable options to the user and, in its earliest versions, offers the user no direct control over important musical parameters such as form and pitch. Berg's AC Toolbox (2003) has a plural idiom affinity: low level tools and objects (such as data sections, masks, and stockpiles) are provided, but they are very general, they are not supplied with defaults, and they can be deployed in a variety of configurations.

3.2.5. Extensibility: Closed and Open

Extensibility refers to the ability of a software system to be extended. This often means adding code, either in the form of plug-ins or other modular software components. In terms of object-oriented systems, this is often done by creating a subclass of a system-defined object, inheriting low-level functionality and a system-compatible interface. An open system allows extensibility: new code can be added to the system by the user. A closed system does not allow the user to add code to the system or change its internal processing in any way other than the parameters exposed to the user.

In terms of CAAC systems, a relationship often exists between the extensibility of a system and its idiom affinity. Systems that have a singular idiom affinity tend to be closed; systems that have a plural idiom affinity tend to be open. All open-source systems, by allowing users to manipulate system source code, have open extensibility. Closed-source systems may or may not provide open extensibility.

Joel Chadabe's and David Zicarelli's M (Zicarelli 1987; Chadabe 1997, p. 316), for instance, is a closed, stand-alone application: though highly configurable, new code, objects, or models cannot be added to the system or interface. Miller Puckette's cross-platform PureData (1997) is an open system: the language is open source and extensible through the addition of compiled modules programmed in C.

3.2.6. Event Production: Generation and Transformation

A distinction can be made between the generation of events from indirect music representations (such as algorithms or lists of musical materials) and the transformation of direct music representations (such as MIDI files) with indirect models. Within some CAAC systems, both processes are available, allowing the user to work with both the organization of generators and the configuration of transformers. Other systems focus on one form over another. As will be detailed in Chapter 5, the division between generators and transformers, like other distinctions, is fluid and contextual.

Andre Bartetzki's Cmask system (1997) allows the generation of event parameters with a library of stochastic functions, generators, masks, and quantizers. Tools for event transformation are not provided. Cope's EMI system (1996) employs a transformative model, producing new music based on analyzed MIDI files, extracting and transforming compositional patterns and signatures. Tools are not provided to generate events without relying on structures extracted from direct music representations.

3.2.7. Sound Source: Internal, Exported, Imported, External

All CAAC systems produce event data for sound production. This event data can be realized by different sound sources. In some cases a system contains the complete definition of sound-production components (instrument algorithms) and is capable of internally producing the sound through an integrated signal processing engine. The user may have complete algorithmic control of not only event generation, but signal processing configuration. Such a system has an internal sound source. In other cases a system may export complete definitions of sound-production components (instrument algorithms) to another system. The user may have limited or complete control over signal processing configuration, but the actual processing is exported to an external system. For example, a system might export Csound instrument definitions or SuperCollider SynthDefs. Such a system has an exported sound source. In a related case a CAAC system may import sound source information from an external system, automatically performing necessary internal configurations. For example, loading instrument definitions into a synthesis system might automatically configure their availability and settings in a CAAC system. Such a system has an imported sound source. In the last case a system may define the sound source only with a label and a selection of sound-source parameters. The user has no control over the sound source except through values supplied to event parameters. Examples include a system that produces Western notation for performance by acoustic instruments or a system that produces a Csound score for use with an external Csound orchestra. Such a system has an external sound source. As with other descriptors, some systems may allow for multiple specifications.

Roger Dannenberg's Nyquist (1997b) is an example of a system with an internal sound source: the language provides a complete synthesis engine in addition to indirect music representations. The athenaCL system is an example of a system that uses an exported sound source: a Csound orchestra file can be dynamically constructed and configured each time an event list is generated. Taube's Common Music supports an imported sound source: Common Lisp Music (CLM) instruments, once loaded, are automatically registered within CM (1997, p. 30). Clarence Barlow's Autobusk system (1990) uses an external sound source: the system provides RT output for MIDI instruments.

3.2.8. User Environment: Language, Batch, Interactive

The user environment is the primary form in which a CAAC system exposes its abstractions to the user. The user environment thus provides the framework in which the user configures system abstractions. A CAAC system may provide multiple environments, or allow users to construct their own environments and interfaces. The primary environment the system presents to the user can, however, be isolated. The overview of user environments provided here will be developed below as a method for general system classification.

Loy (1989, p. 319) attempts to distinguish languages, programs, and (operating) systems. Contemporary systems, however, are not so discrete: a "program" may allow internal scripting or external coding through the program's API; a "language" may only run within a platform-specific program. Particularly in the case of CAAC systems, where at least minimal access to code-level interfaces is common, the division between "language" and "program" is not useful. Such features are here considered aspects of user environment. Language, batch, and interactive environments, while not always discrete, are isolated because they involve different types of computer-user interaction. Loy even considers some systems, such as Koenig's PR1 and PR2, to be languages (1989, p. 324), even though, in the context of computer-user interaction, it has never been possible to program in the "language" of either system.

A language interface provides the user with an artificial language to design and configure music abstractions. There are two forms of languages: text and graphic. A text language is composed with standard text-editors, and includes programming languages, markup-languages, or formal languages and grammars. A graphic language (sometimes called a visual language) is used within a program that allows the organization of software components as visual entities, usually represented as a network of interconnected boxes upon a two-dimensional plane. A box may have a set of inputs and outputs; communication between boxes is configured by drawing graphic lines from inputs to outputs. Laurson (1996) provides a thorough comparison of text and graphic languages. He summarizes differences between the two paradigms: text languages offer compliance with standards, compactness, and speed, whereas graphic languages offer intuitive programming logic, intuitive syntax, defaults, and error checking (1996, p. 16). These differences are not true for all languages: some visual languages offer speed, while some text languages offer an intuitive syntax.

A batch interface is a system that only permits the user to provide input data, usually in the form of a text file or a list of command-line options. The input data, here called a manifest, is processed and the program returns a result. As Roads points out, batch processes refer "… to the earliest computer systems that ran one program at a time; there was no interaction with the machine besides submitting a deck of punched paper cards for execution and picking up the printed output" (1996, p. 845). Modern batch systems, in addition to being very fast, offer considerably greater flexibility of input representation. Though an old model, batch processing is still useful and, for some tasks, superior to interaction. The manifest may resemble a text programming language, but often lacks the expressive flexibility of a complete language. A batch system does not permit an interactive-session: input is processed and returned in one operation. What is desired from the software must be completely specified in the manifest. Curiously, Pope defines a batch system as distinct from RT and "rapid turnaround" systems not by its particular interface or user environment, but by "... the delay between the capture or description of signal, control, or event and its audible effect" (1993, p. 29). More than just a performance constraint, modern batch environments define a particular form of user interaction independent of performance time or process model.

An interactive interface allows the user to issue commands and, for each command, get a response. Interactive interfaces usually run in a session environment: the user works inside the program, executing discrete commands and getting discrete responses. Interactive interfaces often have tools to help the user learn the system, either in the form of help messages, error messages, or user syntax correction. Interactive interfaces often let the user browse the materials that they are working with and the resources available in the system, and may provide numerous different representations of these materials. Such a system may be built with text or graphics. Focusing on interactive systems over interactive interfaces, Roads distinguishes between (1) "... light interactions experienced in a studio-based 'composing environment,' where there is time to edit and backtrack..." and (2) "... real-time interaction experienced in working with a performance system onstage, where ... there is no time for editing" (1996, p. 846). While this distinction is valuable for discussing context-based constraints of system use, many CAAC systems, with either language interfaces or interactive interfaces, support both types of system interaction as described by Roads. Here, use of interaction refers more to user-system interaction in NRT or RT production, rather than user-music interaction in RT production.

An interactive text interface is a program that takes input from the user as text and provides text output. These systems often operate within a virtual terminal descended from the classic DEC VT05 (1975) and VT100 (1978) hardware. The UNIX shell is a common text interface. Contemporary text interfaces interact with the operating system and window manager, allowing a broad range of functionality including the production of graphics. These graphics, in most cases, are static and cannot be used to manipulate internal representations. An interactive text interface system may have a graphic user interface (GUI). Such a system, despite running in a graphic environment, conducts user interaction primarily with text. An interactive graphics interface employs a GUI for the configuration and arrangement of user-created entities. Users can alter musical representations by directly designing and manipulating graphics.

As with other descriptors, these specifications are not exclusive. A CAAC system may offer aspects of both a graphical and a textual programming language. The manifest syntax of a batch system may approach the flexibility of a complete text language. An interactive text or graphics system may offer batch processing or access to underlying system functionality as a language-based API. Despite these overlapping environments, it is nonetheless useful, when possible, to classify a system by its primary user-level interface.

Bill Schottstaedt's Pla system (1983) is an example of a text language. Laurson's Patchwork system (Laurson and Duthen 1989) provides an example of a graphical language. Mikel Kuehn's nGen (2001) is a batch user environment: the user creates a manifest, and this file is processed to produced Csound scores. Joel Chadabe's PLAY system demonstrates an interactive text interface, providing the user a shell-like environment for controlling the system (1978). Finally, Laurie Spiegel's Music Mouse system (1986) provides an example of an interactive graphic system.

3.3. A Classification of Systems

3.3.1. The Primacy of User Environment

Any of the descriptors defined above may be used to partition CAAC systems. This dissertation isolates user environment as the primary method of classification. This choice is based on the notion that CAAC systems are to be used by composers. Composers, before exploring the algorithms or output formats of a system, must navigate the system's environment. As mentioned in Chapter 1, this presentation of systems is not comprehensive, but instead focuses on systems of greater historical and comparative value in the overall context of this study.

3.3.2. Specialized Text Languages

A specialized language, as described above, is a computer programming language, or a symbolic artificial language of any sort, extended to handle CAAC. A language may be extended by offering some combination of specialized, high-level musical abstractions. These tools may include models of musical materials (pitch, rhythm, meter), hierarchical organizations, utilities for external communication (MIDI, OpenSound Control (OSC)), or signal processing facilities. Such languages are the most general CAAC tools. Often a user interacts with such systems by writing and processing code files either in an NRT or an RT process model. Such languages may be used to build larger systems that employ different user environments.

Many CAAC systems have been created by extending the Lisp language into speciality sub-languages. Lisp, through the use of macros, is particularly suited to this approach. The Formes system (Rodet and Cointe 1984), developed in the Vlisp environment, offers the Lisp language with high-level tools for temporal organization of generative processes. This system was originally developed to provide parameter control and generation for IRCAM's CHANT synthesis model (Rodet and Cointe 1984, p. 405). A fundamental unit of the system is the "process," or a dynamic parameter generator (Chadabe 1997, p. 126). The goal of Formes is to provide a language with easy access to and manipulation of collections of these process models, offering "libraries of predefined musical models," while at the same time creating hierarchical tools that are general and compatible with each other (Loy and Abbott 1985, p. 260). The Formes schedular, performing processes organized in a "calculation tree," allows time to selectively activate processes within a complex nested structure (Rodet and Cointe 1984, p. 409). Loy refers to this organization as a "genealogical hierarchy" of objects (1989, p. 364). Fry's Flavors Band, built in Lisp Machine Lisp, provides a specialized Lisp dialect for the creation of "phrase processor" networks. These networks can be modularized, interconnected, and share event streams. The system, while primarily a specialized text language, offers basic GUI facilities in the form of twenty hierarchical menus. These menus facilitate access to documentation, examples, and code evaluation (Fry 1984b, p. 305). Roger Dannenberg has developed a number of Lisp-based languages for composition and synthesis. These include Canon (Dannenberg 1989) and Nyquist (Dannenberg 1997b, 1997a). Rahn's Lisp Kernel (1990b, 1990a), an NRT language specialized for supporting diverse sound sources, and Henkjan Honing's POCO system, implemented in Allegro Common Lisp (1990), provide additional examples of specialized CAAC Lisp environments.

Languages other than Lisp have likewise been extended. Pla, in its earliest form, extended the SAIL language (Schottstaedt 1983, 1989b; Loy and Abbott 1985, p. 257). In addition to the resources of a complete programming language, Pla has high-level constructs for music processing, including models for pitch, rhythm, voice, and section. The "voice" model, in particular, offers a sophisticated example of a generative musical part. Schottstaedt illustrates the use of a voice as a musical line, "encapsulating the knowledge necessary to produce that melody without making any assumptions about the context in which the melody is expressed" (1989b, p. 219). Facilities exist to output event lists in various graphic formats, as well as in Western notation (Loy and Abbott 1985, p. 259).

Taube's Common Music language (1989, 1991, 1996, 1997, 2004), although a specialized Lisp dialect, grew out of Taube's long experience with Pla. Taube considers Pla the "intellectual ancestor" of Common Music (1991, p. 21). Common Music is a language based on Common Lisp. Common Music has historically supported three user environments: a specialized text language, an interactive text interface (called Stella), and an interactive graphic interface (called Capella) (Taube 1997, pp. 29-30). As these environments were later added on top of the system's specialized text language, the text language can be seen as the primary user interface. Common Music supports numerous external sound sources (Csound, CMix, Common Music Notation, and others), as well as imported sound sources when used with Common Lisp Music (1997, p. 30).

The Hierarchical Music Specification Language (HMSL), originally developed in the early 1980s by Larry Polansky and David Rosenboom with input from Tenney (Chadabe 1997, p. 303), offers an extension of the FORTH language for music structuring and generation (Polansky and Rosenboom 1985; Polansky et al. 1990). HMSL implements models derived from perception and cognition theory, and introduces "morphological metrics" as a means of measuring distances and facilitating movement between shapes (Polansky and Rosenboom 1985, p. 243). This language has been ported to the Java language to become the Java Music Specification Language (JMSL), and is now maintained by Phil Burk and Nick Didkovsky (Didkovsky 2001). JMSL supports RT processing and, among other resources, provides tools for the hierarchical organization of musical materials. The LOCO environment, an extension of the LOGO language, was created by Peter Desain and Honing (Desain and Honing 1988; Honing 1990). Pope has created specialized Smalltalk environments including HyperScore (Pope 1987), the Music Object Development Environment (MODE) and, within MODE, the Smalltalk Music Object Kernel (Smoke) (Pope 1992, 1996). Pope's aim with Smoke is a "representation, description language, and interchange format for musical data …" (1996, p. 66); the system offers CAAC functionality with stochastic selection criteria (1996, p. 64) and algorithmic event generators and modifiers (1996, p. 63). James McCartney's SuperCollider, although primarily a language for digital signal processing, has a broad set of tools that can be used for algorithmic design (McCartney 1996, 2002). SuperCollider can be seen as a specialization of the Smalltalk language.

Generalizations about text languages are possible only with a subset of the descriptors defined above. All specialized text languages, depending on their use, can create musical structures anywhere from micro to macro. Specialized text languages, though containing low-level structures for defining musical entities, often have a plural idiom affinity. As all text languages are designed as complete programming languages and, in many cases, are based on a full-featured language, extensibility is always open. Event production is determined entirely by the user, and can employ any variety of generative or transformative techniques.

3.3.3. Specialized Graphic Languages

Graphic languages code software systems with visual objects in a GUI environment. Graphic languages have both advantages and disadvantages over text languages. Graphic languages often offer inexperienced programmers high-level tools for rapid programming, and express many design archetypes in an intuitive fashion. On the other hand graphic languages, when used to program large systems, can be difficult to debug and maintain. For instance, programmatically editing and modifying code is very difficult (if not impossible) in most graphic languages.

There are two primary families of specialized graphic languages for CAAC. The first family is centered around the Max language (Puckette 2002) and its signal processing extensions Max Signal Processing (MSP) (Puckette 1991). The JMax environment, maintained at IRCAM, and the open-source PD environment, led by Miller Puckette, are closely related systems. Max/MSP and PD are developed in C, and allow the graphic language to be extended with text-programmed external modules or embedded interpreters. This extension is necessary in many contexts. As Puckette offers, "musicians have often used Max as a programming environment, at which Max succeeds only very awkwardly … programming as such is better undertaken within the tasks than by building networks of existing tasks" (2002, p. 39). Laurson has criticized Max's interface to text-based language as "neither flexible nor intuitive" (1996, p. 23). In the past, extending Max required using a separate development environment to compile C-coded extensions; newer versions of Max provide interfaces to higher-level text languages such as JavaScript. The Max/MSP family of applications are designed primarily for working within an RT process model with internal and external sound sources.

The second family of graphic languages includes PatchWork (PW), OpenMusic (OM), and PWGL. Patchwork was conceived and initially developed by Laurson (Laurson and Duthen 1989; Laurson 1996); further development was conducted at IRCAM. While PatchWork is no longer maintained, Laurson has reformulated many of its design concepts into the PWGL system (Laurson and Kuuskankare 2002, 2003). Many concepts and design models from PatchWork have been incorporated into IRCAM's OpenMusic (Assayag et al. 1997, 1999). Although stating that PatchWork is "one of the most powerful and versatile programs currently available to aid a composer" Assayag et al. fault the PatchWork source code as being in "tremendous disorder" such that "… major structural changes are extremely difficult and may produce innumerable hidden consequences" (Assayag et al.

1997). OpenMusic reimplemented the PatchWork patch editor, added user interface features, added the ability to do loops and link information between patches, and added the Maquette Editor, an interface that allows "the creation of blocks placed in spatial and/or temporal relationships" (1997). OpenMusic has been popular with composers and researchers at IRCAM, and a wide library of tools, employing many algorithmic models, have been developed for the system. This family of systems is distinguished by an emphasis on producing and manipulating Western notation. Discussing OpenMusic and related CAAC systems, Assayag states that the ideal system "… is thus a language that encapsulates in a consubstantial way the concept of notation, notation of the result (a musical score) but also notation of the process leading to this result (a visual program)" (1998). PatchWork, OpenMusic, and PWGL are all implemented in Lisp, and allow various ways of extending the graphic environment with text-based Lisp code. As Laurson writes of PW, "every Lisp function or CLOS method can automatically be transformed into a PW-box" (1996, p. 23). The PW family of systems were initially designed for working within an NRT process model and with external sound sources (1996, p. 24).

Numerous additional graphic languages have been developed that, although allowing CAAC functionality, focus primarily on tools for synthesis. Scaletti's Kyma system, an object-oriented, Smalltalk-based environment for composition and synthesis, provides a visual programming language as a front end to a dedicated hardware synthesis engine (Scaletti 1987, 1989a, 1989b, 2002; Scaletti and Johnson 1988). The Reaktor system (Native Instruments) is a popular graphic language for synthesis and interface design. Although primarily designed for developing RT virtual instruments, the system is extensible through a graphic programming environment and users have developed instruments employing a variety of CAAC models. Reaktor is an RT system designed for internal and external (MIDI) sound sources.

Generalizations about specialized graphic languages are similar to those possible for text languages. The scale of such systems is determined entirely by the user, though as mentioned before, large-scale systems (potentially useful for producing macro musical structures) can become cumbersome in graphic languages. As languages, idiom affinity is plural, extensibility is open, and all forms of event generation and transformation are possible.

3.3.4. Batch Processors

Batch processors store all necessary specifications for system operation in a manifest. The manifest may use a text or a graphic format to collect data from the user. This data is then processed into musical output. There is no interaction with the user, save reporting if an operation has succeeded or failed.

The early systems of Xenakis (SMP) and Koenig (PR1, PR2) can be seen as batch processors. In all cases initial data is provided by the user and is then processed to produce musical output; scale is macro, process model is NRT, idiom affinity is singular, extensibility is closed, event production is based only on generation, and sound source is external (Western notation for acoustic instruments).

The SCORE system (Smith 1972) was the first batch processor developed to provide an external front end to the Music N score language. SCORE, because of its integration in the event processing of Music V, was called a pre-processor: SCORE was developed "as an improvement on the Pass 1 and Pass 2 stages of processing in Music V" (Loy and Abbott 1985, p. 258). For the parameters of each instrument, arrays of values are either directly specified or assigned generators in the manifest. Events are created by taking values from these arrays for each parameter; an array is looped if more than the available values are necessary (Loy and Abbott 1985, p. 258). SCORE's flexible manifest syntax provides a compact representation of rhythm and pitch sequences, motivic repetitions with transformations, and randomly generated and masked values.

The model of the SCORE system was continued by Michael David Good with Scot (Good 1979) and by Alexander Brinkman with Score11 (Brinkman 1981). Both systems are batch processors designed for use with Music 11. Brinkman's Score11 was later ported for broader use (Gross et al. 2000). Mikel Kuehn's nGen is a portable, cross-platform expansion of Score11. These systems allow the user to define external instruments with variable numbers of parameters. Each parameter can be defined by specifying a collection of nested or sequential generators. Cmask, by Andre Bartetzki (1997), is a batch processor closely related to the SCORE tradition. Cmask specializes in stochastic parameter generators combined with Koenig-inspired dynamic tendency masks. As with Score11 and nGen, the user creates a manifest specifying the parts, their parameters, and specifications for the generators of each parameter.

The SCORE family of CAAC systems, including Scot, Score11, nGen, and Cmask, has many descriptors in common. Generally, these tools are used at the scale of micro musical structures; process model is NRT, idiom affinity is plural, extensibility is closed, event production is generative, and sound source is external (usually limited to Music N languages).

Many of the systems developed by Cope, including EMI, SARA, and Alice, can be seen as batch processors (Cope 1987; 1991; 1992; 1996; 2000). When working with these systems, the user provides a library of complete music representations (MIDI score files) that are then analyzed to produce new music in the style demonstrated by the library. The environment does not provide an interactive interface, though the user can configure various initial settings. Alternatively, Cope describes a one-thousand question yes or no survey that can be used to "… control the program's choices of constraints" (1991, p. 89). These systems specialize in macro structures and have NRT process models, singular idiom-affinities (limited to Western concert music represented as MIDI files), transformative event production methods, closed extensibility, and external sound sources.

3.3.5. Interactive Text Interface Systems

An interactive interface system is often less general than a language: because the system has a user interface, musical constructs and system design are frequently more strongly determined. At the same time, an interactive user interface improves user experience, particularly for users who are not programmers, and can support robust backwards compatibility to architectural changes, as the interface mediates between the user and low-level implementations. As mentioned above, an interactive text interface system may have a GUI.

Truax's POD programs (1973) provide a real-time, interactive environment for composition. Using a text-based interface, the user controls compositional designs and synthesis parameters by supplying command names and necessary command arguments. The system, using a Poisson distribution and user-specified tendency masks to determine event time and frequency, featured an internal sound source, and is seen by Truax as a "MUSIC5 type system with a specific set of compositional subroutines and specialized synthesis instrument" (1976, p. 267). In addition to the features of interactive systems described above, Truax, concerned with the analysis of software systems, offers that interactive systems "create the best situation for observing problem-solving activity…" (1976, p. 239) and provide "new sources of data for the music theorist" (1976, p. 240).

The system PLAY, developed in 1977 by Chadabe and Roger Meyers, is often described as a language. Loy and Abbott describe PLAY as an "interpretively implemented data-flow language" (1985, p. 253); Loy later describes PLAY as a "real-time control language" (1989, p. 341). Although this interpretation is valid, PLAY has an interactive text-based interface: users enter commands, the system provides prompts for necessary data, and real-time processes are executed or dynamically altered. PLAY may be considered a text interface system. Doug Collinge's MOXIE system (Loy and Abbott 1985, p. 255; Loy 1989, p. 353) offers a related model, though with a less robust text interface.

Bernard Bel and James Kippen's BOL Processor can be seen as a text interface system. Although the program uses a GUI environment, the user primarily configures parameters by providing text strings in the system's generative grammar syntax. This system has a micro scale, RT process model, singular idiom affinity, closed extensibility, generative and transformative event production, and external sound source.

Berg's AC Toolbox, built in Lisp, offers a large library of musical structures and tools for parameter event generation and transformation, with outputs to MIDI (RT and NRT), Csound, audio file, and Kyma. Although the program runs within a GUI application and employs numerous windows and dialog boxes, the user enters Lisp code strings to configure and define objects and their parameters. The AC Toolbox offers some features of an interactive graphic interface system. Menu-based object creation, browsing, and preferences are configured with a GUI. More importantly, the system allows masks and shapes to be graphically drawn, stored, and edited; these graphic representations can then be transformed and mapped to any desired numeric representation. Flexible tools are provided for visualizing data, including event timelines and histograms. This system has a scale from micro to macro, NRT and RT process models, plural idiom affinity, open extensibility, generative and transformative event production, and internal and external sound sources.

The athenaCL system provides an interactive text interface. Rather than using a GUI, athenaCL runs within a command-line terminal application (on UNIX platforms) or the

Python interpreter. This text interface provides maximal cross-platform compatibility while providing the benefits of a user interface. The system has its own high-level command syntax (related to UNIX shell commands) and parameter syntax (related to the Python language). All commands can be utilized either as single command-line arguments, or through interactive text-based dialogs, the system prompting the user for all necessary information and providing useful error messages. Although interaction is primarily text-based, facilities are provided for visualizing data as graphical multi-parameter event timelines. This system supports micro and macro scale structures, and has an NRT process model, plural idiom affinity, open extensibility, both generative and transformative event production, internal, external, and exported sound sources, and can function as an interactive text interface system, a batch processor, and as a text-based language extension to Python. The user interface of athenaCL will be described in detail in Chapter 6.

3.3.6. Interactive Graphic Interface Systems

Graphic interface systems have diverse and wide-ranging designs. Though they may have many features in common with text interface systems, the primary user-level interface is provided by graphic or spatially-defined objects exclusively within a GUI environment. Graphic interface systems can be divided into two groups by system extensibility.

The first group of interactive graphic systems has closed extensibility. One of the earliest interactive graphic systems was Laurie Spiegel's Music Mouse, developed in 1986 (Spiegel 1986; Burns 1994, p. 121). This system lets the user, through typed key strokes and the movement of the mouse within a grid, control real-time melodic and harmonic musical gestures. The system M, developed by Chadabe and Zicarelli and first distributed by the company Intelligent Music in 1987 (Chadabe 1997, p. 316), provides a graphical environment to deploy and configure RT algorithmic pattern transformations. The system

Jam Factory, developed in the late 1980s by Zicarelli (1987), provides Markov- and pattern-based tools for CAAC. Both systems present all of their configureable parameters within a single window display. The user edits parameters by selecting boxes, drawing grids, or other visual operations. Clarence Barlow's Autobusk system provides three real-time, independent, algorithmic voices, each configured by a variety of parameters for specialized interval selection (harmonicity and intervalic indigestibility) and meter interpretation (rhythmic indispensability) algorithms (Barlow 1987, 1990). As with M and Jam Factory, all RT options are presented in a single window. Miranda's CAMUS application provides a specialized graphic interface environment for employing Cellular Automata (CA) to generate musical structures (McAlpine and Miranda 1999; Miranda 2000a). Closed interactive graphic systems have many common features. Most are intended for either micro or macro structures, perform RT processing, have a singular idiom affinity, deal primarily with event generation, and rely on MIDI as an external sound source.

The second group of interactive graphic systems has open extensibility. KeyKit (formerly called Keynote), designed by Tim Thompson in 1990, is a MIDI-based system that allows graphically arranging and configuring algorithmic parts (Roads 1996, p. 815). The system may also function as a specialized text-language. Related models can be found in Oppenheim's Dmix environment (Oppenheim 1989, 1990, 1994) and Steven Yi's Java-based system blue (2005). These systems, within graphic environments, allow flexibility in arranging and combining algorithmic tools. These systems can be used for micro or macro structures, have a plural idiom affinity, generative and transformative event production, and provide output to external sound sources.

Chapter 4. Abstractions of Musical Materials

4.1. Introduction

> Unfortunately many authors describe their systems from the perspective of what a prospective user
> has to know to make the program work, instead of presenting the general and specific models which
> the system implements, and the role of the system in the entire process involving the user. At worst,
> the reader is presented with a printout of the program text itself.... The tendency to rely on this
> type of descriptive detail ... generally betrays a lack of concern for making explicit the premises and
> implications of the program.
>
> —Barry Truax (1976, pp. 251-252)

Computers are symbol manipulators (Dijkstra 1989, p. 1401). When the Countess of
Lovelace speaks of the "abstract science of operations" possible with the Analytic Engine,
she speaks of symbol manipulation. She sees the potential for the machine to make music
because she sees that the machine can manipulate and process symbols of any sort, not just
numbers. In the case of CAAC, the computer manipulates symbols that take on musical
interpretations. Some of these symbols may be analogous to Western notational symbols
(pitches, rhythms). Other symbols may be analogous to production phases of musical
practice, either in the form of persons (performers, critics, conductors) or things
(instruments, spaces). Such symbols, as notation or otherwise, are not music. Musical
procedures are used to translate symbols into music.

In the case of software systems, a symbol can take on great complexity, involving both
data and procedural operations. A symbol, in object-oriented programming, becomes an
object. How the object is designed, what features are included, and what operations are
presented are aspects of abstraction. Software abstraction is the process of reducing an entity
or process into a discrete and constrained specification.

Many early CAAC systems, and numerous modern systems, treat musical parameter values exclusively as data symbols. This data is either numeric (such as time or pitch values) or symbolic (such as dynamic symbols or performance articulations). With object-oriented programming, it is possible to model musical materials and procedures as specialized objects. Although not necessarily offering computational advantages, such techniques allow for more intuitive controls, transformations, and interactions of musical materials. The object design and interface directly affect the utility of the component. In the creation of CAAC systems, object design can leverage domain-specific musical knowledge, incorporating this knowledge into the utility of software symbols.

The following three chapters explore in detail the structure of the athenaCL system. This chapter focuses on object design of musical materials, or musical entities most often thought of as "things": pitches, groups of pitches, rhythms, instruments, and orchestras. Chapter 5 focuses on musical entities more often thought of as "actions": processes or transformations. These chapters together demonstrate that the use of specialized objects for musical materials, rather than numeric data-processing, provides advantages at numerous levels, from low-level object interactions to representations presented to the user.

4.2. The Pitch Model

Much musical practice suggests the need for reusable pitch collections. In many musical traditions pre-compositional pitch structures such as modes, scales, chord progressions, sets, and rows have offered musicians valuable models. Certainly, such structures are often the result of analytical reductions. Nonetheless, delimited pitch collections may offer a useful pre-compositional resource.

In athenaCL, reusable pitch material is provided as the Path. The Path consists of any number of Multiset objects. Multiset objects, in turn, consist of any number of Pitch objects.

Paths, as user objects, can be created and stored within athenaCL, and can be analyzed both as state information (sets) and as transformations between those states (map classes or voice leadings). Every user-created Texture (as defined in Chapter 1) contains a reference to a single Path. The Path provides the Texture with a partitioned pitch structure. The Texture can interpret this pitch information in various ways, treating it as chords, melodies, harmonies, motives, or scales.

The production of Event pitch values, from a Pitch in a Multiset to an OutputFormat, requires many steps. Paths are created with various Multiset formats; Textures may interpret Pitches within Multisets as pitch, pitch class, or set class values; these values are selected by the Texture, processed, and then transposed by interval and octave with standard Texture Generator ParameterObjects for "local field" and "local octave" slots. The Texture's Temperament object is then used to fine tune pitch values. Finally, the Pitch is filtered through an Orchestra postMap method to convert the value to the data type and range required by the Texture's Instrument model.

4.2.1. The Pitch

4.2.1.1. Model and Representation

The Pitch object provides a low-level representation of a single discrete pitch entity. The Pitch stores a data attribute for a microtonal pitch space value, and contains methods for transposing, inverting, and converting this value to numerous representations. Generally, the user does not interact directly with Pitch objects, but rather with their higher-level representations in Multisets and Paths. Occasionally the user is required to provide a single Pitch, for example, in the specification boundaries for Xenakis sieves. In these cases Pitch objects are created independently of Multisets or Paths.

The Pitch object provides easy input of and access to the large variety of pitch representations needed for internal processing and specific OutputFormats. Pitch representations supported by the Pitch object include pitch class (pc), MIDI (midi), pitch space real (psReal), pitch space name (psName), PCH (pch), and frequency (fq). Rich representations, such as psReal, PCH, and frequency, include both register position and microtonal tuning. Other representations, such as MIDI and pitch space name do not generally include microtonal tunings. The pitch class representation is the least rich, offering neither register nor microtonal tuning.

The psReal, or pitch space real pitch representation, is the native representation of the Pitch object, and is used throughout athenaCL for internal pitch processing. The psReal uses floating-point numbers to represent pitch space values. The value 0 is fixed at middle C (C4), and pitches can vary to any degree above or below this value. The value of a half-step is 1.0, and floating-point values can be used to provide any degree of microtonal variation. For example, 0.5 would represent C~4, the quarter-tone between C4 and C#4. Alphabetic note-naming conventions will be explained in detail below. A precedent for setting C4 to 0 is found in Mathews' "logarithmic frequency scale," though in his scale the size of the half-step, rather than an integer, is 0.083 (or 1.0 divided by 12), and the size of the octave, rather than 12, is 1 (1969, p. 80).

The MIDI pitch representation, based on the seven-bit integer range (128 values) of the MIDI 1.0 specification (1983), is an integer scale from 0 to 127 where middle C is assigned the value of 60. The Pitch object optionally extends this representation by including microtones (floating-point values) and extending register (below 0 and above 127). For example, 60.5m would represent C~4, the quarter-tone between C4 and C#4. When providing MIDI pitch values, an "m" character must be included to distinguish the pitch from other numerical representations. A MIDI pitch value is equal to a psReal plus 60.

The psName, or pitch space name representation, is the alphabetic note names common to English-speaking practice, reduced to an American Standard Code for Information Interchange (ASCII) compatible notation. The representation consists of a letter (A through G), an accidental (where "~" is a quarter sharp, "#" is a sharp, and "$" is a flat), and an octave register integer (where 4 is the octave containing middle C). This representation, for display, rounds microtonal values to the nearest quarter-tone and assumes enharmonic equivalence. For example, a quarter-tone flat of D4 is C#~4. Though numerous conventions exist for the integer labeling of octave register, the common practice of coding middle C as C4 will be used (1997 Hewlett 1997, p. 52).

The PCH pitch representation, called octave point pitch class, is a representation deployed as part of the Csound score language (Bainbridge 1997, p. 117). Pitch in this representation is a numeric value that, although a real number, is better thought of as two values separated by a decimal point. The leading integer value preceding the decimal point encodes octave; the floating point value following the decimal point encodes pitch class and (optionally) microtones. Presumably to avoid negative values, the octave containing C4 is set at the value of 8. Thus 8.00 is C4; 7.11 is B3, and 8.09 is A4. Microtones can be notated with additional decimal places after the pitch class. Thus 8.005 is C~4, the quarter tone between C4 (8.000) and C#4 (8.010). Although a compact notation, PCH values require cumbersome numerical handling. For example, the value 7.11, transposed up three quarter tones, is 8.005 (not the sum of 7.110 and 0.015).

Frequency, as measured in Hertz, is a real number indicating the cycles per second of a pitch. Because frequency must be mapped to pitch as a logarithmic scale, frequency is often not an intuitive pitch representation for musicians. Frequency is, however, convenient as an input parameter for signal processing algorithms. Pitch objects can be created and represented with floating-point frequency values. When providing frequency values, a "hz" character sequence must be included to distinguish frequency from other numerical representations.

A pitch class representation contains no information about register or microtones: integer values from 0 to 11 represent octave-equivalent pitch types. This represents a higher level of pitch abstraction (less information) than the representations given above. Though post-tonal theory permits this representation to be used with a "movable-Do" mapping (where 0 can represent any pitch class), here 0 always represents C. Although post-tonal theory frequently uses alternative, one-character symbols for integers 10 and 11 (T and E, or A and B), here numerical values will be retained. Pitch class values can be interpreted as psReal values, resulting in a default register assignment within the octave containing C4. Pitch class is equal to a MIDI or psReal value modulo 12.

4.2.1.2. Object Design

There is one Pitch class that is not specialized. Any number of Pitch instances may be created and configured.

A Pitch object is initialized with a pitch value, given either as a number (a float or an integer) or as a string. Optionally, a pitch format string can be provided to distinguish numerical types, such as "m" for MIDI, "pch" for PCH, or "hz" for frequency. If no format string is given, the data will be analyzed and a format will be determined. The raw user data is converted to a psReal for storage. This data is stored in the private data attribute `_real`. The user-supplied data and format are also stored.

After creating the object, the pitch value can be obtained in any representation by use of the object's `get()` method. The desired format string must be provided as an argument to the `get()` method: "midi", "psReal", "psName", "pch", "fq", and "pc." If no format is provided, the pitch value will be returned in the format provided (or interpreted) at initialization. In all cases, the value returned is converted from the internal data format set at initialization.

Additional methods are available to obtain string representations and to transform the pitch space value. The repr() method, by default, returns a string representation of the pitch value in the format specified at initialization. An optional argument for format converts the pitch to the desired string representation. The repr() method is mapped to the __str__() method.

Transformative methods provide the fundamental operations of transposition and inversion. A transposition or inversion can be executed in pitch space, as well as the current octave space (analogous to pitch-class space). The t() method performs a pitch space transposition, while the tMod() method performs a transposition within the local octave. Likewise, the i() method, given an optional pitch axis argument, performs an inversion in pitch space, while the iMod() method, given an optional pitch class axis argument, performs an inversion within the local octave.

4.2.1.3. Diagrams and Examples

The following diagram summarizes important attributes and methods of the Pitch object.

Example 4-1. Pitch Object Class Diagram

```
Class Pitch
Attributes:
   format
   data
   _real
Methods:
   get()
   repr(), __str__()
```

```
t()

tMod()

i()

iMod()
```

The following Python session demonstrates the functionality of the Pitch object.

Example 4-2. Pitch Object in Python

```
>>> from athenaCL.libATH import pitchTools
>>> x = pitchTools.Pitch('c#4') # creating a Pitch from a psName
>>> print x
C#4
>>> x.get('midi') # returning a MIDI representation
61
>>> x.get('fq') # returning a frequency representation
277.18263097687208
>>> x.get('pch') # the pch attribute returns a floating point value
8.0099999999999998
>>> x.repr('pch') # string representations are appropriately rounded.
'8.0100'
>>> x.t(14) # transposing by 14 half steps
>>> print x
D#5
>>> x.iMod() # inversion modulus around a default axis, here C5
>>> print x
A5
>>> # creating a new Pitch from a frequency string
>>> y = pitchTools.Pitch('23hz')
>>> y.t(85.4) # transposing by 85.4 half steps
>>> y.repr('psName') # the Pitch represented as a psName
'G~7'
>>> y.t(-.9) # transposing down by 90 cents
>>> print y # the format set at initialization is retained
```

```
3030.2658
>>> y.repr('psName') # a psName rounded to the nearest quarter tone
'F#~7'
```

4.2.2. The Multiset

4.2.2.1. Model and Representation

Bundles of Pitch objects are collected into Multiset objects. A multiset, in mathematical terms, is a group that allows redundant elements. Here, Multisets can be interpreted as either ordered or unordered collections. Related post-tonal music theory, in comparison, has been concerned primarily with non-redundant, unordered sets (such as Forte-style set-classes (1973)). The Multiset, by storing redundant elements, increases the information in the representation and offers a lower level of abstraction. As such the Multiset, in addition to offering a set interpretation, can encode both a distribution of pitches and an ordered sequence of pitches.

The set class, the pitch-class set, and the Multiset can be seen as three levels of abstraction, each level adding more information. The set class contains only information about the intervals between elements of the set; pitch values, register, distribution, and microtones are lost. The pitch-class set contains information about intervals as well as pitch values; register, distribution, and microtones are lost. The Multiset contains information about pitch, register, distribution, and microtones. The Multiset object, as a lower level of abstraction with more information, can thus provide set class and pitch class representations while at the same time storing a rich data collection. The user is free to create Multisets in any of these formats.

When combined in a Path and interpreted by a Texture, the Multiset offers a pitch group with or without redundancy, and as an ordered or unordered collection. Thus, depending on a Texture's interpretation, a Multiset can encode a linear sequence of ordered pitches (a melody), an unordered distribution of pitches (where distribution is encoded by the number of each unique pitch), or an unordered set of pitch types (a scale or set class). In each case, pitches can be interpreted as pitch values (with register) or pitch-class values. Additionally, the Multiset can be interpreted as a set class, represented by Forte number and normal form (1973).

There are two naming conventions for set classes, one proposed by Forte (1973) and used here, the other proposed by Rahn (1980). Forte names are given as cardinality and index number pairs, with an optional character to encode inversion. For example, the second trichord in its prime form would be 3-2A; the inversion would be notated 3-2B. If there is no inversion (the set is symmetrical), no alphabetic character is provided. An example is provided by the symmetric set 3-1. Internally, the Multiset encodes a Forte name as a list of three values, or an "scTriple." The first element is the cardinality, the second is the index, and the third is either -1 (for an inverted non-symmetrical set), 0 (for a symmetrical set), or 1 (for a non-symmetrical set). Thus 3-2B is encoded as (3,2,-1); 5-1 is encoded as (5,1,0).

As an analytical reduction frequently used in post-tonal music theory, set classes have been thoroughly analyzed and measured. Much of this data is available through the Multiset object and can be used to create and process Multiset objects as set classes. There are two formal methods of determining set class identity. One assumes transposition equivalence (Tn), the other assumes transposition and inversion equivalence (TnI). The Multiset offers all set classes under both Tn and TnI classifications, and all set class operations are switchable between these two formats. The AthenaObject maintains a current setting for Tn/TnI mode. This setting is configurable by the user and is used in all relevant Multiset processing. Set class data available from Multiset objects includes the interval vector (Forte 1973), subset vectors (Lewin 1987), invariance vectors (Morris 1987), and reference data such as common chord and scale names. Additionally, numerous quantitative set class similarity measures are also provided (Castren 1994).

4.2.2.2. Object Design

There is one Multiset class that is not specialized. Any number of Multiset instances may be created and configured.

A Multiset stores a list of Pitch objects in the `psList` attribute. A Multiset object can be initialized either via a pitch space set (a list of floating point psReal values), or as a set-class (notated as a scTriple). External objects can create Pitch groups with different representations, and then convert these values to psReals for Multiset instantiation. If a set class is given at initialization, its normal form is used to create a list of psReal values. Each psReal value is used to initialize a Pitch object, and these objects are appended to the psList.

The MultisetFactory object demonstrates the wide range of pitch representations that can be used to create a Multiset. This utility object is used throughout athenaCL to create Multisets specified by the user either interactively or through command-line arguments. The MultisetFactory accepts user string arguments for pitch class and pitch space representations, Forte set-class notations, MIDI note values, frequency values, Xenakis sieves (Ariza 2005c), and spectral analysis files created with the audio file editor Audacity (after Berg 2003). In all cases user data is converted to psReal pitch values and used to instantiate and return a Multiset.

A Multiset stores an `scTriple` attribute. If the Multiset is initialized via a psReal list, the scTriple is calculated from the normal form of the pitch space set. A Multiset additionally stores a floating point value for duration weighting. This value is initialized at 1. The duration weighting of a Multiset only has meaning in the context of a Path object, to be discussed below. Duration weightings have no absolute value.

All Pitch formats, such as midi, psReal, psName, pc, pch, and fq are available output representations of the Multiset. The `get()` method, given an optional format string, returns a list of values in the desired pitch format and in the same order as the Multiset's internal Pitch objects. Additionally, formats particular only to the Multiset are available. The scTriple can be accessed via the "sc" format string, and the normal form via the "normal" format string. The duration weighting of the Multiset can be accessed via the `dur` attribute.

The Multiset provides numerous methods for retrieving and calculating set-class analysis measures. These include retrieving analysis vectors (`var()`, `icv()`, `cv()`, `xv()`), z-related set information (`z()`, `zObj()`), and referential and subset data (`refData()`, `superSet()`). Complete description of the set-class related utilities available within the Multiset is beyond the scope of this discussion.

As with the Pitch object, the Multiset object offers methods to obtain string representations, to perform transformations, and to retrieve analysis information. The `repr()` method handles the production of string representations, calling each Pitch object's `repr()` method with an optional format string. The `__str__()` method is bound to the `repr()` method. The `setDur()` method is provided to set the duration attribute.

Transformative methods change the Pitch objects of a Multiset in place. Many of these transformations are derived from the Pitch object, such as transposition (`t()` and `tMod()`) and inversion (`i()` and `iMod()`). Additional methods are provided to process the Multiset as an ordered sequence, allowing the Pitch sequence to be reversed (`retro()`), rotated (`rotate()`), and sliced (`slice()`). Additionally, the copy method returns a new Multiset object with the same attributes as the original. The `__len__()` method provides the number of Pitch objects stored in the Multiset.

4.2.2.3. Diagrams and Examples

The following diagram summarizes important attributes and methods of the Multiset object.

Example 4-3. Multiset Class Diagram

```
Class Multiset
Attributes:
   _psList
   _scTriple
   dur
Methods:
   get()
   repr(), __str__()
   setDur()
   t()
   tMod()
   i()
   iMod()
   retro()
   slice()
   rotate()
   copy()
   __len__()
   var(), icv(), cv(), xv()
   z(), zObj()
   refData()
   superSet()
```

The following diagram illustrates the primary object components of the Multiset.

Example 4-4. Component Diagram of a Multiset

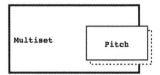

The following Python session demonstrates the functionality of the Multiset object.

Example 4-5. Multiset Object in Python

```
>>> from athenaCL.libATH import SC
>>> # creating a Multiset from three psReal values
>>> x = SC.Multiset((0,4,7))
>>> x.get('fq') # returning values as frequency
(261.62556530059862, 329.62755691286986, 391.99543598174921)
>>> x.get('pch') # returning values as PCH
(8.0, 8.0399999999999991, 8.0700000000000003)
>>> x.get('sc') # returning the scTriple
(3, 11, -1)
>>> x.repr('sc') # returning a Forte set-class notation
'3-11B'
>>> x.i() # inversion in pitch space
>>> # default representation is that provided at initialization
>>> x.repr()
'(0,-4,-7)'
>>> x.repr('sc') # the Forte notation displays the result of inversion
'3-11A'
>>> x.t(5) # transposing by five semitones
>>> x.get('psName') # the set as pitch space names
('F4', 'C#4', 'A#3')
>>> # retrieving the interval class vector of the Multiset as set class.
>>> x.icv()
(0, 0, 1, 1, 1, 0)
```

The following Python session demonstrates the MultisetFactory.

Example 4-6. MultisetFactory Object in Python

```
>>> from athenaCL.libATH import SC
>>> x = SC.MultisetFactory()
>>> a = x(None, '300hz, 1200hz, 20hz') # initialization with frequency strings
>>> a.repr('psName')
'(D~4,D~6,D#~0)'
>>> b = x(None, '3@1|7@2|13@8,c2,c8') # Xenakis sieve notation
>>> b.repr('psName')
'(C#2,D2,E2,G2,G#2,A2,A#2,C#3,E3,G3,A3,A#3,B3,C#4,E4,F#4,G4,A#4,C#5,E5,G5,G#5,
A#5,B5,C#6,D#6,E6,G6,A#6,C7,C#7,E7,F7,G7,A#7,C8)'
>>> c = x(None, '5-4b') # Forte set class notation
>>> c.repr('psName')
'(C4,D#4,E4,F4,F#4)'
>>> c.repr('sc')
'5-4B'
```

4.2.3. The Path

4.2.3.1. Model and Representation

The Path contains an ordered list of one or more Multiset objects. The Path can thus scale from the function of a single pitch (a single Multiset containing a single Pitch) to a pitch group (a single Multiset containing multiple Pitches) to an ordered sequence of pitch-groups (multiple Multisets containing multiple Pitches). The Path satisfies numerous compositional needs for pitch material. A Path can be treated as a single reference pitch, a sequence of melodic fragments or chord changes, a set class, a row, a scale, or a network of voice leadings between chord types. A Path's interpretation is dependent on a Texture or an external object.

In the same manner as the Pitch and the Multiset, the Path can represent pitch material in a variety of formats. When a representation is requested, a list is returned containing, for each Multiset, a list of pitch data in the desired format. Within athenaCL, the Path presents three primary representations to Textures: the pitch space Path "psPath" (psReal values), the pitch class space Path "pcsPath" (pitch class values), and the set class Path "scPath" (set-class normal form).

In addition to the data representations available from the Multiset, a Path provides proportional duration information. The sum of all Multiset dur attributes is calculated, and each Multiset within the Path is given a weight proportional to the Multiset's contribution to the sum. An absolute duration is not calculated until requested, and requires a total time value provided by an external object such as a Texture. For example, if a Path consists of three Multisets, each with a duration weighting of 1, then each Multiset in a temporal realization will be assigned 33.3 percent of the total duration. Alternatively, if a Path consists of three Multisets with duration weightings of 1, 1, and 2, then Multisets in a temporal realization will be assigned 25 percent, 25 percent, and 50 percent of the total duration. This notation is flexible. A user can set durations as decimal proportions (0.25, 0.25, 0.5), whole-number ratios (1, 1, 2), or real-value measures (123, 123, 246); in every case the same proportional distribution will be calculated.

Further, the Path (in Multiset size and number-dependent cases) stores maps and map analysis rankings. A map specifies the movement between each element of a Multiset. For a Path of n Multisets, there are n-1 maps between these Multisets. Maps, within a Path object, provide a complete system of relating any two Multisets of any size from one to six. The map system is based on a complete implementation of the atonal voice leading model of Joseph N. Straus (2003). Complete discussion of this model is beyond the scope of this text, but a brief overview will be provided.

The athenaCL map system contains a stored library of map classes, or transition primitives between Multisets from sizes one to six. If the destination is larger than the source, a single source point may split into two or more destination points. If the destination is smaller than the source, two or more source points may merge onto a single destination point. No map can contain both mergers and splits.

All map classes can be notated in two ways. The first notation is analogous to Forte names for set-classes. In this notation, maps are named by the size of the source set, the size of the destination set, and by an index number. Thus of the 6 maps between sizes 3 and 3, map index number 4 would be notated 3:3-4; of the 540 maps between sizes 3 and 6, map index number 317 would be notated 3:6-317. Also similar to Forte names, index values have no absolute meaning and are a result only of the ordered calculation of maps.

The second notation of map classes symbolically depicts the movement of each element to another. Since a map is abstract and is, by itself, not dependent on values in any particular Multiset, letters are used to designate positions in the destination group. The order of these letters is used to designate positions in the source group. Letters refer to positions starting from the left (or top if represented vertically) and beginning with the letter "a" and continuing to "f"; order positions likewise refer to positions from the left (or top if represented vertically). Thus MC 3:3-4, in this notation, is (bca). This means that the following source and destination positions are exchanged: 1 to 2 (position one to position "b"), 2 to 3 (position two to position "c"), and 3 to 1 (position three to position "a"). For sets of unequal size parentheses are used to show if a position splits or merges. Thus MC 3:6-224 is represented as ((bd)(ae)(cf)). This means that the following splits from source to destination occur: 1 to 2 and 4 (position one to positions "b" and "d"), 2 to 1 and 5 (position two to positions "a" and "e"), and 3 to 3 and 6 (positions three to positions "c" and "f").

Maps can be measured, ranked, and sorted in various ways. One method, developed by Straus (2003), provides measurements of atonal voice leading in pitch class space. Three rankings are defined by Straus: Smoothness, Uniformity, and Balance. Maps within Paths can be ranked and sorted by each of these methods.

The map library contains data only for maps of size six or fewer. Maps are thus not available for all Paths: if a Path has a Multiset consisting of more than six elements no map operations are available. Map operations are also not available if a Path consists of only a single Multiset. When maps are available, a Path can store multiple collections of complete map sequences, called PathVoices. In some cases, it may be useful to use a PathVoice to partition a Path into parts, or separate voices. Only in the case of equal-sized Multisets is unambiguous part extraction possible. The availability of part extraction is encoded in the Path `voiceType` attribute. The `voiceType`, based on the size and number of a Path's Multisets, determines whether maps and parts are available. If a Path has a Multiset with a size greater than six, or a Path consists only of one Multiset, then no map operations, and no parts, are available (a `voiceType` of "none"). If a Path consists of Multisets of equal size, and that size is six or fewer, map operations and parts are available (a `voiceType` of "part"). If all Multisets have six or fewer elements, and Multisets are of varying sizes, then map operations are available, while parts cannot be extracted (a `voiceType` of "map").

4.2.3.2. Object Design

There is one Path class that is not specialized. Any number of Path instances may be created and configured.

The Path is initialized with a string name. It can then be loaded with pitch data in a variety of formats. The method `loadPsList()` accepts a list of lists, with each internal list consisting of psReal values. The method `loadMutlisetList()` accepts a list of Multiset objects. The method `loadDataModel()` accepts a dictionary of all necessary data to store and load the Path derived from the athenaCL XML file representation; the `writeDataModel()` produces such a dictionary for XML storage. After loading data, private methods are called to calculate duration percentages, Path `voiceType`, a default map, and map rankings (if not supplied by `loadDataModel()`). The duration weights of a Path can be supplied as a list with the `loadDur()` method. Whenever weights change, the `durSum` attribute is updated.

Data can be accessed from the Path with methods similar to Multiset and Pitch objects. The `get()` method returns a list of data values conforming to various Pitch and Multiset representations. The `repr()` and `reprList()` methods provide string representations of the Path, either as a single string or as a list of strings. The `len()` method (also mapped to the `__len__()` method) returns the number of Multisets in the Path.

Paths can be transformed in ways similar to Multisets. The `retro()` method reverses the Path; the `slice()` method creates sub-segments of the Path. The `rotate()` method rotates the Path. The `t()` method can transpose one or many Multisets within the Path. The `i()` method can invert one or many Multisets within the Path.

The Path is designed to be referenced by zero or more Textures. For this reason, each Path has a `refCount` attribute that stores the number of Textures that reference the Path. The `refIncr()` and `refDecr()` methods increment and decrement this value, respectively. For a Path to be deleted within athenaCL, the `refCount` must be equal to zero.

4.2.3.3. Diagrams and Examples

The following diagram summarizes important attributes and methods of the Path object. As mentioned above, methods and attributes related to maps will not be described here.

Example 4-7. Path Class Diagram

```
Class Multiset

Attributes:

    voiceType

    multisetPath

    durSum

    refCount

Methods:

    insert()

    retro()

    slice()

    rotate()

    t()

    i()

    reprList()

    repr()

    loadDur()

    loadPsList()

    loadMultisetList()

    loadDataModel()

    writeDataModel()

    copy()

    get()

    len(), __len__()

    refIncr()

    refDecr()
```

The following diagram illustrates the primary object components of the Path.

Example 4-8. Component Diagram of a Path

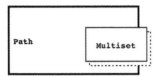

The following Python session demonstrates the functionality of the Path object.

Example 4-9. Path Object in Python

```
>>> from athenaCL.libATH import pitchPath
>>> x = pitchPath.PolyPath() # creating a Path object
>>> x.loadPsList([(3,4),(-4,5,12),(6,4,4,4)]) # loading a list of psReal values
>>> x.repr('psName') # obtaining a pitch space name representation
'(D#4,E4),(G#3,F4,C5),(F#4,E4,E4,E4)'
>>> x.reprList('scPath') # returning a Forte set class name list
['2-1', '3-11A', '2-2']
>>> len(x) # length is the number of Multisets
3
>>> x.rotate(2) # rotating the order of Multisets
>>> x.repr('psName')
'(F#4,E4,E4,E4),(D#4,E4),(G#3,F4,C5)'
>>> x.t(8) # transposition of all Multisets
>>> x.repr('psName')
'(D5,C5,C5,C5),(B4,C5),(E4,C#5,G#5)'
>>> x.get('psPath')
[(14, 12, 12, 12), (11, 12), (4, 13, 20)]
>>> x.get('durPercent') # the duration weights for each Multiset
[0.33333333333333331, 0.33333333333333331, 0.33333333333333331]
```

4.2.4. Compositional Implications

The combined resources of Pitch, Multiset, and Path objects provide numerous flexible and reusable representations of pitch and pitch groups. Roads, in describing the necessity of CAAC systems to support different compositional strategies and representations, provides a pitch group as an example: "… we may want to examine a chord object from several perspectives, such as the set of pitches or pitch intervals in it" (Roads 1985, p. 173). The Multiset provides such an object, and considerably extends the functionality of a chord-type at a lower level with the Pitch, and at a higher level with the Path.

The utility of this model is demonstrated in athenaCL, where a user can provide a group of pitches for use by a Texture in a variety of formats. As already explained, a pitch group can be provided as a set class, as a Xenakis sieve, or as a group of microtonally specified frequencies. If the user desires to work in pitch space, a Path can be created with octave-specific pitches; if not, the Texture's local field and local octave ParameterObjects can function to transpose pitch classes into pitch space. If the user desires to work with microtones, a Path can be created with specific microtonal tunings; if not, the Texture's local field and Temperament objects can modify the final microtonal tuning of Path-derived pitches. For most Textures, local field and local octave transformations can be optionally applied once per event, or once per Multiset. The power of the Path comes from the ease with which it transparently accommodates a wide variety of pitch abstractions and methods of collecting pitch groups.

When multiple Textures share the same Path, large-scale pitch-group deployment can be synchronized, both in terms of access to pitch resources, and in terms of pitch group duration weighting. When multiple Textures share the same Path, the Texture can be configured, as shown above, to read and transform the Path in a variety of ways. One

Texture may transpose the Path with the local octave control; another Texture may read the Path as a pitch class set, stripping register information. The combinations are numerous, flexible, and compositionally satisfying.

In some music, harmonic rhythm, or large-scale deployment of pitch materials, delimits musical structures. Ames uses the term "tonal flux" to describe "the rate at which new pitches enter (and leave) the tonal environment" (1983, p. 164). The Path can be used as a fixed, time-proportional encoding of tonal flux.

The pitch model presented here is strongly informed by post-tonal Western music theory. Although the system does suggest the use of discrete, equal-tempered pitches, there are ample opportunities within athenaCL to vary, and ultimately completely conceal, this model.

4.2.5. Alternative and Related Models

Hiller and Isaacson, in their earliest experiments, use integers to represent pitches. In Experiments One and Two Hiller and Isaacson use a two-octave diatonic pitch scale starting at C3, labeled with integers from 0 to 14. In Experiment Three a chromatic pitch scale is used consisting of two and a half octaves labeled from 0 to 30. This model of using integers to represent pitches is common; Hiller and Isaacson's usage, however, is limited. They demonstrate little concern for integration with alternative representations, and, as the final output format is Western notation, have no interest in microtonal pitch specification. Gill (1963, p. 132) uses a similar system, providing a two octave pitch range labeled alphabetically from "A," past "G," all the way to "N."

SCORE (Smith 1972), and related systems that follow its notation (such as Pla (Schottstaedt 1983)), employs a simple symbolic representation of pitch. For example, "BF5" is interpreted as B-flat in the fifth octave (Loy and Abbott 1985, p. 258), and "CS4" is interpreted as C-sharp in the fourth octave (Smith 1972, p. 10). An "R" is used to designate a rest. The string "REP" can be used to repeat a collection of previous values a certain number of times. For example, "REP 9,3" repeats the previous nine pitches three times. Smith extends this functionality by allowing sequences of pitches (or rhythms) to be marked as motives: the group is demarcated with parenthesis and preceded by an alphabetic symbol. The motive can be recalled by using the "@" symbol followed by the alphabetic symbol. Basic transformations of the motive are then possible, such as retrograde (@-A), transposition (@A13), inversion (@$A), and (in the case of rhythms) augmentation or diminution (@A .6667) (Smith 1972, p. 10). This compact and flexible notation of motives and their transformations is a significant feature of the SCORE family of systems.

Some systems, somewhat analogous to the Multiset and Path, model reusable groups of pitches as either sets, chords, or other combinations. Citron's MUSPEC system permits the user to define a "tonal system," or a collection of symbolically represented pitches. The tonal system can be of variable size, and values from this representation are accessed by positional index values to build scales and harmonic structures used elsewhere in the system. As with the Multiset, Citron's tonal system can encode fixed pitch sequences or proportional pitch distributions, "… the pitch system itself could be a specific tone row or even contain certain notes more than once…" (1970, p. 99). Laurson's PatchWork system features numerous objects for modeling pitch groups. The Chord object groups pitches similarly to the Multiset; pitch data, however, is only available in one representation, transformations are not available, and no set-class or other higher level abstractions are offered (Laurson 1996, p. 99). The Chord-Sequence object, defined as a collection of chords, relates to the Path (1996, p. 110). Again, multiple representations and transformations are not provided.

The extended functionality of the Multiset, particularly its tools for set-class representation and analysis, closely relate to the work of Craig Harris and Alexander

Brinkman (1986). Their tools, limited to analytical application, are not incorporated into a CAAC system. Peter Castine, with Harris and Brinkman, extends this work within the Contemporary Music Analysis Package (CMAP) (Castine et al. 1990; Castine 1991, 1994a, 1994b).

François Pachet, in his model of a system for chordal analysis, introduces an object called a "shape." As he states, "a shape is a temporal object, describing a collection of chords … as well as the rectified harmonic operations…" (2000, p. 97). Shapes "… manifest themselves through well-identified patterns of chords or other shapes…" and "these patterns can be found in most books on Jazz harmony" (2000, p. 98). Pachet provides examples of jazz-derived shapes: a "turnaround shape," a "blues shape," or shapes such as "modal borrowing." Shapes relate to the Path, but again, are narrowly specialized for a particular application.

An early example of a CAAC system with voice-leading specifications is found in Citron's MUSPEC system. Citron describes how voicing input cards can be used to describe motion between two chords with a notation similar to the symbolic map notation presented above: where "structures" are collections of pitches selected from a larger pitch system, "the position of an entry on the voicing card implies the note of the structure in the present chord, while the entry in that position gives the structure note in the next chord to which that voice most move" (1970, p. 102). Generative and computational models of voice-leading have also been explored by Cope in his CAAC system Alice (Cope 2002). His model, employing analysis of a database of MIDI files to generate new MIDI files, analyzes voice leadings as "voice-leading sets" (Cope 2002, p. 122). These transformative archetypes, which are less abstract than the map classes presented above, rely on a set-class interpretation of pitch groups, and are related to the smoothness measure proposed by Straus (2003).

4.3. The Rhythm Model

Rhythm is a unique musical parameter. Rhythm is not simply how long an event sounds, nor is it the time between two events. Some rhythms imply information beyond timing, such as relative amplitudes or local groupings. Rhythm, and rhythm notations, represent ways of thinking about pulse-concepts at a compositional level. A rhythm is defined as a collection of one or more pulses. When actually realized in sound, each pulse of a rhythm is broken into at least three components: a duration (the time until the next event, or delta-time), a sustain (the time the event is maintained), and an accent (a dynamic scalar).

In athenaCL, the user specifies Rhythm objects as collections of Pulse objects. The model and notation used here is designed to be intuitive, clear, and flexible. Pulses are designated as a ratio of a tempo, specified externally to the Pulse or Rhythm objects. Importantly, there is no concept of meter within the Pulse and Rhythm objects. A Pulse itself exists independently of any meter, or any notational beam-structure, though a Rhythm may be designed to imply such formations.

4.3.1. The Pulse

4.3.1.1. Model and Representation

The Pulse object is the duration primitive of athenaCL. The Pulse allows the storage and maintenance of a timing information proportional to an external tempo value measured in beats per minute (BPM). A Pulse includes a duration specified as a ratio, and represented with two integers, a divisor and multiplier. The divisor divides the temporal duration of the beat; the multiplier then scales the resulting value. The multiplier and the divisor together designate a fraction of the BPM-determined beat duration. Pulses accommodate the symbolic representation of Western notation. If the beat is assigned to a quarter note (an arbitrary reference), and a pulse is created with a divisor of 4 and a multiplier of 1, a duration equal to one quarter of the beat will result, or a sixteenth note (one-quarter of a quarter note). If a Pulse is created with a divisor of 3 and a multiplier of 4, a duration equal to four-thirds of a beat will result, or a quarter-note tied to a triplet eighth note. The actual interpretation of a Pulse duration is Texture-dependent. In some cases, Pulse duration may be used to calculate the start time of a subsequent event. In other cases, the timing of a subsequent event may be independent of any previous Pulse.

The Pulse distinguishes between the concept of duration, or the time from one event to the next, and sustain, or the time that an event is maintained regardless of other events. Sustain time is calculated by scaling the ratio-specified duration, and is designated within a Pulse object as a floating-point number greater than zero. A sustain of 1 will result in an event that is maintained as long as the Pulse duration; a sustain of 0.5 will maintain an event for half of its duration. The Western music concept of articulation can be defined in part by sustain: a pulse with a sustain of 0.2, for example, might be considered *staccato*. A pulse with a sustain of 1.5 might be considered *legato*. Sustain is often set by a Texture, but may also be controlled by a Rhythm Generator ParameterObject.

The Pulse also contains accent information. Accent is an amplitude scalar particular to each pulse, within the value range of zero to one. An accent of 0, for example, encodes a measured silence, or a rest. An accent of 1 encodes a fully sounding event. Accent values between 0 and 1 can be used to provide a measure of articulatory dynamic accent to a Pulse, independent of amplitudes calculated at higher procedural levels.

The primary representation of the Pulse, a Pulse triple, is a list of three values: the divisor, the multiplier, and the accent. The Pulse triple provides a convenient notation of a Pulse. The position of the divisor before the multiplier is, at first, possibly counter-intuitive.

The pulse triple (4,1,1) encodes a value that is equal to one-fourth of the beat. Although reversing the notation such that the multiplier precedes the divisor provides a representation closer to a traditional fraction, the notation used here has the advantage of visually organizing pulses by common divisors. For example, it is visually clear that (5,2,1) and (5,9,0) are related pulses: both are based on a division of the beat by five. Visual clarity is also enhanced by replacing accent values of 1 and 0 by the strings "+" and "o" respectively.

The Pulse stores an internal tempo value as the `bpm` attribute; this value can be updated at any time to accommodate dynamic tempi. A Pulse can return data or string representations to other objects in the form of a pulse triple, an accent, a duration, or a sustain value. Duration and sustain values are calculated based on the `bpm` attribute and are returned in seconds.

4.3.1.2. Object Design

There is one Pulse class that is not specialized. Any number of Pulse instances may be created and configured.

A Pulse object is instantiated from a Pulse triple provided either as a string or as a list of values. If the data is a string, private methods are used to parse the string into a list. This list is stored as the `triple` attribute. Each Pulse object stores additional attributes for a BPM value and a sustain scalar. Default values are assigned to these attributes on initialization; they can be later set with the `setBpm()` and `setSus()` methods. The `setAcc()` method is available to alter the accent of a triple, useful for converting a sounding Pulse to a measured silence.

The `__call__()` method can be used to return a three element list containing the calculated duration, sustain value, and accent value. The `__call__()` method takes optional bpm and sustain arguments. These values, if provided, are assigned to internal object attributes. The get() method, with an optional format argument, returns additional Pulse data. The repr() method, with an optional format and bpm argument, returns Pulse data as a string. The scale() method allows the divisor of a Pulse to be multiplied by a value. Thus, a Pulse of (4,1,1), scaled by a factor of 2, results of in a Pulse of (8,1,1). Pulse objects can be compared for equality by comparing Pulse triples. The __eq__() method provides this functionality.

4.3.1.3. Diagrams and Examples

The following diagram summarizes important attributes and methods of the Pulse object.

Example 4-10. Pulse Object Class Diagram

```
Class Pulse
Attributes:
    triple
    sustain
    bpm
Methods:
    __call__()
    get()
    repr(), __str__()
    __eq__()
    setSus()
    setBpm()
    setAcc()
    copy()
    scale()
```

The following Python session demonstrates the functionality of the Pulse object.

Example 4-11. Pulse Object in Python

```
>>> from athenaCL.libATH import rhythm
>>> a = rhythm.Pulse((3,1,1)) # creating a Pulse object.
>>> print a # obtaining the default string representation.
(3,1,+)
>>> # calling the Pulse with an optional BPM argument
>>> a(120) # returns duration, sustain, and accent values
(0.16666666666666666, 0.16666666666666666, 1)
>>> a(60, .5) # the second optional argument sets sustain
(0.33333333333333331, 0.16666666666666666, 1)
>>> a(180) # sustain values are retained
(0.1111111111111111, 0.055555555555555552, 1)
>>> a.repr('sus') # a string representation of calculated sustain
'0.17s'
>>> a.repr('dur') # a string representation of calculated duration
'0.33s'
>>> a.scale(3) # scaling the divisor
>>> a.setAcc(0) # converting a sounding Pulse to a silence
>>> print a
(3,3,o)
>>> a(60) # calling the Pulse at 60 BPM
(1.0, 0.5, 0)
```

4.3.2. The Rhythm

4.3.2.1. Model and Representation

The Rhythm bundles Pulse objects into reusable collections. In the same way that the Multiset bundles Pitch objects to expose their functionality as a group, so the Rhythm object allows many Pulses to be treated as a single unit. Since the Rhythm object bundles and exposes the features of the Pulse, their designs are closely related. The Rhythm accepts initialization data in the form of a list of lists, or a list of Pulse triples. For convenience, a list of on/off values (as 1s and 0s) is also accepted. These integers are converted into beat-length Pulse objects: either (1,1,+) or (1,1,o).

When working in athenaCL, the user designates Rhythms within Textures by suppling a list of Pulses as an argument to a Rhythm Generator ParameterObject. The ParameterObject, not the Texture, thus provides the interface between the user and supplied Rhythms.

4.3.2.2. Object Design

There is one Rhythm class that is not specialized. Any number of Rhythm instances may be created and configured.

Upon initialization, the Rhythm object parses user data and assigns Pulse objects to the `pulseList` attribute. Rhythm methods are available to call corresponding methods for each Pulse of the `pulseList`. The `get()` and `repr()` methods of the Rhythm call the corresponding methods of each Pulse and return the results in a list; `setSus()`, `setAcc()`, and `setBpm()` methods are applied to all Pulses in the `pulseList`.

Unlike Pulse objects, the Rhythm is designed to function as a Python sequence type, providing list-like functionality. The `__len__()` method returns the number of Pulses in the Rhythm; the `__getitme__()`, `__contains__()`, `__delitem__()`, and `__setitem__()` methods are defined such that, given the appropriate Pulse position index, standard list operations can be performed.

4.3.2.3. Diagrams and Examples

The following diagram summarizes important attributes and methods of the Rhythm object.

Example 4-12. Rhythm Object Class Diagram

```
Class Pulse
Attributes:
    pulseList
Methods:
    __call__()
    get()
    repr(), __str__()
    setSus()
    setAcc()
    setBpm()
    __len__()
    __getitem__()
    __contains__()
    __delitem__()
    __setitem__()
```

The following diagram illustrates the primary object components of the Rhythm.

Example 4-13. Component Diagram of a Rhythm

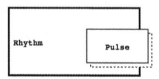

The following Python session demonstrates the functionality of the Rhythm object.

Example 4-14. Pitch Object in Python

```
>>> from athenaCL.libATH import rhythm
>>> a = rhythm.Rhythm([(4,1,1),(5,6,0),(3,2,1),(3,2,1)]) # a list of Pulses
>>> print a # returning a string representation
((4,1,+),(5,6,o),(3,2,+),(3,2,+))
```

```
>>> len(a) # getting the number of Pulses
4
>>> a.setBpm(180) # setting the BPM of all Pulse objects
>>> a.get('dur') # returning calculated durations of each Pulse
[0.083333333333333329, 0.40000000000000002, 0.22222222222222221,
0.22222222222222221]
>>> a[3].get('dur') # getting the duration of the fourth Pulse object
0.22222222222222221
>>> # returning a Pulse triple representation of the second Pulse object
>>> a[1].repr('triple')
'(5,6,o)'
>>> a[3] = rhythm.Pulse((7,2,1)) # assigning a new pulse object to the rhythm
>>> print a
((4,1,+),(5,6,o),(3,2,+),(7,2,+))
>>> # creating a rhythm from a binary Pulse array
>>> b = rhythm.Rhythm((0,1,1,0,1,1))
>>> print b
((1,1,o),(1,1,+),(1,1,+),(1,1,o),(1,1,+),(1,1,+))
```

4.3.3. Compositional Implications

The most significant implication of the Pulse and Rhythm objects is that they free the composer from thinking in terms of meter and bar lines. Pulse durations are specified only in reference to a beat, and do not enforce any notion of larger metrical structure. A consequence of this is that the concept of the tie, as a connection across beam groups or bar lines, is not necessary. Pulses may, in some cases, sum to whole-number groupings (meters); in other cases, Pulses may not easily be partitioned into meters. Accent, applied to a Pulse from a ParameterObject or a Texture, may likewise create a metrical structure. Though this arrangement allows for rhythmic flexibility, problems may arise if the output of a Texture is converted into Western notation. Rhythms can be created that cannot easily, or in any predictable way, be divided into meter and bar formations.

Because Pulse duration and sustain values are evaluated in relation to a provided (or stored) BPM value, dynamic tempi are accommodated. When a Texture processes its Rhythm ParameterObject, BPM values are calculated for each event from an independent Generator ParameterObject. This BPM value is passed to the currently selected Pulse before duration and sustain values are calculated. Dynamic BPM values provide further rhythmic flexibility.

Pulse objects accommodate redundant representations. For example, the Pulse triple (6,2,1) is equal to the Pulse (3,1,1); similarly, the Pulse (1,5,1) is the same as the Pulse (2,10,1). This notation redundancy offers the user flexibility in designing Rhythms. Further, Pulse objects may be algorithmically generated or transformed in multiple ways, including diverse forms of procedural manipulation applied directly to the Pulse triple notation. This opportunity is exploited by the Rhythm Generator ParameterObject GaRhythm. This sub-system, modeling populations of Rhythms as a real-value encoded genetic algorithm, performs "musically meaningful mutation" (Biles 1994, p. 135, 2003) of Pulse objects by individually altering divisor, multiplier, and accent values (Ariza 2002).

Within a Texture, the composer is not limited to using metric, ratio-derived rhythms. As already stated, Pulse and Rhythm objects are provided as arguments to Rhythm Generator ParameterObjects. Rhythm Generator ParameterObjects, however, may use representations other than Pulses. The Rhythm Generator ParameterObject ConvertSecond, for example, allows the user to use an embedded Generator ParameterObject to create durations, without any reference to BPM or beat ratios. The related Rhythm Generator ConvertSecondTriple permits three Generator ParameterObjects to independently supply duration, sustain, and accent values. Further, when working with a Clone, Event time and sustain values are independently transformable, allowing for even more radical alterations of timing information.

4.3.4. Alternative and Related Models

In Experiment Three, Hiller and Isaacson introduce algorithmic rhythm generation. Rhythms are represented as a sequence of evenly spaced pulses in a binary array, where 1 represents sound and 0 represents a silence (Hiller and Isaacson 1959, p. 110). These pulse arrays are organized into larger groupings by taking each of the sixteen permutations of four binary digits and labeling them with integers 0 through 15. These groupings are considered as a single measure of a 4/8 meter. Hiller and Isaacson call these groups rhythm classes. The authors justify this representation based on the nature of the computer itself: "the binary representation of numbers in the machine ... offered a convenient set of symbols ..." (Hiller and Isaacson 1959, p. 110). Perhaps needless to say, justifying musical models based on low-level computer representations is no longer necessary.

Koenig's PR1, in its original form, permitted the user to provide twenty-eight "entry delays"; an entry delay is the time between successive events, or delta-time. In PR1, Koenig notated durations as fractions of a constant tempo, such as 0/0, 1/1, 4/5, 3/5, or 1/8. The ratio 0/0 indicates a note "as fast as possible," or a grace note (Koenig 1970a, p. 35). As Koenig designed PR1 to produce alpha-numeric tables for manual transcription to Western notation, the undefined nature of a 0/0 fraction is not a problem. This representation, as a ratio specification, relates to Pulse objects, though measured silences and dynamic tempi are not directly accommodated. In Koenig's model, the actual calculated duration is based on six discrete tempi provided by the user.

Smith's SCORE system (Smith 1972) also employs a ratio notation of rhythmic durations: "each number entered will be the denominator of any fractional part of a whole note" (Smith 1972, p. 9). The value 4 is then a quarter note, the value 12 is a triplet. This denominator is the same as a Pulse divisor calculated in relation to a whole-note beat; the

Pulse multiplier, as a numerator or otherwise, is not directly configurable. Smith provides for additional flexibility by accommodating floating point denominators. Negative values are used to designate rests. As the SCORE system was designed, in part, to generate Western notation, concepts such as augmentation dots and ties are encoded. Periods are used to designate duration augmentation by one half the duration they follow. All rhythmic values grouped between slashes are "tied" together. The Pulse list (4,5,1), (4,3,0), (4,11,1), (4,1,1), for example, is "4 16 / -8. / 2 8. / 16" in the SCORE notation.

A significant feature of the SCORE representation, as demonstrated above in the discussion of pitch, is the notation of repetitions and motivic transformations. For example, a single value, followed by an "X" and a number, will be repeated that many number of times. Further, as with SCORE pitch representations, the word "REP" can be used to repeat a selection of previous values a given number of times. Likewise, the "@" symbol can be used to recall named, parenthesis-delimited motives, and these motives then can be transformed in various ways.

Mathews demonstrates a Music V PLF composition subroutine that contains a parameter for "duty factor": "the style of playing — legato or staccato — is represented by the duty-factor function … which gives the proportion of the interval between the starting times of successive notes that is occupied by sound" (1969, p. 90). In the same manner as the Pulse object's sustain scalar, Mathews' duty factor is a numeric value between 0 and 1 that scales event sustain independently of duration or delta time. Truax's POD systems provides a related feature called "envelope scaling," whereby the envelope of a sound could be varied independently of the time between events (Buxton 1975, p. 168). As Truax points out, "envelope scaling effects an articulation of the event comparable to conventional staccato or legato markings" (1976, p. 265). These envelope scalings are likewise related to the variable sustain scalar used in the Pulse object.

The PatchWork family of systems (PW, OM, PWGL) employ a hierarchical rhythm notation. This representation, called either a beat-list (Laurson 1996, p. 115) or a rhythm tree (Assayag et al. 2001), encodes rhythms as either beam or measure groups. The use of rhythm trees originated in the design of PatchWork, and was subsequently incorporated into the design of IRCAM's OpenMusic and related systems. The rhythm tree, as many components of these systems, closely relates to Western notation: rhythm trees allow "… complete compatibility with traditional and most complex notation…" and, additionally, are "… directly inspired from OpenMusic's programming language…" Lisp (Assayag et al. 2001).

A rhythm tree is a list in the form (D S), where D (the "beat-count") expresses a duration and S (the "rtm-list") is a list of proportions that take place within D. Each item in S is either a number or a recursively-structured list in the form (D S). Negative S values (as in the SCORE notation) are interpreted as rests. S values followed by a decimal (1.0) are tied to the previous value. The D value may take many forms. The D value may be a floating-point number. The D value may be a question mark, where the necessary numeric value is calculated contextually based on S. Finally, the D value may be a time-signature ratio, where 4//4 or (4 4) is interpreted as the time signature 4/4 (Assayag et al. 2001). For example, the rhythm (1 (2 1)) (Laurson 1996, p. 115) is equivalent to the Pulse list (3,2,1), (3,1,1). Rhythmic flexibility is obtained by embedding additional lists: the rhythm tree (1 (1 (1 (1 1 1)))) (Laurson 1996, p. 118), for example, is equivalent to the Pulse list (2,1,1), (6,1,1), (6,1,1), (6,1,1).

Laurson, anticipating that users might have difficulty editing rhythm trees, offers a graphical editor in PW such that each individual leaf (a sub-list S) can be edited independently and with graphical feedback (1996, pp. 121-122). Even with such aid, the rhythm tree, though compact and powerful, at some levels obscures both the number of pulses and their proportional relationships.

Taube's Common Music supports multiple representations of duration. Symbolic representation of pulse entities is provided by one- or two-character alphabetic notations. For example, W is a whole note, E is an eighth note, TQ is a triplet quarter note. Rhythmic flexibility is obtained by adding dots ("."), parallel to usage in Western notation, or by performing symbolic mathematical operations. For example, the notation h... provides a triple-dotted half note that is equivalent to the Pulse (4,15,1); the notation W-TS provides one triplet sixteenth note less than a whole note (Taube 2004), a duration that is equivalent to the Pulse (6,23,1).

4.4. The Event, SubEvent, and EventSequence Model

As demonstrated in Chapter 2, the digitization of musical structures into discrete events is a fundamental process of many CAAC systems. Where many historical systems have used a fixed number of event parameters, athenaCL Textures create n-dimensional Events, where the number of parameters in each Event is dependent on the Texture's Instrument model. This design effectively includes timbre as a parametric event component. An Instrument may represent a complex synthesis process requiring multiple parameter values for each Event; or an Instrument may require parameter values for control signals, file paths, or other information. Any complex event, if partitioned into discrete parameters, can be expressed as an n-dimensional Event. This is an essential component of the claim made in Chapter 1: any musical structure (imagined or found), taken at a small enough temporal window, can be algorithmically generated. This statement does not claim that any structure can be generated: it only affirms that, at an appropriately small scale, an n-dimensional Event can sufficiently model a complex musical moment.

The athenaCL system uses EventSequences as a means of storage and transport. EventSequence objects are created and processed by Textures and Clones. Textures add

Events (or SubEvents that are expanded to Events) to an EventSequence. A Texture may add Events to an EventSequence in the order of their temporal deployment (linear Event generation) or in a different order than their temporal deployment (non-linear Event generation). Clones process a Texture-produced EventSequence and create a new, modified EventSequence. Clones, through the use of Filter ParameterObjects, transform values of each parameter field as a complete array.

4.4.1. The Event and SubEvent

The Event object is a Python dictionary with a defined collection of key and value pairs. All Textures create Events (with the `makeEvent()` method) by supplying standard and auxiliary parameter values. Standard parameters include instrument number, a start time, a tempo (in BPM), a Pulse triple (if available), a duration (in seconds), a sustain value (in seconds), an accent (between 0 and 1), an amplitude (typically between 0 and 1), a pitch space value (as a psReal), and a panning value (between 0 and 1). Auxiliary parameter values are supplied in an *n*-dimensional list. Additionally, an optional comment string may be supplied for each Event.

The Event stores detailed timing information: calculated duration and sustain values, as well as BPM and Pulse triples, are retained. Though this information may seem redundant, it provides a rich representation, enabling a wide variety of EventSequence output conversions and Event transformations. For example, start time and sustain are the only temporal values necessary to create a Csound event list. However, if Western notation is desired as an output, it is useful (if possible) to retain, for each Event, the user-supplied or Texture-generated Pulse triple. Where a duration given in seconds may not clearly reflect a notated rhythm, the ratio provided by a Pulse triple can always be properly notated. For example, with a Pulse such as (3,1,0), a triplet eighth rest will always be properly represented, regardless of dynamic tempi or modified sustain values. Similarly, storing a BPM value for each Event may also be considered redundant, as duration and sustain values have already been calculated. Yet, since BPM values produced by a Texture may be dynamic, storing the BPM of each Event enables Clones to process Events with BPM-dependent Rhythm Generator ParameterObjects. By retaining the tempo used to calculate duration and sustain values for each Event, Event transformations specified with Pulse notations are then possible.

Events may be silences: an accent of 0 encodes a silent Event. Storing empty Events, however, may be superfluous for some OutputFormats. For instance, Csound event lists have no need to represent silent Events. Alternative OutputFormats such as Western notation, however, benefit from complete information concerning measured silences. Within athenaCL, the calculation and storage of silent Events is switchable for every Texture: the silenceMode attribute allows users to specify if silences should be calculated and stored, or if they should be ignored and skipped.

The SubEvent is designed to enable a group of related, partial Event structures to be added to an EventSequence. The use and context of SubEvents is defined by a Texture: a SubEvent may be a series of ornaments that surround an Event, or a number of points that interpolate between two Events. SubEvents are Event dictionaries that lack a complete representation: they may contain values only for start time, sustain, amplitude, pitch space, and panning. When a SubEvent is added to an EventSequence, it is expanded into a complete Event by inheriting missing parameters from a supplied parent Event. The storePolyEvent() method allows the Texture to add any number of SubEvents to an EventSequence. A parent Event, from which missing parameters are taken, must be supplied.

4.4.2. The EventSequence

4.4.2.1. Model and Representation

With the `storeEvent()` and `storePolyEvent()` methods, Textures add Events to EventSequence objects. Each Texture and Clone contains a single EventSequence object. The EventSequence object provides methods and functionality similar to a Python list, with additional methods for sorting, changing, and accessing Event data.

4.4.2.2. Object Design

There is one EventSequence class that is not specialized. Any number of EventSequence instances may be created and configured.

The EventSequence object consists of a list of Event dictionaries. Events are added to this list with the `append()` or `__setitem__()` methods. Each Event, as any item in a list, can be accessed from an EventSequence by its integer index value. As all Events within a single EventSequence have the same number (and name) of dictionary keys, an EventSequence can be treated as a table, where Events are rows and Event key values are columns. The `__getitem__()` method will, for a given index, return the entire Event dictionary (a row of the table). Alternatively, methods can process the columns of the EventSequence: methods `getArray()` and `setArray()` allow external objects to obtain, for example, all amplitude values of all Events, modify them, and replace them in their corresponding Event Dictionaries.

Clones perform transformations on EventSequences. Processing EventSequence arrays (table columns) is one way Clones operate on EventSequences. Another way, for example, is by using the EventSequence's `retrograde()` method, which transforms the order and time relationships within an EventSequence. There are two types of retrograde transformations available: event inversion (the reversal of events with forward time values), and time inversion (the reverse of events and time values). In Chapter 5 the Clone will be discussed in detail.

Additionally, the EventSequence calculates and stores meta-data about its internal Events. The meta-data of primary concern is the absolute start and end time of the complete EventSequence. Although Textures have user-specified time ranges, algorithmically generated Events may deviate from this range. Absolute start and end times cannot be known until all Events have been added to the EventSequence. The EventSequence start time is found with the Event having the smallest start time; the EventSequence end time is found with with the Event having the largest sum of start time and sustain value. The EventSequence can be sorted with the sort() method, though this is only necessary for particular OutputFormats. The sort() method is called by the Performer object (to be explained in Chapter 6).

4.4.2.3. Diagrams and Examples

The following diagram summarizes important attributes and methods of the EventSequence object.

Example 4-15. EventSequence Class Diagram

```
Class EventSequence
Attributes:
  _eventList
  _eventData
Methods:
  append()
  __len__()
  keys()
  __getitem__()
```

```
__setitem__()

__delitem__()

getArray()

setArray()

clear()

sort()

updatePre()

updatePost()

getTimeRangeAbs()

retrograde()

copy()
```

The following diagram illustrates the primary object components of the EventSequence.

Example 4-16. Component Diagram of an EventSequence

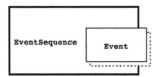

Since the EventSequence is normally created and modified by Textures, its full functionality will not be demonstrated here. The following Python session demonstrates basic functionality of the EventSequence object.

Example 4-17. EventSequence Object in Python

```
>>> from athenaCL.libATH import eventList
>>> # minimal Event dictionaries may be created
>>> event01 = {'time':2.3, 'sus':4}
>>> event02 = {'time':2.8, 'sus':0.2}
>>> event03 = {'time':4.0, 'sus':1.3}
>>> a = eventList.EventSequence() # creating an EventSequence object
```

```
>>> a.append(event01) # appending Events to the EventSequence
>>> a.append(event02)
>>> a.append(event03)
>>> a.updatePost() # updating the EventSequence
>>> # EventSequences support list-like operations
>>> len(a)
3
>>> a[0] # accessing a complete Event by index position
{'sus': 0.5, 'time': 2.2999999999999998}
>>> a.keys() # getting a list of all index positions
[0, 1, 2]
>>> a.getArray('time') # getting an array, or a column of Event data
[2.2999999999999998, 2.7999999999999998, 4.0]
>>> a.getArray('sus')
[4, 0.20000000000000001, 1.3]
>>> a.setArray('sus', [.5, .5, .5]) # editing an array of Event data
>>> a.getArray('sus')
[0.5, 0.5, 0.5]
>>> a.getTimeRangeAbs() # accessing meta-data
(2.2999999999999998, 5.2999999999999998)
```

4.4.3. Compositional Implications

The Event and EventSequence are music representations. In terms of the representation categories established by Eleanor Selfridge-Field, they may be seen as an expansion of a sound-related code (with precise non-metric time and pitch values) with aspects of a music notation code (with ratio-specific Pulse triples) (1997b, p. 28). As with other representations, "assumptions concerning end use determine what elements of information are to be considered essential" (Selfridge-Field 1997b, p. 14). The end use of the EventSequence is conversion into a wide variety of OutputFormats; a priority is placed on sound-related formats over notation formats, though an attempt to accommodate notation, to some degree, is made.

The Event object, as described above, provides a rich representation. The detail contained within the Event is greater than that provided by many alternative CAAC systems. This design provides diverse algorithmic control as well as support for a wide variety of OutputFormats. Many CAAC systems, for example, encode timbre simply as a program or channel number. By allowing the Event to store any number of additional Instrument- or Orchestra-specific parameters, both a simple MIDI instrument and a complex, multi-parameter Csound instrument are supported with the same model. Many systems store only two time values per event: start time and duration. With the storage of BPM, Pulse triple, and sustain value, in addition to start time and duration, the Event supports powerful temporal Clone transformations. The inclusion of panning as a standard Event parameter is also uncommon. Within athenaCL, the panning parameter, like amplitude, is an abstract value between 0 and 1. Ultimate interpretation of this value is Instrument- or Orchestra-dependent. With this model, diverse OutputFormat-dependent panning configurations are supported. For example, with the CsoundNative Orchestra a Texture's panning parameter can control stereo or quadraphonic panning. Depending on Instrument and Csound configuration, the Event parameter is mapped to the appropriate range. If a MIDI file is created, the same value is mapped to the necessary MIDI specification. If an Orchestra or Instrument requires more than one parameter for panning, this can be accommodated with additional auxiliary parameters.

The EventSequence does not enforce event adjacency. The term event adjacency means that, within a series of events, all events are temporally adjacent and there are no temporal gaps between any two events. Enforcing event adjacency means that there is no "empty" time between notes or rests in a series of events. This concept is inherited from Western notation: a measure is considered incorrect if all beat values are not filled with at least one voice of notes or rests. EventSequences, contrary to this, make no restriction on temporal event position, gaps, or overlaps. This allows Textures to create Events in any desired arrangement.

The EventSequence is a utility object. As such, it is not directly created or edited by the user. Only by configuring Textures and Clones does the user generate or transform EventSequences. These EventSequences are then collected and, depending on EventMode and OutputEngines, processed into OutputFormats. Because the EventSequence is an intermediary, its compositional influence is minimal. EventSequences cannot be imported or loaded into athenaCL (as MIDI files or otherwise), and are not stored in the athenaCL XML data format. EventSequences are the result of the algorithmic processes of Textures and Clones, and represent one possible structure variant. Their use is as a medium for translation to OutputFormats.

4.4.4. Alternative and Related Models

Leach and Fitch describe the musical "event" as an occurrence parallel to natural phenomena and kinetic energy, such as the fall of a stone down a cliff. An event, in this context, essentially contains anticipation and climax: "in every sequence of notes there must now be a note that is classified as the major event of the sequence" (1995, p. 25). Leach and Fitch introduce the concept of "sub-events" as smaller events that, in the context of numerous events, lead to a major event. These sub-events can be found before or after the major event. To continue the falling-stone analogy, sub-events are the minor collisions of the stone with the mountainside on its way toward final impact (1995, p. 25). The Event and SubEvent, as used in athenaCL, are free of such teleological associations. Although a Texture may be designed to implement such models, they are not encoded in the object design. A SubEvent, for instance, could be more musically relevant than its parent Event, and there is no demand that an EventSequence contains a single major event. Directed motion, and relationships between Events, is variable and exclusively the domain of Texture processing.

The inclusion of panning as an algorithmically generated event parameter can be found in Tenney's 1963 PLF-5 subroutine (1969, p. 58). As with other event, synthesis, and function table selection parameters for Music IV, Tenney allowed panning to be varied with generative procedures. PLF-5, as well as Tenney's earlier PLF subroutines, was designed to support specific instrument designs; the number and type of event parameters was fixed for each subroutine.

Truax's POD system offers an early example of a variable-size event parameter specification. Truax states that the event is "the basic perceptual unit posited by the program." Events contain data for frequency, time delay, maximum amplitude, and sound object number; the sound object number, in turn, provides "the data representation of the sounding object without those parameters determined in the event data" (1976, p. 260), that is, specific parameters dependent on the particular synthesis method applied. Truax provides examples of sound object parameters such as waveform and panning specifications (1973, p. 9) and, in the case of FM synthesis, modulation index and envelope (1976, p. 260). This design is parallel to the *n*-dimensional event list of athenaCL. In a similar manner to that described by Truax, a Texture, using a CsoundNative FM instrument for example, will be assigned additional parameters for modulation index and envelope control. The number of Event parameters changes to accommodate timbre.

While Fry notes that events in his Flavors Band system are designed primarily to model "… the pitch-time structure of a score" (1984b, p. 297), he offers, based on a standard Lisp feature, variable sized property lists "that can hold any number of additional properties"; further, "… properties may be added, deleted, and read by phrase processors as an event progresses through a network" (1984b, p. 297). Though Fry suggests the use of event property lists for timbre specification, their primary use is to "… hold amplitude, and sometimes scales, or voicings of chords" (1984b, p. 297). Within the Lisp Kernel system, Rahn provides a very general data structure for events. The goal of this design is a representation "… that is general enough that each of the data structures employed by other programs could be translated into it" (1990a, p. 42). In this model events, or "note-structures," are implemented as a flat list of alternating properties and values, where values themselves are embedded lists (1990a, p. 44). In order to "… accommodate any event-oriented representation of music" (1990a, p. 43), the type and number of property and value pairs is variable.

Tipei refers to a related event model in his MP1 system (1975), where events are modeled within an *n*-dimensional vector space (1994, p. 5). As this system produces scores in Western notation for acoustic instruments, the variable dimensions of these vectors are not explicitly applied to synthesis parameters.

The configuration of Textures and Clones is the primary user-level representation of musical structures in athenaCL. Many CAAC systems have focused on storing and manipulating event lists as a primary, user-level representation. This approach, found as early as Buxton et al. (1978; Buxton 1978), has encouraged the design of systems based on hierarchical and nested event lists.

Buxton defines an event as having, at a minimum, a start and an end time. Events, in this model, are very general and designed for hierarchical nesting: "any musical event … can be made up of composite musical events … hence the basis for our hierarchy" (1978, p. 27).

In one of the first applications of object-oriented design to event structures, Buxton proposes a model where event lists, as events, can be deployed in multiple instances at multiple hierarchical levels. Buxton describes a design, where "… each appearance of a particular sub-score constitutes an instance rather than a master copy of that sub-score …" and further, "any changes to the original are reflected in each instance …" (1978, p. 65). Combining "arbitrary hierarchical (tree) structures" with object-oriented deployment of event list instances provides a flexible model. As Buxton states, this design provides "… the ability to deal with any (user-defined) sub-set of a score in the same manner, and with the same ease, as with a single note …" (1978, p. 89).

Pope, employing a related model as a component of the Smoke environment, describes events as "… simply property lists or dictionaries; they can have named properties whose values are arbitrary …" and scale to all durations, "… from tens of milliseconds to tens of seconds" (1996, p. 59). Pope's event list model is closely related to that proposed by Buxton et al. (1978): "event lists are events themselves and can therefore be nested into trees… they can also map their properties onto their component events … an event can be 'shared' by being in more than one event list at different relative start times and with different properties mapped onto it" (1996, p. 63). A similar arrangement is found in Oppenheim's Dmix system, where EventLists are modeled as collections of TerminalEvents (single events or messages) or embedded EventLists (1989, p. 229).

Though potentially powerful, hierarchical event structures have been criticized. Roads, in considering the use of grammars in CAAC systems, states that "… musical structure cannot always be segmented into neat hierarchical groupings" and further, "if we want to manipulate musical structures that extend beyond strictly hierarchical groupings, more powerful representations are needed" (1985, p. 170). Similarly, Selfridge-Field states that, "while it is often convenient for analytical purposes to view music as hierarchical in nature, it is only within the bounds of certain specific attributes that musical information can be thought of as being hierarchical" (1997a, p. 568). The association of analytic techniques of Western music with hierarchical event structures is important. Hierarchical structures may be directly inspired, or at least informed, by a particular idiom-affinity: notated Western music. Hierarchical structures may not be as prevalent in musical practices not so reliant on notation. Smalley, in discussing spectro-morphological music, states, "… there is no consistent low-level unit, and therefore no simple equivalent of the structure of tonal music with its neat hierarchical stratification from the note upwards, through motif, phrase, period, until we encompass the whole work" (1986, p. 80). Hierarchical structures are certainly prevalent in common-practice Western notated music; their utility in other musical idioms has been less thoroughly demonstrated.

The hierarchical event list offers creative and powerful production models. The athenaCL system does not forbid such models: hierarchical subsystems, of any complexity, may be embedded within a TextureModule, and offer any range of useful hierarchical constructions and manipulations. With such a Texture the user would be able to directly configure and manipulate hierarchical forms. Importantly, such models are contained within TextureModules: their influence need not spill out into the rest of the system. No matter how a Texture internally represents Events, the EventSequence provides a temporary, flat representation designed to accommodate conversion into diverse OutputFormats.

4.5. The Instrument and Orchestra Model

The athenaCL system integrates algorithmic parts (Textures) with internal, external, and exported sound production systems. When created, a Texture is assigned an Instrument, and all Clones inherit their parent Texture's Instrument. A TextureModule is independent of any particular sound production system, and thus any Texture can be used with any Instrument.

An Orchestra is a container of Instruments, and provides their public interface. The terms Instrument and Orchestra, despite historical associations, are very general. Traditional production models should not be inferred from these terms. An Instrument refers to an entity that responds to a parametric event specification; an Orchestra is simply a collection of Instruments.

Instrument objects, in most cases, encode a model of a sound source or sound production device. Such a sound source may require standard Event parameters, such as amplitude and duration, as well as any number of additional auxiliary parameters.

Textures, and users of Textures, must be informed of the parametric demands of a particular Instrument. These demands include the number of auxiliary parameter values (those beyond standard parameters), as well as documentation and default values for these auxiliary parameters. Further, OutputEngines, when converting an EventSequence to an OutputFormat, require information about the Instrument's pitch, amplitude, and panning specifications. These specifications, such as the absolute range of amplitude values, may be different for each Instrument. Finally, the OutputEngine may need to interact with external systems to activate, or even create, the sound sources expected by an OutputFormat. The Instrument object may contain source code in specialized languages to instantiate the sound source. When using Instruments from athenaCL's built-in Csound instrument collection (provided by the CsoundNative Orchestra), for example, Csound orchestra files are dynamically created for use with EventSequences converted to Csound score files.

External objects access Instruments through an Orchestra, a model of a collection of related Instruments. Instruments in an Orchestra are related by sound production system. Examples of Orchestras include the built-in Csound instruments (CsoundNative), external Csound definitions (CsoundExternal), and General MIDI (GeneralMidi and

GeneralMidiPercussion). In some cases, an Orchestra may contain unique, sub-classed object definitions for each Instrument. In other cases, an Orchestra may use a single, generic object to provide a common specification for numerous Instruments. The Orchestra manages the interaction between external objects and these internal objects.

All Orchestras, through their internal Instrument specifications, provide methods for transforming Event pitch space, amplitude, and panning parameters. This facility, as stated above, is necessary because OutputFormats require diverse representations of these parameters. These transformations are configured by "postMap" values and methods: these specifications map values, after EventSequence production, from native athenaCL representations to Instrument-specific representations. As sound sources frequently require diverse numerical representations along different numerical scales, Instrument-specific transformations allow Textures to be configured without consideration for final OutputFormat. As already mentioned, within Textures and Clones pitch space values are stored as psReals, and amplitude and planing values are specified within the unit interval. These values, combined with Instrument-specific postMap specifications, can be converted to any OutputFormat. This facility is provided by Orchestras and OutputEngines, to be explained in more detail in Chapter 6.

When creating a Texture within athenaCL, the user must always specify an Instrument. The user never directly specifies an Orchestra, but rather selects an EventMode. The EventMode determines what Orchestra is active, and thus what Instruments are available for Texture creation. EventModes also determine the nature of initial Texture configuration. Every Texture stores both an Instrument number and an Orchestra name within its instrument parameter; this parameter may be edited after Texture creation. Details of the EventMode system will be explained in Chapter 6. As is the case with many components of athenaCL (such as ParameterObjects and TextureModules), additional Orchestras and Instruments can be added to the system by subclassing parent classes.

4.5.1. The Instrument

4.5.1.1. Model and Representation

Instrument objects, used exclusively through an Orchestra interface, provide data necessary for configuring a Texture's auxiliary parameters, documentation of parameter values, and EventSequence postMap values. Additionally, Instruments may contain source code or specifications for creating or controlling external sound sources.

All Instruments are identified by a number. The interpretation of this number is dependent on the sound source. In the case of Csound-based sound sources, Instrument numbers are used as Csound orchestra and score instrument numbers. In the case of MIDI-based sound sources, Instrument numbers may refer to General MIDI (GM) programs (as in Orchestra GeneralMidi) or to pitch values (as in Orchestra GeneralMidiPercussion).

4.5.1.2. Object Design

There are many Instrument sub-classes, each specialized by one or more levels of inheritance. As Instruments are always encapsulated within Orchestras, Instrument sub-classes may not be polymorphic. Within an Orchestra, a single instance of each Instrument sub-class is stored.

The richness of an Instrument sub-class representation depends on the demands of the sound source and the role of the Orchestra. All Instruments inherit from a parent Instrument class. Some Instruments have one level of inheritance: InstrumentMidi, for example, is a sub-class of Instrument. In this case, one instance is used to represent all MIDI Instruments. Each MIDI-related Orchestra (GeneralMidi and GeneralMidiPercussion) contains a single, multi-purpose Instrument object. Other Instruments in other Orchestras may have two levels of inheritance: InstrumentCsound, for example, is a sub-class of Instrument, and is in turn sub-classed to create a separate object for each Instrument available (class Inst80, for example).

Each Instrument contains an `auxNo` attribute to specify the number of auxiliary parameter fields required for use by a Texture. For some Instruments, the number of auxiliary fields is configurable. This is the case with InstrumentCsoundExternal: the number of auxiliary parameters is determined by the user, and passed to the Instrument at Texture instantiation. An Instrument object additionally contains attributes for postMap values (`postMapPs`, `postMapAmp`, and `postMapPan`). These attributes consist of three values: a minimum, a maximum, and a mapping-type string (after Taube (1991)). Through the Orchestra's `postMap()` method, these values are made available for Event processing.

An Instrument may contain optional attributes such as an Instrument number (`instNo`) and a description string (`info`). In other cases this information may be provided by the Orchestra. The Instrument may specify dictionaries of parameter documentation and parameter defaults (`pmtrInfo` and `pmtrDefault`). Parameter defaults may be provided for both auxiliary and standard parameters. If a highly specialized Instrument contains source code for instantiating an external sound source, this data is stored as a string in the `orcCode` attribute. In the case of the CsoundNative orchestra, for example, an Instrument contains a partial Csound instrument definition that is built into a complete Csound orchestra by the Orchestra object.

4.5.1.3. Diagrams and Examples

The inheritance diagram below provides an example of Instrument inheritance.

Example 4-18. Instrument Inheritance: Inst32

```
Instrument
|
InstrumentCsound
|
Inst32
```

The following diagram summarizes important attributes and methods of the InstrumentCsound object.

Example 4-19. Instrument Object Class Diagram

```
Class InstrumentCsound
Attributes:
    name
    auxNo
    pmtrInfo
    pmtrDefault
    postMapPs
    postMapAmp
    postMapPan
    instNo
    info
    orcCode
Methods:
    getPresetDict()
```

As the public interface to Instruments is provided through the Orchestra, demonstration of isolated Instrument objects is limited: the following Python session demonstrates only basic features.

Example 4-20. Instrument Object in Python

```
>>> from athenaCL.libATH.libOrc import csoundNative
>>> a = csoundNative.Inst32() # creating a CsoundNative instrument object
>>> a.info # viewing instrument documentation
'A simple sampler with a proportional linear envelope and a variable low-pass
filter.'
>>> a.name # instrument name
'samplerUnitEnvelope'
>>> a.auxNo # the number of required auxiliary values
7
>>> a.pmtrDefault['pmtr8'] # a default parameter value
('c', 0.5)
>>> a.getPresetDict() # a complete dictionary of default parameter values
{'auxQ0': ('c', 0.5), 'auxQ1': ('c', 0.5), 'auxQ2': ('c', 18000), 'auxQ3':
('c', 8000), 'auxQ4': ('c', 1), 'auxQ5': ('c', 0), 'auxQ6': ('sampleSelect',
('drum01.aif', 'latch01.aif'))}
>>> a.postMapAmp # postMap amplitude specification
(0, 9, 'linear')
>>> from athenaCL.libATH.libOrc import generalMidi
>>> b = generalMidi.InstrumentMidi() # creating a MIDI Instrument
>>> # MIDI Instrument names are provided by Orchestra, not Instrument
>>> b.name
'generic'
>>> b.auxNo # MIDI instruments have no auxiliary parameters
0
>>> b.postMapAmp # MIDI amplitude values specified between 0 and 127
(0, 127, 'linear')
```

4.5.2. The Orchestra

4.5.2.1. Model and Representation

The Orchestra object provides a public interface to a collection of Instruments. Within an Orchestra, one or more Instrument objects exist. As mentioned above, in some cases the Orchestra will provide an interface to Instruments by using numerous specialized objects, while in other cases the Orchestra will provide an interface to Instruments by using a single Instrument object augmented with Orchestra-bound specifications. Orchestra objects are used for obtaining all Instrument data, such as the number of auxiliary parameters, presets, documentation, and postMap specifications. In some cases, Orchestras create external sound sources.

4.5.2.2. Object Design

There are many Orchestra sub-classes, each specialized by one or more levels of inheritance. All Orchestra sub-classes are polymorphic and may be used interchangeably. Any number of Orchestra instances may be created.

As Orchestra sub-classes have different design demands, unique internal, private structures are necessary. All Orchestras feature a `name` attribute as well as a method to test if an Instrument number is valid (`instNoValid()`). The method `instNoList()` returns either a list of valid Instrument numbers or None when a discrete list cannot be specified (as is the case with the CsoundExternal orchestra).

Most Orchestra methods are designed to obtain Instrument-specific data. Methods such as `getInstInfo()`, `getInstPreset()`, `getInstName()`, `getInstAuxNo()`, `getInstPmtrInfo()`, and `postMap()` all take an Instrument number as an argument, and return data specific to the requested Instrument.

The `postMap()` method takes an Instrument number, parameter name, value, and Orchestra map mode as arguments. Instrument number is used to obtain Instrument-specific postMap values. These values are used to map and limit the value argument. In the case of pitch, the value is additionally converted to the necessary Orchestra-determined output representation (such as frequency or PCH). The Orchestra map mode (`orcMapMode`) allows a Texture to optionally turn off postMap value mapping while performing necessary format conversions.

4.5.2.3. Diagrams and Examples

The inheritance diagram below provides an example of Orchestra inheritance. In all cases Orchestras inherit directly from the Orchestra parent class.

Example 4-21. Orchestra Inheritance: CsoundNative

```
Orchestra
|
CsoundNative
```

The following diagram summarizes important attributes and methods of the Orchestra object.

Example 4-22. Orchestra Object Class Diagram

```
Class Orchestra
Attributes:
   name
Methods:
   instNoValid()
   instNoList()
   constructOrc()
   getInstInfo()
```

```
getInstPreset()

getInstName()

getInstAuxNo()

getInstPmtrInfo()

postMap()
```

The following diagram illustrates the primary object components of the Orchestra.

Example 4-23. Component Diagram of an Orchestra

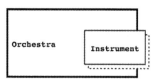

The following Python session demonstrates the functionality of the Orchestra object.

Example 4-24. Orchestra Object in Python

```
>>> from athenaCL.libATH.libOrc import generalMidi
>>> a = generalMidi.GeneralMidi() # creating the GeneralMidi orchestra
>>> a.name # the name of the orchestra
'generalMidi'
>>> a.instNoValid(34) # testing if an instrument number is valid
1
>>> a.instNoValid(129)
0
>>> a.getInstName(34) # getting an instrument name
'pickedBass'
>>> a.getInstAuxNo(34) # getting the number of required auxiliary parameters
0
>>> # the postMap method can be used to map and format Event parameters
>>> # the first argument is the Instrument number
>>> a.postMap(20, 'ps', 0) # mapping a psReal value to a MIDI format
60
```

```
>>> a.postMap(20, 'amp', .5) # mapping an amplitude value to a MIDI format
64
>>> b = csoundNative.CsoundNative() # creating the CsoundNative orchestra
>>> b.instNoList() # returning a list of available Instrument numbers
(3, 5, 11, 12, 13, 14, 15, 20, 21, 22, 23, 30, 31, 32, 33, 34, 50, 51, 52, 60,
61, 62, 70, 71, 80, 81)
>>> b.getInstAuxNo(32) # getting the number of auxiliary parameters
7
>>> b.getInstName(32) # getting an instrument name
'samplerUnitEnvelope'
>>> b.getInstPmtrInfo(32, 3) # getting documentation for a parameter
'low-pass filter end cutoff frequency in Hz'
>>> b.postMap(32, 'ps', 0) # mapping a psReal value to a Csound PCH format
8.0
>>> b.postMap(32, 'amp', .5) # mapping an amplitude value to a Csound range
4.5
```

4.5.3. Compositional Implications

The Instrument and Orchestra model allow the composer to work in diverse
OutputFormats within a uniform environment. Many alternative systems are designed for
use with a particular sound source, be it Western notation, Csound, or MIDI. Further, it is
compositionally useful to produce multiple OutputFormats of the same structure
simultaneously. For example, a Csound score and orchestra, produced with the
CsoundNative Orchestra, can be generated at the same time as a MIDI file or a text format.
The Csound-rendered digital audio might be used in one context, while the same material, as
MIDI data, might be used in a related context.

The ability of each Instrument to store defaults for auxiliary parameters assists the user
in learning parameter function and value ranges. For example, when creating a Texture with

an Instrument from the CsoundNative Orchestra, the user is provided with default values and documentation for each auxiliary parameter.

The use of defaults, in general, is an important issue. All athenaCL user objects, once created from a minimum specification, are provided with defaults. Buxton, one of the first authors to consider the implications of using defaults, states that their use is "pedagogically useful in that we are able to 'hide' from the novice user details which are beyond [her/his] current level of competence … in too many previous systems the necessity of specifying every last detail (correctly), before being able to assess the musical results is an impediment to composers' access" (Buxton 1978, p. 25). A similar concern motivated the use of defaults in athenaCL. Buxton, as well as others, acknowledge the legitimate arguments against the use of defaults. Their use in athenaCL, however, is often transparent. In most cases defaults are simply a starting point or a place holder; many options and their defaults are silent until activated.

4.5.4. Alternative and Related Models

Modular output formats that are independent of primary system representations have been used in numerous systems. In describing the MUSICOMP system, Hiller refers to "sound synthesis routines" that, he states, "… are not actual synthesis programs but rather routines that prepare and organize data that serve as input to sound-generating programs described elsewhere" (1969, p. 72). Truax, separating event data from sound object data in the POD system, describes how one sound object "… could equally well be specified by an entirely different set of parameters in the case of a different synthesis program" (1976, p. 261). With this design, "the compositional strategy is independent of the synthesis model being used…" (1976, p. 261). Truax's POD system provides an early example of a system with modular outputs and diverse instrument models.

Rahn describes how the Lisp Kernel system, supporting outputs for MIDI, Music IV, Csound, and the NeXT Music Kit, frees the composer from "… consideration of what synthesis system or device will be used for the output at an intermediate stage of composition" (1990b, p. 186). This is implemented with a variable internal representation that is then re-mapped or extended for various output formats: output formats are accommodated by "… reordering the parameters as needed, filtering out parameters that a particular output device may not be able to use, and supplying defaults for any parameters needed by the output device which are not part of the internal representation of the notes" (1990b, p. 186). Through the use of instrument-specific templates and defaults (1990a, p. 46), multiple outputs are accommodated, though a direct link to instrument models is not provided. Although flexible, the lack of a direct link between internal representation and output may, in some cases, force the user to accept default configurations for parameters and settings that otherwise may offer powerful control.

Holtzman describes how his Generative Grammar Definition Language (GGDL) allows the manipulation of abstract objects independent of any output, such that the mapping of output is "… completely separate and, from the point of view of the system, completely arbitrary" (1994, p. 231). Holtzman offers note events, performance variables, or direct waveform specifications as example outputs. This complete separation between model and output, while providing flexibility, is not always advantageous. A complete separation prohibits the generative part (such as the Texture) from expanding to the needs of diverse OutputFormats. Some Instruments, for example, require more parameters than others; some parameter values require diverse formats and representations. By using the Instrument definition to configure Textures, greater control of diverse OutputFormats is provided. The athenaCL system does not offer a complete separation between model and output: though TextureModules are independent of Instruments, a Texture, once instantiated, must have a declared Instrument, and this Instrument and Orchestra may not be compatible with all OutputFormats. This dependency, however, is minimal and provides greater output flexibility.

Common Music provides an additional example of a modular output design: "one of the central features of Common Music might be termed 'connectivity,' the ability to write compositions for different sound synthesis packages without changing the manner in which compositions are described. Common Music has been designed to support the incremental addition of new output formats…" (1991, p. 21). As Taube points out, earlier models of modular output formats can be found in Pope's HyperScore (Pope 1987) and Rahn's Lisp Kernel (Rahn 1990a).

The model of Common Music informed the Instrument model presented here. In particular, the use of normalized standard parameter values (for pitch, amplitude, and panning), combined with Instrument-based postMap specifications, was inspired by Taube (1991). Although his model does not include panning or pitch, Taube describes output-dependent amplitude scaling: "a logical amplitude is a number between 0 and 1.0 … an amplitude value is computed from the weight of the logical amplitude, a minimum and maximum amplitude value, and a power curve" (1991, p. 29). In athenaCL, this model was extended to panning and pitch.

Chapter 5. Abstractions of Musical Procedures

5.1. Introduction

Repeat, again and again: A beautiful numeric structure may be different from a beautiful visual structure may be different from a beautiful sonic structure may be different from a beautiful verbal structure may be different from...

—Warren Burt (1996, p. 170)

A musical procedure is any process of creating ordered or unordered events or event components. Often, musical procedures are used to create dynamic or static time-domain trajectories. Any process of information generation or transformation, when abstracted into software and applied to one or more musical parameters, can become a musical procedure. Some abstractions of musical procedures may be processes analogous to production phases of traditional Western composition: the selection and ordering of pitches from a collection, the permutation of a defined series, or the assignment of values based on a random operation. Other abstractions of musical procedures may have no direct analogue to production phases of Western composition.

Historically, CAAC has been concerned with the collection, exploration, and deployment of these abstractions of musical procedures. A focus on particular procedures and algorithms has led some to a false teleology: new technologies, once applied to musical processes, are heralded as an improvement over previous models, or, in fewer cases, an answer to broad compositional problems. This false teleology, when applied to technology in general, relates to the concept of technological determinism (Heilbroner 1967; Skinner 1976; Bimber 1990). This concept has diverse interpretations and has been investigated in many fields; computer music systems in particular provide a valuable focus (Di Scipio 1997; Hamman 2002). Hamman, in the context of software for creative production, defines technological determinism as the assumption that (1) technology progresses from lower to higher levels and (2) technological development follows a single unified sequence of stages (2002, p. 95). Hamman argues that these assumptions must be rejected, for in the general case, "the falseness of this conditioned interpretive response has socially debilitating effects, projecting the view that technical progress follows a purely pragmatic and instrumental course and that there is little that human beings can do to alter that course" (2002, p. 95). In the case of composition systems, this debilitation is not only a passivity to the influence of software tools, but a disregard for collections of tools considered "old" in favor of fashionable "new" technologies. Musical procedures, whether abstracted in software or otherwise, are not scientific theories that can be tested or proven. Unlike hardware or software technologies, musical procedures do not go out of date. They are creative tools. The science of CAAC is in the design, organization, and interaction of these tools; the art is in their use and in their products.

This confusion has led some, as discussed in Chapter 3, to classify CAAC systems by algorithm type. This is mistaken not only because algorithm types will continue to expand and develop, but because, from the perspective of composers, how a musical procedure is used, interpreted, and deployed is of greater importance than the particular type of algorithm. In many cases, completely contrasting algorithm types can be used in similar production models to produce similar results. For most listeners, the outputs of Hiller and Isaacson's historic counterpoint, generated with random pitches filtered through Fux-based rules (1959), Schottstaedt's Fux-modeled best-first search techniques (1989a), or Cope's recent Fux-inspired back-tracking learning algorithm (2004) may all sound remarkably similar. In many cases, algorithm interpretation and deployment is more important than particular technologies or algorithm types.

In describing athenaCL, it is useful to organize musical procedures by production orientation: where, and on what, do the algorithms operate. There are then two types of algorithms for modeling musical procedures: generators and transformers. This division between generators and transformers was applied to devices of the "classic tape studio" as early as 1962: a survey of twenty international studios, titled *Rèpertoire International des Musiques Expèrimentales*, supplied lists of equipment in three categories: sound generators, sound transformers or modifiers, and sound mixers and recorders (Ciamaga 1975, pp. 72-73). Generators and transformers, further, can operate on two scales: one-dimensional or multi-dimensional. These divisions are not rigid: the interpretation of a procedure may change depending on its deployment. A loose contextual frame, however, is valuable.

A generator is a musical procedure that produces values. The values produced may be numeric or symbolic. The generator may be configured by numerous parameters. Some or all of these parameters may be controlled by internal or external generators. When called to produce a value, a generator, in some cases, may not require additional information. In other cases, a generator may require contextual information, such as the current time of evaluation from an external clock. A generator has its analogue in the voltage-controlled studio, where an oscillator can be used to produce a signal without additional inputs or controls. Likewise, a pink or white noise "generator" produces a signal without any input.

A transformer is a musical procedure that changes or alters existing values. The values transformed may be numeric or symbolic. Like generators, transformers may be configured by numerous parameters. Some or all of these parameters may be controlled by internal or external generators. Unlike a generator, however, when called to produce a value a transformer must be supplied with values to transform. A transformer has its analogue in the voltage-controlled studio, where a filter (in most cases) requires an input signal to produce an altered output signal.

Both generators and transformers can operate at a variety of scales. If a procedure is one-dimensional, it either produces or processes one value, or one bundle of related values. If a procedure is multi-dimensional, it produces or processes multiple independent values.

As defined here, there are then four possibilities of musical procedures: one- and multi-dimensional generators, and one- and multi-dimensional transformers. In athenaCL, these four procedure types are provided by the Generator ParameterObject, the Texture, the Filter ParameterObject, and the Clone respectively. Together, they offer three levels of algorithmic design. Generator and Filter ParameterObjects occupy the lowest level. The Texture, at a higher level, embeds ParameterObjects and offers meta-parametric control. The Clone, at the highest level, embeds ParameterObjects and offers post-Textural control. The following diagram illustrates these three levels of algorithmic design.

Example 5-1. Three Levels of Algorithmic Design

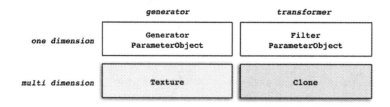

Generators and transformers can embed one another. An argument, for instance, may be provided by a separate, autonomous procedure. When the argument is required, the embedded procedure is called to produce a value. The embedding of procedures within procedures produces a hierarchical tree, where each nested node is either a constant or a procedure, and evaluation transverses the tree, higher nodes calling lower nodes.

Generators and transformers can contain complete subsystems of any complexity. The common transformative processes of selection and mapping provide an example. Selection is the process of choosing an item from a list. Selection can be seen as a transformative process. A list of values is the required external input. A selector transforms this list into one resulting (chosen) value. Mapping is the process of taking a value within a scale (often the unit interval) and translating that value to another scale. Such subsystems may be embedded within a generator or transformer.

Any algorithm type can be used to build either generators or transformers at any scale. For example, a genetic algorithm, as a generator, can be used to produce a sequence of rhythms. A genetic algorithm, as a transformer, might analyze a pattern of pitches and return a transformed, evolved variation. Algorithm type alone does not necessarily suggest implementation as a generator or a transformer.

This chapter demonstrates the design of procedural abstractions. Within athenaCL, one dimensional generators and transformers are modularized and deployed as ParameterObjects. ParameterObjects come in various varieties including the Generator, Rhythm Generator, Filter, and Static ParameterObject. Multi-dimensional generators and transformers are modularized and deployed as Textures and Clones.

5.2. The One-Dimensional Generator and Transformer

The ParameterObject is a multi-purpose, reusable object for one-dimensional parameter generation and transformation. ParameterObjects are specialized through one or more levels of single inheritance. Each of the main types (Generator, Rhythm Generator, Filter, and Static) have a specialized subclass of the Parameter parent class. These classes are then further sub-classed to create individual, specialized ParameterObjects with a common interface.

Within athenaCL, ParameterObjects are used to fill slots in Textures and Clones. A Texture collects values produced by ParameterObjects as input values, and then uses these values to generate new Events and EventSequences. A Clone uses ParameterObjects to process and configure transformations of EventSequences.

Users directly create and edit ParameterObjects by supplying an ordered, comma-separated list of arguments. The first argument is always the name of the ParameterObject. Additional arguments may be strings, numbers, or lists. Some arguments may be embedded ParameterObjects, the argument position filled with a sub-list of additional arguments. Though ParameterObjects are, in all cases, objects, names are provided to the user with leading lower-case characters.

With the use of a modified Python syntax, the athenaCL Interpreter and Command objects facilitate ParameterObject creation. Rather than demanding that the user supply complete Python language statements, a number of shorthands are permitted. The complete string provided by the user is pre-processed before being used to instantiate the ParameterObject. The motivations for this design are compactness and ease of use. First, all parentheses are converted to brackets, forcing all notations of groups into lists rather than tuples. This aspect of Python syntax, explained in Chapter 1, allows the specification of single-element groups without the use of a comma. Second, all character sequences are automatically quoted, allowing the entry of strings without delimiting characters. Third, automatic acronym expansion allows ParameterObject names and parameter control strings, given as short acronyms without periods, to be expanded into verbose, human-readable notations.

All ParameterObjects supply four main features. The first feature is argument checking. Because users directly configure and instantiate ParameterObjects with a list of arguments, it is necessary that, if a mistake is made, the object is able to return detailed, informative error messages. This is done by type checking and validating each argument, as well as by providing default arguments for missing values. The second feature is the production of concise and human-readable string representations. This is done by providing a formatted version of the argument list with expanded acronyms and high-level notations. The third feature is use of the __call__() method to return calculated or transformed values. Depending on the ParameterObject, the __call__() method may require particular information at evaluation, such as a time value from an external clock. The fourth feature is the reset() method. As ParameterObjects store state information over repeated execution, it is occasionally necessary to return them to their initial state.

ParameterObjects modularize algorithmic processes into reusable components, applicable to a wide variety of parameters. The design and use of ParameterObjects is one of the three ways the athenaCL system exposes algorithmic design to users. ParameterObjects are algorithm independent: they can model and use any algorithm type, with any degree of internal complexity. The accumulation of a library of diverse and robust ParameterObjects is a long-term goal of the system. The ParameterObject asserts the importance of providing a user with a practical model of, and interface to, specialized musical procedures.

5.2.1. The Selector

5.2.1.1. Model and Representation

The Selector object is designed to fulfill the basic transformative process of selection from a list of values. The Selector, strictly speaking, is not a ParameterObject. This object does not inherit from the Parameter parent class and is not a user-instantiated object. Instead, the Selector is a utility object designed to handle zero-parameter selection procedures. Selection procedures that require more parameters, if desired, can be built separately as a ParameterObject component or a shared utility object. The Selector, as a zero-parameter transformer, requires only the name of the selection method and a list of values from which to make selections. No additional configuration parameters are required at initialization or during selection. Selection methods include randomChoice, randomWalk, randomPermutate, orderedCyclic, and orderedOscillate. The Selector, when available, is embedded in other ParameterObjects and configured by providing a selection method within the ParameterObject's argument list.

5.2.1.2. Object Design

There is one Selector class that is not specialized. Any number of Selector instances may be created and configured.

The Selector, on initialization, takes a list of values and a control string. The list of values is assigned to src and is stored. Each value in the src is then copied and appended to the ref list attribute. This list is used to read and process values. The control string determines the selection method, and is assigned to the control attribute.

Similar to ParameterObjects, the Selector's primary functionality is made available through the __call__() method. This method, calling private methods as needed, returns a value based on the desired selection method. The reset() method allows the Selector to be reset to its initial state; the update() method permits a new list of values to be applied to the Selector.

5.2.1.3. Diagrams and Examples

The following diagram summarizes important attributes and methods of the Selector.

Example 5-2. Selector Class Diagram

```
Class Selector
Attributes:
    src
```

```
    control
    ref
Methods:
    __call__()
    reset()
    update()
```

The following Python session demonstrates the functionality of the Selector. In each example the same source list is given to the Selector. Python list comprehension is used to demonstrate twelve evaluations of the __call__() method.

Example 5-3. Selector in Python

```
>>> from athenaCL.libATH.libPmtr import basePmtr
>>> x = basePmtr.Selector([0,1,2,3], 'randomChoice')
>>> [x() for y in range(12)]
[1, 0, 0, 2, 3, 2, 2, 3, 0, 1, 0, 3]
>>>
>>> x = basePmtr.Selector([0,1,2,3], 'randomWalk')
>>> [x() for y in range(12)]
[1, 2, 1, 0, 1, 2, 3, 0, 1, 2, 1, 0]
>>>
>>> x = basePmtr.Selector([0,1,2,3], 'randomPermutate')
>>> [x() for y in range(12)]
[2, 3, 0, 1, 0, 3, 1, 2, 0, 2, 3, 1]
>>>
>>> x = basePmtr.Selector([0,1,2,3], 'orderedCyclic')
>>> [x() for y in range(12)]
[0, 1, 2, 3, 0, 1, 2, 3, 0, 1, 2, 3]
>>>
>>> x = basePmtr.Selector([0,1,2,3], 'orderedOscillate')
>>> [x() for y in range(12)]
[0, 1, 2, 3, 2, 1, 0, 1, 2, 3, 2, 1]
```

5.2.2. The Generator ParameterObject

5.2.2.1. Model and Representation

The Generator ParameterObject is designed to provide an interface to a wide variety of generative procedures. In some cases these procedures are common generators such as the production of random values, wave forms, or break-point functions. In other cases, a Generator may be designed to fulfill specialized needs, such as providing scaled values of a Xenakis sieve, or selected file paths of audio files from a specified directory. Generator ParameterObjects, as one-dimensional procedures, return a single value when called. The Rhythm Generator, to be discussed below, is a specialized Generator ParameterObject.

The complete list of athenaCL Generator ParameterObjects, as well as their documentation, can be found in Section B.1.

5.2.2.2. Object Design

There are many Generator ParameterObject sub-classes, each specialized by one or more levels of inheritance. All Generator sub-classes are polymorphic and may be used interchangeably. Any number of Generator instances may be created and configured.

Generator ParameterObjects are directly sub-classed from the Parameter parent class, sharing Parameter public methods and attributes. Depending on the design of the Generator, however, extensive private methods or additional Python modules may be used for internal processing.

The Generator __call__() method requires two arguments: a time value (t) and a reference dictionary (refDict). Whenever a Generator is called within a Texture, the Texture provides an event start time and this reference dictionary. The reference dictionary stores temporary data concerning the current state of the Texture, including the current Multiset,

Pitch, and tempo (BPM). The result of the __call__() operation is stored in the currentValue attribute before being returned. For some Generators, __call__() arguments are optional.

Both Generator and Rhythm Generator ParameterObjects have, in addition to the __call__() method, a postEvent() method. The postEvent() method allows a ParameterObject to modify an Event dictionary. After all values for an Event have been calculated, and before that Event is added to the EventSequence, each Generator and Rhythm Generator ParameterObject may call its postEvent() method on the Event dictionary. The order that ParameterObjects access the Event is based on a ParameterObject's priority attribute. This integer value is defined by the ParameterObject class.

Generator ParameterObjects that produce or process lists of data, such as BasketGen or SieveList, embed a Selector object to perform value selection. Whenever a ParameterObject's reset() method is called, all embedded objects are likewise reset, including internal ParameterObjects and Selectors.

Numerical Generator ParameterObjects often embed mapping functionality. Mapping is provided by minimum and maximum arguments. These arguments may be provided as numbers, or as a list of arguments for an embedded ParameterObject. For example RandomUniform or WaveSine have minimum and maximum parameter arguments. These arguments scale the internal unit-interval output to whatever scale is specified between the minimum and maximum. Minimum and maximum arguments can be Generator ParameterObjects, allowing the production of dynamic, masked value mapping.

5.2.2.3. Diagrams and Examples

The inheritance diagram below provides an example of Generator ParameterObject inheritance. In some cases, a collection of related ParameterObjects inherit from a common sub-class of Parameter, providing shared functionality.

Example 5-4. Generator ParameterObject Inheritance: RandomUniform

```
Parameter
|
_Random
|
RandomUniform
```

The following class diagram summarizes important attributes and methods of the Generator ParameterObject.

Example 5-5. Generator ParameterObject Class Diagram

```
Class Parameter
Attributes:
    args
    argTypes
    argNames
    argDefaults
    doc
    parent
    priority
    outputFmt
    currentValue
Methods:
    checkArgs()
    reprDoc()
    repr(), __str__()
```

```
__call__()
reset()
postEvent()
```

The following Python session demonstrates the functionality of the RandomUniform and BasketGen Generator ParameterObjects. RandomUniform provides a random uniform distribution with arguments for minimum and maximum values. Minimum and maximum arguments can be embedded ParameterObjects. BasketGen provides basic functionality from the Selector: the user provides a selection method and a list of values from which selections are made.

Example 5-6. Generator ParameterObject in Python

```
>>> from athenaCL.libATH.libPmtr import parameter
>>> x = parameter.factory(['ru', 0, 1]) # ru is expanded to RandomUniform
>>> x.repr() # string representations start with a lower-case character
'randomUniform, (constant, 0), (constant, 1)'
>>> [x(t) for t in range(12)] # call the object 12 times
[0.51467950304488186, 0.33223242458055902, 0.20062809650001023,
0.93186898020217312, 0.96310544779767293, 0.17003733606347682,
0.8688317670322192, 0.45870860367568689, 0.13905691211600524,
0.088496054418016667, 0.41475385775295059, 0.84069988035300813]
>>> # bg is expanded to BasketGen; rp is expanded to randomPermutate
>>> x = parameter.factory(['bg', 'rp', ['a','b','c']])
>>> x.repr()
'basketGen, randomPermutate, (a,b,c)'
>>> [x(t) for t in range(12)] # call the object 12 times
['a', 'b', 'a', 'c', 'b', 'a', 'b', 'c', 'c', 'a', 'b', 'b']
```

5.2.3. The Rhythm Generator ParameterObject

5.2.3.1. Model and Representation

Rhythm Generators are ParameterObjects specialized to produce complete Event timing information. This specialization is necessary for two reasons. First, Textures provide tempo as a configurable parameter slot controllable by a Generator. Rhythm Generators must receive a BPM value in order to calculate duration and sustain values from Pulse objects. Second, Rhythm Generators, with the __call__() method, return three values rather than one: a duration time, a sustain time, and an accent value. The meaning of these values, and the nature of Pulse and Rhythm representations, have been explained in Chapter 4.

The complete list of athenaCL Rhythm Generator ParameterObjects, as well as their documentation, can be found in Section B.2.

5.2.3.2. Object Design

There are many Rhythm Generator ParameterObject sub-classes, each specialized by one or more levels of inheritance. All Rhythm Generator sub-classes are polymorphic and may be used interchangeably. Any number of Rhythm Generator instances may be created and configured.

The design of the Rhythm Generator is similar to that of the Generator ParameterObject. All Rhythm Generators inherit from the RhythmParameter class. When called, the currentValue attribute is set to the list of calculated duration, sustain, and accent values. Unique to Rhythm Generators, a string representation of the currently active Pulse object, if available, is set to the currentPulse attribute. If a Pulse object representation is not in use, the currentPulse attribute is set to None.

Rhythm Generators that produce or process lists of Pulses, such as Loop or GaRhythm, embed a Selector object to perform Pulse selection. In some cases Rhythm Generators may alter user-provided Pulses or generate new Pulse sequences. In other cases Rhythm Generators may alter the sustain scalar (sus) or accent (acc) attribute of Pulse objects.

Rhythm Generator ParameterObjects may use any rhythm specification, and may provide timing values independent of a Texture's tempo. As mentioned in Chapter 4, the ConvertSecond object provides an example: this Rhythm Generator operates without Pulse objects and is independent of a Texture's tempo. Unlike other Rhythm Generators, this ParameterObject interprets the numerical output of an embedded Generator ParameterObject as duration and sustain values, effectively simulating Pulse object processing by returning a three-value triple. In this case, duration and sustain are always equal and accent never codes a rest.

5.2.3.3. Diagrams and Examples

The inheritance diagram below provides an example of Rhythm Generator ParameterObject inheritance. All Rhythm Generators inherit from the RhythmParameter parent class.

Example 5-7. Rhythm Generator Inheritance: Loop

```
Parameter
|
RhythmParameter
|
Loop
```

The following diagram summarizes important attributes and methods of the Rhythm Generator.

Example 5-8. Rhythm Generator Class Diagram

```
Class Rhythm Generator
Attributes:
    args
    argTypes
    argNames
    argDefaults
    doc
    parent
    priority
    outputFmt
    currentValue
    currentPulse
Methods:
    checkArgs()
    reprDoc()
    repr(), __str__()
    __call__()
    reset()
    postEvent()
```

The following Python session demonstrates the functionality of the Rhythm Generator.

Example 5-9. Rhythm Generator in Python

```
>>> from athenaCL.libATH.libPmtr import parameter
>>> # 'l' is expanded to Loop; 'oc' is expanded to orderedCyclic
>>> x = parameter.factory(['l', ((5,2,1),(7,1,0),(3,5,1)), 'oc'],
'rthmPmtrObjs')
>>> x.repr() # string representation expands acronyms
'loop, ((5,2,+),(7,1,o),(3,5,+)), orderedCyclic'
>>> # calling the object returns duration, sustain value, and accent
>>> x(0, {'bpm':60}) # a bpm value must be provided in a refDict
(0.14285714285714285, 0.14999999999999999, 0)
```

```
>>> x(0, {'bpm':60}) # multiple calls calculate each Pulse in order
(1.6666666666666665, 1.75, 1)
>>> x(0, {'bpm':60})
(0.40000000000000002, 0.42000000000000004, 1)
>>> x(0, {'bpm':60})
(0.14285714285714285, 0.14999999999999999, 0)
>>> x(0, {'bpm':60})
(1.6666666666666665, 1.75, 1)
```

5.2.4. The Filter ParameterObject

5.2.4.1. Model and Representation

The Filter is a one-dimensional transformer. Filter ParameterObjects process a complete
EventSequence value array (a column of event data), and return an array of equal size. The
EventSequence and its facilities for providing such arrays have been explained in Chapter 4.
Rather than processing and generating one value at a time, Filters process and generate a
one-dimensional array. For example, all amplitude values of an EventSequence may be
processed at once, permitting operations such as rotation, averaging, or reversal. Filters,
depending on design, may embed Generator, Rhythm Generator, or additional Filter
ParameterObjects.

The complete list of athenaCL Filter ParameterObjects can be found in Section B.3.

5.2.4.2. Object Design

There are many Filter ParameterObject sub-classes, each specialized by one or more levels of
inheritance. All Filter sub-classes are polymorphic and may be used interchangeably. Any
number of Filter instances may be created and configured.

The primary difference in design between Filter and Generator ParameterObjects is the
type of arguments provided to the __call__() method. Filter ParameterObjects require a

value array, a time array, and reference dictionary array. All arrays are the same length, and provide, respectively, the values to be processed, the times at which time-dependent embedded ParameterObjects should be evaluated, and necessary reference values. As with Generator ParameterObjects, time and reference values are not required by all Filters.

5.2.4.3. Diagrams and Examples

The inheritance diagram below provides an example of Filter ParameterObject inheritance. All Filter ParameterObjects inherit from the FilterParameter parent class.

Example 5-10. Filter Inheritance: PipeLine

```
Parameter
|
FilterParameter
|
PipeLine
```

The following diagram summarizes important attributes and methods of the Filter ParameterObject.

Example 5-11. Filter ParameterObjects Class Diagram

```
Class Filter ParameterObjects
Attributes:
    args
    argTypes
    argNames
    argDefaults
    doc
    parent
    outputFmt
    inputFmt
```

```
Methods:
    checkArgs()
    reprDoc()
    repr(), __str__()
    __call__()
    reset()
```

The following Python session demonstrates basic functionality of a Filter ParameterObject.

Example 5-12. Filter ParameterObjects in Python

```
>>> from athenaCL.libATH.libPmtr import parameter
>>> # or expands to orderRotate
>>> x = parameter.factory(['or', 3], 'filterPmtrObjs') # creating an object
>>> x.repr() # returning a string representation
'orderRotate, 3'
>>> x([0,1,2,3,4,5,6], None, None) # processing an array of values
[3, 4, 5, 6, 0, 1, 2]
```

5.2.5. The Static ParameterObject

5.2.5.1. Model and Representation

Static ParameterObjects are designed to maintain user-configured static data for use in internal Texture and Clone processing. There are two types of Static ParameterObjects: TextureStatic and CloneStatic, each designed to work only with Textures and Clones respectively. Where Generator and Rhythm Generator ParameterObjects are often used to suggest Event values, Static ParameterObjects return values to configure internal Texture and Clone processing. A Texture may additionally configure internal processing by defining dynamic parameter slots. These slots may use Generator, Rhythm Generator, or Filter ParameterObjects to provide values for internal Texture processing.

The complete list of athenaCL Static ParameterObjects can be found in Section B.4 and Section B.5.

5.2.5.2. Object Design

There are many Static ParameterObject sub-classes, each specialized by one or more levels of inheritance. All Static ParameterObject sub-classes are polymorphic and may be used interchangeably. Unlike Generator and Filter ParameterObjects, Static ParameterObjects are not used in the object composition of Textures or Clones, but instead have a fixed assignment based on Texture or Clone sub-class specification. Any number of Static ParameterObject instances may be created and configured.

Static ParameterObjects differ from Generators in that, instead of returning a generated value, the `__call__()` method is used to obtain data from the user-provided argument list. This provides access within internal Texture or Clone processing to user-provided values, while at the same time using the same interface and error checking mechanisms shared by all ParameterObjects. Unique to Static ParameterObjects, all arguments are named and stored in the `argNames` attribute. After initialization, values read from the argument list are stored as a dictionary of name and value pairs.

5.2.5.3. Diagrams and Examples

The inheritance diagram below provides an example of TextureStatic inheritance. The StaticParameterTexture class, in some cases, is further specialized to provide common functionality to a number of related Static ParameterObjects.

Example 5-13. TextureStatic Inheritance: LoopWithinSet

```
Parameter
|
```

```
StaticParameterTexture

|

_SwitchOnOff

|

LoopWithinSet
```

The following inheritance diagram provides an example of CloneStatic inheritance. All CloneStatic ParameterObjects are subclasses of generic TextureStatic ParameterObjects.

Example 5-14. CloneStatic Inheritance: RetrogradeMethodToggle

```
Parameter

|

StaticParameterTexture

|

StaticParameterClone

|

RetrogradeMethodToggle
```

The following diagram summarizes important attributes and methods of the Static ParameterObject.

Example 5-15. Static ParameterObjects Class Diagram

```
Class Static ParameterObjects
Attributes:
    args
    argTypes
    argNames
    argDefaults
    doc
    parent
    outputFmt
    currentValue
```

```
Methods:
    checkArgs()
    getArgs()
    reprDoc()
    repr(), __str__()
    __call__()
    reset()
```

The following Python session demonstrates the functionality of the Static
ParameterObjects.

Example 5-16. Static ParameterObjects in Python

```
>>> from athenaCL.libATH.libPmtr import parameter
>>> # lws expands to LoopWithinSet
>>> x = parameter.factory(['lws', 'on'], 'textPmtrObjs')
>>> x.repr() # returning a string representation
'loopWithinSet, on'
>>> x('onOff') # returning the value of the "onOff" argument
'on'
```

5.2.6. Compositional Implications

The ParameterObjects of athenaCL offer a core library of algorithmic processing utilities.
Where many such libraries already exist, the ParameterObject promotes modeling reusable
tools from the perspective of the user rather than a programing API. The design of a
ParameterObject interface, namely its argument list and format, becomes a task very similar
to that of designing a signal processing instrument, such as a Csound instrument or a
SuperCollider SynthDef. The designer must choose which parameters to expose to the user
and in what format. Various levels of abstraction can be provided by specialized
ParameterObjects for various needs; different ParameterObjects may share common
features but provide unique interfaces. Within the context of the system, however,

ParameterObjects all offer a uniform level of abstraction. For composers, this offers a wide range of tools that are modular, interchangeable, and deployable in a wide range of contexts. Emphasizing the importance of an algorithmic procedure's interface, Roads states that what is important to musicians is "… the quality of interaction they have with the algorithm … each algorithm — even those that are formally equivalent — represents musical processes in a different way, giving the composer unique 'handles' to manipulate" (1996, p. 908).

Pope states that the term "algorithmic composition" implies that "… the composer builds a program (the algorithm) that then composes (all or only some features of) the music" (1995). This building of algorithms, however, need not happen at the code level. The combination and deployment of ParameterObjects allows flexible design of algorithmic processes without writing low-level code-based algorithms. Highly specialized ParameterObjects, such as those employing the Xenakis sieve, demonstrate the flexibility of the ParameterObject abstraction (Ariza 2005c).

Giuseppe Englert claims that "a compositional algorithm must … satisfy the following postulate: that the dynamic equilibrium between the correlation and contrast of events be guaranteed over large spans of time" (1981, p. 133). Though Englert proposes a one-dimensional Intersecting Sine Function Polynomial (ISFP) generator as an example, many useful algorithms would be excluded from his definition. Such demands, at the level of a single compositional algorithm, are too severe. Even if the musical effects of such an equilibrium are desired, they can be obtained by selective use and deployment of any algorithm. Such demands of correlation and contrast might be better placed on, and more easily implemented with, a multi-dimensional generator such as a Texture.

In many contexts, choice and application of mapping supersedes concerns for algorithmic design. As Burt observes, "mostly, when we talk about algorithmic processes, we are talking about mappings of one kind or another…" (1996, p. 169). When using athenaCL ParameterObjects, it is possible to control mapping within a single object (using the minimum and maximum arguments, or others as specified), or through the combination of multiple ParameterObjects (such as the Mask or OperatorMultiply ParameterObjects). Even so, Burt continues: "… mappings are only the beginning … how we perceive the mapping, in what contexts, how we observe, how we have learned to observe, are often the crucial factors in any judgments … as to how 'interesting' or 'dull' the results of the mappings are" (1996, p. 169). The TextureModule, explained below, plays one role in providing context to mappings; remaining contextual interpretations are beyond the scope of algorithmic implementation, and are left to the user.

The facility of postEvent processing allows the design of ParameterObjects that modify Event values. Although currently only used by Rhythm Generators, this facility provides for interesting parameter interactions. An example is provided by the Rhythm Generator BinaryAccent. This ParameterObject both supplies a different Pulse and increases an Event amplitude value whenever the first Pitch in the current Multiset has been selected by a Texture. The current Pitch and Multiset is provided to the ParameterObject through the refDict passed by the Texture. The ParameterObject, after determining if such a condition has been satisfied, executes a scaling function on the Event's amplitude with the postEvent() method.

Within athenaCL, Rhythm generation is treated as a special case of parameter generation. This provides composers with powerful and intuitive Event timing controls. Where CAAC systems have often treated rhythm simply as a numerical process applied to time, the Pulse object and specialized Rhythm Generators support more diverse conceptions of rhythm. The utility of specialized Generators for rhythm production is demonstrated by the PulseSieve and RhythmSieve objects. These Rhythm Generators employ the Xenakis sieve to generate and select Pulse sequences, or to transform and filter a provided Pulse sequence (Ariza 2005c). Such operations would be difficult to model without a generator specialized for rhythm production.

5.2.7. Alternative and Related Models

The Selector object closely relates to the selection methods deployed by Koenig in PR1 and PR2. PR1's series and alea methods are the same as the Selector's randomPermutate and randomChoice selection methods. PR2's sequence method is the same as the Selector's orderedCyclic selection method. The remaining selection methods of PR2 require more than zero parameters, and are thus not compatible with the Selector.

ParameterObject mapping functionality, provided by dynamic minimum and maximum arguments, is closely related to Koenig's tendency mask selection method first used in PR2 (1970a). A related model of selection within dynamic boundaries can be seen in the early work of Tenney (Mathews 1963; Tenney 1969). Koenig's tendency mask, however, performs selection based only on mapping values from a random uniform distribution within break-point line segment boundaries. Alternative distributions, and alternative boundary generators, are not supported. The "Low" and "High" arguments used to configure value generators in Berg's AC Toolbox (where low and high are either constants or embedded generators) generalize Koenig's tendency mask into a flexible mapping technique for a wide variety of applications. ParameterObject minimum and maximum values are modeled after this design.

The concept of reusable, modular parameter generators is common to many CAAC systems. The "process" model of Formes can be seen in part as a one-dimensional ParameterObject. Rodet and Cointe state that "the role of each process is to ensure the calculation of a particular musical characteristic, such as an aspect of phrasing, vibrato, loudness control, or timbre" (1984, p. 407). These processes can then be organized and embedded in a variety of arrangements: "... processes can be organized in a structure that reflects some aspects of the desired musical structure, by combination in sequence, in parallel, and hierarchically" (1984, p. 408). Chadabe describes how in Formes many independent processes "... unfolding at different rates and applying to different aspects of the sounds and music, ... unfold together" (1997, p. 126). A related model is found in the "item streams" of Taube's Common Music, such as Sequence, Cycle, Heap, Random, Palindrome, Accumulation, Graph, Function, and Item (1991, p. 26). Taube relates item streams to Pope's EventGenerators (EGens), deployed in the HyperScore system (Taube 1991, p. 30). Pope's EventGenerators, however, are multi-dimensional generators that return a complete EventList, and are thus more like Textures than PararmeterObjects (1989, p. 251).

Berg's AC Toolbox offers a large library of Generator objects, covering numerous diverse and historical approaches to one-dimensional parameter generation. Generators frequently come in two varieties: one to produce values within ranges, another to make selections from stockpiles. Further, the AC Toolbox offers a number of other object types, including Shapes, Masks, and Stockpiles, each of which can be used, once properly converted or "read," within particular Generators. Generators, in turn, can be used to create Shapes, Masks, and Stockpiles. Selection methods are not typically embedded in Generators. This design is more modular and flexible than the embedded selection methods and subsystems of athenaCL ParameterObjects. The tradeoff, however, is less uniform levels of abstraction at the system level: some object types in the AC Toolbox, in order to be embedded, need to be converted to the appropriate format with an external utility function. In athenaCL, there are only a handful of different ParameterObject types, and all completely encapsulate output functionality: external utility functions are not required.

Modular parameter transformers are also common to many CAAC systems. Oppenheim's Dmix environment permits the application of modifiers to alter or replace event parameters; modifier types include Functions, Tables, Filters, Quantizers, and ModifierInterpolators (1989, p. 228). In a similar manner, Honing's POCO system features a collection of transformation tools that "generate new or modified musical information" and include tools for matching, filtering, scaling, and merging musical information (1990, p. 366). The AC Toolbox offers a large collection of modular modifiers called Transformers. These tools are designed for use with the Transform method, to be described below.

In general, parameter interaction and calculation order are handled in athenaCL by the Texture. Koenig, in PR2, provides an early example of allowing users to directly alter parameter calculation order. Although athenaCL does not offer user-level configuration of ParameterObject calculation order (except when configurable with TextureStatic ParameterObjects), the postEvent() method permits ParameterObjects to revise values produced by other ParameterObjects. The calculation order of ParameterObjects can take any form in athenaCL, and is exclusively dependent on TextureModule design.

5.3. The Multi-Dimensional Generator and Transformer

The ParameterObject is the lowest level of algorithmic design in athenaCL, offering a one-dimensional generative and transformative tool. The Texture and the Clone, at a higher level of algorithmic design, offer multi-dimensional Event generation and transformation. Like the ParameterObject, the Texture and the Clone are designed to be reusable, modular, and flexible. Unlike the ParameterObject, the Texture is opaque: since its output is the result of internal processing of ParameterObject values and other configurable and non-configurable settings, the Events it produces are not determined solely by its inputs. The Clone offers both single EventSequence array transformations (via Filter ParameterObjects) and complete EventSequence transformations (via settings provided by CloneStatic ParameterObjects).

5.3.1. The Temperament

5.3.1.1. Model and Representation

Each Texture stores a single Temperament object. The Temperament object is designed to provide reusable algorithmic pitch transformations. Temperament processing is performed on pitch values after local field and octave transpositions are applied to a Path-derived Pitch. Temperament objects can be divided into two groups, based on the type of pitch transformation employed. The first group of Temperaments is designed to emulate historic Western or alternative tuning systems, and functions by mapping pitch classes to microtonally-tuned pitches. This process is deterministic: for a given pitch class, the same tempered pitch value is always returned. The second group of Temperaments is designed to apply algorithmic, non-deterministic processes to pitches. For example, a random amount of variation can be applied to a pitch value. These processes are designed to provide various degrees of context-free pitch inflection.

Although some of the functionality of the Temperament can be provided by careful use of a Path or a Texture's local field control, the Temperament object adds a useful and intuitive construct. By default, all Textures are assigned a twelve-tone equal Temperament (the TwelveEqual object). Temperaments are instantiated by use of a factory object.

A complete list of current Temperaments is found in Section C.1.

5.3.1.2. Object Design

There are many Temperament sub-classes, each specialized by one or more levels of inheritance. All Temperament sub-classes are polymorphic and may be used interchangeably. Within a Texture, there is typically a single Temperament sub-class.

The Temperament provides attributes to store the name of the temperament type (name) and a documentation string (doc). The parent class defines a __call__() method that takes a psReal as a required argument. The psReal is split into a list of octave, pitch class, and microtone, and these values are temporarily assigned to local attributes. Each Temperament subclass defines a _translatePitch() method that accesses the pitch information given to the __call__() method, performs a translation or transformation, and then re-assigns new pitch values. The __call__() method calls this _translatePitch() method, joins the split pitch elements back into a psReal, and then returns the tempered pitch value.

5.3.1.3. Diagrams and Examples

The inheritance diagram below provides an example of Temperament inheritance.

Example 5-17. Temperament Inheritance: Pythagorean

```
Temperament
 |
Pythagorean
```

The following diagram summarizes important attributes and methods of the Temperament object.

Example 5-18. Temperament Class Diagram

```
Class Temperament
Attributes:
```

```
    name
    doc
Methods:
  __call__()
  _translatePitch()
```

The following Python session demonstrates basic functionality of the Temperament. Temperaments designed to model Pythagorean tuning and random noise are created and used to translate psReal pitch values.

Example 5-19. Temperament in Python

```
>>> from athenaCL.libATH import temperament
>>> # creating a historical Temperament
>>> a = temperament.factory('pythagorean')
>>> a.name # the name of the Temperament type
'Pythagorean'
>>> a(9) # an equal-tempered psReal of 9 (A4), is returned six cents sharp
9.0600000000000005
>>> a(3)
2.9399999999999999
>>> a(3.2) # a microtonally specified psReal is proportionally shifted
3.1400000000000001
>>> a(3+(12*2)) # psReal shifted two octaves (D#6)
26.940000000000001
>>> # creating an algorithmic Temperament
>>> b = temperament.factory('noisemedium')
>>> b.name
'NoiseMedium'
>>> b.doc # examining the documentation string
'Provide uniform random +/- 10 cent noise on each pitch'
>>> b(9)
9.0856754499789716
>>> b(9)
```

```
8.9815941517806177
>>> b(3)
2.9729603698919114
>>> b(3)
2.9469239959249669
```

5.3.2. The Texture

5.3.2.1. Model and Representation

The Texture, as a model of a multi-dimensional generative part, is the second level of
algorithmic design in athenaCL. The creation, configuration, and arrangement of Texture
instances are the primary compositional tasks of athenaCL users. Every Texture class, or
TextureModule, inherits a common interface from the Texture parent class. Users create and
modify instances of TextureModules. TextureModules can be designed, at the code level, to
perform a wide variety of compositional tasks. A TextureModule might specialize in
generating linear monophonic Events, vertical chordal collections, or non-linear polyphonic
Events. Because the EventSequence does not enforce event adjacency (as described in
Chapter 4), Textures are free to create Events in any order and with any degree of layered
density. All Textures provide a variable user-level interface in the form of configurable
Generator and Static ParameterObjects.

The name "Texture" originated from a conception of broad structural archetypes of
musical shapes, and is used in this context to mean any sort of musical gesture, phrase, form,
or structure. This use of the term contrasts with the usage proposed by Smalley, for whom a
texture, "… is concerned with internal behavior patterning, energy directed inwards or
reinjected, self-propagating …" and further, "instead of being provoked to act" a texture
"… merely continues behaving" (1986, p. 82). Smalley contrasts texture with gesture, the
two together offering the "fundamental structuring strategies…" (1986, p. 82). Texture, as

defined here, is a considerably broader concept, and includes both of Smalley's notions of texture and gesture. Other writers support this usage. Wallace Berry, placing texture as a fundamental property of musical structures, delineates numerous classes of textural types and progressions (1987). David Huron suggests that the term texture, like timbre or sonority, offers an "apparent universality" not found in other music descriptors (1989, p. 131). Referring to texture as "the number and diversity of activities in a sound field," Huron states that as "number and diversity exist in any and all sound fields (including silence), ... texture is a property of all sounded activity" (1989, p. 133).

A complete listing of available TextureModules is found in Section C.2.

5.3.2.2. Object Design

There are many Texture sub-classes, each specialized by both one or more levels of inheritance and object composition. Object composition occurs both during and after instantiation with the assignment of variable ParameterObjects, a Path, and a Temperament. The number and type of TextureStatic ParameterObjects and TextureDynamic slots are dependent on sub-class specialization. All Texture sub-classes are polymorphic and may be used interchangeably. Any number of Texture instances may be created and configured.

All Textures have both configurable attributes and a collection of embedded ParameterObjects. The configurable attributes are simple settings used in EventSequence generation and by OutputEngines. These include settings for method of Path interpretation (pitchMode and polyMode), MIDI channel and program numbers, mute status, user-supplied name, rest calculation (silenceMode), and Orchestra postMap settings (postMapMode).

Textures contain a variable number of standard slots for Generator ParameterObjects. Standard Generator slots include tempo (BPM), pitch transposition in pitch space (local field), pitch transposition in octaves (local octave), amplitude, and panning. Standard slots also exist for instrument, time range, and Path, although these are not filed with normal Generator ParameterObjects. The instrument and time range slots use specialized, single-use Generator ParameterObjects; the Path slot contains a reference to an external Path object.

Standard slots are used to suggest corresponding values in the resultant EventSequence. The amplitude slot, for example, takes a Generator ParameterObject that suggests EventSequence amplitude values. The values produced from standard slots, however, are only recommendations. A Texture is opaque: it takes these values only as input. The TextureModule, in its design, is responsible for interpreting these values and processing them into Events or SubEvents. The method the TextureModule uses to do this is completely TextureModule-dependent.

The standard slots represent common Event parameters. Auxiliary slots are used to provide Generators for additional parameters required by the sound source. The number of auxiliary parameters is TextureModule independent, and is assigned at Texture instantiation based on the selected Instrument and Orchestra. As the TextureModule is designed to be independent of any particular Instrument, in most cases the TextureModule will provide each Event with the exact values produced by the appropriate auxiliary Generators. In all cases, however, the TextureModule interprets the raw values produced by standard and auxiliary slots before writing them to Events.

All standard slots assume, by default, particular value scales. BPM expects floating point BPM values. Panning and amplitude values, while postMap mode is active, are normalized within the unit interval. Local field and local octave values are normalized at the half-step and the octave per unit respectively. Auxiliary slots, because they are instrument specific (and the Texture is Instrument independent), have no assumed value scale. Instead, the user must provide values within the appropriate scale for the desired Instrument. Information concerning Instrument parameters, as explained in Chapter 4, is supplied by the Orchestra object in the form of default auxiliary values and parameter documentation strings. The number of auxiliary slots required by the Instrument is set at Texture creation and stored in the Texture's auxNo attribute.

In addition to standard and auxiliary slots, a TextureModule may define any number of additional slots in order to produce values necessary for internal Texture processing. These additional slots come in two varieties: static and dynamic. Texture static slots provide configurable, static options specific to the particular TextureModule. These slots accept only TextureStatic ParameterObjects. Texture dynamic slots provide variable data inputs for TextureModule processing that, depending on design, may use Generator, Rhythm Generator, or Filter ParameterObjects. The number of static and dynamic slots, declared in the TextureModule, is stored as textPmtrNo and dynPmtrNo respectively.

The TextureModule thus provides a variable number of inputs, or ParameterObject slots. The user configures these slots with any ParameterObject of the appropriate type, and can configure these ParameterObjects in whatever way necessary, embedding additional ParameterObjects within ParameterObjects to any desired depth. The values produced for all slots are taken by the TextureModule, processed, and used to create Events or SubEvents. Again, the Texture is opaque: exactly what the TextureModule does with these inputs is completely left to the specification of the TextureModule.

All ParameterObjects are stored within the Texture in two forms. The first form is the raw argument list provided by the user. The second form is the instantiated object. Two dictionaries, the pmtrQDict and the pmtrObjDict store arguments and objects respectively for all slots.

All Textures store a reference to a Path object. As explained in Chapter 4, Paths offer multiple interpretations of ordered pitch groups. By configuring a Texture's `pitchMode` attribute, the user can specify which interpretation of the Path will be used. Thus the Path can be interpreted in either pitch space (ps), pitch class space (pcs), or as a set class (sc). The TextureModule is responsible for using this interpretation when taking pitches from the Path. The TextureModule, further, is responsible for partitioning its time range into segments that correspond to the proportional durations of each Multiset in a Path. Each duration segment uses only the pitches provided by the corresponding Multiset of the Path. The order that pitches are taken from Multisets is completely TextureModule dependent.

After pitches are taken from the Path, they are processed in at least three additional ways: by the local field, by the local octave, and with the Temperament. The standard slot "local field" provides a Generator that can be used for producing Event transposition values. These transposition values are floating point, positive or negative values, where one-half step is equal to 1.0. The local field parameter can thus be used to provide any range of pitch modification, from the level of microtonal variation to large-interval transpositions. Similarly, the standard slot "local octave" provides a Generator that can be used to produce octave transpositions, where values, to the nearest positive or negative integer, designate octave transpositions of the Path-derived pitches. For greater flexibility, most TextureModules provide static slots to allow the user to select when new values are drawn from field and octave Generators. In such cases, the TextureStatic ParameterObject LevelFieldMonophonic, for example, permits the user to select if new field values are drawn for each Multiset or for each Event.

The third step of pitch processing is done by a Temperament object. The Temperament, explained above, provides a reusable, specialized transformer designed for processing pitch values. Temperament objects are configured as a Texture attribute, the user providing only the desired Temperament name.

All TextureModules are subclasses of the Texture parent class. The Texture parent class provides the core functionality of the Texture, including loading data (the `load()` and `loadDefault()` methods), storing data, reading values from ParameterObjects ("get" prefixed methods, such as `getPan()`), editing ParameterObjects (`editPmtrObj()` and `updatePmtrObj()`), providing string representations (`repr()`), and creating EventSequences (`makeEvent()`, `storeEvent()`, `storePolyEvent()`). The code of any particular TextureModule subclass is thus relatively small, defining only `name` and `author` attributes, static and dynamic slots, documentation, and the essential EventSequence generating method `_scoreMain()`. When a Texture is called to create an EventSequence, the inherited method `score()` is called. This method, in turn, calls the parent class `_scorePre()` method, the sub-class `_scoreMain()` method, and the parent class `_scorePost()` method. The `_scorePre()` and `_scorePost()` methods provide utility operations common to all TextureModules. The `_scoreMain()` method is where musical structures are created: each TextureModule, with its own specialized `_scoreMain()` method, can model diverse methods of EventSequence production.

The `_scoreMain()` method may use any processing necessary, or any external modules, to produce an EventSequence. EventSequence production usually involves reading pitches from the Path with the `getPitchGroup()` method (with pitches taken from the Path in the desired pitchMode), obtaining values from all standard and auxiliary ParameterObjects (with the get-prefixed methods), and creating an Event with the `makeEvent()` method. These Events are then passed to the `storeEvent()` or `storePolyEvent()` methods. These methods pass a complete Event to each ParameterObject's `postEvent()` method, in the order determined by the ParameterObject's `priority` attribute. The resulting Event is then added to the Texture's EventSequence object (`esObj`). The `storePolyEvent()` method requires a list of SubEvents and a parent Event. Missing SubEvent values are inherited from the parent Event, and the resulting Events are passed to the `storeEvent()` method. A Texture's `getScore()` method can be called to return a copy of the complete EventSequence.

5.3.2.3. Diagrams and Examples

The diagram below demonstrates TextureModule inheritance. All TextureModules inherit from the Texture base-class.

Example 5-20. Texture Inheritance: LineGroove

```
Texture
|
LineGroove
```

The following diagram summarizes important attributes and methods of the Texture.

Example 5-21. Texture Class Diagram

```
Class Texture
Attributes:
    name
    doc
    mute
    esObj
    refDict
    pmtrQDict
    pmtrObjDict
    auxNo
    textPmtrNo
    dynPmtrNo
Methods:
    stateUpdates()
```

```
stateClear()

getRefDict()

getRefClone()

load()

loadDefault()

copy()

repr()

updatePmtrObj()

editPmtrObj()

getPitchGroup()

getMultiset()

getTimeRange()

getInst()

getOrc()

getField()

getOct()

getPan()

getAmp()

getRhythm()

getAux()

getTextStatic()

getTextDynamic()

reprDoc()

makeEvent()

storeEvent()

storePolyEvent()

_scorePre()

_scoreMain()

_scorePost()

score()

getScore()

clearScore()
```

The following diagram illustrates the primary object components of the Texture.

Example 5-22. Component Diagram of a Texture

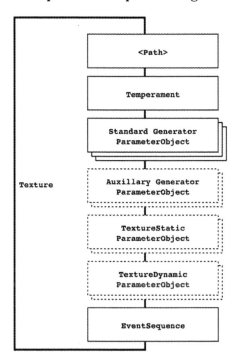

The following diagram illustrates the generation of one parameter value of one Event. The sequence of steps is as follows: (1) a Value is produced by a Generator ParameterObject, (2) the Value is processed by specialized, TextureModule-dependent Event processing (3) the Value, with all other parameter values, is formed into an Event, (4) the Event is processed by each ParameterObject's postEvent() method, (5) the Event is added to the EventSequence.

Example 5-23. Activity Diagram of Texture Event Value Production

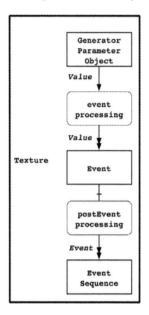

The following diagram illustrates the generation of one Pitch value of one Event. The sequence of steps is as follows: (1) a Texture contains a reference to a Path, (2) the Texture selects a Pitch from the Path, (3) the Pitch is modified by the value produced by the local field Generator ParameterObject, (4) the Pitch is modified by the value produced by the local octave Generator ParameterObject, (5) the Pitch is modified by the Temperament object, (6) the Pitch, with all other parameter values, is formed into an Event, (7) the Event is processed by each ParameterObject's postEvent() method, (8) the Event is added to the EventSequence.

Example 5-24. Activity Diagram of Texture Event Pitch Production

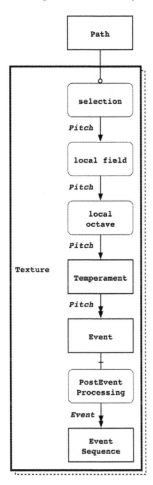

The following Python session demonstrates elementary functionality of the Texture. The TextureModule LineGroove, a simple monophonic linear Event generator, is loaded with default values, the score() method is called, and the resulting EventSequence object is examined.

Example 5-25. The Texture in Python

```
>>> from athenaCL.libATH import pitchPath
```

```
>>> from athenaCL.libATH.libTM import texture
>>> x = pitchPath.PolyPath() # creating an empty Path
>>> x.loadPsList([(3,4),(-4,5,12),(6,4,4,4)]) # loading three pitch groups
>>> # to create an object with the Texture factory, a TextureModule
>>> # and a Texture name must be provided
>>> a = texture.factory('LineGroove', 'a') # creating a Texture
>>> a.loadDefault(3, x) # loading an Instrument number and a Path reference
>>> a.repr() # returning a string representation
'LineGroove: a'
>>> a.pmtrQDict # the ParameterObject argument dictionary
{'panQ': ('constant', 0.5), 'rhythmQ': ('binaryAccent', ((4, 5), (4, 5))),
'fieldQ': ('constant', 0), 'octQ': ('constant', 0), 'inst': ('staticInst', 3,
'csoundNative'), 'beatT': ('c', 120), 'textQ2': ('levelFieldMonophonic',
'set'), 'textQ3': ('levelOctaveMonophonic', 'event'), 'textQ0':
('parallelMotionList', [], 0.0), 'ampQ': ('constant', 0.90000000000000002),
'tRange': ('staticRange', (0, 20)), 'textQ1': ('nonRedundantSwitch', 'on')}
>>> a.score() # calling the score() method to create an EventSequence
1
>>> a.esObj._eventList[:2] # examining the first two Events
[{'acc': 1, 'ps': 3, 'amp': 0.97200000000000009, 'bpm': 120, 'pulse':
'(4,5,+)', 'comment': [3], 'sus': 1.0, 'aux': [], 'time': 0, 'inst': 3, 'dur':
0.625, 'pan': 0.5}, {'acc': 1, 'ps': 4, 'amp': 0.90000000000000002, 'bpm':
120, 'pulse': '(4,5,+)', 'comment': [4], 'sus': 0.875, 'aux': [], 'time':
0.625, 'inst': 3, 'dur': 0.625, 'pan': 0.5}]
```

5.3.3. The Clone

5.3.3.1. Model and Representation

The Clone is a model of the multi-dimensional transformative part, and provides the third

level of algorithmic design in athenaCL. The Clone processes a Texture-produced

EventSequence and transforms it into a new EventSequence. A single Texture may have any

number of Clones. Clones are in all cases linked to a single Texture, and can only be created or modified after Texture creation. Although this relationship is not one of object-oriented inheritance, it is useful to think of a Clone as having a "parent" Texture. Unlike the specialization of Textures through TextureModules, there is only one Clone type.

The name "Clone" is perhaps a misnomer. In early versions of athenaCL, working with identical copies of Texture-generated material was not possible. As Textures often employ non-deterministic procedures, a copy of a Texture, even with identical parameter settings, would likely produce a unique EventSequence. The Clone developed as a way of copying and temporally shifting the Events produced by a Texture. This allowed for the production of exact copies, or "clones" of a Texture's EventSequence. This temporal shift has been subsequently generalized as one of many transformative processes.

5.3.3.2. Object Design

There is one Clone class. Clones are specialized by object composition. Object composition occurs both during and after instantiation with the assignment of variable Filter ParameterObjects. The number and type of CloneStatic ParameterObjects is fixed and dependent on the class definition. Any number of Clone instances may be created and configured.

Clones, like Textures, define a number of slots that can be configured by the user with ParameterObjects. Standard slots directly correspond to values in the EventSequence of the Texture, and are filled only with Filter ParameterObjects. Depending on the parent Texture's Instrument, a Clone may also have auxiliary slots. Additional static options are configured with CloneStatic ParameterObjects. Clones, like Textures, have attributes in addition to slots. The mute attribute, however, is the only attribute not inherited from the parent Texture; Clones may be muted independently of their parent Texture. As such, a Texture may be muted and used as a generator of an unheard EventSequence that is subsequently processed by a Clone. All other attributes, such as auxNo, MIDI channel and program, silenceMode, and postMapMode are inherited from the parent Texture.

Clones have seven standard slots: time, sustain, accent, local field, local octave, amplitude, and panning. Clones do not process rhythm values with the same representation used by Textures, but rather as Events with independent duration, sustain, and accent values. The time slot modifies Event start times, and can be used to shift or scale a sequence either by a constant or a dynamic value. A wide range of temporal transformations are thus possible. The sustain slot modifies Event sustain values. The accent slot allows the transformation of sounding events to measured silences. Since each Event stores a BPM value (as discussed in Chapter 4), Clone-bound Filter ParameterObjects can transform temporal values with embedded Rhythm ParameterObjects. In such cases, for each Event, the Event's BPM value is supplied to the Rhythm Generator embedded within the Filter, a value is produced, and the Filter performs the necessary Event value transformation.

The standard slots local field and local octave, as with their Texture-based counterparts, transform Event pitch space values. The amplitude and panning slots likewise transform corresponding Event values. Auxiliary parameter slots allow a Clone to transform Instrument-specific parameter values generated by a Texture. A Clone, depending on the Instrument of its parent Texture, can thus alter these Instrument-specific parameter values with Filter ParameterObjects. Finally, a Clone has slots for CloneStatic ParameterObjects. Rather than the processing of EventSequence arrays with Filter ParameterObjects, these slots are used to configure high-level Clone EventSequence processing. Such processes include multi-parameter holistic modifications to the EventSequence such as various forms of retrograde transformations.

Clone object design is parallel to Texture object design. Clones store their user-assigned name, and the name of their parent Texture. User-supplied ParameterObject argument lists are stored in the pmtrQDict. These argument lists are used to instantiate Filter or CloneStatic ParameterObjects, and these objects are stored in the pmtrObjDict.

As with Textures, a loadDefault() method is provided to load an instantiated Clone with basic options. The load() method is used to load a complete Clone specification, provided from an athenaCL XML file. The copy() and repr() methods provide duplicate objects and string representations respectively. The updatePmtrObj() method is used to edit and reinitialize ParameterObjects stored in the pmtrObjDict.

Numerous get-prefixed methods, such as getTime(), getSus(), getAcc(), getAmp(), getPan(), getField(), getOct(), and getAux() are used to process value arrays obtained from an EventSequence. These methods share a common form. Each accepts a value array, an evaluation time array, and a reference dictionary array. The arguments are passed to the appropriate Filter ParameterObject, the Filter returns a new value array, and this modified array is then reinserted into the EventSequence.

The Clone score() method takes as arguments an EventSequence and a reference dictionary from its parent Texture. This method then calls the _scorePre(), _scoreMain(), and _scorePost() methods. The _scoreMain() method is where EventSequence transformations take place. This method calculates the necessary time evaluation array (configurable between either Texture time points or post-Filter Clone time points), calls each get-prefixed method to obtain and replace value arrays, and performs multi-parameter EventSequence transformations.

The CloneManager, stored in the AthenaObject, is a utility object that provides an interface to the collection of all Clones. The CloneManager is needed, in part, to manage the multiple links between a single Texture and any number of associated Clones. This object facilitates the creation, renaming, editing, and deletion of Clones.

5.3.3.3. Diagrams and Examples

The following diagram summarizes important attributes and methods of the Clone.

Example 5-26. Clone Class Diagram

```
Class Clone
Attributes:
    name
    nameParent
    mute
    refDict
    auxNo
    auxFmt
    pmtrObjDict
    pmtrQDict
Methods:
    load()
    loadDefault()
    copy()
    repr()
    updatePmtrObj()
    getTime()
    getSus()
    getAcc()
    getAmp()
    getPan()
    getField()
    getOct()
    getAux()
    getCloneStatic()
```

```
_scorePre()

_scoreMain()

_scorePost()

score()

getScore()

clearScore()
```

The following diagram illustrates the primary object components of the Clone.

Example 5-27. Component Diagram of a Clone

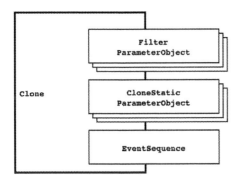

The following diagram illustrates the transformation of one value array of one EventSequence. The sequence of steps is as follows: (1) a Clone is given a copy of the parent Texture's EventSequence, (2) a value Array is extracted from the EventSequence, (3) the Array is processed by a Filter ParameterObject, (4) the modified Array is returned to the EventSequence, (5) the Clone performs multi-parameter EventSequence transformations.

Example 5-28. Activity Diagram of Clone EventSequence Transformation

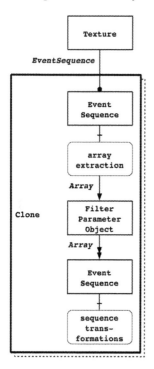

The following Python session demonstrates the functionality of the Clone.

Example 5-29. The Clone in Python

```
>>> from athenaCL.libATH import pitchPath
>>> from athenaCL.libATH.libTM import texture
>>> from athenaCL.libATH import clone
>>> x = pitchPath.PolyPath() # creating a Path
>>> x.loadPsList([(3,4),(-4,5,12),(6,4,4,4)]) # loading three pitch groups
>>> a = texture.factory('LineGroove', 'a') # creating a Texture
>>> a.loadDefault(3, x) # loading an Instrument number and a Path reference
>>> # to create a Clone, a Clone name and the parent Texture name
>>> # must be provided
>>> b = clone.Clone('b', 'a') # creating a Clone
>>> b.loadDefault(a.auxNo, a.getAuxOutputFmt()) # loading the Clone
```

```
>>> # the Clone must be provided with an EventSequence from a Texture
>>> b.score(a.getScore(), a.getRefClone()) # transforming an EventSequence
1
>>> b.esObj._eventList[:2] # examining the first two Events
[{'acc': 1, 'ps': 4, 'amp': 0.90000000000000002, 'bpm': 120, 'comment': [4],
'inst': 3, 'pulse': '(4,5,+)', 'time': 0.5, 'sus': 0.875, 'aux': [], 'dur':
0.625, 'pan': 0.5}, {'acc': 1, 'ps': 3, 'amp': 0.97200000000000009, 'bpm':
120, 'comment': [3], 'inst': 3, 'pulse': '(4,5,+)', 'time': 1.125, 'sus': 1.0,
'aux': [], 'dur': 0.625, 'pan': 0.5}]
```

5.3.4. Compositional Implications

The Texture supports diverse paradigms of CAAC, embedding complete generative systems of various complexities and designs. Where many systems offer a single method of combining parameter generators, the Texture offers reusable, specialized Event production methods with a common interface. In allowing different design paradigms to operate side by side, athenaCL offers composers diverse compositional options within a single environment. The model of the Texture is one of the most important design features of athenaCL.

The Texture offers the potential for Event production not possible by single-parameter generation alone. A Texture, as a multi-dimensional generator, can offer holistic, contextual modes of production. The TextureModule MonophonicOrnament offers an example (Ariza 2003). This TextureModule produces various types of discrete Event ornamentation upon a Path-derived melodic line. Because ornamentation often involves coordinating many Event parameter values within a single gesture, it is difficult, if not impossible, to imagine a configuration of individual parameter generators that would result in an ornamented melodic line.

Designing numerous specialized models of algorithmic procedures, in the same manner as ParameterObjects, elevates the multi-dimensional generative part into a modular and reusable system component. The Texture thus allows the generative part to be treated like a signal processing instrument, such as a Csound instrument or a SuperCollider SynthDef. As is the case with the ParameterObject, the design of a Texture requires interface design choices. The designer must choose which parameters to expose to the user, what to internalize, and in what context the Texture is to be used. Koenig, without considering that a single system could provide diverse answers to this problem, writes, "the fundamental difficulty in developing composing programs is indubitably in determining the dividing-line between the automatic process and the dynamic influence exerted by the composer by means of input data and dialogue … when there are few data and little dialogue, automata are expected to produce the composition; when there are a lot of data and dialogue, the responsibility remains the composer's, the computer being degraded to an intelligent typewriter" (1980a). The Texture, by offering a variable user-level interface and opaque internal processing, provides a reusable component that can create generative models within the entire range of dialog possibilities expressed by Koenig.

Concerning the future of CAAC systems, Berg has stated that "the necessary compositional abstractions are not hierarchical descriptions of entire compositions, but generators of musical material or gestures" (1996, p. 26). Berg continues: "without the development of some new generators of parametric material, the idea of composing with a computer has little future" (1996, p. 25). The Texture supports the creation of numerous individual, specialized generators of parametric material. These generators, further, are not limited to linear, single-parameter generation or to hierarchical descriptions, though such models, if desired, may be accommodated. As multi-dimensional generators with dynamic inputs, the diversity of generative models the Texture can accommodate is great. The ultimate goal of this design is the accumulation of numerous TextureModules, each reflecting unique, if not personal and idiomatic, methods of generating musical parts. This addresses the challenge posed by Laske: "… the kind of musical knowledge that, if implemented, would improve computer music tools is often not public or even shared among experts, but personal, idiosyncratic knowledge" (1992a, p. 20). The Texture offers a repository for this idiosyncratic knowledge.

The Clone leverages the power of the Texture, and extends it further with modular, parametric, and holistic transformations. The utility of the Clone is Texture independent: Clones can accommodate any Texture or Instrument model within athenaCL. Processing a generative part (the Texture) with any number of multi-parameter transformers (Clones) enables the production and configuration of sonic structures not easily deployed within a single Texture. Further, rather than an intractable web of nested dependencies, the Clone offers a single, transparent hierarchical relationship with the Texture. By using a Filter ParameterObject that permits numerous embedded Filters to operate in series (such as PipeLine), this singular relationship does not limit transformations to one level of processing. A Clone can thus, with a single parameter or many parameters, perform numerous levels of transformative processing within a contained, tractable entity.

5.3.5. Alternative and Related Models

Many CAAC systems do not modularize the generative part: the system itself is the generative part. This is the case with many Music N event generators, including Score-11, nGen, and Cmask. These systems provide a wide variety of powerful generators to be configured for each parameter (slot) of a multi-parameter instrument. Higher-level interaction and control at the event level or above, however, is limited to single-parameter generation alone, or possibly interactions between parameter values. The system itself, in terms of athenaCL, is one TextureModule.

Within Music V Mathews offers two layers of CAAC processing. These layers permit multi-dimensional event generation and transformation and are called PLay First pass (PLF) and PLay Second pass (PLS) respectively. (PLF and PLS routines were first deployed in Music III (Mathews 2005); PLF and PLS routines were called A and B routines in Music4BF and Music360 (Rogers 1975).) This design provides an interesting parallel to athenaCL's use of Textures and Clones. In Music V, the process of rendering an audio file from a score and orchestra definition is divided into three stages. Mathews states that this is done for "… both conceptual and computational reasons" (1969, p. 38). Pass I is the "composer sequence" stage: note cards (events) from the score are read and functions and parameters are set. Additionally, instruction cards can provide parameters for Fortran-coded PLF subroutines which, among other things, generate additional note cards. As Mathews states, "most of the composing power of the program resides in Pass I" (1969, p. 38). Pass II is the "time sequence" stage: note cards are sorted by start time. No additional note cards can be added, and event order cannot be changed. However, PLS subroutines can be used to transform existing note card parameters. Built-in metronome functions, as start time and duration transformations, are performed as Pass II operations. Pass III is the "sound generation" stage: note cards are read and, with the supplied instrument definitions, audio is rendered.

Mathews states that the use of PLF subroutines, and compositional subroutines in general, offer "… some of the most interesting but difficult directions in which computer sound generation can be developed" (1969, p. 78). Mathews provides an example of a PLF subroutine that, from a pre-defined motive, creates a sequence of events from numerous transposed and time-scaled motive instances. The PLF subroutines, in the same manner as instrument definitions, are defined to accept an ordered list of parameter values. The designer of the subroutine is free to declare as many parameters as needed. As a note card must declare an instrument number, so each PLF instruction card must declare a PLF routine number between one and five. The PLF subroutines offer a modular, parametric, and reusable method of multi-dimensional event generation. These subroutines can be seen in part as an athenaCL TextureModule consisting only of constant-value parameter slots, or TextureStatic ParameterObjects. With the addition of one-dimensional generators to supply parameter values, the Texture becomes a more powerful, flexible, and reusable tool than PLF subroutines.

Mathews demonstrates the use of a PLS subroutine to perform pitch quantizing: the pitch parameters of events, generated with a PLF subroutine, are shifted to the nearest step of a pre-defined scale (1969, p. 94). The PLS subroutines, as with PLF, are defined to accept an ordered list of parameter values and, when called with an instruction card, must declare a PLS routine number between one and five. The PLS subroutines offer a modular, parametric, and reusable method of multi-dimensional event transformation. These subroutines can be seen in part as an athenaCL Clone consisting only of constant-value parameter slots, or CloneStatic ParameterObjects. In the example presented above, a PLS routine transforms PLF-generated events; in the same manner, a Clone can be used to transform Texture-generated events. Where a Clone is always linked to a single Texture, PLS routines can operate on any events in the Pass II stage, and Mathews' frequently suggests their use for "… relations involving several voices at a particular time" (1969, p. 94).

In the design of a more general, reusable generative part, there is a need for two kinds of slots: slots that configure event parameter values, and slots that configure and control the part itself. This division is demonstrated in Truax's POD system. Truax describes the distribution of events as a syntactic field, where event time and frequency values are controlled by a Poisson distribution. The application of this distribution is configured with parameters for the total number of events, frequency masks, and amplitude and sound object selection methods (1976, p. 262). The system also provides "performance variables" and additional options to control the Poisson distribution itself. Some performance variables configure the speed and direction used in reading the calculated Poisson values (Buxton 1975, p. 23), while other options control initial and final density values and average time delay (Buxton 1975, p. 58). A parallel model in athenaCL would employ a TextureModule that, in additional to standard slots for amplitude and pitch selection, would provide the part-level density and performance variables Truax describes as TextureStatic or TextureDynamic ParameterObjects.

Hiller, within later versions of MUSICOMP, provides subroutines for phrase-generation and imitation. Hiller suggests that with such tools composers can "… begin to think of larger units than isolated notes…" (1969, p. 81). In describing his PHRASE system (1978), Hiller again affirms his desire to create generative parts from resources greater than individual parameters: "in contrast to earlier computer algorithms for music composition, program PHRASE can be used to compose themes, motives and phrases and … to imitate these phrases in a number of ways"; further, the system "… transcends the manipulation of just individual musical elements because it can handle substantial groups of elements which can be time related as a piece unfolds," (Hiller 1978, p. 193). A Texture, as a multi-dimensional generative part, is capable of phrase-level event production.

Fry's "phrase processors," deployed in his Flavors Band system, model low-level generative and transformative procedures. Phrase processors are not used in isolation as musical parts; rather, "a musical style is represented as a phrase-processing network" (1984b, p. 296). Though Flavors Band contains over sixty phrase processors, their design is not uniform. For example, while all operate on complete event specifications and accept configuration arguments, some phrase processors are one-dimensional transformers (such as "transpose" or "swing"), others are zero-input multi-dimensional generators (such as "notes"), while others are one-input multi-dimensional transformers (such as "context-mapper"). This heterogeneity, while promoting diversity, complicates the system. Additionally, Flavors Band has "event array accessors," "designed to store intermediate event streams to be used and modified in numerous other places" (1984b, p. 300), as well as additional programming utilities in the form of generative and utility functions. While sharing many features of ParameterObjects, Textures, and Clones, the degree of generality proposed by the phrase processor decreases ease of use: "… flexibility had a higher priority than ease of use … Flavors Band is not simple to use" (Fry 1984b, p. 308).

Textures in athenaCL relate to the voice model of Pla. In Pla, a voice is a template for a voice instance, and each instance may have unique flavors. Schottstaedt describes the code necessary to produce a voice: "the voice body is simply a block of code that can, if it wants, instruct that a note or musical event be placed in the note list" (1989b, p. 219). Each voice instance has parameters for duration as well as generators for other musical parameters as needed. Parameter generators in Pla, in addition to the standard algorithmic techniques, can edit preexisting note lists, react to output or behavior of other voices, and can communicate between voices via messages. As Roads describes, the Pla voice "can be embedded in expressions, be passed parameters, create other voices, read and edit note lists, and serve as a background process that handles multivoice phrasing or scheduling" (Roads 1985, p. 173). These facilities are an extension of SAIL's parallel process run-time facility (Loy and Abbott 1985, p. 258), and are also found in Loy's SAIL-coded MUSBOX system (Loy 1989, p. 343). Oppenheim compares the voiceLoop of Dmix to the Pla voice; each voiceLoop, as a scheduled, Smalltalk-based macro for a generative part, permits the user to access any object within the entire Dmix environment (1990, p. 256). Because Texture EventSequences are not created in real-time, and Textures have no external dependencies other than the Path, such inter-Texture communication is not currently conceivable within athenaCL. However, it is possible for a TextureModule to internally model a system consisting of multiple independent, interacting agents.

As mentioned above, Pope's EventGenerators, like Textures, are multi-dimensional generators that describe particular musical archetypes. As Pope states, "examples of simple event generators are chords, trills, and scales; one can, for example, define a chord given its root, type, and inversion, or a trill given its notes, duration and frequency, or a scale given its base, goal, and gamut" (1995). Elsewhere Pope describes more general, higher-level EventGenerators such as Cluster, Cloud, and Ostinato that, through specialization, may include stochastic, Markov-based, and other generative processes (1989, p. 251).

Taube, in early versions of Common Music, describes "gesture streams," a type of item stream that returns multiple valued items. Gesture streams offer a multi-dimensional generator that, in some cases, provide "… a more natural and efficient means to organize … material than using separate item streams for each of the types of values …" (1989, p. 317). In addition to gesture streams, Common Music models the generative part as "collections": "collections may occupy more than one time period in a single performance, they may contain other collections to any depth level" (1997, p. 31). Taube describes six collection types: thread, merge, heap, algorithm, network, and layout. Collections have features similar to both Textures and ParameterObjects. Textures cannot, however, embed other Textures. A TextureModule, as already mentioned, could be designed to manipulate internal nested hierarchical structures if desired.

Berg's AC Toolbox features numerous varieties of Sections, objects that offer functionality similar to Textures. AC Toolbox Section varieties include data, note, structured, and density. Additionally, MIDI Objects and Csound Objects offer part-structures, similar to Sections, specialized for particular output formats. The different types of Sections are somewhat analogous to the various methods of multi-dimensional event generation offered by Textures. The slots of a Section are configured with Generators, Transformers, or other system objects. Sections, however, are transparent structures: they combine the output of Generators into events without internal intervention. This contrasts with a Texture, which is opaque: the Texture acts as an intermediary between ParameterObjects and Events, and accepts a variable number of additional inputs (TextureStatic and TextureDynamic parameters) to configure internal Texture processing.

The AC Toolbox offers transformative methods related to those offered by the Clone. These methods, each transforming one object into a new object, include Backwards, Filter, and Transform. The Backwards method creates a new object in reverse. The Filter method creates a new object by transforming particular parameters of an existing object with signal-processing modeled filters such as "Low-Pass" and "Band-Reject." The Transform method creates a new object by applying modular Transformers to each parameter of a Section, where rhythm values are treated as separate Tempo, Attack, and Duration values. As with Sections, the wide variety of transformative types promotes flexibility and modularity. The Clone, by offering a single type of transformative object linked to a Texture, offers a related model within a uniform level of abstraction.

Chapter 6. System Architecture

6.1. Introduction

> If a composition is a program, then, just as it can be proven that there are noncomputable functions, it can be proven that there are noncomposable sounds … there must be sounds which are noncomposable on a digital computer.
>
> —Carla Scaletti (1989a, p. 65)

Working with a computer is an aesthetic experience. This experience has changed as the computer has become increasingly transparent, the computer now little more than a thin visual display and an input device. Where the physicality of a closet-sized "mini-computer" in the 1970s perhaps conditioned experience more than any particular software, the physicality of contemporary machines approaches zero, and the software provides the primary aesthetic experience.

The appearance, configuration, and functionality of software form an aesthetic entity. In the case of software for creative production, the aesthetic experience offered is perhaps more significant than with conventional software. While writing, composing, designing, or programming, the software should support the user's desired aesthetic environment, rather than obfuscate or supplant it. In complex GUI-based interfaces, this demand is primarily met by making the interface configurable, either with themes, colors, fonts, or other user-controlled options. There is, however, a frequent trade-off: the more complex and refined the GUI components become, the less configurable options are exposed to the user. An alternative way to support the user's aesthetic environment is to make the interface simpler, and thus more configurable. The maximally simple computer interface is provided by the text-based interactive command line.

The athenaCL system uses an interactive command-line interface for many reasons. The most important, from the perspective of users, is aesthetic. Not only is the command-line environment highly configurable, it is fast, ergonomic, and portable. A user, with the command line, can move twenty files to a different directory in a fraction of the time it would take a windowed, point-and-click approach. The physical detriments of using the mouse or trackpad are widely known and felt. Finally, the syntax of the command-line, consisting only of text, can always be automated and controlled by a lower- or higher-level system. Although the promises of comfort and ease offered by point-and-click environments have convinced many, there are numerous things that can be done more effectively with slightly simpler technology.

This chapter examines the large-scale system architecture of athenaCL. The AthenaObject, the central storage unit of user-created objects, is discussed. Of particular architectural importance is the EventMode production model. This sub-system of athenaCL allows users to create Textures with specific Instrument models, while at the same time generating multiple OutputFormats. The EventMode sub-system is modular: new OutputFormats can be incrementally added to the system, providing, along with TextureModules and ParameterObjects, an expanding library of compatible resources. The primary interface components of athenaCL are the Command and Interpreter objects. Together, they form the outer layer of the system. The Interpreter and Command objects offer a high-level, flexible front-end to AthenaObject processing, capable of being used interactively through the command line or programmatically with a Python script.

Unlike Chapters 4 and 5, this chapter does not explore comparisons to related systems. User-level interfaces have already been described in Chapter 2, and the components described in this chapter support the previously-described distinctions. Further, the components of system architecture described here are either too specific (like the EventMode) or too general (like the Command) for useful comparisons.

6.2. The Architecture of athenaCL

The AthenaObject stores instances of both utility objects, such as the External, and user objects, such as Paths, Textures, and Clones. When using athenaCL, the user, through the Interpreter, builds and processes components of an AthenaObject. Storage of the AthenaObject, as an XML file or otherwise, provides a complete data representation of user-created objects. The Interpreter creates or loads a single AthenaObject, and passes references to this object to Commands for processing.

6.2.1. The External

The External is a utility object designed to manage files and file-paths external to athenaCL. The External scans the athenaCL package directory structure, finding all essential directories and storing their file paths.

The External provides error logging and internet-based error reporting to a central on-line server. Error messages, collected by the Interpreter, are passed to the External; the External stores these error messages in a locally-written log file. Upon quitting a session, the Interpreter gives the user the option of submitting the log to the server. The External parses the log, packages it as a Hyper Text Markup Language (HTML) form POST request, connects to the server, and passes the data. An automated error reporting facility is of great utility, both for users, who can effortlessly report errors, and for the system, which gains in reliability from diverse testing in real-world environments.

Additionally, the External manages the athenaCL preferences file. This file, located in appropriate platform-specific locations and written in XML, stores user data maintained between multiple sessions. This data includes Interpreter and graphic preferences, OutputFormat selections, and recent file paths. The External provides methods to obtain and store preference values, as well as to update preference files made with earlier versions of athenaCL.

When the AthenaObject is instantiated, a single External object is created and stored as an attribute. The External is accessed by Commands and the Interpreter through the AthenaObject.

6.2.2. The AthenaObject

6.2.2.1. Model and Representation

The AthenaObject is the collection of all objects necessary for EventSequence creation and processing, including Paths, Textures, Clones and related utility objects. The AthenaObject also stores a list of available commands, resources for obtaining documentation, and command correction utilities. In most scenarios, the AthenaObject is created by an Interpreter and is passed a Terminal object (to be described below). An External, as mentioned above, is created by the AthenaObject upon initialization.

The AthenaObject is primarily a storage facility: all objects processed by athenaCL are contained within the AthenaObject. An AthenaObject provides a complete representation of a user session. When users save their work in athenaCL, the AthenaObject, coded into human-readable XML, is written to a file. An AthenaObject, processed with Commands in an Interpreter, can be reloaded or merged with an already-loaded AthenaObject.

6.2.2.2. Object Design

There is one AthenaObject class that is not specialized. Within an Interpreter, one AthenaObject instance is created and configured.

The AthenaObject consists primarily of attributes for user-defined object collections. Such collections include the `pathLib` dictionary, the `textureLib` dictionary, and the `cloneLib` CloneManager object. Additional attributes include the string names of currently-active objects, such as `activeSetMeasure`, `activePath`, `activeTextureModule`, `activeTexture`, and `activeEventMode`. The `aoInfo` dictionary is used to store version information, a user's command history, and recently-used file paths. The `tniMode` attribute stores a boolean value to determine if Multisets, as set-classes, are interpreted in Tn or TnI classification. This distinction is explained in Chapter 4.

As each EventMode has an associated Orchestra (to be explained below), the AthenaObject method `setEventMode()` sets the `activeEventMode` attribute with a string name and the `orcObj` attribute with a local Orchestra object. This Orchestra is referenced when users create new Textures: the Orchestra determines what Instruments are available, as well as how auxiliary parameters are configured. Orchestras and Instruments are introduced in Chapter 4; their use by Textures is explained in Chapter 5.

In addition to storing user-created objects, the AthenaObject maintains a hierarchical list of Command names for presentation to the user. Utility methods provide tools for obtaining Command documentation strings and correcting user-provided Command strings. Although the Interpreter is responsible for creating and finding available Commands, the command tools in the AthenaObject provide common user-level resources that are often needed at hierarchical levels below that of the Interpreter.

6.2.2.3. Diagrams and Examples

The following diagram summarizes important attributes and methods of the AthenaObject.

Example 6-1. AthenaObject Class Diagram

```
Class AthenaObject
Attributes:
    external
    help
    termObj
    orcObj
    activeSetMeasure
    pathLib
    activePath
    activeTextureModule
    textureLib
    activeTexture
    cloneLib
    activeEventMode
    aoInfo
    tniMode
Methods:
    setEventMode()
    cmdCorrect()
    compareVersion()
```

The following diagram illustrates the primary object components of the AthenaObject.

Example 6-2. Component Diagram of an AthenaObject

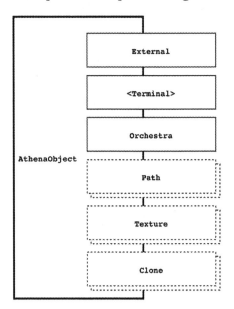

The following Python session demonstrates basic functionality of the AthenaObject. Demonstration of user objects within the AthenaObject, such as the Path, Texture, and Clone, requires the use of Interpreter and Command objects described below.

Example 6-3. AthenaObject in Python

```
>>> from athenaCL import athenaObj
>>> ao = athenaObj.AthenaObject() # creating an AthenaObject
>>> # obtaining a file-based preference from the External
>>> ao.external.getPref('athena', 'eventMode')
'midi'
>>> ao.external.libATHpath # the external stores local file paths
'/Users/ariza/_x/src/athenaCL/libATH'
>>> ao.tniMode # attribute for Multiset set-class representations
0
>>> ao.aoInfo['version'] # current system version number
'1.4.1'
```

```
>>> # comparing the current version to the most recent on-line version
>>> ao.compareVersion()
('current', '1.4.1')
>>> # correcting the case of a user-supplied command
>>> ao.cmdCorrect('tin')
'TIn'
```

6.2.3. The Performer and PolySequence

The Performer is a utility object created and managed by the EventMode. The Performer
`flattenSome()` and `flattenAll()` methods, for a given list of Textures or a complete
AthenaObject, calls each Texture's or Clone's `score()` method. In the case of Clones, the
Performer passes a copy of the parent-Texture's EventSequence to the Clone's `score()`
method. The resulting EventSequences, from both Textures and Clones, are stored in a
PolySequence, a nested dictionary containing EventSequences and meta-data necessary for
OutputEngine processing.

PolySequence meta-data, obtained for each Texture and Clone, includes mute status,
Instrument and Orchestra data, MIDI settings, and Orchestra postMap mode. The
Performer has a `sort()` method to optionally sort all EventSequences contained in the
PolySequence, and a `reset()` method to reinitialize the PolySequence.

The Performer thus "performs" Textures and Clones, calling their `score()` methods
and retrieving their EventSequences. The PolySequence is simply an intermediary data
structure to be read by OutputEngines for final output production. The Performer "flattens"
the complex object data of Textures and Clones into structured static data.

6.2.4. The OutputFormat

The OutputFormat is a simple representation of an output type. In all current cases, outputs
are files, but in future cases, outputs may be expanded to other forms. When representing a

file type, an OutputFormat describes the appropriate file extension (such as ".sco" or ".mid"), and is used to create a complete file path from a root file path provided to the EventMode. (To provide clear command organization within athenaCL, OutputFormats are presented to the user as EventOutputs; the two terms are synonymous.)

Users configure output settings by selecting any number of OutputFormats and an EventMode. Users can select desired OutputFormats independently of particular OutputEngines or EventModes. The list of selected OutputFormats is stored as a user preference and retained between Interpreter sessions. For example, if a user desires a MIDI file, selecting the OutputFormat "midiFile" will, the next time outputs are created, cause the appropriate OutputEngine to be allocated by the EventMode and a MIDI file to be written. Some OutputFormats, even when selected, will be used only if an appropriate EventMode is active. The "csoundOrchestra" OutputFormat, for example, will only be created if the "csoundNative" EventMode is active.

A complete list of current OutputFormats is found in Appendix D.

6.2.5. The OutputEngine

6.2.5.1. Model and Representation

An OutputEngine transforms a PolySequence into one or more OutputFormats. PolySequences, as described above, are collections of EventSequences. The data created by the OutputEngine may be an event list format, such as a MIDI file, Csound score, or a pulse code modulation (PCM) audio file. The OutputEngine may also create related support files, such as Csound orchestra code or utility scripts. OutputEngines, like ParameterObjects and TextureModules, are modular components that can embed additional modules and subsystems. OutputEngines are utility objects; they are created and managed by the EventMode, not by the user.

A complete list of current OutputEngines is found in Appendix D.

6.2.5.2. Object Design

There are many OutputEngine sub-classes that are specialized by one or more levels of inheritance. All OutputEngines are polymorphic and may be used interchangeably. Within an EventMode, no more than one instance of each OutputEngine sub-class is created and configured.

OutputEngine objects are created and managed by the EventMode, based on the EventMode type and a list of OutputFormat requests. On initialization the OutputEngine stores the type of EventMode that created it, as well as a reference dictionary of EventMode-prepared file paths. OutputEngine class names are prefixed by the word "Engine."

OutputEngines process a PolySequence to produce event list files. Every OutputEngine requires a local Orchestra object; this Orchestra is used for Orchestra postMap processing of pitch, amplitude, and panning values, as well as the creation of necessary Orchestra-related support files. The type of Orchestra object used within an OutputEngine, in some cases, is dependent only on the OutputEngine type. In other cases, the type of Orchestra object is dependent on the EventMode that created the OutputEngine. For example, the EngineCsoundNative OutputEngine will always use a CsoundNative Orchestra. This is necessary for properly calculating Orchestra postMap values, as well as generating necessary resources such as the Csound orchestra file. The EngineText, however, will use whatever Orchestra is specified by the EventMode. As text event-list files are independent of any specific sound source, Orchestra postMap values may reflect any Orchestra, and no additional support files need be generated.

OutputEngines are never directly selected by users, but are selected by the EventMode based on the combination of EventMode type and user OutputFormat request. Multiple OutputEngines are gathered by the EventMode and are used to process a single PolySequence. This design allows for the creation of multiple outputs from a single source. Depending on user-configuration, every time a Texture's or Clone's score() method is called a unique EventSequence is created. Although this is a source of useful algorithmic variation, at times a single variant is desired in multiple OutputFormats. The Performer "flattens" one collection of EventSequences from all Textures and Clones into a PolySequence; this PolySequence then provides all OutputEngines access to the exact same collection of EventSequences.

Each sub-classed OutputEngine contains attributes that define its compatibility with other Orchestras and OutputFormats. The orcIncompat attribute is used to name any Orchestras that are incompatible with this OutputEngine. For example, the EngineCsoundNative object is incompatible with Textures and Clones created with any Orchestra other than CsoundNative; the EngineMidiFile, EngineCsoundExternal, and EngineText, on the other hand, are all compatible with Textures created with any Orchestra. What determines OutputEngine and Orchestra compatibility is the extent of an OutputEngine's reliance on specific Instrument models and auxiliary parameter configurations to produce its output. For example, a Texture created with the CsoundNative Orchestra will have an Instrument number and a prescribed number of auxiliary parameters. Such Textures can be processed by the EngineText, as it is not necessary for the OutputEngine to know anything about the Texture's Instrument or auxiliary parameters. However, if a Texture is created with the GeneralMidi Orchestra, an Instrument number may be selected that has no representation in the CsoundNative Orchestra. If this Texture is processed by the EngineCsoundNative, no Instrument information would be available, and proper Csound orchestra and score construction would be impossible; if the Instrument number does exist, the Texture may not define the necessary auxiliary parameters.

When a Texture is created, the Texture's Instrument is selected from those available under the current EventMode-specified and AthenaObject-stored Orchestra. If the user changes EventMode and creates new Textures, a heterogeneous collection of Texture-bound Orchestras may result. OutputEngines are designed to handle such diverse collections. Using the specification given by the `orcIncompat` attribute, each OutputEngine collected by the EventMode examines each Texture's Orchestra, and creates a list of compatible Textures and Instrument numbers ("compatNames" and "compatInsts"). When the OutputEngine creates an OutputFormat, incompatible Textures (and their child Clones) are skipped. Incompatibilities, if necessary, can be resolved by editing a Texture's Instrument under the desired EventMode.

Each sub-classed OutputEngine defines attributes for available and minimum OutputFormats (`outAvailable` and `outMin`). The OutputEngine thus defines what OutputFormats it can write, as well as a minimum of OutputFormats that it will always write when called by an EventMode. The user, within athenaCL, configures a list of desired OutputFormats. This list, independent of any particular EventMode or OutputEngine, is passed to each OutputEngine when called. Each user-requested OutputFormat, if available from the OutputEngine, is then created. If a requested OutputFormat is not available from a particular OutputEngine, it is ignored. If none of the OutputFormats requested by the user are supported by the OutputEngine, and the OutputEngine has been allocated and called by the EventMode, the OutputEngine always creates its declared minimum OutputFormats.

The parent class _OutputEngine defines a `write()` method. This method calls three methods defined in each sub-class: `_writePre()`, `_write()`, and `_writePost()`. Together, these methods perform all operations necessary to write the requested or minimum OutputFormats. The `write()` method takes a PolySequence object and a list of requested OutputFormats as arguments. The OutputFormat request is stored as `outRequest`, and all OutputFormat names, once completed, are appended to the `outComplete` list.

6.2.5.3. Diagrams and Examples

The inheritance diagram below provides an example of OutputEngine inheritance.

Example 6-4. OutputEngine Inheritance: EngineCsoundExternal

```
_OutputEngine
|
EngineCsoundExternal
```

The following diagram summarizes important attributes and methods of the OutputEngine.

Example 6-5. OutputEngine Class Diagram

```
Class OutputEngine
Attributes:
   ref
   emName
   orcIncompat
   orcObj
   outComplete
   outRequest
   outAvailable
   outMin
   compatNames
```

```
  compatInsts
Methods:
  write()
```

The following diagram illustrates the role of the Performer, PolySequence, and OutputFormat in EventSequence production. The sequence of steps is as follows: (1) a Performer, given a reference to an AthenaObject, calls Texture and Clone score() methods (2) a Texture generates Events, (3) Events are formed into an EventSequence, (4) a copy of the EventSequence is passed to the Clone; another copy is passed to the PolySequence, (5) the Clone, with Filter ParameterObjects, performs array transformations on the EventSequence, (6) the Clone performs sequence transformations on the EventSequence, (7) a copy of the transformed EventSequence is passed to the PolySequence, (8) the Performer passes a reference to the PolySequence to one or more OutputEngines.

Example 6-6. Activity Diagram of the Performer, PolySequence, and OutputFormat

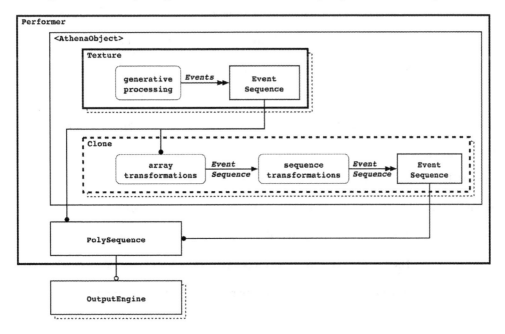

6.2.6. The EventMode

6.2.6.1. Model and Representation

The EventMode represents a complex event list production system. The EventMode type, stored as a string within an AthenaObject, determines Texture configuration, Instrument availability, and the function of some Commands. The EventMode object, when created by a Command, is responsible for instantiating and processing a Performer object, selecting OutputEngines, and passing the Performer's PolySequence to OutputEngines. The EventMode manages the translation of Texture and Clone EventSequences into a variety of sometimes conflicting sound-source dependent OutputFormats.

The EventMode exists as a single class that has different types. There are no EventMode subclasses. When working in athenaCL, an EventMode type, stored as a string, is always active, and the user can select a different EventMode at any time. Each EventMode type, when selected, assigns a default Orchestra to the AthenaObject. A single Orchestra class may be used by more than one EventMode type. This Orchestra, based on the active EventMode, determines what Instruments are available for creating new Textures, and determines how auxiliary Texture parameter slots are configured. For example, the EventMode "midi" assigns the GeneralMidi Orchestra to the AthenaObject; Textures created while this EventMode is active must use an Instrument defined by GeneralMidi. These MIDI Instruments require no auxiliary parameter slots. The EventMode "csoundExternal" assigns the CsoundExternal Orchestra to the AthenaObject; Textures created while this EventMode is active may define any Instrument number and any number of auxiliary slots. The EventMode type thus alters what options are available when Textures are created. After instantiation, Textures retain their internal Instrument and Orchestra settings unless edited.

When used to process Textures and Clones into OutputFormats, an EventMode object is created by a Command object. The EventMode object is not stored in the AthenaObject. Given a type, a reference to an AthenaObject, and a list of OutputFormat requests, the EventMode selects and instantiates all necessary OutputEngines. The EventMode then creates a Performer, generates a PolySequence, and then passes a reference to this PolySequence to each collected OutputEngine.

6.2.6.2. Object Design

There is one EventMode class. The EventMode is specialized by object composition. Object composition occurs after instantiation with the assignment of variable OutputEngines and an Orchestra. Within a Command, no more than one EventMode instance is created and configured.

On initialization, the EventMode is given a reference to an AthenaObject and an EventMode type string. The EventMode type, in most cases, is the same as the user-selected `activeEventMode` stored in the AthenaObject. In some cases it is useful to create an EventMode object in a mode different than that selected by the user, for instance, to produce a MIDI file of a temporary Texture.

The `setRootPath()` method is used to set a root file path from which all other OutputFormat file paths are derived. The file path must have an XML extension (.xml). The method `_engineAllocate()`, given a list of OutputFormat requests, collects the necessary OutputEngine objects in a list. All EventMode types mandate the allocation of at least one OutputEngine; even when a user provides an empty OutputFormat request, a single OutputEngine will be allocated based on the current EventMode type. Given an empty OutputFormat request, the OutputEngine will, in turn, always produce its minimum OutputFormats.

For example, when the user, through a Command object, creates a "csoundNative" EventMode, the EngineCsoundNative is always allocated, regardless of OutputFormat request. Some EventMode types share the same default OutputEngine allocation. This is the case with the "midi" and "midiPercussion" EventMode types: both will always allocate the EngineMidiFile. Some OutputEngines are completely independent of EventMode type. These OutputEngines are allocated exclusively when one of their OutputFormats is found in the user-supplied OutputFormat request. Whenever a "textTab" or "textSpace" OutputFormat is requested, for example, the EngineText OutputEngine is allocated.

6.2.6.3. Diagrams and Examples

The following diagram summarizes important attributes and methods of the EventMode.

Example 6-7. EventMode Class Diagram

```
Class EventMode
Attributes:
   name
   ao
   rootPath
Methods:
   _engineAllocate()
   setRootPath()
   process()
```

The following diagram illustrates the role of the EventMode in Performer, OutputEngine, and OutputFormat creation. The sequence of steps is as follows: (1) the EventMode, given a reference to an AthenaObject, passes this reference to a Performer, (2) after the Performer processes Textures and Clones into a PolySequence, the EventMode passes references to this PolySequence to one or more OutputEngines, (3) the

OutputEngine processes the PolySequence, performing Orchestra postMap processing, (4) the OutputEngine performs OutputFormat specific formatting, (5) the OutputEngine writes one or more OutputFormats.

Example 6-8. Activity Diagram of the EventMode

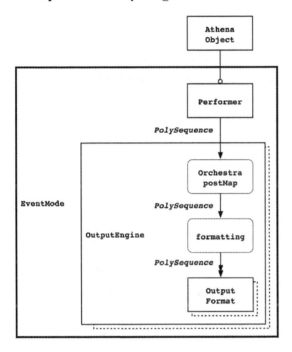

The following Python session demonstrates basic functionality of the EventMode. As Textures or Clones are required to produce OutputFormats, the demonstration below is limited.

Example 6-9. EventMode in Python

```
>>> from athenaCL import athenaObj
>>> from athenaCL.libATH import eventList
>>> ao = athenaObj.AthenaObject() # creating an AthenaObject
>>> # an AthenaObject will always have an activeEventMode attribute
```

```
>>> em = eventList.factory(ao.activeEventMode, ao) # creating an EventMode
>>> em.name # examining the EventMode type
'midi'
>>> em.reprDoc() # getting EventMode documentation
(['EventMode: midi; ', '1 active OutputEngine:\n'], [['EngineMidiFile',
'Translates events to a standard MIDI file. Compatible with all Orchestras;
GeneralMidi orchestra will be used for all conversions. EventOutput available:
midiFile']])
>>> em.setRootPath('/Users/ariza/out.xml') # providing a root file path
>>> # processing the EventMode creates all requested OutputFormats
>>> ok, msg, outComplete = em.process(None, ['midiFile'])
>>> # no Textures have been created, so no outputs completed
>>> print outComplete
[]
```

6.2.7. Compositional Implications

The OutputEngine, OutputFormat, and EventMode together support the flexible production of a wide variety of event list outputs, as well as the ability to create numerous types of event lists simultaneously. Further, Textures created with diverse and potentially incompatible Orchestra and Instrument models can be accommodated in a single environment.

This model supports OutputFormats that are closely related to a particular sound source, as well as those that are not. For example, future OutputFormats that support Western notation, such as SCORE language files, MusicXML, or LilyPond, can be added to the system simply as OutputEngines and appropriate OutputFormats. These formats do not require unique Orchestras or Instrument models. Future output formats that employ alternative sound sources, such as SuperCollider, can be added as a dedicated Orchestra model and as an appropriate OutputEngine and OutputFormat. This design supports

OutputFormats that are Orchestra dependent, as well as OutputFormats that are Orchestra independent. Internal, external, and exported sound sources can thus all be accommodated.

Despite the complexity demonstrated at the code level, the EventMode model, to the user, is flexible and intuitive. Depending on desired sound source and output needs, the user can simply select an EventMode and create Textures. If the user requires multiple OutputFormats, any combination can be selected and stored as a user preference. Depending on the active EventMode, the desired outputs, if available, will be created. If the user creates a collection of Textures with mixed Orchestras, or changes EventMode after Texture creation, warnings will be given during OutputFormat creation for any Textures with incompatible Orchestras. Such incompatibilities, if desired, can be resolved by editing the Texture's Instrument parameter under the new EventMode. This design integrates specific Instrument and Orchestra models, diverse OutputFormats, and output-independent Textures and Clones.

6.3. The Interface of athenaCL

The interface of athenaCL is designed for speed, portability, and ease of use. The interactive command-line interface is one of the few user interface archetypes capable of meeting these needs. Most graphical and GUI-based environments are comparatively slow (in both data-entry and window drawing and repositioning) and are frequently platform dependent. For users only familiar with GUI environments, a text-based interface may not immediately provide ease of use. Such users, unless they are familiar with common command-line environments such as a UNIX shell or a text-based FTP program, are presented with initial challenges. Anticipating these difficulties, the athenaCL interface attempts to make the command-line easier for novices. This is done in three ways.

First, all Commands follow a hierarchical naming scheme. Command names are built from a two character prefix followed by a short, UNIX-style command name. The two character prefix is an acronym formed from system component names. For example, EventMode is given the prefix EM; TextureInstance is given the prefix TI. UNIX-style command names are added to these prefixes, and refer to operations applied within the domain of the prefix. When possible, well-known UNIX command names are used. For example, UNIX commands such as "ls" (listing the files in a directory) and "rm" (removing a file) are combined with a prefix and used to list or remove athenaCL components. The Command "EMls" thus provides a list of all EventModes; the Command "TIrm" removes (deletes) a Texture. Command case distinctions are used only for visual clarity; the Interpreter ignores upper- or lower-case distinctions.

Second, all Commands function both interactively (where the Interpreter prompts the user for each necessary argument) and non-interactively (where the user supplies all necessary arguments with the Command name in a space delimited list). Interactive Commands are easier for the novice while non-interactive Commands are faster for the expert; by providing dual functionality, both are satisfied. Further, novices can become experts with experience. Given an unfamiliar Command, a user can simply enter the Command's name and the Interpreter will provide prompts for each argument. If the Command is frequently used, the user will learn the necessary arguments and their order. With this knowledge, the user can execute the Command non-interactively, providing a list of arguments following the Command name. Non-interactive Command use is invariably faster, as less typing and screen display is necessary. Once learned, non-interactive Command strings can be used to programmatically control and automate athenaCL, either from a UNIX shell script or a Python script.

Third, limited graphical and GUI tools are available to inform and extend text-based interaction. Numerous Commands provide graphical output, producing images and graphs to provide information that cannot be clearly shown in text, such as event data for each ParameterObject of a Texture. Numerous graphical output formats are supported, including Portable Network Graphics (PNG), Joint Photographic Experts Group (JPEG), Adobe Encapsulated PostScript (EPS), and the Tk-based Python GUI environment TkInter. Additionally, GUI-based file and directory selection dialogs can optionally be used, allowing users to browse their file system visually. As browsing a directory structure in a text-based interface is awkward for some, optional GUI file dialogs provide a useful resource.

6.3.1. The Command Object

6.3.1.1. Model and Representation

The Command object encapsulates a user-level process performed on components in the AthenaObject. Commands are created and controlled by the Interpreter. Each Command made available to the user is a subclass of the parent Command class. Each sub-class inherits a common interface of basic operations, methods, and utility objects for parsing user argument strings and interactively obtaining data from the user.

The complete list of user commands, as well as their documentation, is found in Appendix E.

6.3.1.2. Object Design

There are many Command sub-classes, each specialized by one or more levels of inheritance. All Command sub-classes are polymorphic and may be used interchangeably. Any number of Command instances may be created and configured.

The design of the Command object is based in part on a widely used command design pattern (Gamma et al. 1994, p. 60). All Commands are either standard Command objects or sub-Commands. Standard Commands gather data from the user, perform necessary processing, perform operations on the AthenaObject, and return a text-based response or graphical display. Though data in the AthenaObject may be altered by a standard Command, no data (other than status messages) is returned to the Interpreter. Sub-Commands, designated by the subCmd attribute, gather and process data like Commands, but return a dictionary to the Interpreter for further processing. Sub-Commands are necessary to perform operations only possible at the level of the Interpreter, such as quitting the program or reinitializing the AthenaObject.

On initialization the Command takes a reference to an AthenaObject, command environment settings, and an optional argument string. The command environment settings (cmdEnviron), obtained from the Interpreter, are stored in a dictionary and include settings for threading, threading poll duration, debug status flag, and verbosity level. The do() method, defined in the Command parent class, provides the primary interface for Commands. Command sub-classes override the methods gather(), process(), and display() to provide command functionality. The gather() method is responsible for obtaining argument values. This is done by either checking and parsing the argument string given at Command initialization, or by interactively obtaining values from the user. The process() method performs an operation. This operation may create or edit objects in the AthenaObject (such as Textures, Paths, or Clones), produce outputs, set preferences, or obtain reference data. The display() method returns a string based on the results of the process() method.

The do() method performs the gather(), process(), and display() methods in sequence, first checking which steps are necessary (set with the gatherSwitch and processSwitch attributes). The do() method handles errors, spawns threads if necessary, marks completed stages (set with the gatherStatus and processStatus attributes), and calls optional graphical display methods (determined by the gfxSwitch attribute). The do() method returns a status flag and a message string.

The Command's log() method is used to obtain a string representation of the arguments necessary to recreate the Command. The log() method constructs this string based on the results of the gather() method, and can thus return a complete command-line argument string from data gathered interactively. The Interpreter stores each log() string in a history list, and enables the user to arbitrarily execute commands and their arguments from this history.

Though a Command history is maintained, Command objects are temporary: they are created, used, and discarded. Future development may provide additional functionality: by extending and storing Command objects, multiple levels of undo are possible. Command objects, expanded with an unprocess() method capable of undoing what was done with the process() method, will be stored in an ordered list. When a user desires to undo an operation, the previous Command's unprocess() method is called. If further undo operations are desired, the same method is called for each previous Command stored in sequence.

6.3.1.3. Diagrams and Examples

The inheritance diagram below provides an example of Command inheritance. In cases when numerous Commands share functionality, a common sub-class may be used.

Example 6-10. Command Inheritance: AOl

```
Command
|
```

```
_CommandAO
|
AO1
```

The following diagram summarizes important attributes and methods of the Command.

Example 6-11. Command Class Diagram

```
Class Command
Attributes:
    termObj
    args
    cmdEnviron
    gatherSwitch
    gatherStatus
    processSwitch
    processStatus
    gfxSwitch
    subCmd
Methods:
    gather()
    process()
    unprocess()
    log()
    result()
    display()
    displayGfx()
    do()
```

The following diagram illustrates the primary object components of the Command.

Example 6-12. Component Diagram of a Command

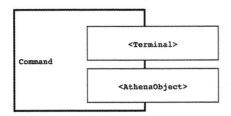

The following Python session demonstrates basic functionality of the Command.

Example 6-13. Command in Python

```
>>> from athenaCL import athenaObj
>>> from athenaCL.libATH import command
>>> # a cmdEnviron dictionary must be provided to each Command object
>>> # this dictionary is supplied by the Interpreter
>>> cmdEnviron = {'threadAble':0, 'pollDur':10, 'debug':0, 'verbose':1}
>>> cmd = command.PIn(ao, cmdEnviron) # the PIn command, for PathInstance new
>>> # since no command arguments were provided at object creation,
>>> # the do() method interactively obtains necessary arguments
>>> cmd.do()
name this PathInstance: path01
enter a pitch set, sieve, spectrum, or set-class: 5|7,c2,c4
    SC 8-23 as (C2,F2,G2,A#2,D3,D#3,G#3,A3)? (y, n, or cancel): y
    add another set? (y, n, or cancel): n
(1, 'PI path01 added to PathInstances.\n')
>>> # the AthenaObject pathLib dictionary stores Paths by name
>>> # the new Path, when printed, returns a set-class representation
>>> print ao.pathLib['path01']
8-23
>>> # the same Command can be created with complete arguments
>>> cmd = command.PIn(ao, cmdEnviron, 'path02 c#2,d2 a#8,a7')
>>> cmd.do() # with provided arguments, the do() method is not interactive
(1, 'PI path02 added to PathInstances.\n')
```

```
>>> # the AthenaObject now contains two Paths
>>> ao.pathLib.keys() # the Python dictionary keys() method returns all names
['path01', 'path02']
>>> print ao.pathLib['path02']
2-1,2-1
>>> # the PIls Command provides a list display of Paths
>>> cmd = command.PIls(ao, cmdEnviron)
>>> # the do() method returns a status and a message string
>>> print cmd.do()[1] # obtaining just the message from the Command
PathInstances available:
{name,TIrefs,PVgroups,scPath}
    path01          0  1  8-23
  + path02          0  1  2-1,2-1
```

6.3.2. The Terminal

The Terminal is a utility object that models the text-based output device used during an athenaCL Interpreter session. The object contains the Interpreter session type, display configuration information, and abstractions of operations that can be performed on the display. Some session types, such as those done through a standard command-line interface program on a UNIX-based system (such as xterm or Terminal.app), offer complete control of character width and height, cursor position, and display redraw. In session types where such tools are not available, the Terminal object supplies default values. The Interpreter creates and stores a single Terminal instance, passing references to other objects as needed. Cross-platform, cross-interface, interactive dialog functions, designed to obtain strings and file-paths from the user, require a Terminal as an argument to determine session type and output configuration.

6.3.3. The Interpreter

6.3.3.1. Model and Representation

The Interpreter is the highest-level abstraction of the athenaCL architecture. When the user starts an athenaCL session, an Interpreter instance is created. The Interpreter performs setup operations, creates necessary utility objects, and loads preferences. When used interactively, the Interpreter provides an input prompt ("::") and waits to receive Command requests. When used programmatically, the Interpreter instance may receive Command strings from a method. The Interpreter, in addition to creating and running Command objects, provides resources for parsing Command strings, supplying Command help, logging errors, configuring display options, running multiple Commands as a list or an internal script, managing Command history, and completing sub-Command operations.

6.3.3.2. Object Design

There is one Interpreter class that is not specialized. Any number of Interpreter instances may be created and configured.

The design of the Interpreter is based in part on the cmd.py command-line framework distributed with Python. Upon initialization, the Interpreter is passed optional arguments for session type, threading activation, verbosity, and debug status. A Terminal object is created with the provided session type, and is stored in the Interpreter as termObj. An AthenaObject, with a reference to this Terminal object, is created and stored as ao. A command environment dictionary (cmdEnviron) is created for use with Command instances.

Once initialized, operations can be performed on the AthenaObject through the Interpreter in multiple ways. If the Interpreter is used non-interactively by an external system (such as a Python script), the method cmd() can be called with complete command-line argument strings to create and process Commands. If the Interpreter is used interactively, the method cmdLoop() is called. This method creates the outermost loop of user interaction, displaying a command prompt, waiting for input, and creating and processing Command requests. When a Command string is received, it is passed to the cmdExecute() method which, after creating and configuring the necessary Command object, calls the Command's do() method, obtains the result, stores the Command log() string, and catches and reports any errors.

If the Command is a sub-Command, a data dictionary is returned by the Command and passed to the appropriate Interpreter method. Sub-Command methods within the Interpreter are prefixed by the label "proc." The proc_quit() method, for example, destroys the AthenaObject and exits the main Interpreter loop. The proc_shell() method, on UNIX-based systems, allows command-line arguments to be passed to the operating system shell; the proc_py() method starts a Python interpreter inside the athenaCL Interpreter.

6.3.3.3. Diagrams and Examples

Example 6-14. Interpreter Class Diagram

```
Class Interpreter
Attributes:
    sessionType
    verbose
    debug
    echo
    termObj
    ao
    cmdEnviron
Methods:
    cmd()
    cmdLoop()
```

```
cmdExecute()
runScript()
proc_quit
proc_shell
proc_py
```

The following diagram illustrates the primary object components of the Interpreter.

Example 6-15. Component Diagram of an Interpreter

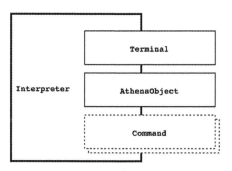

The following Python session demonstrates the functionality of the Interpreter.

Example 6-16. Command in Python

```
>>> from athenaCL import athenaObj
>>> x = athenaObj.Interpreter('cgi') # creating a "cgi" interpreter
>>> ok, msg = x.cmd('AUpc 60hz') # calling the AUpc pitch converter Command
>>> if ok: print msg
AthenaUtility Pitch Converter
format          fq
name            A#~1
midi            35
pitch-class     11
pch             5.1051
frequency       60.0000
pitch-space     -25.49
```

```
>>> ok, msg = x.cmd('EOls') # listing active OutputFormats
>>> if ok: print msg
EventOutput active:
{name}
    audioFile
    csoundBatch
    csoundData
    csoundOrchestra
    csoundScore
    maxColl
  + midiFile
    textSpace
    textTab
  + xmlAthenaObject
>>> # calling the cmdLoop() method is best done through a module
>>> from athenaCL import athenacl
athenaCL 1.4.1 (on darwin via terminal threading off)
Enter "cmd" to see all commands. For help enter "?".
Enter "c" for copyright, "w" for warranty, "r" for credits.
::
```

6.3.4. Compositional Implications

The athenaCL interface can run on nearly any operating system on nearly any platform (all varieties of GNU/Linux, BSD, MacOS, and Windows). Further, with Python ports available for mobile phones and personal digital assistants (PDAs), athenaCL will be able to run on hand-held and embedded devices. AthenaObject XML files created on any platform can be loaded on any other platform, allowing complete platform independence.

Interface design for music systems is a difficult problem. As Pennycook says, no single interface will satisfy all users: "a user interface that satisfies the needs of one musician in an efficient, well-ordered way may be awkward or even counterproductive for another musician" (1985, p. 270). The interactive command-line interface of athenaCL will not be suitable for all users. However, CAAC is often a data-intensive task, involving the specification of numerous carefully configured values and components. A text-based interface allows the rapid viewing and editing of this text-based data. Roads, in describing the differences between linguistic and gestural inputs, states that "in some cases, a linguistic specification is much more efficient than gestural input would be ... this is the case when a single command applies to a massive group of events, or when a short list of commands replaces dozens of pointing and selecting gestures" (1996, p. 785); these are precisely the circumstances where a command-line environment excels.

Todd Winkler suggests that by "... modeling interaction with physical objects," GUI environments are easier and more intuitive, and that "GUI is slowly replacing older command-line interfaces, which require typing in somewhat cryptic commands to get the computer to do something" (1998, p. 48). Winkler ignores, however, that many compositional entities, such as a multi-dimensional gesture or a process, have no obvious physical representation. Command names, further, need not be cryptic; they may instead reflect a clear labeling scheme and system organization. And although command-line interfaces are used by a minority of computer users, they are still being developed and refined, and are unlikely to ever be replaced. Command-line interfaces, such as the UNIX shell, are at the core of most modern operating systems.

Many composers desire to use CAAC tools without writing code. This may be because they do not know how to program, or because they want to work faster than programming permits. As Oppenheim states, during the "implementation" of musical ideas "... the composer should not have to spend time writing code or consulting operating manuals" (1989, p. 227). The interactive command-line interface of athenaCL provides CAAC tools without the demands of a programming environment. If desired, however, programmatic control of the athenaCL Interpreter is easily accomplished. With such an arrangement, athenaCL Commands can be automated, scripted, and provided with diverse interfaces. Higher-level systems, built in Python or other languages (such as C or Java), may be constructed with alternative interfaces (GUI- or HTML-based, for example) and used to create and control single or multiple athenaCL Interpreters. The portability of Python, the modular design of athenaCL, and athenaCL's discrete Command language all support the development of a wide range of alternative control environments. An embedded Interpreter provides the full range of athenaCL functionality to nearly any form of higher-level environment. Possible applications of an embedded athenaCL Interpreter include server-side CGI scripts (through a web browser), interactive environments, multi-media and entertainment software, and specialized GUI applications.

Alternatively, the Interpreter and Commands can be bypassed, and any of the lower-level athenaCL components can be used as an API, providing the Python language with a library of specialized CAAC tools and objects. Within the flexibility of a general purpose language, even more diverse applications of athenaCL are possible. Schottstaedt expresses hope that "the compositional tools of the future do not restrict composers to anything less than the full power of a real [programming] language" (1989b, p. 224). Used as an API, athenaCL offers this "full power." With the provided interface, however, athenaCL offers CAAC tools to a broad audience.

Chapter 7. Postscript

Our machines have become a part of our sensibility. We now no longer expect human beings to labor in a manner more suited to machines. In fact, we find it undesirable to do anything that we perceive as possible for a machine to do, even when our parents or grandparents might have found such activity quite usual, if not especially pleasant. We appreciate, or at least tolerate, our machines until they somehow impinge on some activity regarded distinctly as a human endeavor. Then we collide with the idea, take stock, and decide whether to fight or flee.

—F. Richard Moore (1980, p. 215)

No specification was ever prepared for the design of athenaCL. No system functioned as a model for its initial form. Rather, I set off programming a system well before I understood what it needed to do, not to mention how it related to the preceding fifty years of research. My initial goals were simple: to build a tool to produce Csound score files, with a facility to handle Forte set-class pitch representations. Inspired by my initial progress, and convinced of the open-source development principle "release early and release often" (Raymond 2001), I distributed the software publicly.

From my current vantage five years later, attempting to build such a system from scratch seems remarkably unwise. Despite being a composer, I had studied only the fundamentals of C programming, had but a few months of experience with Csound and Max/MSP, and had just begun studying Python. I underestimated the size of the programming task, and was largely unaware of the range of alternative software options. Had I been wiser, I would have studied an alternative system, perhaps expanding it to meet my needs. No system at the time, however, offered an easy to use, cross-platform, open-source model. With only a vague idea of how to proceed, I began to develop a system employing Paths and Textures.

Every original component of the system has since been replaced, remodeled, and refined. The utility of the system has expanded to such a degree that the original model seems but a trivial experiment. Now, after examining the history of the field, studying the wide range of alternative software models, and refining the design of athenaCL into a comprehensive system, I am confident that athenaCL contributes, at least in part, to the paradigms of CAAC systems.

Most important, the system works, has been used productively by many (including myself), and continues to grow. Xenakis, looking back upon his initial experiments with the IBM 7090, stated, "stochastically speaking, my venture should have encountered failure" (1992, p. 134). Although for different reasons, my project likewise had a high probability of failure. Many single-developer, small-audience, non-commercial software systems find their place among the detritus of half-finished projects or, worse, well-conceived vaporware. Loy, after his thorough survey of composition systems, describes how "many languages become dead tongues when their implementors move on…" and that "it is remarkable how few … are generally available" (1989, p. 373). Such a statement is a strong argument for public code repositories and open-source development: even if abandoned, projects can be studied and resumed by others.

There are many factors that contributed to the progress of this system. Yet perhaps more than any single factor, it was the Python language itself that sustained the development of athenaCL. Had I attempted such a project in another language, I suspect it would have been abandoned long ago. The Python language allowed me to develop a design that took me five years to understand.

Future development of the athenaCL system will proceed along three lines. The first is the further development of modular components. Numerous additional algorithmic models and techniques can be included; implemented as ParameterObjects and Textures, these models will expand system resources. Support for additional music representations and synthesis languages, as Orchestras, OutputEngines, and EventModes, will provide even more diverse sonic production and greater interoperability.

The second is code profiling and optimization. The system has been created more for concerns of design clarity than for speed. Although Python supports this luxury, there are likely many ways the Python code can be improved to increase performance. As Textures and ParameterObjects grow in complexity, and as Events scale to smaller levels, processing speed becomes more significant. If native Python optimizations are not sufficient, Python supports the use of compiled C libraries within Python code. Redesigning performance-sensitive components of athenaCL as compiled C libraries would offer tremendous performance improvements, and can be integrated incrementally into the system.

The third is the creation of an external server for scheduling and performing AthenaObjects generated from remote athenaCL Interpreters. This design will allow one or more users to create small chunks of algorithmic materials (collections of Textures and Clones), and then send the resulting structures to a server. The server will schedule and temporally deploy the AthenaObject's EventSequences, optionally creating new EventSequences or temporal transformations as necessary. The server, via MIDI and OSC protocols, will provide RT communication, sending event data to external sound sources built in Max/MSP, SuperCollider, or other systems. This model will provide deferred RT performance.

The server and scheduler will extend the model suggested by athenaCL. With the development of numerous small, useful musical models in athenaCL, a higher level system, deploying these lower-level tools, may have the flexibility to create larger, more sophisticated, and more responsive algorithmic structures.

Appendix A. Notes on Included Compositions

In support of this dissertation, three digital audio compositions are included: *onomatopoeticized* (2004), *agoralalia* (2002), and *swarmmeme* (2003). Each of these works employs athenaCL at various compositional scales. Further, these works in part demonstrate the progress of the athenaCL system and the expansion of its resources. Of the many athenaCL features used in these compositions, a few are worth particular mention: *agoralalia* uses a system for generating rhythmic variations with genetic algorithms (Ariza 2002); *swarmmeme* employs a model of heterophony and ornamentation based on the analysis of Csángó laments and funeral music (Ariza 2003); and *onomatopoeticized* uses pitch groups and polyrhythms generated with Xenakis sieves (Ariza 2004b).

These compositions are not clinical demonstrations of the athenaCL system. No work employs athenaCL exclusively: in all cases athenaCL output is interpreted, edited, processed, and combined with other digital materials during musical realization.

Example A-1. Compact Disc Track Listing and Timing

```
1. onomatopoeticized (2004) 8:31
2. agoralalia      (2002) 8:10
3. swarmmeme       (2003) 7:52
```

Appendix B. ParameterObject Reference and Examples

B.1. Generator ParameterObjects

B.1.1. accumulator (a)

accumulator, initValue, parameterObject

Description: For each evaluation, this Generator adds the result of the Generator ParameterObject to the stored cumulative numeric value; the initialization value argument initValue is the origin of the cumulative value.

Arguments: (1) name, (2) initValue, (3) parameterObject {generator}

Sample Arguments: a, 0, (bg,rc,(1,3,4,7,-11))

Example B-1. accumulator Demonstration 1

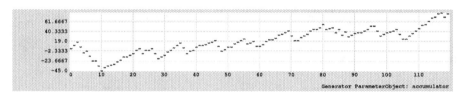

accumulator, 0, (basketGen, randomChoice, (1,3,4,7,-11))

Example B-2. accumulator Demonstration 2

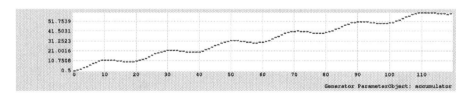

accumulator, 0, (waveSine, event, 20, 0, (constant, -0.5), (constant, 1.5))

B.1.2. analysisSelect (as)

analysisSelect, fileNameList, selectionString

Description: Given a list of file names (fileNameList), this Generator provides a complete file path to the file found within either the libATH/sadir or the user-selected sadir. Values are chosen from this list using the selector specified by the selectionString argument.

Arguments: (1) name, (2) fileNameList, (3) selectionString {"randomChoice", "randomWalk", "randomPermutate", "orderedCyclic", "orderedOscillate"}

Sample Arguments: `as, (), rc`

B.1.3. basketGen (bg)

basketGen, selectionString, valueList

Description: Choose values from a user-supplied list (valueList). Values can be strings or numbers. Values are chosen from this list using the selector specified by the selectionString argument.

Arguments: (1) name, (2) selectionString {"randomChoice", "randomWalk", "randomPermutate", "orderedCyclic", "orderedOscillate"}, (3) valueList

Sample Arguments: `bg, rc, (0,0.25,0.25,1)`

Example B-3. basketGen Demonstration 1

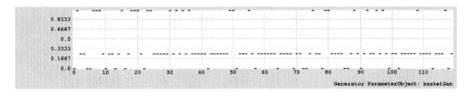

`basketGen, randomChoice, (0,0.25,0.25,1)`

Example B-4. basketGen Demonstration 2

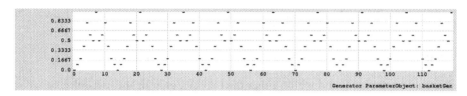

```
basketGen, orderedOscillate, (0,0.1,0.2,0.4,0.8,0.6,0.5,1)
```

Example B-5. basketGen Demonstration 3

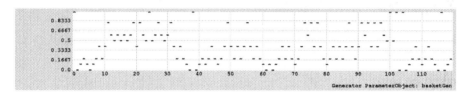

```
basketGen, randomWalk, (0,0.1,0.2,0.4,0.8,0.6,0.5,1)
```

B.1.4. breakPointLinear (bpl)

breakPointLinear, stepString, edgeString, pointList

Description: Provides a linear break-point function from a list of (x,y) coordinate pairs (pointList). A step type (stepString) determines if x values in the pointList refer to events or real-time values. Interpolated y values are the output of the Generator. The edgeString argument determines if the break-point function loops, or is executed once at the given coordinates.

Arguments: (1) name, (2) stepString {"event", "time"}, (3) edgeString {"loop", "single"}, (4) pointList

Sample Arguments: `bpl, e, 1, ((0,1),(6,0.3),(12,0.3),(18,0),(24,0.6))`

Example B-6. breakPointLinear Demonstration 1

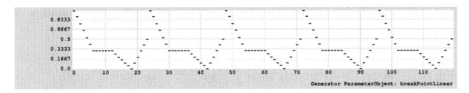

breakPointLinear, event, loop, ((0,1),(6,0.3),(12,0.3),(18,0),(24,0.6))

Example B-7. breakPointLinear Demonstration 2

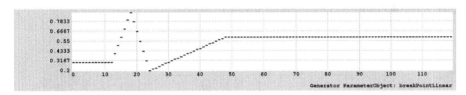

breakPointLinear, event, single, ((12,0.3),(18,0.9),(24,0.2),(48,0.6))

Example B-8. breakPointLinear Demonstration 3

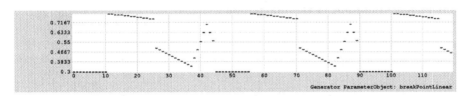

breakPointLinear, event, loop,
((0,0.3),(10,0.3),(11,0.8),(25,0.75),(26,0.5),(37,0.35),(42,0.7),(45,0.5))

B.1.5. breakPointPower (bpp)

breakPointPower, stepString, edgeString, pointList, exponent

Description: Provides an exponential break-point function from a list of (x,y) coordinate pairs (pointList). A step type (stepString) determines if x values in the pointList refer to events or real-time values. Interpolated y values are the output of the Generator.

The edgeString argument determines if the break-point function loops, or is executed once at the given coordinates. The exponent argument may be any positive or negative numeric value.

Arguments: (1) name, (2) stepString {"event", "time"}, (3) edgeString {"loop", "single"}, (4) pointList, (5) exponent

Sample Arguments: `bpp, e, l, ((0,1),(6,0.3),(12,0.3),(18,0),(24,0.6)), -1.5`

Example B-9. breakPointPower Demonstration 1

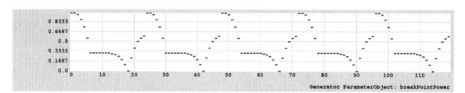

`breakPointPower, event, loop, ((0,1),(6,0.3),(12,0.3),(18,0),(24,0.6)), -1.5`

Example B-10. breakPointPower Demonstration 2

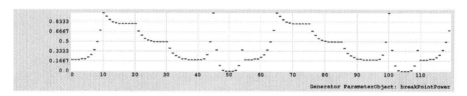

```
breakPointPower, event, loop,
((0,0.2),(10,1),(20,0.8),(30,0.5),(40,0.2),(45,1),(50,0),(55,1)), 3.5
```

Example B-11. breakPointPower Demonstration 3

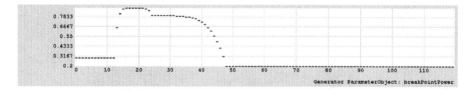

```
breakPointPower, event, single, ((12,0.3),(18,0.9),(24,0.8),(48,0.2)), -4
```

B.1.6. constant (c)

constant, value

Description: Return a constant string or numeric value.

Arguments: (1) name, (2) value

Sample Arguments: c, 0

Example B-12. constant Demonstration 1

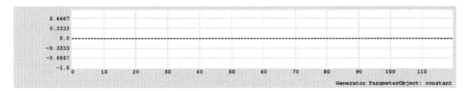

```
constant, 0
```

B.1.7. constantFile (cf)

constantFile, absoluteFilePath

Description: Given an absolute file path, a constant file path is returned as a string. Note: symbolic links (aliases or shortcuts) and home directory symbols (~) are expanded into complete paths.

Arguments: (1) name, (2) absoluteFilePath

Sample Arguments: cf,

B.1.8. cyclicGen (cg)

cyclicGen, directionString, min, max, increment

Description: Cycles between static minimum (min) and maximum (max) values with a static increment value. Cycling direction and type is controlled by the directionString argument.

Arguments: (1) name, (2) directionString {"upDown", "downUp", "up", "down"}, (3) min, (4) max, (5) increment

Sample Arguments: `cg, ud, 0, 1, 0.13`

Example B-13. cyclicGen Demonstration 1

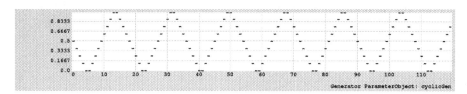

`cyclicGen, upDown, 0, 1, 0.13`

Example B-14. cyclicGen Demonstration 2

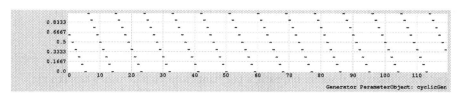

`cyclicGen, down, 0, 1, 0.13`

B.1.9. directorySelect (ds)

directorySelect, directoryFilePath, fileExtension, selectionString

Description: Within a user-provided directory (directoryFilePath) and all sub-directories, this Generator finds all files named with a file extension that matches the fileExtension argument, and collects these complete file paths into a list. Values are chosen from this list using the selector specified by the selectionString argument. Note: the fileExtension argument string may not include a leading period (for example, use "aif", not ".aif"); symbolic links (aliases or shortcuts) and home directory symbols (~) are expanded into complete paths.

Arguments: (1) name, (2) directoryFilePath, (3) fileExtension, (4) selectionString {"randomChoice", "randomWalk", "randomPermutate", "orderedCyclic", "orderedOscillate"}

Sample Arguments: `ds, ., aif, rw`

B.1.10. fibonacciSeries (fs)

fibonacciSeries, start, length, min, max, selectionString

Description: Provides values derived from a contigous section of the Fibonacci series. A section is built from an initial value (start) and as many additional values as specified by the length argument. Negative length values reverse the direction of the series. The resulting list of values is normalized within the unit interval. Values are chosen from this list using the selector specified by the selectionString argument. After selection, this value is scaled within the range designated by min and max; min and max may be specified with ParameterObjects.

Arguments: (1) name, (2) start, (3) length, (4) min, (5) max, (6) selectionString {"randomChoice", "randomWalk", "randomPermutate", "orderedCyclic", "orderedOscillate"}

Sample Arguments: `fs, 200, 20, 0, 1, oc`

Example B-15. fibonacciSeries Demonstration 1

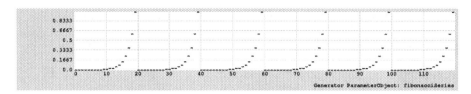

```
fibonacciSeries, 200, 20, (constant, 0), (constant, 1), orderedCyclic
```

Example B-16. fibonacciSeries Demonstration 2

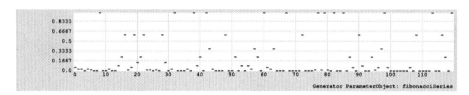

```
fibonacciSeries, 40, 20, (constant, 0), (constant, 1), randomChoice
```

Example B-17. fibonacciSeries Demonstration 3

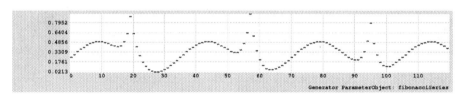

```
fibonacciSeries, 400, 20, (waveSine, event, 35, 0, (constant, 0.5), (constant,
0)), (cyclicGen, upDown, 0.6, 1, 0.03), orderedOscillate
```

B.1.11. henonBasket (hb)

henonBasket, xInit, yInit, parameterObject, parameterObject, valueCount, valueSelect, min, max, selectionString

Description: Performs the Henon map, a non-linear two-dimensional discrete deterministic dynamical system. For some parameter settings the system exhibits chaotic behavior, for others, periodic behavior; small changes in initial parameters may demonstrate the butterfly effect. Variables x and y describe coordinate positions; values a (alpha) and b (beta) configure the system. As the output range cannot be predicted, as many values as specified by the valueCount argument, as well as any combination of variables with the valueSelect argument, are generated and stored at initialization. These values are then scaled within the unit interval. Values are chosen from this list using the selector specified by the selectionString argument. After selection, this value is scaled within the range designated by min and max; min and max may be specified with ParameterObjects. Note: some values may cause unexpected results; alpha values should not exceed 2.0.

Arguments: (1) name, (2) xInit, (3) yInit, (4) parameterObject {a value}, (5) parameterObject {b value}, (6) valueCount, (7) valueSelect {"x", "y", "xy", "yx"}, (8) min, (9) max, (10) selectionString {"randomChoice", "randomWalk", "randomPermutate", "orderedCyclic", "orderedOscillate"}

Sample Arguments: `hb, 0.5, 0.5, 1.4, 0.3, 1000, x, 0, 1, oc`

Example B-18. henonBasket Demonstration 1

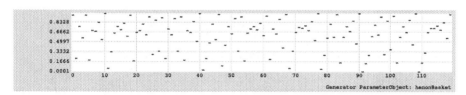

```
henonBasket, 0.5, 0.5, (constant, 1.4), (constant, 0.3), 1000, x, (constant,
0), (constant, 1), orderedCyclic
```

Example B-19. henonBasket Demonstration 2

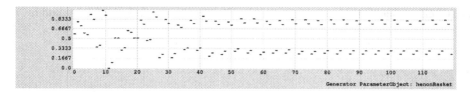

```
henonBasket, 0.5, 0.5, (constant, 0.5), (constant, 0.8), 1000, yx, (constant,
0), (constant, 1), orderedCyclic
```

Example B-20. henonBasket Demonstration 3

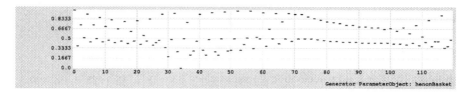

```
henonBasket, 0.5, 0.5, (cyclicGen, upDown, 0, 0.9, 0.05), (constant, 0.3),
1000, xy, (constant, 0), (constant, 1), orderedCyclic
```

B.1.12. iterateGroup (ig)

iterateGroup, parameterObject, parameterObject

Description: Allows the output of a source ParameterObject to be grouped (a value is held and repeated a certain number of times), to be skipped (a number of values are generated and discarded), or to be bypassed. A numeric value from a control ParameterObject is used to determine the source ParameterObject behavior. A positive value (rounded to the nearest integer) will cause the value provided by the source ParameterObject to be repeated that many times. After output of these values, a new control value is generated. A negative value (rounded to the nearest integer) will cause that many number of values to be generated and discarded from the source ParameterObject, and force the selection of a new control value. A value of 0 is treated as a bypass, and forces the selection of a new control value. Note: if the control ParameterObject fails to produce positive values after many attempts, a value will be automatically generated from the selected ParameterObject.

Arguments: (1) name, (2) parameterObject {source Generator}, (3) parameterObject {group or skip control Generator}

Sample Arguments: ig, (ws,e,30,0,0,1), (bg,rc,(-3,1,-1,5))

Example B-21. iterateGroup Demonstration 1

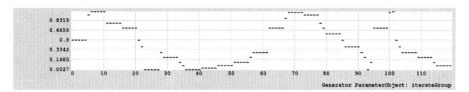

```
iterateGroup, (waveSine, event, 30, 0, (constant, 0), (constant, 1)),
(basketGen, randomChoice, (-3,1,-1,5))
```

Example B-22. iterateGroup Demonstration 2

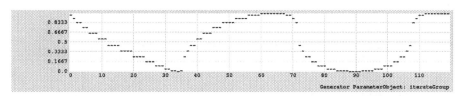

```
iterateGroup, (waveCosine, event, 30, 0, (constant, 0), (constant, 1)),
(waveTriangle, event, 20, 0, (constant, 4), (constant, -1))
```

B.1.13. iterateHold (ih)

iterateHold, parameterObject, parameterObject, parameterObject, selectionString

Description: Allows a variable number of outputs from a source ParameterObject, collected and stored in a list, to be held and selected. Values are chosen from this list using the selector specified by the selectionString argument. A numeric value from a size ParameterObject is used to determine how many values are drawn from the source ParameterObject. A numeric value from a refresh count ParameterObject is used to determine how many events must pass before a new size value is drawn and the source ParameterObject is used to refill the stored list. A refresh value of zero, once encountered, will prohibit any further changes to the stored list. Note: if the size ParameterObject fails to produce a non-zero value for the first event, an alternative count value will be assigned.

Arguments: (1) name, (2) parameterObject {source Generator}, (3) parameterObject {size Generator}, (4) parameterObject {refresh count Generator}, (5) selectionString {"randomChoice", "randomWalk", "randomPermutate", "orderedCyclic", "orderedOscillate"}

Sample Arguments: `ih, (ru,0,1), (bg,rc,(2,3,4)), (bg,oc,(12,24)), oc`

Example B-23. iterateHold Demonstration 1

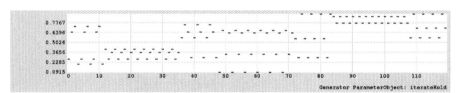

```
iterateHold, (randomUniform, (constant, 0), (constant, 1)), (basketGen,
randomChoice, (2,3,4)), (basketGen, orderedCyclic, (12,24)), orderedCyclic
```

Example B-24. iterateHold Demonstration 2

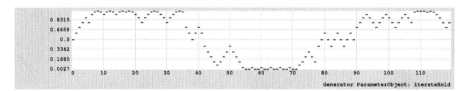

```
iterateHold, (waveSine, event, 30, 0, (constant, 0), (constant, 1)),
(basketGen, randomChoice, (3,4,5)), (basketGen, orderedCyclic, (6,12,18)),
orderedOscillate
```

B.1.14. iterateWindow (iw)

iterateWindow, parameterObjectList, parameterObject, selectionString

Description: Allows a ParameterObject, selected from a list of ParameterObjects, to generate values, to skip values (a number of values are generated and discarded), or to bypass value generation. A numeric value from a control ParameterObject is used to determine the selected ParameterObject behavior. A positive value (rounded to the nearest integer) will cause the selected ParameterObject to produce that many new values. After output of these values, a new ParameterObject is selected. A negative value (rounded to the nearest integer) will cause the selected ParameterObject to generate and discard that many values, and force the selection of a new ParameterObject. A value equal to 0 is treated as a bypass, and forces the selection of a new ParameterObject. ParameterObject selection is determined with a string argument for a selection method. Note: if the control ParameterObject fails to produce positive values after many attempts, a value will be automatically generated from the selected ParameterObject.

Arguments: (1) name, (2) parameterObjectList {a list of Generators}, (3) parameterObject {generate or skip control Generator}, (4) selectionString {"randomChoice", "randomWalk", "randomPermutate", "orderedCyclic", "orderedOscillate"}

Sample Arguments: iw, ((ru,0,1),(wt,e,30,0,0,1)), (bg,oc,(8,4,-2)), oc

Example B-25. iterateWindow Demonstration 1

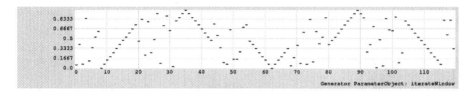

```
iterateWindow, ((randomUniform, (constant, 0), (constant, 1)), (waveTriangle,
event, 30, 0, (constant, 0), (constant, 1))), (basketGen, orderedCyclic,
(8,4,-2)), orderedCyclic
```

Example B-26. iterateWindow Demonstration 2

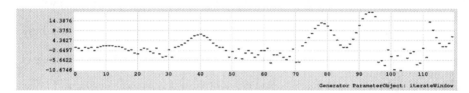

```
iterateWindow, ((randomUniform, (constant, 1), (accumulator, 0, (constant,
-0.2))), (waveSine, event, 15, 0.25, (accumulator, 1, (constant, 0.4)),
(constant, 1))), (basketGen, orderedCyclic, (8,8,-11)), randomChoice
```

B.1.15. lorenzBasket (lb)

lorenzBasket, xInit, yInit, zInit, parameterObject, parameterObject, parameterObject, valueCount, valueSelect, min, max, selectionString

Description: Performs the Lorenz attractor, a non-linear three-dimensional discrete deterministic dynamical system. The equations are derived from a simplified model of atmospheric convection rolls. For some parameter settings the system exhibits chaotic behavior, for others, periodic behavior; small changes in initial parameters may demonstrate the butterfly effect. Variables x, y, and z are proportional to convective intensity, temperature difference between descending and ascending currents, and the difference in vertical temperature profile from linearity. Values s (sigma), r, and b are the Prandtl number, the quotient of the Rayleigh number and the critical Rayleigh number, and the geometric factor. As the output range cannot be predicted, as many values as specified by the valueCount argument, as well as any combination of variables with the valueSelect argument, are generated and stored at initialization. These values are then scaled within the unit interval. Values are chosen from this list using the selector specified by the selectionString argument. After selection, this value is scaled within the range designated by min and max; min and max may be specified with ParameterObjects. Note: some values may cause unexpected results; r should not exceed 90.

Arguments: (1) name, (2) xInit, (3) yInit, (4) zInit, (5) parameterObject {r value}, (6) parameterObject {s value}, (7) parameterObject {b value}, (8) valueCount, (9) valueSelect {"x", "y", "z", "xy", "xz", "yx", "yz", "zx", "zy", "xyz", "xzy", "yxz", "yzx", "zxy", "zyx"}, (10) min, (11) max, (12) selectionString {"randomChoice", "randomWalk", "randomPermutate", "orderedCyclic", "orderedOscillate"}

Sample Arguments: `lb, 1.0, 1.0, 1.0, 28, 10, 2.67, 1000, xyz, 0, 1, oc`

Example B-27. lorenzBasket Demonstration 1

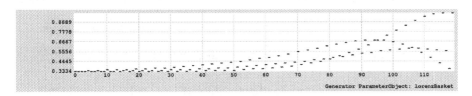

```
lorenzBasket, 1.0, 1.0, 1.0, (constant, 28), (constant, 10), (constant, 2.67),
1000, xyz, (constant, 0), (constant, 1), orderedCyclic
```

Example B-28. lorenzBasket Demonstration 2

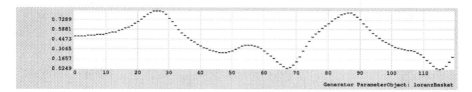

```
lorenzBasket, 0.5, 1.5, 10, (cyclicGen, down, 1, 80, 1.5), (constant, 10),
(constant, 12.4), 1000, x, (constant, 0), (constant, 1), orderedCyclic
```

B.1.16. logisticMap (lm)

logisticMap, initValue, parameterObject, min, max

Description: Performs the logistic map, or the Verhulst population growth equation. The logistic map is a non-linear one-dimensional discrete deterministic dynamical system. For some parameter settings the system exhibits chaotic behavior, for others, periodic behavior; small changes in initial parameters may demonstrate the butterfly effect. Variable x represents the population value; value p represents a combined rate for reproduction and starvation. The p argument allows the user to provide a static or dynamic value to the equation. Certain p-value presets can be provided with strings: "bi", "quad", or "chaos". If a number is provided for p, the value will be used to create a constant ParameterObject. The equation outputs values within the unit interval. These values are scaled within the range designated by min and max; min and max may be specified with ParameterObjects.

Arguments: (1) name, (2) initValue, (3) parameterObject {p value}, (4) min, (5) max

Sample Arguments: lm, 0.5, (wt,e,90,0,2.75,4), 0, 1

Example B-29. logisticMap Demonstration 1

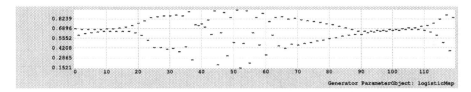

```
logisticMap, 0.5, (waveTriangle, event, 90, 0, (constant, 2.75), (constant,
4)), (constant, 0), (constant, 1)
```

Example B-30. logisticMap Demonstration 2

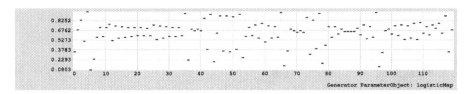

```
logisticMap, 0.1, (basketGen, randomWalk, (3,3,3,3.2,3.2,3.2,3.9,3.9,3.9)),
(constant, 0), (constant, 1)
```

Example B-31. logisticMap Demonstration 3

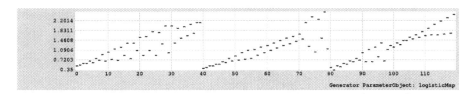

```
logisticMap, 0.5, (iterateGroup, (basketGen, randomChoice, (3,3.2,3.57)),
(basketGen, randomChoice, (5,7,9))), (breakPointLinear, event, loop,
((0,0.5),(60,0),(120,0.5)))), (breakPointLinear, event, loop, ((0,0.5),(40,3)))
```

B.1.17. mask (m)

mask, boundaryString, parameterObject, parameterObject, parameterObject

Description: Given values produced by two boundary parameterObjects in parallel, the Generator ParameterObject value is fit within these values. The fit is determined by the boundaryString: limit will fix the value at the nearest boundary; wrap will wrap the value through the range defined by the boundaries; reflect will bounce values in the opposite direction through the range defined by the boundaries.

Arguments: (1) name, (2) boundaryString {"limit", "wrap", "reflect"}, (3) parameterObject {first boundary}, (4) parameterObject {second boundary}, (5) parameterObject {generator of masked values}

Sample Arguments: m, l, (ws,e,60,0,0.5,0), (wc,e,90,0,0.5,1), (ru,0,1)

Example B-32. mask Demonstration 1

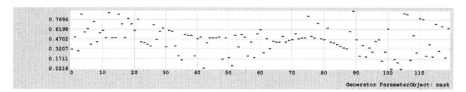

```
mask, limit, (waveSine, event, 60, 0, (constant, 0.5), (constant, 0)),
(waveCosine, event, 90, 0, (constant, 0.5), (constant, 1)), (randomUniform,
(constant, 0), (constant, 1))
```

Example B-33. mask Demonstration 2

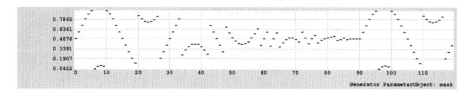

```
mask, wrap, (breakPointLinear, event, loop, ((0,0),(90,0.5))),
(breakPointLinear, event, loop, ((0,1),(90,0.5))), (waveSine, event, 30, 0,
(constant, 0), (constant, 1))
```

Example B-34. mask Demonstration 3

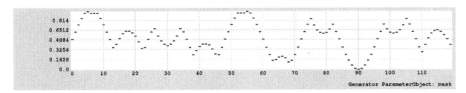

```
mask, reflect, (waveSine, event, 60, 0.25, (constant, 0.7), (constant, 1)),
(breakPointLinear, event, loop, ((0,0.4),(90,0),(120,0.4))), (waveSine, event,
24, 0, (constant, 0), (constant, 1))
```

B.1.18. markovGeneratorAnalysis (mga)

markovGeneratorAnalysis, parameterObject, valueCount, maxAnalysisOrder,
parameterObject

Description: Produces values by means of a Markov analysis of values provided by a source Generator ParameterObject; the analysis of these values is used with a dynamic transition order Generator to produce new values. The number of values drawn from the source Generator is specified with the valueCount argument. The maximum order of analysis is specified with the maxAnalysisOrder argument. Markov transition order is specified by a ParameterObject that produces values between 0 and the maximum order available in the Markov transition string. If generated-orders are greater than those available, the largest available transition order will be used. Floating-point order values are treated as probabilistic weightings: for example, a transition of 1.5 offers equal probability of first or second order selection.

Arguments: (1) name, (2) parameterObject {source Generator}, (3) valueCount, (4) maxAnalysisOrder, (5) parameterObject {output order value}

Sample Arguments: mga, (ws,e,30,0,0,1), 30, 2,

(mv,a{1}b{0}c{2}:{a=10|b=1|c=2},(c,0))

Example B-35. markovGeneratorAnalysis Demonstration 1

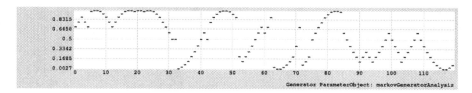

markovGeneratorAnalysis, (waveSine, event, 30, 0, (constant, 0), (constant,
1)), 30, 2, (markovValue, a{1}b{0}c{2}:{a=10|b=1|c=2}, (constant, 0))

Example B-36. markovGeneratorAnalysis Demonstration 2

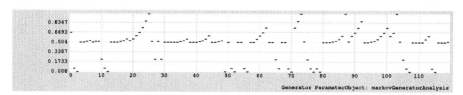

markovGeneratorAnalysis, (breakPointPower, event, loop,
((0,0.5),(10,1),(15,0)), 2), 15, 2, (basketGen, randomWalk, (0,1,2,2,1))

Example B-37. markovGeneratorAnalysis Demonstration 3

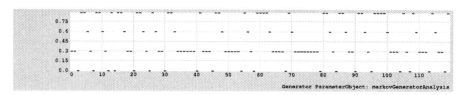

markovGeneratorAnalysis, (basketGen, orderedCyclic,
(0.3,0.3,0.3,0,0.9,0.9,0.6)), 28, 2, (markovValue,
a{1}b{0}c{2}:{a=10|b=1|c=2}, (constant, 0))

B.1.19. markovValue (mv)

markovValue, transitionString, parameterObject

Description: Produces values by means of a Markov transition string specification and a dynamic transition order generator. Markov transition order is specified by a ParameterObject that produces values between 0 and the maximum order available in the Markov transition string. If generated-orders are greater than those available, the largest available transition order will be used. Floating-point order values are treated as probabilistic weightings: for example, a transition of 1.5 offers equal probability of first or second order selection.

Arguments: (1) name, (2) transitionString, (3) parameterObject {order value}

Sample Arguments: mv, a{.2}b{.5}c{.8}d{0}:{a=5|b=4|c=7|d=1}, (c,0)

Example B-38. markovValue Demonstration 1

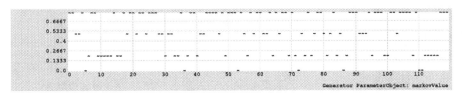

markovValue, a{.2}b{.5}c{.8}d{0}:{a=5|b=4|c=7|d=1}, (constant, 0)

B.1.20. noise (n)

noise, resolution, parameterObject, min, max

Description: Fractional noise (1/fn) Generator, capable of producing states and transitions between 1/f white, pink, brown, and black noise. Resolution is an integer that describes how many generators are used. The gamma argument determines what type of noise is created. All gamma values are treated as negative. A gamma of 0 is white noise; a gamma of 1 is pink noise; a gamma of 2 is brown noise; and anything greater is black noise. Gamma can be controlled by a dynamic ParameterObject. The value produced by the noise generator is scaled within the unit interval. This normalized value is then scaled within the range designated by min and max; min and max may be specified by ParameterObjects.

Arguments: (1) name, (2) resolution, (3) parameterObject {gamma value as string or number}, (4) min, (5) max

Sample Arguments: n, 100, pink, 0, 1

Example B-39. noise Demonstration 1

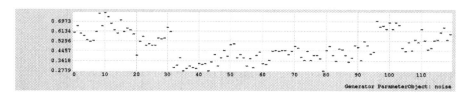

noise, 100, (constant, 1), (constant, 0), (constant, 1)

Example B-40. noise Demonstration 2

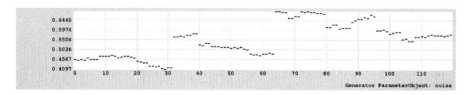

noise, 100, (constant, 3), (constant, 0), (constant, 1)

Example B-41. noise Demonstration 3

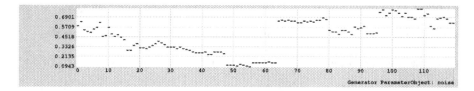

```
noise, 100, (waveTriangle, event, 120, 0, (constant, 1), (constant, 3)),
(constant, 0), (constant, 1)
```

Example B-42. noise Demonstration 4

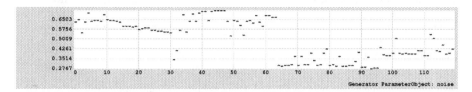

```
noise, 100, (basketGen, randomChoice, (3,3,3,3,2,1)), (constant, 0),
(constant, 1)
```

B.1.21. operatorAdd (oa)

operatorAdd, parameterObject, parameterObject

Description: Adds the value of the first ParameterObject to the second
ParameterObject.

Arguments: (1) name, (2) parameterObject {first value}, (3) parameterObject {second
value}

Sample Arguments: oa, (ws,e,30,0,0,1), (a,0.5,(c,0.03))

Example B-43. operatorAdd Demonstration 1

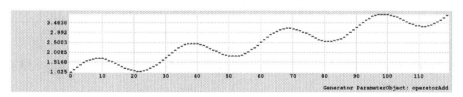

```
operatorAdd, (waveSine, event, 30, 0, (constant, 0), (constant, 1)),
(accumulator, 0.5, (constant, 0.03))
```

B.1.22. operatorDivide (od)

operatorDivide, parameterObject, parameterObject

Description: Divides the value of the first ParameterObject object by the second ParameterObject. Division by zero, if encountered, returns the value of the first ParameterObject unaltered.

Arguments: (1) name, (2) parameterObject {first value}, (3) parameterObject {second value}

Sample Arguments: od, (ws,e,30,0,0,1), (a,0.5,(c,0.03))

Example B-44. operatorDivide Demonstration 1

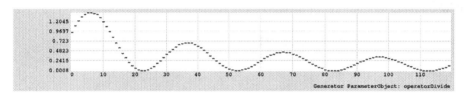

```
operatorDivide, (waveSine, event, 30, 0, (constant, 0), (constant, 1)),
(accumulator, 0.5, (constant, 0.03))
```

B.1.23. operatorMultiply (om)

operatorMultiply, parameterObject, parameterObject

Description: Multiplies the value of the first ParameterObject by the second.

Arguments: (1) name, (2) parameterObject {first value}, (3) parameterObject {second value}

Sample Arguments: om, (ws,e,30,0,0,1), (a,0.5,(c,0.03))

Example B-45. operatorMultiply Demonstration 1

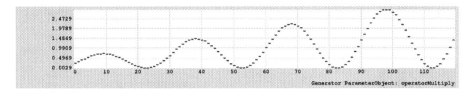

```
operatorMultiply, (waveSine, event, 30, 0, (constant, 0), (constant, 1)),
(accumulator, 0.5, (constant, 0.03))
```

B.1.24. operatorPower (op)

operatorPower, parameterObject, parameterObject

Description: Raises the value of the first ParameterObject to the power of the second ParameterObject.

Arguments: (1) name, (2) parameterObject {first value}, (3) parameterObject {second value}

Sample Arguments: op, (ws,e,30,0,0,1), (a,0.5,(c,0.03))

Example B-46. operatorPower Demonstration 1

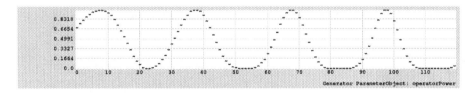

```
operatorPower, (waveSine, event, 30, 0, (constant, 0), (constant, 1)),
(accumulator, 0.5, (constant, 0.03))
```

B.1.25. operatorSubtract (os)

operatorSubtract, parameterObject, parameterObject

Description: Subtracts the value of the second ParameterObject from the first ParameterObject.

Arguments: (1) name, (2) parameterObject {first value}, (3) parameterObject {second value}

Sample Arguments: os, (ws,e,30,0,0,1), (a,0.5,(c,0.03))

Example B-47. operatorSubtract Demonstration 1

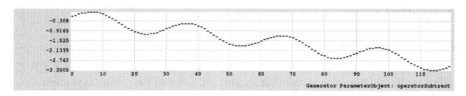

```
operatorSubtract, (waveSine, event, 30, 0, (constant, 0), (constant, 1)),
(accumulator, 0.5, (constant, 0.03))
```

B.1.26. pathRead (pr)

pathRead, pathFormatString

Description: Extracts pitch information from the current Multiset within a Texture's Path. Data can be presented in a variety of formats including representations of the Multiset as "forte", "mason", or data on the current active pitch as "fq" (frequency), "ps" (psReal), "midi" (midi pitch values), "pch" (Csound pitch octave format), or "name" (alphabetic note names).

Arguments: (1) name, (2) pathFormatString {"forte", "mason", "fq", "ps", "midi", "pch", "name"}

Sample Arguments: pr, forte

B.1.27. quantize (q)

quantize, parameterObject, parameterObject, stepCount, parameterObject, parameterObject

Description: Dynamic grid size and grid position quantization. For each value provided by the source ParameterObject, a grid is created. This grid is made by taking the number of steps specified by the stepCount integer from the step width Generator ParameterObject. The absolute value of these widths are used to create a grid above and below the reference value, with grid steps taken in order. The value provided by the source ParameterObject is found within this grid, and pulled to the nearest grid line. The degree of pull can be a dynamically allocated with a unit-interval quantize pull ParameterObject. A value of 1 forces all values to snap to the grid; a value of .5 will cause a weighted attraction.

Arguments: (1) name, (2) parameterObject {grid reference value Generator}, (3) parameterObject {step width Generator}, (4) stepCount, (5) parameterObject {unit interval measure of quantize pull}, (6) parameterObject {source Generator}

Sample Arguments: `q, (c,0), (c,0.25), 1, (c,1), (ru,0,1)`

Example B-48. quantize Demonstration 1

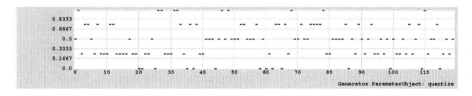

```
quantize, (constant, 0), (constant, 0.25), 1, (constant, 1), (randomUniform,
(constant, 0), (constant, 1))
```

Example B-49. quantize Demonstration 2

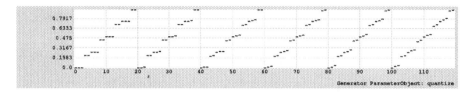

```
quantize, (constant, 0), (basketGen, orderedCyclic, (0.05,0.2)), 2,
(breakPointLinear, event, loop, ((0,1),(120,0.5))), (wavePowerUp, event, 20,
-2, 0, (constant, 0), (constant, 1))
```

Example B-50. quantize Demonstration 3

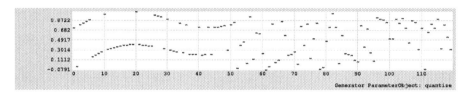

```
quantize, (waveSine, event, 60, 0, (constant, 1.25), (constant, 1.75)),
(cyclicGen, upDown, 0.3, 0.9, 0.006), 1, (breakPointLinear, event, loop,
((0,1),(40,1),(120,0.25))), (randomUniform, (constant, 0), (constant, 1))
```

B.1.28. randomBeta (rb)

randomBeta, alpha, beta, min, max

Description: Provides random numbers between 0 and 1 within a Beta distribution. This value is scaled within the range designated by min and max; min and max may be specified with ParameterObjects. Note: alpha and beta values should be between 0 and 1; small alpha values increase the probability of events on the lower boundary; small beta values increase the probability of events on the upper boundary.

Arguments: (1) name, (2) alpha, (3) beta, (4) min, (5) max

Sample Arguments: rb, 0.5, 0.5, 0, 1

Example B-51. randomBeta Demonstration 1

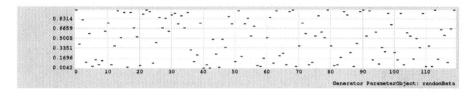

```
randomBeta, 0.5, 0.5, (constant, 0), (constant, 1)
```

Example B-52. randomBeta Demonstration 2

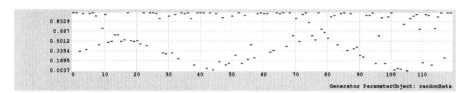

```
randomBeta, 0.2, 0.2, (waveSine, event, 60, 0, (constant, 0), (constant,
0.5)), (constant, 1)
```

B.1.29. randomBilateralExponential (rbe)

randomBilateralExponential, lambda, min, max

Description: Provides random numbers between 0 and 1 within a bilateral exponential distribution. This value is scaled within the range designated by min and max; min and max may be specified with ParameterObjects.

Arguments: (1) name, (2) lambda, (3) min, (4) max

Sample Arguments: rbe, 0.5, 0, 1

Example B-53. randomBilateralExponential Demonstration 1

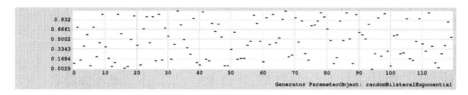

randomBilateralExponential, 0.5, (constant, 0), (constant, 1)

Example B-54. randomBilateralExponential Demonstration 2

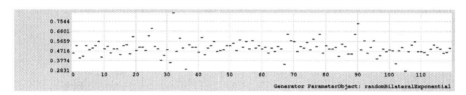

randomBilateralExponential, 10.0, (constant, 0), (constant, 1)

Example B-55. randomBilateralExponential Demonstration 3

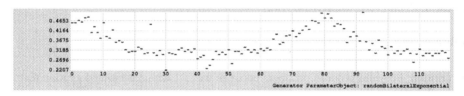

randomBilateralExponential, 20.0, (constant, 0), (breakPointPower, event,
loop, ((0,1),(40,0.6),(80,1)), 2)

B.1.30. randomCauchy (rc)

randomCauchy, alpha, mu, min, max

Description: Provides random numbers between 0 and 1 within a Cauchy distribution.
This value is scaled within the range designated by min and max; min and max may be
specified with ParameterObjects. Note: suggested values: alpha = 0.1, mu = 0.5.

Arguments: (1) name, (2) alpha, (3) mu, (4) min, (5) max

Sample Arguments: `rc, 0.1, 0.5, 0, 1`

Example B-56. randomCauchy Demonstration 1

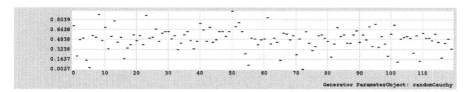

randomCauchy, 0.1, 0.5, (constant, 0), (constant, 1)

Example B-57. randomCauchy Demonstration 2

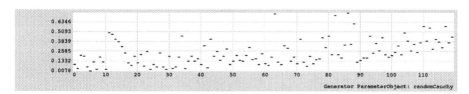

randomCauchy, 0.1, 0.1, (constant, 1), (breakPointPower, event, loop,
((0,0),(120,0.3)), 2)

Example B-58. randomCauchy Demonstration 3

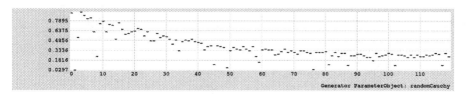

randomCauchy, 0.1, 0.9, (constant, 0), (breakPointPower, event, loop,
((0,1),(120,0.3)), 2)

B.1.31. randomExponential (re)

randomExponential, lambda, min, max

Description: Provides random numbers between 0 and 1 within an exponential distribution. This value is scaled within the range designated by min and max; min and max may be specified with ParameterObjects. Lambda values should be between 0 and 1. Lambda values control the spread of values; larger values increase the probability of events near the minimum.

Arguments: (1) name, (2) lambda, (3) min, (4) max

Sample Arguments: `re, 0.5, 0, 1`

Example B-59. randomExponential Demonstration 1

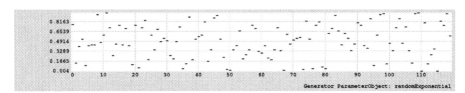

`randomExponential, 0.5, (constant, 0), (constant, 1)`

Example B-60. randomExponential Demonstration 2

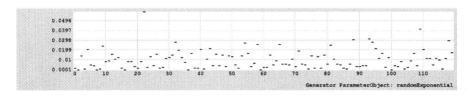

`randomExponential, 100.0, (constant, 0), (constant, 1)`

Example B-61. randomExponential Demonstration 3

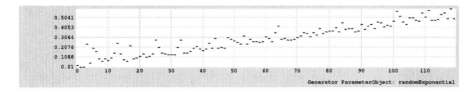

```
randomExponential, 10.0, (breakPointLinear, event, loop, ((0,0),(120,0.5)))),
(breakPointLinear, event, loop, ((0,0.5),(120,1)))
```

B.1.32. randomGauss (rg)

randomGauss, mu, sigma, min, max

Description: Provides random numbers between 0 and 1 within a Gaussian distribution. This value is scaled within the range designated by min and max; min and max may be specified with ParameterObjects. Note: suggested values: mu = 0.5, sigma = 0.1.

Arguments: (1) name, (2) mu, (3) sigma, (4) min, (5) max

Sample Arguments: rg, 0.5, 0.1, 0, 1

Example B-62. randomGauss Demonstration 1

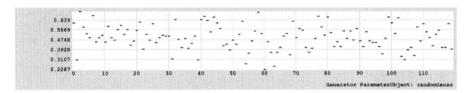

```
randomGauss, 0.5, 0.1, (constant, 0), (constant, 1)
```

Example B-63. randomGauss Demonstration 2

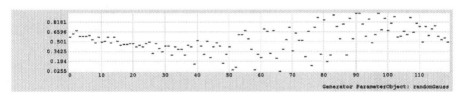

```
randomGauss, 0.5, 0.5, (waveSine, event, 120, 0.25, (constant, 0), (constant,
0.5)), (waveSine, event, 120, 0.5, (constant, 1), (constant, 0.5))
```

B.1.33. randomInverseExponential (rie)

randomInverseExponential, lambda, min, max

Description: Provides random numbers between 0 and 1 within an inverse exponential distribution. This value is scaled within the range designated by min and max; min and max may be specified with ParameterObjects.

Arguments: (1) name, (2) lambda, (3) min, (4) max

Sample Arguments: `rie, 0.5, 0, 1`

Example B-64. randomInverseExponential Demonstration 1

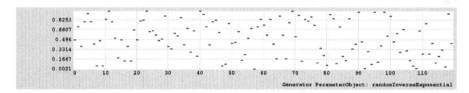

`randomInverseExponential, 0.5, (constant, 0), (constant, 1)`

Example B-65. randomInverseExponential Demonstration 2

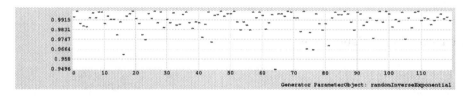

`randomInverseExponential, 100.0, (constant, 0), (constant, 1)`

Example B-66. randomInverseExponential Demonstration 3

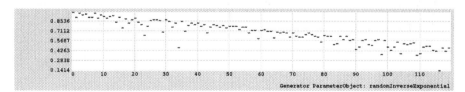

```
randomInverseExponential, 10.0, (breakPointLinear, event, loop,
((0,0.5),(120,0))), (breakPointLinear, event, loop, ((0,1),(120,0.5)))
```

B.1.34. randomInverseLinear (ril)

randomInverseLinear, min, max

Description: Provides random numbers between 0 and 1 within a linearly increasing distribution. This value is scaled within the range designated by min and max; min and max may be specified with ParameterObjects. Note: values are distributed more strongly toward max.

Arguments: (1) name, (2) min, (3) max

Sample Arguments: `ril, 0, 1`

Example B-67. randomInverseLinear Demonstration 1

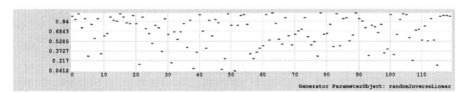

```
randomInverseLinear, (constant, 0), (constant, 1)
```

Example B-68. randomInverseLinear Demonstration 2

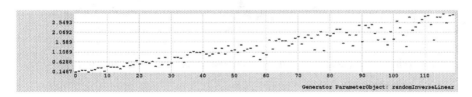

```
randomInverseLinear, (accumulator, 0, (constant, 0.01)), (accumulator, 0.2,
(constant, 0.03))
```

B.1.35. randomInverseTriangular (rit)

randomInverseTriangular, min, max

Description: Provides random numbers between 0 and 1 within an inverse triangular distribution. This value is scaled within the range designated by min and max; min and max may be specified with ParameterObjects. Note: values are distributed more strongly away from the mean of min and max.

Arguments: (1) name, (2) min, (3) max

Sample Arguments: `rit, 0, 1`

Example B-69. randomInverseTriangular Demonstration 1

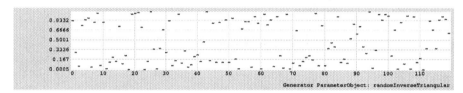

```
randomInverseTriangular, (constant, 0), (constant, 1)
```

Example B-70. randomInverseTriangular Demonstration 2

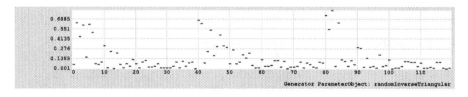

```
randomInverseTriangular, (constant, 0), (wavePowerDown, event, 40, 0, 2,
(constant, 1), (constant, 0.1))
```

B.1.36. randomLinear (rl)

randomLinear, min, max

Description: Provides random numbers between 0 and 1 within a linearly decreasing distribution. This value is scaled within the range designated by min and max; min and max may be specified with ParameterObjects. Note: values are distributed more strongly toward min.

Arguments: (1) name, (2) min, (3) max

Sample Arguments: r1, 0, 1

Example B-71. randomLinear Demonstration 1

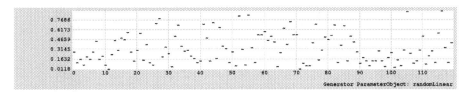

```
randomLinear, (constant, 0), (constant, 1)
```

Example B-72. randomLinear Demonstration 2

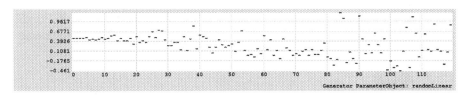

```
randomLinear, (accumulator, 0.5, (constant, -0.01)), (accumulator, 0.5,
(constant, 0.01))
```

B.1.37. randomTriangular (rt)

randomTriangular, min, max

Description: Provides random numbers between 0 and 1 within a triangular distribution. This value is scaled within the range designated by min and max; min and max may be specified with ParameterObjects. Note: values are distributed more strongly toward the mean of min and max.

Arguments: (1) name, (2) min, (3) max

Sample Arguments: rt, 0, 1

Example B-73. randomTriangular Demonstration 1

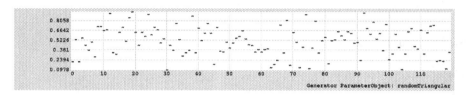

randomTriangular, (constant, 0), (constant, 1)

Example B-74. randomTriangular Demonstration 2

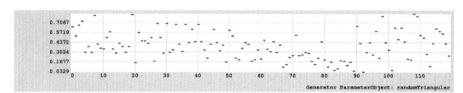

randomTriangular, (constant, 0), (wavePowerDown, event, 90, 0, -1.5,
(constant, 1), (constant, 0))

B.1.38. randomUniform (ru)

randomUniform, min, max

Description: Provides random numbers between 0 and 1 within an uniform distribution. This value is scaled within the range designated by min and max; min and max may be specified with ParameterObjects. Note: values are evenly distributed between min and max.

Arguments: (1) name, (2) min, (3) max

Sample Arguments: `ru, 0, 1`

Example B-75. randomUniform Demonstration 1

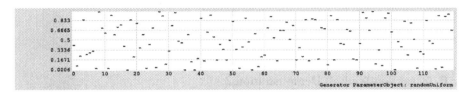

```
randomUniform, (constant, 0), (constant, 1)
```

Example B-76. randomUniform Demonstration 2

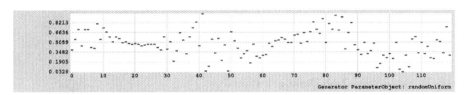

```
randomUniform, (waveSine, event, 60, 0, (constant, 0.5), (constant, 0)),
(waveSine, event, 40, 0.25, (constant, 1), (constant, 0.5))
```

B.1.39. randomWeibull (rw)

randomWeibull, alpha, beta, min, max

Description: Provides random numbers between 0 and 1 within a Weibull distribution. This value is scaled within the range designated by min and max; min and max may be specified with ParameterObjects. Note: suggested values: alpha = 0.5, beta = 2.0.

Arguments: (1) name, (2) alpha, (3) beta, (4) min, (5) max

Sample Arguments: `rw, 0.5, 2.0, 0, 1`

Example B-77. randomWeibull Demonstration 1

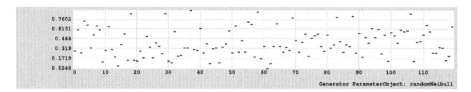

randomWeibull, 0.5, 2.0, (constant, 0), (constant, 1)

Example B-78. randomWeibull Demonstration 2

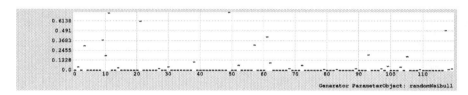

randomWeibull, 0.9, 0.1, (constant, 0), (constant, 1)

Example B-79. randomWeibull Demonstration 3

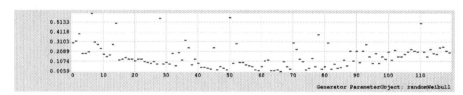

randomWeibull, 0.1, 0.9, (waveSine, event, 240, 0, (constant, 0), (constant, 0.4)), (constant, 1)

B.1.40. sieveFunnel (sf)

sieveFunnel, logicalString, length, min, max, parameterObject

Description: Using the user-supplied logical string, this Generator produces a Xenakis sieve segment within the z range of zero to one less than the supplied length. Values produced with the fill value Generator ParameterObject are funneled through this sieve:

given a fill value, the nearest sieve value is selected and returned. Note: the fill value ParameterObject min and max should be set to 0 and 1.

Arguments: (1) name, (2) logicalString, (3) length, (4) min, (5) max, (6) parameterObject {fill value generator}

Sample Arguments: `sf, 3|4, 24, 0, 1, (ru,0,1)`

Example B-80. sieveFunnel Demonstration 1

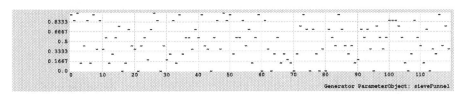

```
sieveFunnel, 3@0|4@0, 24, (constant, 0), (constant, 1), (randomUniform,
(constant, 0), (constant, 1))
```

Example B-81. sieveFunnel Demonstration 2

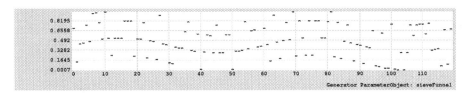

```
sieveFunnel, 5@0|13@0, 14, (waveSine, event, 60, 0, (constant, 0), (constant,
0.25)), (waveSine, event, 60, 0, (constant, 0.75), (constant, 1)),
(randomUniform, (constant, 0), (constant, 1))
```

Example B-82. sieveFunnel Demonstration 3

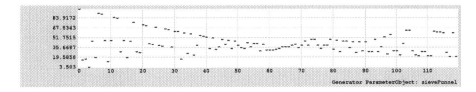

```
sieveFunnel, 13@5|13@7|13@11, 20, (accumulator, 0, (waveSine, event, 30, 1,
(constant, -0.75), (constant, 1.75))), (breakPointPower, event, loop,
((0,100),(160,20)), 2), (randomBeta, 0.4, 0.3, (constant, 0), (constant, 1))
```

B.1.41. sieveList (sl)

sieveList, logicalString, zMin, zMax, format, selectionString

Description: Produces a Xenakis sieve as a raw, variable format sieve segment list. A z is defined by the range of integers from zMin to zMax. Depending on format type, the resulting segment can be given as an integer, width, unit, or binary segment. Values are chosen from this list using the selector specified by the selectionString argument.

Arguments: (1) name, (2) logicalString, (3) zMin, (4) zMax, (5) format {"integer", "width", "unit", "binary"}, (6) selectionString {"randomChoice", "randomWalk", "randomPermutate", "orderedCyclic", "orderedOscillate"}

Sample Arguments: `sl, 3|4, -12, 12, int, oc`

Example B-83. sieveList Demonstration 1

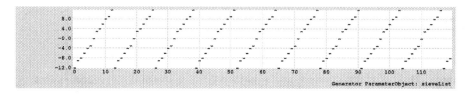

```
sieveList, 3@0|4@0, -12, 12, integer, orderedCyclic
```

B.1.42. sampleSelect (ss)

sampleSelect, fileNameList, selectionString

Description: Given a list of file names (fileNameList), this Generator provides a complete file path to the file found within either the libATH/ssdir or the user-selected ssdir. Values are chosen from this list using the selector specified by the selectionString argument.

Arguments: (1) name, (2) fileNameList, (3) selectionString {"randomChoice", "randomWalk", "randomPermutate", "orderedCyclic", "orderedOscillate"}

Sample Arguments: `ss, (), rc`

B.1.43. valueSieve (vs)

valueSieve, logicalString, length, min, max, selectionString

Description: Using the user-supplied logical string, this Generator produces a Xenakis sieve segment within the z range of zero to one less than the supplied length. The resulting list of values is normalized within the unit interval. Values are chosen from this list using the selector specified by the selectionString argument. After selection, this value is scaled within the range designated by min and max; min and max may be specified with ParameterObjects.

Arguments: (1) name, (2) logicalString, (3) length, (4) min, (5) max, (6) selectionString {"randomChoice", "randomWalk", "randomPermutate", "orderedCyclic", "orderedOscillate"}

Sample Arguments: `vs, 3&19|4&13@11, 360, 0, 1, oo`

Example B-84. valueSieve Demonstration 1

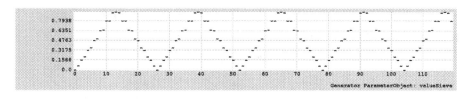

```
valueSieve, 3@0&19@0|4@0&13@11, 360, (constant, 0), (constant, 1),
```

```
orderedOscillate
```

Example B-85. valueSieve Demonstration 2

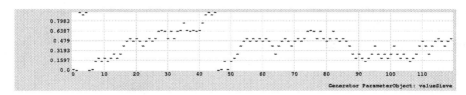

```
valueSieve, 3@0&19@0|4@0&13@11|5@2&15@2, 120, (constant, 0), (constant, 1),
randomWalk
```

Example B-86. valueSieve Demonstration 3

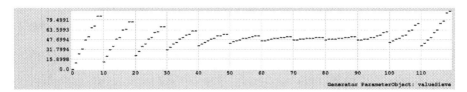

```
valueSieve, 3@0&19@0|4@0&13@11, 240, (breakPointPower, event, single,
((0,0),(80,48),(120,30)), -1.25), (breakPointPower, event, single,
((0,100),(80,52),(120,100)), 1.25), orderedCyclic
```

Example B-87. valueSieve Demonstration 4

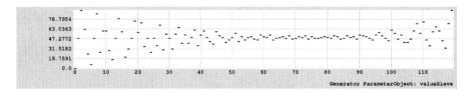

```
valueSieve, 3@0&19@0|4@0&13@11, 120, (breakPointPower, event, single,
((0,0),(80,48),(120,30)), -1.25), (breakPointPower, event, single,
((0,100),(80,52),(120,100)), 1.25), randomPermutate
```

B.1.44. waveCosine (wc)

waveCosine, stepString, secPerCycle, phase, min, max

Description: Provides cosinusoid oscillation between 0 and 1 at a rate given in either time or events per period. This value is scaled within the range designated by min and max; min and max may be specified with ParameterObjects. Depending on the stepString argument, the period rate (frequency) may be specified in spc (seconds per cycle) or eps (events per cycle). The phase argument is specified as a value between 0 and 1. Note: conventional cycles per second (cps or Hz) are not used for frequency.

Arguments: (1) name, (2) stepString {"event", "time"}, (3) secPerCycle, (4) phase, (5) min, (6) max

Sample Arguments: `wc, e, 30, 0, 0, 1`

Example B-88. waveCosine Demonstration 1

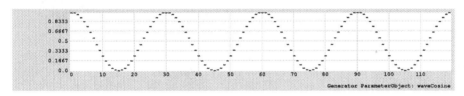

`waveCosine, event, 30, 0, (constant, 0), (constant, 1)`

Example B-89. waveCosine Demonstration 2

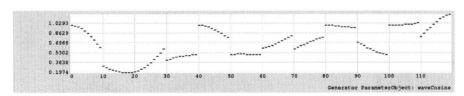

`waveCosine, event, 40, 0, (wavePulse, event, 20, 0, (constant, 1), (constant, 0.5)), (accumulator, 0, (constant, 0.01))`

B.1.45. wavePulse (wp)

wavePulse, stepString, secPerCycle, phase, min, max

Description: Provides a pulse (square) wave between 0 and 1 at a rate given in either time or events per period. This value is scaled within the range designated by min and max; min and max may be specified with ParameterObjects. Depending on the stepString argument, the period rate (frequency) may be specified in spc (seconds per cycle) or eps (events per cycle). The phase argument is specified as a value between 0 and 1. Note: conventional cycles per second (cps or Hz) are not used for frequency.

Arguments: (1) name, (2) stepString {"event", "time"}, (3) secPerCycle, (4) phase, (5) min, (6) max

Sample Arguments: `wp, e, 30, 0, 0, 1`

Example B-90. wavePulse Demonstration 1

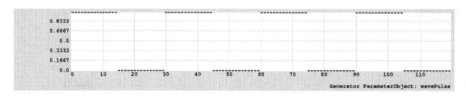

```
wavePulse, event, 30, 0, (constant, 0), (constant, 1)
```

Example B-91. wavePulse Demonstration 2

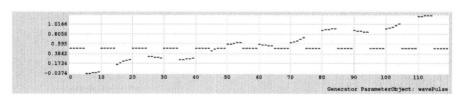

```
wavePulse, event, 10, 0, (accumulator, 0, (waveSine, event, 30, 0.75,
(constant, -0.01), (constant, 0.03))), (constant, 0.5)
```

B.1.46. wavePowerDown (wpd)

wavePowerDown, stepString, secPerCycle, phase, exponent, min, max

Description: Provides a power down wave between 0 and 1 at a rate given in either time or events per period. This value is scaled within the range designated by min and max; min and max may be specified with ParameterObjects. Depending on the stepString argument, the period rate (frequency) may be specified in spc (seconds per cycle) or eps (events per cycle). The phase argument is specified as a value between 0 and 1. Note: conventional cycles per second (cps or Hz) are not used for frequency.

Arguments: (1) name, (2) stepString {"event", "time"}, (3) secPerCycle, (4) phase, (5) exponent, (6) min, (7) max

Sample Arguments: `wpd, e, 30, 0, 2, 0, 1`

Example B-92. wavePowerDown Demonstration 1

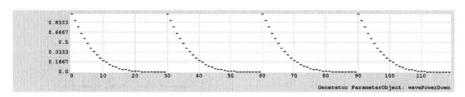

```
wavePowerDown, event, 30, 0, 2, (constant, 0), (constant, 1)
```

Example B-93. wavePowerDown Demonstration 2

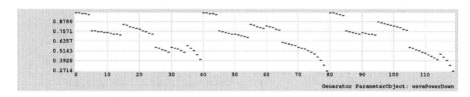

```
wavePowerDown, event, 40, 0, -1.5, (wavePulse, event, 30, 0, (constant, 0),
(constant, 0.2)), (wavePulse, event, 20, 0.25, (constant, 1), (constant, 0.8))
```

B.1.47. wavePowerUp (wpu)

wavePowerUp, stepString, secPerCycle, phase, exponent, min, max

Description: Provides a power up wave between 0 and 1 at a rate given in either time or events per period. This value is scaled within the range designated by min and max; min and max may be specified with ParameterObjects. Depending on the stepString argument, the period rate (frequency) may be specified in spc (seconds per cycle) or eps (events per cycle). The phase argument is specified as a value between 0 and 1. Note: conventional cycles per second (cps or Hz) are not used for frequency.

Arguments: (1) name, (2) stepString {"event", "time"}, (3) secPerCycle, (4) phase, (5) exponent, (6) min, (7) max

Sample Arguments: `wpu, e, 30, 0, 2, 0, 1`

Example B-94. wavePowerUp Demonstration 1

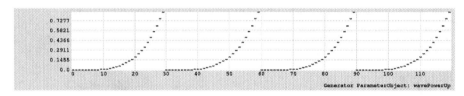

`wavePowerUp, event, 30, 0, 2, (constant, 0), (constant, 1)`

Example B-95. wavePowerUp Demonstration 2

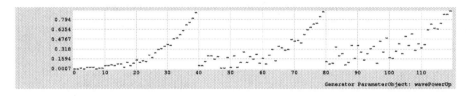

`wavePowerUp, event, 40, 0, 2, (randomUniform, (constant, 0), (accumulator, 0, (constant, 0.005))), (constant, 1)`

B.1.48. waveSine (ws)

waveSine, stepString, secPerCycle, phase, min, max

Description: Provides sinusoid oscillation between 0 and 1 at a rate given in either time or events per period. This value is scaled within the range designated by min and max; min and max may be specified with ParameterObjects. Depending on the stepString argument, the period rate (frequency) may be specified in spc (seconds per cycle) or eps (events per cycle). The phase argument is specified as a value between 0 and 1. Note: conventional cycles per second (cps or Hz) are not used for frequency.

Arguments: (1) name, (2) stepString {"event", "time"}, (3) secPerCycle, (4) phase, (5) min, (6) max

Sample Arguments: ws, e, 30, 0, 0, 1

Example B-96. waveSine Demonstration 1

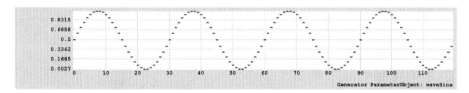

waveSine, event, 30, 0, (constant, 0), (constant, 1)

Example B-97. waveSine Demonstration 2

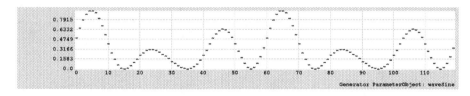

waveSine, event, 20, 0, (constant, 0), (waveSine, event, 60, 0.25, (constant, 0.25), (constant, 1))

B.1.49. waveSawDown (wsd)

waveSawDown, stepString, secPerCycle, phase, min, max

Description: Provides a saw-down wave between 0 and 1 at a rate given in either time or events per period. This value is scaled within the range designated by min and max; min and max may be specified with ParameterObjects. Depending on the stepString argument, the period rate (frequency) may be specified in spc (seconds per cycle) or eps (events per cycle). The phase argument is specified as a value between 0 and 1. Note: conventional cycles per second (cps or Hz) are not used for frequency.

Arguments: (1) name, (2) stepString {"event", "time"}, (3) secPerCycle, (4) phase, (5) min, (6) max

Sample Arguments: `wsd, e, 30, 0, 0, 1`

Example B-98. waveSawDown Demonstration 1

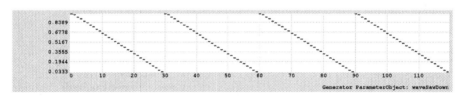

`waveSawDown, event, 30, 0, (constant, 0), (constant, 1)`

Example B-99. waveSawDown Demonstration 2

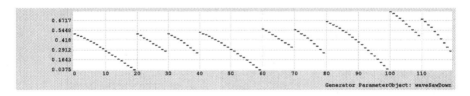

`waveSawDown, event, 20, 0, (wavePowerUp, event, 120, 0, 1.5, (constant, 0.5), (constant, 1)), (wavePowerDown, event, 40, 0.25, 1.5, (constant, 0.5),`

```
(constant, 0))
```

B.1.50. waveSawUp (wsu)

waveSawUp, stepString, secPerCycle, phase, min, max

Description: Provides a saw-up wave between 0 and 1 at a rate given in either time or events per period. This value is scaled within the range designated by min and max; min and max may be specified with ParameterObjects. Depending on the stepString argument, the period rate (frequency) may be specified in spc (seconds per cycle) or eps (events per cycle). The phase argument is specified as a value between 0 and 1. Note: conventional cycles per second (cps or Hz) are not used for frequency.

Arguments: (1) name, (2) stepString {"event", "time"}, (3) secPerCycle, (4) phase, (5) min, (6) max

Sample Arguments: `wsu, e, 30, 0, 0, 1`

Example B-100. waveSawUp Demonstration 1

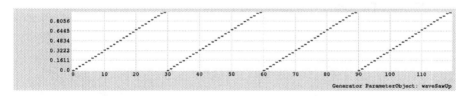

```
waveSawUp, event, 30, 0, (constant, 0), (constant, 1)
```

Example B-101. waveSawUp Demonstration 2

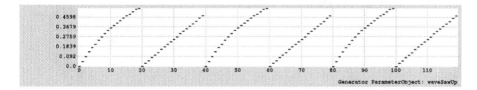

```
waveSawUp, event, 20, 0, (wavePowerDown, event, 40, 0, 1.5, (constant, 1),
(constant, 0.5)), (constant, 0)
```

B.1.51. waveTriangle (wt)

waveTriangle, stepString, secPerCycle, phase, min, max

Description: Provides a triangle wave between 0 and 1 at a rate given in either time or events per period. This value is scaled within the range designated by min and max; min and max may be specified with ParameterObjects. Depending on the stepString argument, the period rate (frequency) may be specified in spc (seconds per cycle) or eps (events per cycle). The phase argument is specified as a value between 0 and 1. Note: conventional cycles per second (cps or Hz) are not used for frequency.

Arguments: (1) name, (2) stepString {"event", "time"}, (3) secPerCycle, (4) phase, (5) min, (6) max

Sample Arguments: `wt, e, 30, 0, 0, 1`

Example B-102. waveTriangle Demonstration 1

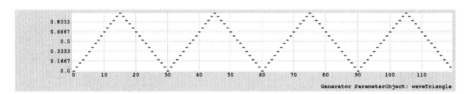

```
waveTriangle, event, 30, 0, (constant, 0), (constant, 1)
```

Example B-103. waveTriangle Demonstration 2

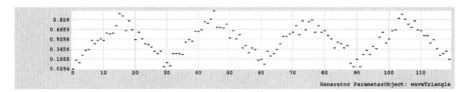

```
waveTriangle, event, 30, 0, (randomUniform, (constant, 0), (constant, 0.3)),
(randomUniform, (constant, 0.7), (constant, 1))
```

B.2. Rhythm ParameterObjects

B.2.1. binaryAccent (ba)

binaryAccent, pulseList

Description: Deploys two Pulses based on event pitch selection. Every instance of the first pitch in the current set of a Texture's Path is assigned the second Pulse; all other pitches are assigned the first Pulse. Amplitude values of events that have been assigned the second pulse are increased by a scaling function.

Arguments: (1) name, (2) pulseList {a list of Pulse notations}

Sample Arguments: `ba, ((3,1,1),(3,2,1))`

B.2.2. convertSecond (cs)

convertSecond, parameterObject

Description: Allows the use of a Generator ParameterObject to create rhythm durations. Values from this ParameterObject are interpreted as equal Pulse duration and sustain values in seconds. Accent values are fixed at 1. Note: when using this Rhythm Generator, tempo information (bpm) has no effect on event timing.

Arguments: (1) name, (2) parameterObject {duration values in seconds}

Sample Arguments: `cs, (ru,0.25,2.5)`

Example B-104. convertSecond Demonstration 1

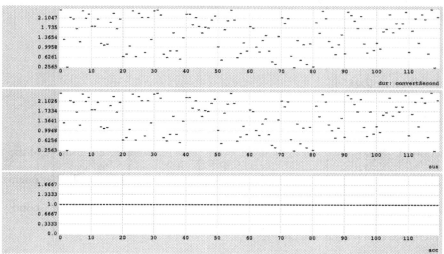

```
convertSecond, (randomUniform, (constant, 0.25), (constant, 2.5))
```

B.2.3. convertSecondTriple (cst)

convertSecondTriple, parameterObject, parameterObject, parameterObject

Description: Allows the use of three Generator ParameterObjects to directly specify duration, sustain, and accent values. Values for duration and sustain are interpreted as values in seconds. Accent values must be between 0 and 1, where 0 is a measured silence and 1 is a fully sounding event. Note: when using this Rhythm Generator, tempo information (bpm) has no effect on event timing.

Arguments: (1) name, (2) parameterObject {duration values in seconds}, (3) parameterObject {sustain values in seconds}, (4) parameterObject {accent values between 0 and 1}

Sample Arguments: `cst, (ws,e,30,0,0.25,2.5), (ws,e,60,0.25,0.25,2.5),` `(bg,rc,(0,1,1,1))`

Example B-105. convertSecondTriple Demonstration 1

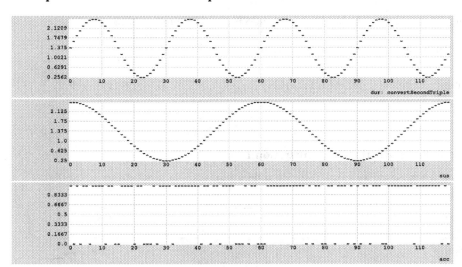

```
convertSecondTriple, (waveSine, event, 30, 0, (constant, 0.25), (constant,
2.5)), (waveSine, event, 60, 0.25, (constant, 0.25), (constant, 2.5)),
(basketGen, randomChoice, (0,1,1,1))
```

B.2.4. gaRhythm (gr)

gaRhythm, pulseList, crossover, mutation, elitism, selectionString

Description: Uses a genetic algorithm to create rhythmic variants of a source rhythm. Crossover rate is a percentage, expressed within the unit interval, of genetic crossings that undergo crossover. Mutation rate is a percentage, expressed within the unit interval, of genetic crossings that undergo mutation. Elitism rate is a percentage, expressed within the unit interval, of the entire population that passes into the next population unchanged. All rhythms in the final population are added to a list. Pulses are chosen from this list using the selector specified by the control argument.

Arguments: (1) name, (2) pulseList {a list of Pulse notations}, (3) crossover, (4) mutation, (5) elitism, (6) selectionString {"randomChoice", "randomWalk", "randomPermutate", "orderedCyclic", "orderedOscillate"}

Sample Arguments: `gr, ((3,1,1),(3,1,1),(6,1,1),(6,3,1),(3,1,0)), 0.7, 0.06, 0.01, oc`

Example B-106. gaRhythm Demonstration 1

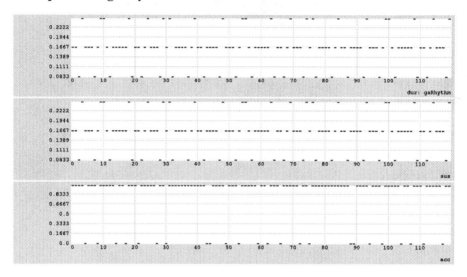

```
gaRhythm, ((3,1,+),(3,1,+),(6,1,+),(6,3,+),(3,1,o)), 0.7, 0.06, 0.01,
orderedCyclic
```

B.2.5. loop (l)

loop, pulseList, selectionString

Description: Deploys a fixed list of rhythms. Pulses are chosen from this list using the selector specified by the selectionString argument.

Arguments: (1) name, (2) pulseList {a list of Pulse notations}, (3) selectionString {"randomChoice", "randomWalk", "randomPermutate", "orderedCyclic", "orderedOscillate"}

Sample Arguments: 1, ((3,1,1),(3,1,1),(8,1,1),(8,1,1),(8,3,1),(3,2,0)), rp

Example B-107. loop Demonstration 1

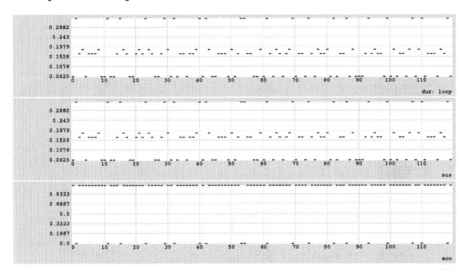

```
loop, ((3,1,+),(3,1,+),(8,1,+),(8,1,+),(8,3,+),(3,2,o)), randomPermutate
```

B.2.6. markovPulse (mp)

markovPulse, transitionString, parameterObject

Description: Produces Pulse sequences by means of a Markov transition string specification and a dynamic transition order generator. The Markov transition string must define symbols that specify valid Pulses. Markov transition order is specified by a ParameterObject that produces values between 0 and the maximum order available in the Markov transition string. If generated-orders are greater than those available, the largest available transition order will be used. Floating-point order values are treated as probabilistic weightings: for example, a transition of 1.5 offers equal probability of first or second order selection.

Arguments: (1) name, (2) transitionString, (3) parameterObject {order value}

Sample Arguments: `mp, a{3,1,1}b{2,1,1}c{3,2,0}:{a=3|b=4|c=1}, (c,0)`

Example B-108. markovPulse Demonstration 1

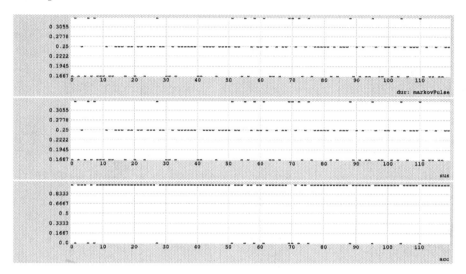

`markovPulse, a{3,1,1}b{2,1,1}c{3,2,0}:{a=3|b=4|c=1}, (constant, 0)`

B.2.7. markovRhythmAnalysis (mra)

markovRhythmAnalysis, parameterObject, pulseCount, maxAnalysisOrder, parameterObject

Description: Produces Pulse sequences by means of a Markov analysis of a rhythm provided by a source Rhythm Generator ParameterObject; the analysis of these values is used with a dynamic transition order Generator to produce new values. The number of values drawn from the source Rhythm Generator is specified with the pulseCount argument. The maximum order of analysis is specified with the maxAnalysisOrder argument. Markov transition order is specified by a ParameterObject that produces values between 0 and the maximum order available in the Markov transition string. If generated-orders are greater than those available, the largest available transition order will be used. Floating-point order values are treated as probabilistic weightings: for example, a transition of 1.5 offers equal probability of first or second order selection.

Arguments: (1) name, (2) parameterObject {source Rhythm Generator}, (3) pulseCount, (4) maxAnalysisOrder, (5) parameterObject {output order value}

Sample Arguments: `mra,`

`(1,((4,3,1),(4,3,1),(4,2,0),(8,1,1),(4,2,1),(4,2,1)),oc), 12, 2,`

`(cg,u,0,2,0.25)`

Example B-109. markovRhythmAnalysis Demonstration 1

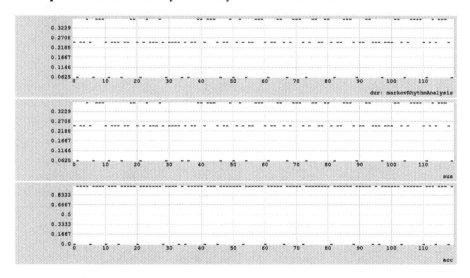

```
markovRhythmAnalysis, (loop,
((4,3,+),(4,3,+),(4,2,o),(8,1,+),(4,2,+),(4,2,+)), orderedCyclic), 12, 2,
(cyclicGen, up, 0, 2, 0.25)
```

B.2.8. pulseSieve (ps)

pulseSieve, logicalString, sieveLength, pulse, selectionString, articulationString

Description: Using the user-supplied logical string, this Generator produces a Xenakis sieve segment within the z range of zero to one less than the supplied length. This sieve, as a binary or width segment, is interpreted as a pulse list. The length of each pulse and the presence of rests are determined by the user-provided Pulse object and the articulationString argument. An articulationString of "attack" creates durations equal to the provided Pulse for every non-zero binary sieve segment value; an articulationString of "sustain" creates durations equal to the Pulse times the sieve segment width, or the duration of all following rests until the next Pulse. Values are chosen from this list using the selector specified by the selectionString argument.

Arguments: (1) name, (2) logicalString, (3) sieveLength, (4) pulse {a single Pulse notation}, (5) selectionString {"randomChoice", "randomWalk", "randomPermutate", "orderedCyclic", "orderedOscillate"}, (6) articulationString {"attack", "sustain"}

Sample Arguments: `ps, 3|4|5@2, 60, (3,1,1), oc, a`

Example B-110. pulseSieve Demonstration 1

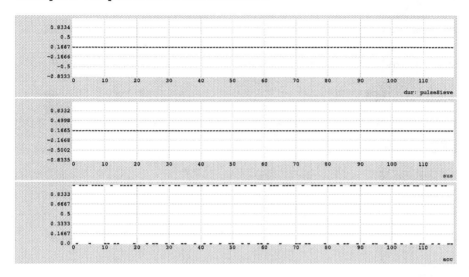

```
pulseSieve, 3@0|4@0|5@2, 60, (3,1,+), orderedCyclic, attack
```

Example B-111. pulseSieve Demonstration 2

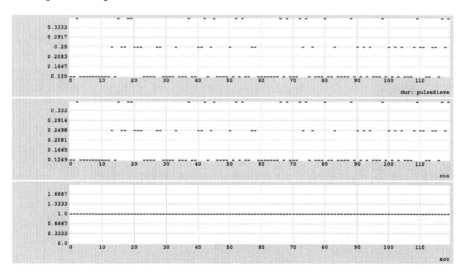

```
pulseSieve, 3@0|4@0|5@2, 60, (4,1,+), randomChoice, sustain
```

B.2.9. pulseTriple (pt)

pulseTriple, parameterObject, parameterObject, parameterObject, parameterObject

Description: Produces Pulse sequences with four Generator ParameterObjects that directly specify Pulse triple values and a sustain scalar. The Generators specify Pulse divisor, multiplier, accent, and sustain scalar. Floating-point divisor and multiplier values are treated as probabilistic weightings. Note: divisor and multiplier values of 0 are not permitted and are replaced by 1; the absolute value is taken of all values.

Arguments: (1) name, (2) parameterObject {pulse divisor}, (3) parameterObject {pulse multiplier}, (4) parameterObject {accent value between 0 and 1}, (5) parameterObject {sustain scalar greater than 0}

Sample Arguments: `pt, (bg,rc,(6,5,4,3)), (bg,rc,(1,2,3)), (bg,rc,(1,1,1,0)), (ru,0.5,1.5)`

Example B-112. pulseTriple Demonstration 1

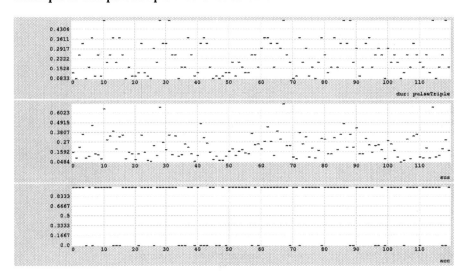

```
pulseTriple, (basketGen, randomChoice, (6,5,4,3)), (basketGen, randomChoice,
```

```
(1,2,3)), (basketGen, randomChoice, (1,1,1,0)), (randomUniform, (constant,
0.5), (constant, 1.5))
```

B.2.10. rhythmSieve (rs)

rhythmSieve, logicalString, sieveLength, selectionString, parameterObject

Description: Using the user-supplied logical string, this Generator produces a Xenakis sieve segment within the z range of zero to one less than the supplied length. The resulting binary sieve segment is used to filter any non-rest Pulse sequence generated by a Rhythm ParameterObject. The sieve is interpreted as a mask upon the ordered positions of the generated list of Pulses, where a sieve value retains the Pulse at the corresponding position, and all other Pulses are converted to rests. Note: any rests in the generated Pulse sequence will be converted to non-rests before sieve filtering.

Arguments: (1) name, (2) logicalString, (3) sieveLength, (4) selectionString {"randomChoice", "randomWalk", "randomPermutate", "orderedCyclic", "orderedOscillate"}, (5) parameterObject {Rhythm Generator}

Sample Arguments: rs, 3|4|5, 60, rw, (1,((3,1,1),(3,1,1),(3,5,1)))

Example B-113. rhythmSieve Demonstration 1

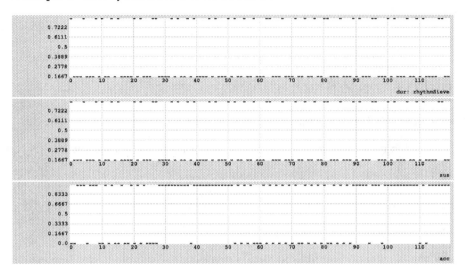

```
rhythmSieve, 3@0|4@0|5@0, 60, randomWalk, (loop, ((3,1,+),(3,1,+),(3,5,+)),
randomPermutate)
```

B.3. Filter ParameterObjects

B.3.1. bypass (b)

bypass

    Description: Each input value is returned unaltered.

    Arguments: (1) name

    Sample Arguments: b

Example B-114. bypass Demonstration 1

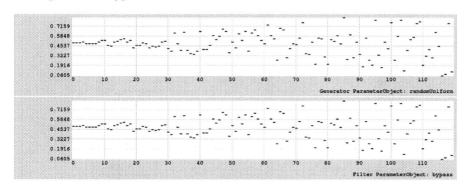

```
randomUniform, (breakPointLinear, event, loop, ((0,0.5),(120,0))),
(breakPointLinear, event, loop, ((0,0.5),(120,1)))
bypass
```

B.3.2. filterAdd (fa)

filterAdd, parameterObject

Description: Each input value is added to a value produced by a user-supplied ParameterObject.

Arguments: (1) name, (2) parameterObject {operator value generator}

Sample Arguments: `fa, (ws,e,30,0,0,1)`

Example B-115. filterAdd Demonstration 1

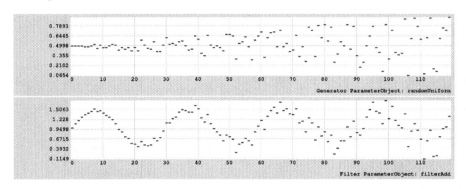

```
randomUniform, (breakPointLinear, event, loop, ((0,0.5),(120,0))),
(breakPointLinear, event, loop, ((0,0.5),(120,1)))
filterAdd, (waveSine, event, 30, 0, (constant, 0), (constant, 1))
```

B.3.3. filterMultiplyAnchor (fma)

filterMultiplyAnchor, anchorString, parameterObject

Description: All input values are first shifted so that the position specified by anchor is zero; then each value is multiplied by the value produced by the parameterObject. All values are then re-shifted so that zero returns to its former position.

Arguments: (1) name, (2) anchorString {"lower", "upper", "average", "median"}, (3) parameterObject {operator value generator}

Sample Arguments: fma, lower, (wc,e,30,0,0,1)

Example B-116. filterMultiplyAnchor Demonstration 1

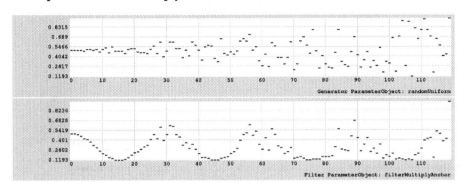

```
randomUniform, (breakPointLinear, event, loop, ((0,0.5),(120,0))),
(breakPointLinear, event, loop, ((0,0.5),(120,1)))
filterMultiplyAnchor, lower, (waveCosine, event, 30, 0, (constant, 0),
(constant, 1))
```

B.3.4. orderBackward (ob)

orderBackward

> Description: All values input are returned in reversed order.

> Arguments: (1) name

> Sample Arguments: ob

Example B-117. orderBackward Demonstration 1

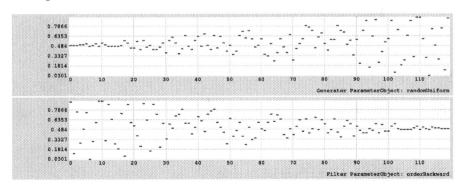

```
randomUniform, (breakPointLinear, event, loop, ((0,0.5),(120,0))),
(breakPointLinear, event, loop, ((0,0.5),(120,1)))
orderBackward
```

B.3.5. orderRotate (or)

orderRotate, rotationSize

Description: Rotates all input values as many steps as specified; if the number of steps is greater than the number of input values, the modulus of the input length is used.

Arguments: (1) name, (2) rotationSize

Sample Arguments: or, 40

Example B-118. orderRotate Demonstration 1

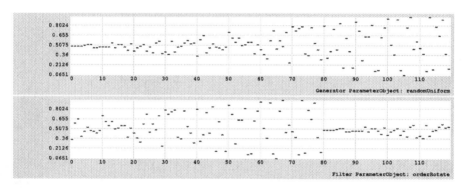

```
randomUniform, (breakPointLinear, event, loop, ((0,0.5),(120,0))),
(breakPointLinear, event, loop, ((0,0.5),(120,1)))
orderRotate, 40
```

B.3.6. pipeLine (pl)

pipeLine, filterParameterObjectList

Description: Provide a list of Filter ParameterObjects; input values are passed through each filter in the user-supplied order from left to right.

Arguments: (1) name, (2) filterParameterObjectList {a list of sequential Filter ParameterObjects}

Sample Arguments: `pl, ((or,40),(ob))`

Example B-119. pipeLine Demonstration 1

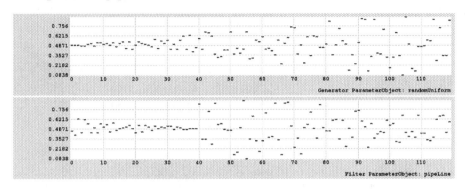

```
randomUniform, (breakPointLinear, event, loop, ((0,0.5),(120,0))),
(breakPointLinear, event, loop, ((0,0.5),(120,1)))
pipeLine, ((orderRotate, 40), (orderBackward))
```

B.3.7. replace (r)

replace, parameterObject

Description: Replace input values with values produced by a Generator ParameterObject.

Arguments: (1) name, (2) parameterObject {generator to replace original values}

Sample Arguments: `r, (ru,0,1)`

Example B-120. replace Demonstration 1

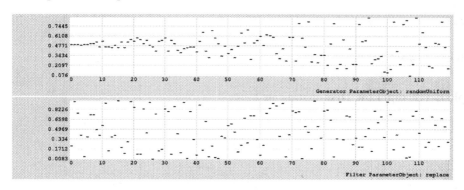

```
randomUniform, (breakPointLinear, event, loop, ((0,0.5),(120,0))),
(breakPointLinear, event, loop, ((0,0.5),(120,1)))
replace, (randomUniform, (constant, 0), (constant, 1))
```

B.4. TextureStatic ParameterObjects

B.4.1. levelFieldMonophonic (lfm)

levelFieldMonophonic, level

Description: Toggle between selection of local field (transposition) values per set of the Texture's Path, or per event.

Arguments: (1) name, (2) level {"set", "event"}

Sample Arguments: lfm, event

B.4.2. levelFieldPolyphonic (lfp)

levelFieldPolyphonic, level

Description: Toggle between selection of local field (transposition) values per set of the Texture's Path, per event, or per polyphonic voice event.

Arguments: (1) name, (2) level {"set", "event", "voice"}

Sample Arguments: `lfp, event`

B.4.3. levelOctaveMonophonic (lom)

levelOctaveMonophonic, level

Description: Toggle between selection of local octave (transposition) values per set of the Texture's Path, or per event.

Arguments: (1) name, (2) level {"set", "event"}

Sample Arguments: `lom, event`

B.4.4. levelOctavePolyphonic (lop)

levelOctavePolyphonic, level

Description: Toggle between selection of local octave (transposition) values per set of the Texture's Path, per event, or per polyphonic voice event.

Arguments: (1) name, (2) level {"set", "event", "voice"}

Sample Arguments: `lop, event`

B.4.5. loopWithinSet (lws)

loopWithinSet, onOff

Description: Controls if pitches in a set are repeated by a Texture within the set's duration fraction.

Arguments: (1) name, (2) onOff {"on", "off"}

Sample Arguments: `lws, on`

B.4.6. maxTimeOffset (mto)

maxTimeOffset, time

Description: Used to select an offset time in seconds. Offset is applied with the absolute value of a gaussian distribution after the Texture-generated event start time.

Arguments: (1) name, (2) time

Sample Arguments: `mto, 0.04`

B.4.7. nonRedundantSwitch (nrs)

nonRedundantSwitch, onOff

Description: Toggle selection of pitches between either random selection or random permutation.

Arguments: (1) name, (2) onOff {"on", "off"}

Sample Arguments: `nrs, on`

B.4.8. ornamentLibrarySelect (ols)

ornamentLibrarySelect, libraryName

Description: Selects a library of ornaments to use with a Texture.

Arguments: (1) name, (2) libraryName {"chromaticGroupC", "diatonicGroupA", "diatonicGroupB", "microGroupA", "microGroupB", "microGroupC", "trillGroupA", "off"}

Sample Arguments: `ols, diatonicGroupA`

B.4.9. ornamentMaxDensity (omd)

ornamentMaxDensity, percent

Description: Controls maximum percent of events that are ornamented. Density value should be specified within the unit interval.

Arguments: (1) name, (2) percent

Sample Arguments: `omd, 1`

B.4.10. parallelMotionList (pml)

parallelMotionList, transpositionList, timeDelay

Description: List is a collection of transpositions created above every Texture-generated base note. The timeDelay value determines the amount of time in seconds between each successive transposition in the transpositionList.

Arguments: (1) name, (2) transpositionList, (3) timeDelay

Sample Arguments: `pml, (), 0.0`

B.5. CloneStatic ParameterObjects

B.5.1. retrogradeMethodToggle (rmt)

retrogradeMethodToggle, name

Description: Selects type of retrograde transformation applied to Texture events.

Arguments: (1) name, (2) name {"timeInverse", "eventInverse", "off"}

Sample Arguments: `rmt, off`

B.5.2. timeReferenceSource (trs)

timeReferenceSource, name

Description: Selects time reference source used in calculating ParameterObjects.

Arguments: (1) name, (2) name {"cloneTime", "textureTime"}

Sample Arguments: `trs, textureTime`

Appendix C. Temperament and TextureModule Reference

C.1. Temperaments

C.1.1. Temperament Interleave24Even

Even steps of a 24 tone equal tempered scale

C.1.2. Temperament Interleave24Odd

Odd steps of a 24 tone equal tempered scale

C.1.3. Temperament Just

Static Just tuning

C.1.4. Temperament MeanTone

Static Mean Tone tuning

C.1.5. Temperament NoiseHeavy

Provide uniform random +/- 15 cent noise on each pitch

C.1.6. Temperament NoiseLight

Provide uniform random +/- 5 cent noise on each pitch

C.1.7. Temperament NoiseMedium

Provide uniform random +/- 10 cent noise on each pitch

C.1.8. Temperament Pythagorean

Static Pythagorean tuning

C.1.9. Temperament Split24Lower

Lower half of a 24 tone equal tempered scale

C.1.10. Temperament Split24Upper

Upper half of a 24 tone equal tempered scale

C.1.11. Temperament TwelveEqual

Twelve tone equal temperament

C.2. TextureModules

C.2.1. TextureModule LineGroove

This TextureModule performs each set of a Path as a simple monophonic line; pitches are chosen from sets in the Path randomly but non-redundantly.

C.2.2. TextureModule LineCluster

This TextureModule performs each set of a Path as a chord cluster, randomly choosing different voicings.

C.2.3. TextureModule MonophonicOrnament

This TextureModule performs each set of a Path as a literal line; pitches are chosen from sets in order, and are optionally repeated within a single set's duration. Algorithmic ornamentation is added to a line based on two factors: the selection of an ornament repertory, and the specification of ornament density.

C.2.4. TextureModule LiteralHorizontal

This TextureModule performs each set of a Path as a literal horizontal line; pitches are chosen from sets in fixed order, and are optionally repeated within a single set's proportional duration.

C.2.5. TextureModule DroneArticulate

This TextureModule treats each pitch in each set of a Path as an independent voice; each voice is written one at time over the complete time range of each set in the Texture.

C.2.6. TextureModule LiteralVertical

This TextureModule performs each set of a Path as a literal verticality; pitches are chosen from sets in fixed order, and are optionally repeated within a single set's proportional duration.

C.2.7. TextureModule IntervalExpansion

This TextureModule performs each set of a Path as a literal line; pitches are chosen from sets in order, and are optionally repeated within a single set's duration. Algorithmic ornamentation is added to a line based on two factors: the selection of an ornament repertory, and the specification of ornament density.

C.2.8. TextureModule DroneSustain

This TextureModule performs a simple vertical presentation of the Path, each set sustained over the complete duration proportion of the set within the Texture. Note: rhythm and bpm values have no effect on event durations.

Appendix D. OutputFormat and OutputEngine Reference

D.1. OutputFormats

D.1.1. acToolbox

acToolbox: AC Toolbox Environment file. (.act)

D.1.2. audioFile

audioFile: Pulse Code Modulation (PCM) file. (.synth.aif)

D.1.3. csoundBatch

csoundBatch: Platform specific script or batch file. (.bat)

D.1.4. csoundData

csoundData: Csound XML unified file format. (.csd)

D.1.5. csoundOrchestra

csoundOrchestra: Csound orchestra file. (.orc)

D.1.6. csoundScore

csoundScore: Csound score file. (.sco)

D.1.7. maxColl

maxColl: Max coll object data format. (.max.txt)

D.1.8. midiFile

midiFile: Standard MIDI file. (.mid)

D.1.9. textSpace

textSpace: Space delimited event list. (.space.txt)

D.1.10. textTab

textTab: Tab delimited event list. (.tab.txt)

D.1.11. xmlAthenaObject

xmlAthenaObject: athenaCL native XML format. (.xml)

D.2. OutputEngines

D.2.1. EngineAcToolbox

Translates each Texture and each Clone into a Section and writes an Environment file for loading within Paul Berg's AC Toolbox. A Parallel Section, containing references to each of these Sections, is also provided. Compatible with all Orchestras; GeneralMidi Orchestra will be used for event postMap conversions.

D.2.2. EngineAudioFile

Translates events to audio samples, and writes an audio file. Each event's amplitude is scaled between -1 and 1. Event timing and other event parameter data are stripped. Compatible with all Orchestras.

D.2.3. EngineCsoundExternal

Translates events to a Csound score for use with an external orchestra. Event parameters instrument number, start time, and duration are always the first three parameters. Additional event parameters taken from auxiliary parameters. Compatible with all Orchestras.

D.2.4. EngineCsoundNative

Translates events to a Csound score for use with the native Csound orchestra. All event parameters are retained. Compatible only with the CsoundNative Orchestra.

D.2.5. EngineCsoundSilence

Translates Texture and Clone events to a Csound score for use with the Csound Silence system by Michael Goggins. Event parameters follow a standard number and order. Standard panning control applied to x pan event parameter. Compatible only with the CsoundSilence Orchestra.

D.2.6. EngineMaxColl

Translates events to a Max coll object data format for use inside Max/MSP. All values are converted to MIDI integer values. Events, for each Texture or Clone, are stored as triples of MIDI pitch, MIDI velocity, and event time span. All events for Textures or Clones are labeled with numbered keys, starting from 1. Compatible with all Orchestras; GeneralMidi Orchestra will be used for event postMap conversions.

D.2.7. EngineMidiFile

Translates events to a standard (type 1) MIDI file. Compatible with all Orchestras; in all cases events are translated with the GeneralMidi Orchestra.

D.2.8. EngineText

Translate events to a plain text file. All event parameter values are separated by a delimiter (tab or space) and ended with a return carriage. Compatible with all Orchestras; EventMode Orchestra will be used for event postMap conversions.

Appendix E. Command Reference

E.1. AthenaHistory Commands

E.1.1. AH

AthenaHistory: Commands: Displays a list of all AthenaHistory commands.

E.1.2. AHexe

AHexe: AthenaHistory: Execute: Execute a command or a command range within the current history.

E.1.3. AHls

AHls: AthenaHistory: List: Displays a listing of the current history.

E.1.4. AHrm

AHrm: AthenaHistory: Remove: Deletes the stored command history.

E.2. AthenaObject Commands

E.2.1. AO

AthenaObject: Commands: Displays a list of all AthenaObject commands.

E.2.2. AOals

AOals: AthenaObject: Attribute List: Displays raw attributes of the current AthenaObject.

E.2.3. AOl

AOl: AthenaObject: Load: Load an athenaCL XML AthenaObject. Loading an AthenaObject will overwrite any objects in the current AthenaObject.

E.2.4. AOmg

AOmg: AthenaObject: Merge: Merges a selected XML AthenaObject with the current AthenaObject.

E.2.5. AOrm

AOrm: AthenaObject: Remove: Reinitialize the AthenaObject, destroying all Paths, Textures, and Clones.

E.2.6. AOw

AOw: AthenaObject: Save: Saves an AthenaObject file, containing all Paths, Textures, Clones, and environment settings.

E.3. AthenaPreferences Commands

E.3.1. AP

AthenaPreferences: Commands: Displays a list of all AthenaPreferences commands.

E.3.2. APcc

APcc: AthenaPreferences: Customize Cursor: Lets the user customize the cursor prompt tool by replacing any of the standard characters with any string. The user may optionally select to restore system defaults.

E.3.3. APcurs

APcurs: AthenaPreferences: Cursor: Toggle between showing or hiding the cursor prompt tool.

E.3.4. APdir

APdir: AthenaPreferences: Directories: Lets the user select or enter directories necessary for writing and searching files. Directories that can be entered are the "scratch" directory, the "user ssdir", and the "user sadir". The scratch directory is used for writing temporary files with automatically-generated file names. Commands such as SCh, PIh, and those that produce graphics (depending on format settings specified with APgfx) use this directory. The user ssdir and sadir are used within ParameterObjects that search for files. With such ParameterObjects, the user can specify any file within the specified directory simply by name. To find the the file's complete file path, all directories are recursively searched in both the user ssdir and the libATH/ssdir. Directories named "_exclude" will not be searched. If files in different nested directories do not have unique file names, correct file paths may not be found.

E.3.5. APdlg

APdlg: AthenaPreferences: Dialogs: Toggle between different dialog modes. Not all modes are available on every platform or Python installation. The "text" dialog mode works without a GUI, and is thus available on all platforms and Python installations.

E.3.6. APgfx

APgfx: AthenaPreferences: Graphics: Toggle between different graphic output formats. All modes may not be available on every platform or Python installation. This command uses the active graphic output format; this can be selected with the "APgfx" command. Output in "tk" requires the Python Tkinter GUI installation; output in "png" and "jpg" requires the Python Imaging Library (PIL) library installation; output in "eps" and "text" do not require any additional software or configuration.

E.3.7. APr

APr: AthenaPreferences: Refresh: When refresh mode is active, every time a Texture or Clone is edited, a new event list is calculated in order to test ParameterObject compatibility and to find absolute time range. When refresh mode is inactive, editing Textures and Clones does not test event list production, and is thus significantly faster.

E.3.8. APwid

APwid: AthenaPreferences: Width: Manually set the number of characters displayed per line during an athenaCL session. Use of this preference is only necessary on platforms that do not provide a full-featured terminal envrionment.

E.4. AthenaScript Commands

E.4.1. ASexe

ASexe: AthenaScript: Execute: Runs an AthenaScript if found in the libATH/libAS directory. Not for general use.

E.5. AthenaUtility Commands

E.5.1. AU

AthenaUtility: Commands: Displays a list of all AthenaUtility commands.

E.5.2. AUbeat

AUbeat: AthenaUtility: Beat: Simple tool to calculate the duration of a beat in BPM.

E.5.3. AUbug

AUbug: AthenaUtility: Bug: causes a bug to test the error reporting system.

E.5.4. AUdoc

AUdoc: AthenaUtility: Documentation: Opens the athenaCL documentation in a web browser. Attempts to load documentation from a local copy; if this fails, the on-line version is loaded.

E.5.5. AUlog

AUlog: AthenaUtility: Log: If available, opens the athenacl-log file used to store error messages.

E.5.6. AUpc

AUpc: AthenaUtility: Pitch Converter: Enter a pitch, pitch name, or frequency value to display the pitch converted to all formats. Input is converted to traditional pitch names (where middle C = C4), MIDI pitch numbers (where middle C = 60), pitch class values (where C = 0), Csound PCH values (where middle C = 8.00), frequency (where A4 = 440.0 hz), and pitch space real values (where middle C = 0.0). Values can be input as traditional pitch names, frequency, MIDI, pch, and pitch space real note values. Plain numbers are interpreted as pitch-space real values. When pitch names are used, a sharp is represented as "#"; a flat is represented as "$"; a quarter-sharp is represented as "~"; multiple accidentals are valid. When providing a value, a format string may need to be provided. To designate a frequency, include "hz" with the number; to designate MIDI input value, include a "m" with the number. To designate a pch input value, include a "pch" with the number. Input values can include microtones as symbols or floating-point values.

E.5.7. AUsys

AUsys: AthenaUtility: System: Displays a list of all athenaCL properties and their current status.

E.5.8. AUup

AUup: AthenaUtility: Update: Checks on-line to see if a new version of athenaCL is available; if so, the athenaCL download page will be opened in a web browser.

E.6. CsoundPreferences Commands

E.6.1. CP

CsoundPreferences: Commands: Displays a list of all CsoundPreferences commands.

E.6.2. CPapp

CPapp: CsoundPreferences: Application: Select the file path to the executable Csound application.

E.6.3. CPauto

CPauto: CsoundPreferences: Auto Score Render Control: Turn on or off auto score render, causing athenaCL to automatically render (ELr) and hear (ELh) audio files every time a Csound score is created with ELn.

E.6.4. CPch

CPch: CsoundPreferences: Channels: Choose the number of audio channels used in creating the Csound orchestra. Channel options are mono, stereo, and quad (1, 2, and 4 channels).

E.6.5. CPff

CPff: CsoundPreferences: FileFormat: Choose which audio file format (AIF, WAVE, or SoundDesignerII) is created by Csound.

E.7. EventList Commands

E.7.1. EL

EventList: Commands: Displays a list of all EventList commands.

E.7.2. ELh

ELh: EventList: Hear: If possible, opens and presents to the user the last audible EventList output (audio file, MIDI file) created in the current session.

E.7.3. ELn

ELn: EventList: New: Create a new event list, in whatever formats are specified within the active EventMode and EventOutput. Generates new events for all Textures and Clones that are not muted. Specific output formats are determined by the active EventMode (EMo) and selected output formats (EOo).

E.7.4. ELr

ELr: EventList: Render: Renders the last event list created in the current session with the Csound application specified by CPapp.

E.7.5. ELv

ELv: EventList: View: Opens the last event list created in the current session as a text document.

E.7.6. ELw

ELw: EventList: Save: Write event lists stored in Textures and Clones, in whatever formats specified within the active EventMode and EventOutput; new event lists are not generated, and output will always be identical.

E.8. EventMode Commands

E.8.1. EM

EventMode: Commands: Displays a list of all EventMode commands.

E.8.2. EMi

EMi: EventMode: Instruments: Displays a list of all instruments available as defined within the active EventMode. The instrument assigned to a Texture determines the number of auxiliary parameters and the default values of these parameters.

E.8.3. EMls

EMls: EventMode: List: Displays a list of available EventModes.

E.8.4. EMo

EMo: EventMode: Select: Select an EventMode. EventModes determine what instruments are available for Textures, default auxiliary parameters for Textures, and the final output format of created event lists.

E.8.5. EMv

EMv: EventMode: View: Displays documentation for the active EventMode. Based on EventMode and selected EventOutputs, documentation for each active OutputEngine used to process events is displayed.

E.9. EventOutput Commands

E.9.1. EO

EventOutput: Commands: Displays a list of all EventOutput commands.

E.9.2. EOls

EOls: EventOutput: List: List all available EventOutput formats.

E.9.3. EOo

EOo: EventOutput: Select: Adds a possible output format to be produced when an event list is created. Possible formats are listed with EOls.

E.9.4. EOrm

EOrm: EventOutput: Remove: Removes a possible output format to be produced when an event list is created. Possible formats can be seen with EOls.

E.10. MapClass Commands

E.10.1. MC

MapClass: Commands: Displays a list of all MapClass dictionary commands.

E.10.2. MCcm

MCcm: MapClass: Comparison: Displays all possible maps and analysis data between any two sets of six or fewer members. Maps can be sorted by Joseph N. Straus's atonal voice-leading measures Smoothness, Uniformity, or Balance. Full analysis data is provided for each map, including vectors for each measure, displacement, offset, max, and span.

E.10.3. MCgrid

MCgrid: MapClass: Grid: Creates a grid of all minimum displacements between every set class of two cardinalities. Cardinalities must be six or fewer. Note: for large cardinalities, processing time may be long. Note: values calculated between different-sized sets may not represent the shortest transitional distance.

E.10.4. MCnet

MCnet: MapClass: Network: Creates a graphical display of displacement networks between set classes.

E.10.5. MCopt

MCopt: MapClass: Optimum: Finds an optimum voice leading and minimum distance for any two sets of six or fewer elements.

E.10.6. MCv

MCv: MapClass: View: Displays a listing of MapClasses for a given size class (source to destination size) and between a range of indexes. MapClasses are notated in two possible notations. An index notation specifies a source:destination size pair followed by an index number. For example: 3:4-35 is the thirty fifth map class between sets of 3 and 4 elements. A spatial notation uses names and order position to code transitions. For example: (cd(ab)).

E.11. PathInstance Commands

E.11.1. PI

PathInstance: Commands: Displays a list of all PathInstance commands.

E.11.2. PIals

PIals: PathInstance: Attribute List: Displays a listing of raw attributes of the selected Path.

E.11.3. PIcp

PIcp: PathInstance: Copy: Create a copy of a selected Path.

E.11.4. PIdf

PIdf: PathInstance: Duration Fraction: Provide a new list of duration fractions for each pitch group of the active Path. Duration fractions are proportional weightings that scale a total duration provided by a Texture. When used within a Texture, each pitch group of the Path will be sustained for this proportional duration. Values must be given in a comma-separated list, and can be percentages or real values.

E.11.5. PIe

PIe: PathInstance: Edit: Edit a single Multiset in the active Path.

E.11.6. PIh

PIh: PathInstance: Hear: Creates a temporary Texture with the active Path and the active TextureModule, and uses this Texture to write a short sample EventList as a temporary MIDI file. This file is written in the scratch directory specified by APdir command. If possible, this file is opened and presented to the user.

E.11.7. PIls

PIls: PathInstance: List: Displays a list of all Paths.

E.11.8. PImv

PImv: PathInstance: Move: Rename a Path, and all Texture references to that Path.

E.11.9. PIn

PIn: PathInstance: New: Create a new Path from user-specified pitch groups. Users may specify pitch groups in a variety of formats. A Forte set class number (6-23A), a pitch-class set (4,3,9), a pitch-space set (-3, 23.2, 14), standard pitch letter names (A, C##, E~, G#), MIDI note numbers (58m, 62m), frequency values (222hz, 1403hz), a Xenakis sieve (5&3|11), or an Audacity frequency-analysis file (import) all may be provided. Pitches may be specified by letter name (psName), pitch space (psReal), pitch class, MIDI note number, or frequency. Pitch letter names may be specified as follows: a sharp is represented as "#"; a flat is represented as "$"; a quarter sharp is represented as "~"; multiple sharps, quarter sharps, and flats are valid. Octave numbers (where middle-C is C4) can be used with pitch letter names to provide register. Pitch space values (as well as pitch class) place C4 at 0.0. MIDI note numbers place C4 at 60. MIDI note-numbers and frequency values must contain the appropriate unit as a string ("m" or "hz"). Xenakis sieves are entered using logic constructions of residual classes. Residual classes are specified by a modulus and shift, where modulus 3 at shift 1 is notated 3@1. Logical operations are notated with "&" (and), "|" (or), "^" (symmetric difference), and "-" (complementation). Residual classes and logical operators may be nested and grouped by use of braces ({}). Complementation can be applied to a single residual class or a group of residual classes. For example: -{7@0|{-5@2&-4@3}}. When entering a sieve as a pitch set, the logic string may be followed by two comma-separated pitch notations for register bounds. For example "3@2|4, c1, c4" will take the sieve between c1 and c4. Audacity frequency-analysis files can be produced with the cross-platform open-source audio editor Audacity. In Audacity, under menu View, select Plot Spectrum, configure, and export. The file must have a .txt extension. To use the file-browser, enter "import"; to select the file from the prompt, enter the complete file path, optionally followed by a comma and the number of ranked pitches to read.

E.11.10. PIo

PIo: PathInstance: Select: Select the active Path. Used for "PIret", "PIrot", "PIslc", "PScpa", "PScpb", and "TIn".

E.11.11. PIopt

PIopt: PathInstance: Optimize: Creates a new Path from a voice-leading optimization of the active Path. All pitch groups will be transposed to an optimized transposition, and a new PathVoice will be created with optimized voice leadings. Note: PathVoices are not preserved in the new Path.

E.11.12. PIret

PIret: PathInstance: Retrograde: Creates a new Path from the retrograde of the active Path. All PathVoices are preserved in the new Path.

E.11.13. PIrm

PIrm (name): PathInstance: Remove: Delete a selected Path.

E.11.14. PIrot

PIrot: PathInstance: Rotation: Creates a new Path from the rotation of the active Path. Note: since a rotation creates a map not previously defined, PathVoices are not preserved in the new Path.

E.11.15. PIslc

PIslc: PathInstance: Slice: Creates a new Path from a slice of the active Path. All PathVoices are preserved in the new Path.

E.11.16. PIv

PIv: PathInstance: View: Displays all properties of the active Path.

E.12. PathSet Commands

E.12.1. PS

PathSet: Commands: Displays a list of all PathSet commands.

E.12.2. PScma

PScma: PathSet: Comparison A: Analyze the active Path as a sequence of set classes. Compare each adjacent pair of pitch groups, as set classes, using the active SetMeasure. A SetMeasure is activated with the "SMo" command.

E.12.3. PScmb

PScmb: PathSet: Comparison B: Analyze the active Path as a Sequence of set classes. Compare each set class with a reference set class, employing the active SetMeasure.

E.13. PathVoice Commands

E.13.1. PV

PathVoice: Commands: Displays a list of all PathVoice commands.

E.13.2. PVan

PVan: PathVoice: Analysis: Displays Smoothness, Uniformity, and Balance analysis data for each map in the active PathVoice of the active Path.

E.13.3. PVauto

PVauto: PathVoice: Auto: Create a new PathVoice with mappings chosen automatically from either the first or last ranked map of a user-selected ranking method (Smoothness, Uniformity, or Balance). A new PathVoice is created, all maps being either first or last of the particular ranking.

E.13.4. PVcm

PVcm: PathVoice: Comparison: Displays Smoothness, Uniformity, and Balance analysis data for an ordered partition of all maps available between any two sets in the active Path.

E.13.5. PVcp

PVcp: PathVoice: Copy: Duplicate an existing PathVoice within the active Path. To see all PathVoices enter "PVls".

E.13.6. PVe

PVe: PathVoice: Edit: Choose a new map for a single position within the active PathVoice and Path.

E.13.7. PVls

PVls: PathVoice: List: Displays a list of all PathVoices associated with the active Path.

E.13.8. PVn

PVn: PathVoice: New: Create a new PathVoice (a collection of voice leadings) for the active Path. Each PathVoice voice leading may be selected by rank or map. Rank allows the user to select a map based on its Smoothness, Uniformity, or Balance ranking.

E.13.9. PVo

PVo: PathVoice: Select: Select an existing PathVoice within the active Path. To see all PathVoices enter "PVls".

E.13.10. PVrm

PVrm: PathVoice: Delete: Delete an existing PathVoice within the active Path. To see all PathVoices enter "PVls".

E.13.11. PVv

PVv: PathVoice: View: Displays the active Path and the active PathVoice.

E.14. SetClass Commands

E.14.1. SC

SetClass: Commands: Displays a list of all SetClass dictionary commands.

E.14.2. SCcm

SCcm: SetClass: Comparison: Compare any two user-selected pitch groups (as set classes) with all available Set Class similarity measures (SetMeasures). For each SetMeasure the calculated similarity value, a proportional graph of that value within the SetMeasure's range, and the measure's range (between minimum and maximum) are displayed.

E.14.3. SCf

SCf: SetClass: Find: Search all set classes with various search methods. Search methods include searching by common name (such as major, all-interval, phrygian, or pentatonic), z-relation, or superset.

E.14.4. SCh

SCh: SetClass: Hear: Creates a temporary Texture with the selected set and the DroneSustain TextureModule, and uses this Texture to write a short sample EventList as a temporary MIDI file. This file is written in the scratch directory specified by APdir command. If possible, this file is opened and presented to the user.

E.14.5. SCmode

SCmode: SetClass: Mode: Sets system-wide Tn (set classes not differentiated by transposition) or Tn/I (set classes not differentiated by transposition and inversion) state for all athenaCL set class processing. To view active SCmode state, enter "AUsys".

E.14.6. SCs

SCs: SetClass: Search: Search all set classes with the active SetMeasure for similarity to a pitch group (as a set class) and within a similarity range. The user must supply a pitch group and a percent similarity range. Similarity ranges are stated within the unit interval (between 0 and 1). To change the active SetMeasure, enter "SMo".

E.14.7. SCv

SCv: SetClass: View: Displays all data in the set class dictionary for the user-supplied pitch groups. Users may specify pitch groups in a variety of formats. A Forte set class number (6-23A), a pitch-class set (4,3,9), a pitch-space set (-3, 23.2, 14), standard pitch letter names (A, C##, E~, G#), MIDI note numbers (58m, 62m), frequency values (222hz, 1403hz), a Xenakis sieve (5&3|11), or an Audacity frequency-analysis file (import) all may be provided. Pitches may be specified by letter name (psName), pitch space (psReal), pitch class, MIDI note number, or frequency. Pitch letter names may be specified as follows: a sharp is represented as "#"; a flat is represented as "$"; a quarter sharp is represented as "~"; multiple sharps, quarter sharps, and flats are valid. Octave numbers (where middle-C is C4) can be used with pitch letter names to provide register. Pitch space values (as well as pitch class) place C4 at 0.0. MIDI note numbers place C4 at 60. MIDI note-numbers and frequency values must contain the appropriate unit as a string ("m" or "hz"). Xenakis sieves are entered using logic constructions of residual classes. Residual classes are specified by a modulus and shift, where modulus 3 at shift 1 is notated 3@1. Logical operations are notated with "&" (and), "|" (or), "^" (symmetric difference), and "-" (complementation). Residual classes and logical operators may be nested and grouped by use of braces ({}). Complementation can be applied to a single residual class or a group of residual classes. For example: -{7@0|{-5@2&-4@3}}. When entering a sieve as a pitch set, the logic string may be followed by two comma-separated pitch notations for register bounds. For example "3@2|4, c1, c4" will take the sieve between c1 and c4. Audacity frequency-analysis files can be produced with the cross-platform open-source audio editor Audacity. In Audacity, under menu View, select Plot Spectrum, configure, and export. The file must have a .txt extension. To use the file-browser, enter "import"; to select the file from the prompt, enter the complete file path, optionally followed by a comma and the number of ranked pitches to read. For all pitch groups the SCv command interprets the values as a set class. The Normal Form, Invariance Vector and all N Class Vectors (for the active Tn/TnI mode) are displayed. N-Class Vectors, when necessary, are displayed in 20 register rows divided into two groups of 10 and divided with a dash (-). The output of this command is configured by the active system Tn/TnI mode; to change the set class Tn/TnI mode enter the command "SCmode".

E.15. SetMeasure Commands

E.15.1. SM

SetMeasure: Commands: Displays a list of all SetMeasure dictionary commands.

E.15.2. SMls

SMls: SetMeasure: List: Displays a list of all available SetMeasures.

E.15.3. SMo

SMo: SetMeasure: Select: Sets the active SetMeasure, or computational method of set class comparison, used for "SCf", "PScpa", "PScpb" commands.

E.16. TextureClone Commands

E.16.1. TC

TextureClone: Commands: Displays a list of all TextureClone commands.

E.16.2. TCals

TCals: TextureClone: Attribute List: Displays raw attributes of the active Clone.

E.16.3. TCdoc

TCdoc: TextureClone: Documentation: Displays documentation for each auxiliary parameter field from the associated Texture, as well as argument formats for static Clone options.

E.16.4. TCe

TCe: TextureClone: Edit: Edit attributes of the active Clone.

E.16.5. TCls

TCls: TextureClone: List: Displays a list of all Clones associated with the active Texture.

E.16.6. TCmap

TCmap: TextureClone: Map: Displays a graphical map of the parameter values of the active Clone. With the use of one optional argument, the TCmap display can be presented in two orientations. A TCmap diagram can position values on the x-axis in an equal-spaced orientation for each event (event-base), or in a time-proportional orientation, where width is relative to the time of each event (time-base). As Clones process values produced by a Texture, all TCmap displays are post-TM. This command uses the active graphic output format; this can be selected with the "APgfx" command. Output in "tk" requires the Python Tkinter GUI installation; output in "png" and "jpg" requires the Python Imaging Library (PIL) library installation; output in "eps" and "text" do not require any additional software or configuration.

E.16.7. TCmute

TCmute: TextureClone: Mute: Toggle the active Clone (or any number of Clones named with arguments) on or off. Muting a Clone prevents it from producing EventOutputs.

E.16.8. TCn

TCn: TextureClone: New: Creates a new Clone associated with the active Texture.

E.16.9. TCo

TCo: TextureClone: Select: Choose the active Clone from all available Clones associated with the active Texture.

E.16.10. TCrm

TCrm: TextureClone: Remove: Deletes a Clone from the active Texture.

E.16.11. TCv

TCv: TextureClone: View: Displays all editable attributes of the active Clone, or a Clone named with a single argument.

E.17. TextureEnsemble Commands

E.17.1. TE

TextureEnsemble: Commands: Displays a list of all TextureEnsemble commands.

E.17.2. TEe

TEe: TextureEnsemble: Edit: Edit a user-selected attribute for all Textures.

E.17.3. TEmap

TEmap: TextureEnsemble: Map: Provides a text-based display and/or graphical display of the temporal distribution of Textures and Clones. This command uses the active graphic output format; this can be selected with the "APgfx" command. Output in "tk" requires the Python Tkinter GUI installation; output in "png" and "jpg" requires the Python Imaging

Library (PIL) library installation; output in "eps" and "text" do not require any additional software or configuration.

E.17.4. TEmidi

TEmidi: TextureEnsemble: MidiTempo: Edit the tempo written in a MIDI file. Where each Texture may have an independent tempo, a MIDI file has one tempo. The tempo written in the MIDI file does not effect playback, but may effect transcription into Western notation. The default tempo is 120 BPM.

E.17.5. TEv

TEv: TextureEnsemble: View: Displays a list of ParameterObject arguments for a single attribute of all Textures.

E.18. TextureInstance Commands

E.18.1. TI

TextureInstance: Commands: Displays a list of all TextureInstance commands.

E.18.2. TIals

TIals: TextureInstance: Attribute List: Displays raw attributes of a Texture.

E.18.3. TIcp

TIcp: TextureInstance: Copy: Duplicates a user-selected Texture.

E.18.4. TIdoc

TIdoc: TextureInstance: Documentation: Displays auxiliary parameter field documentation for a Texture's instrument, as well as argument details for static and dynamic Texture parameters.

E.18.5. TIe

TIe: TextureInstance: Edit: Edit a user-selected attribute of the active Texture.

E.18.6. TIls

TIls: TextureInstance: List: Displays a list of all Textures.

E.18.7. TImap

TImap: TextureInstance: Map: Displays a graphical map of the parameter values of the active Texture. With the use of two optional arguments, the TImap display can be presented in four orientations. A TImap diagram can position values on the x-axis in an equal-spaced orientation for each event (event-base), or in a time-proportional orientation, where width is relative to the time of each event (time-base). A TImap diagram can display, for each parameter, direct ParameterObject values as provided to the TextureModule (pre-TM), or the values of each parameter of each event after TextureModule processing (post-TM). This command uses the active graphic output format; this can be selected with the "APgfx" command. Output in "tk" requires the Python Tkinter GUI installation; output in "png" and "jpg" requires the Python Imaging Library (PIL) library installation; output in "eps" and "text" do not require any additional software or configuration.

E.18.8. TImidi

TImidi: TextureInstance: MIDI: Set the MIDI program and MIDI channel of a Texture, used when a "midiFile" EventOutput is selected. Users can select from one of the 128 GM MIDI programs by name or number. MIDI channels are normally auto-assigned during event list production; manually entered channel numbers (1 through 16) will override this feature.

E.18.9. TImode

TImode: TextureInstance: Mode: Set the pitch, polyphony, silence, and orcMap modes for the active Texture. The pitchMode (either "sc", "pcs", or "ps") designates which Path form is used within the Texture: "sc" designates the set class Path, which consists of non-transposed, non-redundant pitch classes; "pcs" designates the pitch class space Path, retaining set order and transposition; "ps" designates the pitch space Path, retaining order, transposition, and register.

E.18.10. TImute

TImute: TextureInstance: Mute: Toggle the active Texture (or any number of Textures named with arguments) on or off. Muting a Texture prevents it from producing EventOutputs. Clones can be created from muted Textures.

E.18.11. TImv

TImv: TextureInstance: Move: Renames a Texture, and all references in existing Clones.

E.18.12. TIn

TIn: TextureInstance: New: Creates a new instance of a Texture with a user supplied Instrument and Texture name. The new instance uses the active TextureModule, the active

Path, and an Instrument selected from the active EventMode-determined Orchestra. For some Orchestras, the user must supply the number of auxiliary parameters.

E.18.13. TIo

TIo: TextureInstance: Select: Select the active Texture from all available Textures.

E.18.14. TIrm

TIrm: TextureInstance: Remove: Deletes a user-selected Texture.

E.18.15. TIv

TIv: TextureInstance: View: Displays all editable attributes of the active Texture, or a Texture named with a single argument.

E.19. TextureModule Commands

E.19.1. TM

TextureModule: Commands: Displays a list of all TextureModule commands.

E.19.2. TMls

TMls: TextureModule: List: Displays a list of all TextureModules.

E.19.3. TMo

TMo: TextureModule: Select: Choose the active TextureModule. This TextureModule is used with the "TIn" and "TMv" commands.

E.19.4. TMv

TMv: TextureModule: View: Displays documentation for the active TextureModule.

E.20. TextureParameter Commands

E.20.1. TP

TextureParameter: Commands: Displays a list of all TextureParameter commands.

E.20.2. TPexp

TPexp: TextureParameter: Export: Write a file containing ParameterObject output.

E.20.3. TPls

TPls: TextureParameter: List: Displays a list of all ParameterObjects.

E.20.4. TPmap

TPmap: TextureParameter: Map: Displays a graphical map of any ParameterObject. User must supply parameter library name, the number of events to be calculated, and appropriate parameter arguments. This command uses the active graphic output format; this can be selected with the "APgfx" command. Output in "tk" requires the Python Tkinter GUI installation; output in "png" and "jpg" requires the Python Imaging Library (PIL) library installation; output in "eps" and "text" do not require any additional software or configuration.

E.20.5. TPv

TPv: TextureParameter: View: Displays documentation for one or more ParameterObjects. All ParameterObjects that match the user-supplied search string will be displayed. ParameterObject acronyms are accepted.

E.21. TextureTemperament Commands

E.21.1. TT

TextureTemperament: Commands: Displays a list of all TextureTemperament commands.

E.21.2. TTls

TTls: TextureTemperament: List: Displays a list of all temperaments available.

E.21.3. TTo

TTo: TextureTemperament: Select: Choose a Temperament for the active Texture. The Temperament provides fixed or dynamic mapping of pitch values. Fixed mappings emulate historical Temperaments, such as MeanTone and Pythagorean; dynamic mappings provide algorithmic variation to each pitch processed, such as microtonal noise.

E.22. Other Commands

E.22.1. cmd

cmd: Displays a hierarchical menu of all athenaCL commands.

E.22.2. help

help: To get help for a command or any available topic, enter "help" or "?" followed by a search string. If no command is provided, a menu of all commands available is displayed.

E.22.3. py

Begins an interactive Python session inside the current athenaCL session.

E.22.4. pypath

pypath: Lists all file paths in the Python search path.

E.22.5. q

q: Exit athenaCL.

E.22.6. quit

quit: Exit athenaCL.

E.22.7. shell

On UNIX-based platforms, the "shell" or "!" command executes a command-line argument in the default shell.

References

Abelson, H. and G. Sussman. 1985. *Structure and Interpretation of Computer Programs*. Cambridge: MIT Press.

Ambler, S. W. 2002. "Be Realistic About the UML: It's Simply Not Sufficient." Internet: http://www.agilemodeling.com/essays/realisticUML.htm.

Ames, C. 1983. "Stylistic Automata in Gradient." In *The Music Machine*. C. Roads, ed. Cambridge: MIT Press.

———. 1987. "Automated Composition in Retrospect: 1956-1986." *Leonardo* 20(2): 169-185.

———. 1990. "Statistics and Compositional Balance." *Perspectives of New Music* 28(1): 80-111.

Ames, C. and M. Domino. 1992. "Cybernetic Composer: An Overview." In *Understanding Music with AI: Perspectives on Music Cognition*. M. Balaban, K. Ebcioglu and O. Laske, eds. Cambridge: AAAI Press / MIT Press. 186-205.

Anonymous. 1956a. "'Brain' Computes New Tune for TV." *New York Times* July 3: 51.

———. 1956b. "The first ballad to be composed by an electronic computer." *International Musician* 55: 21.

———. 1956c. "Syncopation by Automation." In *Data from ElectroData*. Pasadena: Burroughs Corporation (ElectroData Division). 2.

Ariza, C. 2002. "Prokaryotic Groove: Rhythmic Cycles as Real-Value Encoded Genetic Algorithms." In *Proceedings of the International Computer Music Conference*. San Francisco: International Computer Music Association. 561-567.

———. 2003. "Ornament as Data Structure: An Algorithmic Model based on Micro-Rhythms of Csángó Laments and Funeral Music." In *Proceedings of the International Computer Music Conference*. San Francisco: International Computer Music Association. 187-193.

———. 2004a. "algorithmic.net." Internet: http://www.algorithmic.net.

———. 2004b. "An Object Oriented Model of the Xenakis Sieve for Algorithmic Pitch, Rhythm, and Parameter Generation." In *Proceedings of the International Computer Music Conference*. San Francisco: International Computer Music Association. 63-70.

———. 2005a. *athenaCL Tutorial Manual: Second Edition.*

———. 2005b. "Navigating the Landscape of Computer-Aided Algorithmic Composition Systems: A Definition, Seven Descriptors, and a Lexicon of Systems and Research." In *Proceedings of the International Computer Music Conference*. San Francisco: International Computer Music Association. 765-772.

———. 2005c. "The Xenakis Sieve as Object: A New Model and a Complete Implementation." *Computer Music Journal* 29(2): 40-60.

Arsenault, L. M. 2002. "Iannis Xenakis's Achorripsis: The Matrix Game." *Computer Music Journal* 26(1): 58-72.

Assayag, G. and J. Baboni, K. Haddad. 2001. *OpenMusic 4.0 User's Manual and Reference*. Paris: IRCAM — Centre Georges Pompidou.

Assayag, G. and C. Rueda, M. Laurson, C. Agon, O. Delerue. 1999. "Computer-Assisted Composition at IRCAM: From PatchWork to OpenMusic." *Computer Music Journal* 23(3): 59-72.

Assayag, G. 1998. "Computer Aided Composition Today." *IRCAM Music Representation Team.*

Assayag, G. and C. Agon, J. Fineberg, P. Hanappe. 1997. "An Object Oriented Visual Environment for Musical Composition." In *Proceedings of the International Computer Music Conference*. San Francisco: International Computer Music Association. 364-367.

Babbage, C. 1832. *On the Economy of Machinery and Manufactures*. London: Charles Knight.

Bailey, R. W. 1974. "Computer-assisted poetry: the writing machine is for everybody." In *Computers in the Humanities*. J. L. Mitchell, ed. Minneapolis: University of Minnesota Press. 283-295.

Bainbridge, D. 1997. "Csound." In *Beyond MIDI: the Handbook of Musical Codes*. E. Selfridge-Field, ed. Cambrdige: MIT Press. 111-142.

Baker, R. 1963a. "MUSICOMP: Music-Simulator for Compositional Procedures for the IBM 7090 Electronic Digital Computer." *Tehcnical Report No. 9, University of Illinois, Experimental Music Studio*.

———. 1963b. *A Statistical Analysis of the Harmonic Practice of the 18th and 19th Centuries*. D.M.A. Dissertation, University of Illinois.

Balaban, M. and K. Ebcioglu, O. E. Laske. 1992. *Understanding Music with AI: Perspectives on Music Cognition*. Cambridge: AAAI Press / MIT Press.

Balestrini, N. 1968. "Tape Mark I." In *Cybernetic Serendipity*. J. Reichardt, ed. London: Studio International, W. & J. Mackay. 55-56.

Banks, J. D. and P. Berg, R. Rowe, D. Theriault. 1979. "SSP — A Bi-Parametric Approach to Sound Synthesis." In *Sonological Reports*. Utrecht: Institute of Sonology. 5.

Barbaud, P. 1960. "Musique Algorithmique." *Esprit* 28(280): 92-97.

———. 1966. *Initiation à la composition algorithmique*. Paris: Dunod.

Barlow, C. 1987. "Two Essays on Theory." *Computer Music Journal* 11(1): 44-60.

———. 1990. "Autobusk: An algorithmic real-time pitch and rhythm improvisation programme." In *Proceedings of the International Computer Music Conference.* San Francisco: International Computer Music Association. 166-168.

Baroni, M. and R. Jacoboni. 1975. "Analysis and generation of Bach's chorale melodies." In *Proceedings of the 1st International Congress on the Semiotics of Music.* G. Stefani, ed. Pesaro: Centro di Iniziativa Culturale.

Bartetzki, A. 1997. "CMask, a Stochastic Event Generator for Csound." Internet: http://gigant.kgw.tu-berlin.de/~abart/CMaskMan/CMask-Manual.htm.

Baudot, J. A. 1964. *La machine à écrire.* Montreal: Les Editions du Jour.

———. 1968. "Automatic sentence generation." In *Cybernetic Serendipity.* J. Reichardt, ed. London: Studio International, W. & J. Mackay. 58.

Bel, B. 1992. "Symbolic and Sonic Representations of Sound Object Structures." In *Understanding Music with AI: Perspectives on Music Cognition.* M. Balaban, K. Ebcioglu and O. Laske, eds. Cambridge: AAAI Press / MIT Press. 65-109.

———. 1996. "A Flexible Environment for Music Composition in non-European Contexts." *Journees d'Informatique Musicale.*

———. 1998. "Migrating Musical Concepts: An Overview of the Bol Processor." *Computer Music Journal* 22(2): 56-64.

Bel, B. and J. Kippen. 1992. "Bol Processor Grammars." In *Understanding Music with AI: Perspectives on Music Cognition.* M. Balaban, K. Ebcioglu and O. Laske, eds. Cambridge: AAAI Press / MIT Press. 366-400.

Berg, P. and R. Rowe, D. Theriault. 1980. "SSP and Sound Description." *Computer Music Journal* 4(1): 25-35.

Berg, P. 1978. *A User's Manual for SSP*. Utrecht: Institute of Sonology.

———. 1979. "PILE - A Language for Sound Synthesis." *Computer Music Journal* 3(1): 30-41.

———. 1996. "Abstracting the Future: The Search for Musical Constructs." *Computer Music Journal* 20(3): 24-27.

———. 2003. *Using the AC Toolbox*. Den Haag: Institute of Sonology, Royal Conservatory.

Berry, W. 1987. *Structural Functions in Music*. New York: Dover.

Bidlack, R. A. 1992. "Chaotic Systems as Simple (but Complex) Compositional Algorithms." *Computer Music Journal* 16(3): 33-47.

Biles, J. A. 1994. "GenJam: A Genetic Algorithm for Generating Jazz Solos." In *Proceedings of the International Computer Music Conference*. San Francisco: International Computer Music Association. 131-137.

———. 2003. "GenJam in Perspective: A Tentative Taxonomy for GA Music and Art Systems." *Leonardo* 36(1): 43-45.

Bimber, B. 1990. "Karl Marx and the Three Faces of Technological Determinism." *Social Studies of Science* 20(2): 333-351.

Birkhoff, G. D. 1933. *Aesthetic Measure*. Cambridge: Harvard University Press.

Blum, T. 1979. "Herbert Brün: Project Sawdust." *Computer Music Journal* 3(1): 6-7.

Boehm-Davis, D. A. and R. W. Holt, A. C. Schultz. 1992. "The Role of Program Structure in Software Mainenance." *International Journal of Man-Machine Studies* 36: 21-63.

Bousfield, T. 1998. *A Practical Guide to AutoCAD AutoLISP*. New York: Addison Wesley.

Breton, A. 1969. *Manifestoes of Surrealism.* Translated by R. Seaver and H. R. Lane. Ann Arbor: University of Michigan Press.

Brinkman, A. 1981. "Data Structures for a Music-11 Preprocessor." In *Proceedings of the International Computer Music Conference.* San Francisco: International Computer Music Association.

Brooks, F. P. and A. Hopkins, P. Neumann, W. V. Wright. 1957. "An Experiment in Musical Composition." *IRE Transcripts on Electronic Computers* 6: 175-182.

Brower, B. 1961. "Why 'Thinking Machines' Cannot Think." *New York Times* February 19: 213.

Bruce, K. B. 2002. *Foundations of Object-Oriented Languages: Types and Semantics.* Cambridge: MIT Press.

Brün, H. 1968. "Composition with Computers." In *Cybernetic Serendipity.* J. Reichardt, ed. London: Studio International, W. & J. Mackay. 20.

———. 1969. "Infraudibles." In *Music by Computer.* H. von Foerster and J. W. Beauchamp, eds. New York: John Wiley & Sons. 117-120.

———. 1970. "From Musical Ideas to Computers and Back." In *The Computer and Music.* H. B. Lincoln, ed. Ithaca: Cornell University Press. 23-36.

———. 1971. "Technology and the Composer." In *Music and Technology (Proceedings of the Stockholm Meeting organized by UNESCO).* Paris: La Revue Musicale. 181-192.

———. 1980. "Dust, More Dust, Dustiny." In *UNESCO Computer Music: Report on an internationl project including the international workshop held at Aarhus, Denmark in 1978.* M. Battier and B. Truax, eds. Canadian Commission for UNESCO. 85-86.

Buchner, A. 1978. *Mechanical Musical Instruments*. Translated by I. Irwin. Westport: Greenwood Press.

Burns, K. H. 1994. *The History and Development of Algorithms in Music Composition, 1957-1993*. D.A. Dissertation, Ball State University.

Burt, W. 1996. "Some Parentheses Around Algorithmic Composition." *Organised Sound* 1(3): 167-172.

Busoni, F. 1962. "Sketch of a New Esthetic of Music." In *Three Classics in the Aesthetics of Music*. Translated by T. Baker. New York: Dover. 73-102.

Buxton, W. 1975. *Manual for the POD Programs*. Utrecht: Institute of Sonology, University of Utrecht.

———. 1978. *Design Issues in the Foundation of a Computer-Based Tool for Music Composition*. Toronto: Technical Report Computer Systems Research Group.

Buxton, W. and W. Reeves, R. Baecker, L. Mezei. 1978. "The Use of Hierarchy and Instance in a Data Structure for Computer Music." *Computer Music Journal* 2(4): 10-20.

Castine, P. 1991. "Contemporary Music Analysis Package (CMAP) for the Macintosh." *Computing in Musicology* 7: 73-75.

———. 1994a. "The Development of Set-Theoretic Analysis Tools for Macintosh." In *Les Actes de "Journees Informatique Musicales"*. Bordeaux: LaBRI Université Bordeaux I.

———. 1994b. *Set Theory Objects. Abstractions for Computer-Aided Analysis and Composition of Serial and Atonal Music*. Frankfurt am Main: Peter Lang.

Castine, P. and A. Brinkman, C. Harris. 1990. "Contemporary Music Analysis Package (CMAP) for Macintosh." In *Proceedings of the International Computer Music Conference*. San Francisco: International Computer Music Association.

Castren, M. 1994. *RECREL: A Similarity Measure for Set-Classes*. Helsinki: Sibelius Academy.

Chadabe, J. 1975a. "System Composing." In *Proceedings of the Second Annual Music Computation Conference*. J. Beauchamp and J. Melby, eds. Urbana, Illinois: Office of Continuing Education and Public Service in Music. 7-10.

————. 1975b. "The Voltage-controlled Synthesizer." In *The Development and Practice of Electronic Music*. J. H. Appleton and R. C. Perera, eds. Englewood Cliffs: Prentice-Hall. 138-188.

————. 1978. "An Introduction to the Play Program." *Computer Music Journal* 2(1).

————. 1997. *Electric Sound: The Past and Promise of Electronic Music*. New Jersey: Prentice-Hall.

Chomsky, N. 1957. *Syntactic Structures*. The Hague: Mouton.

Chowning, J. 1973. "The Synthesis of Complex Audio Spectra by Means of Frequency Modulation." *Journal of the Audio Engineering Society* 21(7): 526-534.

Ciamaga, G. 1975. "The Tape Studio." In *The Development and Practice of Electronic Music*. J. H. Appleton and R. C. Perera, eds. Englewood Cliffs: Prentice-Hall. 68-137.

Citron, J. 1970. "MUSPEC." In *The Computer and Music*. H. B. Lincoln, ed. Ithaca: Cornell University Press. 97-111.

Cohen, H. 1986. "Off the shelf." *The Visual Computer* 2: 191-194.

Cohen, J. E. 1962. "Information Theory and Music." *Behavioral Science* 7(2): 137-163.

Cointe, P. and X. Rodet. 1984. "Formes: An object and time oriented system for music composition and synthesis." In *Proceedings of the 1984 ACM Symposium on LISP and functional programming*. Austin: ACM Press. 85-95.

Cony, E. 1956. "Canny Computers: Machines Write Music, Play Checkers, Tackle New Tasks in Industry." *Wall Street Journal* 148(56): 1.

Cope, D. 1987. "An Expert System for Computer-Assisted Music Composition." *Computer Music Journal* 11(4): 30-46.

———. 1991. *Computers and Musical Style*. Oxford: Oxford University Press.

———. 1992. "Computer Modeling of Musical Intelligence in EMI." *Computer Music Journal* 16(2): 69-83.

———. 1993. "Algorithmic Composition [re]Defined." In *Proceedings of the International Computer Music Conference*. San Francisco: International Computer Music Association. 23-25.

———. 1996. *Experiments in Music Intelligence*. Madison, WI: A-R Editions.

———. 1997. "The Composer's Underscoring Environment: CUE." *Computer Music Journal* 21(3): 20-37.

———. 2000. *The Algorithmic Composer*. Madison, WI: A-R Editions.

———. 2002. "Computer Analysis and Composition Using Atonal Voice-Leading Techniques." *Perspectives in New Music* 40(1): 121-146.

———. 2004. "A Musical Learning Algorithm." *Computer Music Journal* 28(3): 12-27.

Cross, I. 1993. "The Chinese Music Box." *Interface* 22: 165-172.

Dannenberg, R. B. 1989. "The Canon Score Language." *Computer Music Journal* 13(1): 47-56.

———. 1997a. "The Implementation of Nyquist, A Sound Synthesis Language." *Computer Music Journal* 21(3): 71-82.

————. 1997b. "Machine Tongues XIX: Nyquist, a Language for Composition and Sound Synthesis." *Computer Music Journal* 21(3): 50-60.

Darreg, I. 1957. "The Electronic Computer Takes Up Music Lessons." Internet: http://sonic-arts.org/darreg/dar6.htm.

Day, R. and J. Powell. 1993. "The vision, the potential and the virtual reality: technologies to inform architectural design." In *Companion to Contemporary Architectural Thought*. B. Farmer and H. Louw, eds. London: Routledge. 166-173.

Degazio, B. 1997. "The Evolution of Musical Organisms." *Leonardo Music Journal* 7: 27-33.

————. 2004. "The Transformation Engine." In *Proceedings of the International Computer Music Conference*. San Francisco: International Computer Music Association. 528-531.

Desain, P. 1990. "LISP as a Second Language: Functional Aspects." *Perspectives of New Music* 28(1): 192-222.

Desain, P. and H. Honing. 1988. "LOCO: A Composition Microworld in Logo." *Computer Music Journal* 12(3): 30-42.

Di Scipio, A. 1994. "Formal Processes of Algorithmic Composition Challenging the Dualistic Paradigm of Computer Music." In *Proceedings of the International Computer Music Conference*. San Francisco: International Computer Music Association. 202-208.

————. 1995. "On Different Approaches to Computer Music as Different Models of Compositional Design." *Perspectives of New Music* 331-2: 360-402.

————. 1997. "Towards a Critical Theory of (Music) Technology. Computer Music and Subversive Rationalization." In *Proceedings of the International Computer Music Conference*. San Francisco: International Computer Music Association. 62-65.

Didkovsky, N. 2001. "Java Music Specification Language." Internet:

    http://www.algomusic.com/jmsl/JMSL_presentation_March_2001/index.html.

Dijkstra, E. W. 1989. "On the Cruelty of Really Teaching Computing Science."

    Communications of the ACM 32(12): 1398-1404.

Divilbiss, J. L. 1964. "The Real-Time Generation of Music with a Digital Computer." *Journal*

    of Music Theory 8: 99.

Dodge, C. 1988. "Profile: A musical fractal." *Computer Music Journal* 12(3): 10-14.

Dodge, C. and T. A. Jerse. 1997. *Computer Music: Synthesis, Composition, and Performance*. New

    York: Shirmer Books.

Doornbusch, P. 2004. "Computer Sound Synthesis in 1951: The Music of CSIRAC."

    Computer Music Journal 28(1): 10-25.

Détienne, F. 2001. *Software Design - Cognitive Aspects*. London: Springer.

Ebcioglu, K. 1984. "An Expert System for Schenkerian Synthesis of Chorales in the Style of

    J. S. Bach." In *Proceedings of the International Computer Music Conference*. San Francisco:

    International Computer Music Association. 135-142.

————. 1987. "Report on the CHORAL Project: An Expert System for Chorale

    Harmonization." In *Research report no. RC 12628*. Yorktown Heights: IBM, Thomas J.

    Watson Research Center.

————. 1988. "An Expert System for Harmonizing Four-part Chorales." *Computer Music*

    Journal 12(3): 43-51.

Eco, U. 1989. *The Open Work*. Translated by A. Cancogni. Cambridge: Harvard University

    Press.

Englert, G. 1981. "Automated Composition and Composed Automation." *Computer Music Journal* 5(4): 30-35.

Fencl, Z. 1966. "Komponující algoritmus a obsah informace." *Kybernetica* 2: 243.

Ferentzy, E. N. 1965. "On Formal Music Analysis-Synthesis: Its Application in Music Education." *Computational Linguistics* 4: 107.

Fishwick, P. A. 2002. "Aesthetic Programming: Crafting Personalized Software." *Leonardo* 35(4).

Forte, A. 1973. *The Structure of Atonal Music*. New Haven: Yale University Press.

Fry, C. 1980. "Computer Improvisation." *Computer Music Journal* 4(3): 48-58.

———. 1983. "Flavors Band: Beyond Computer Improvisation and/or a Meta-Composition Language." In *Proceedings of the International Computer Music Conference*. San Francisco: International Computer Music Association. 31-54.

———. 1984a. "Flavors Band." *Computer Music Journal* 8(4): 20-34.

———. 1984b. "Flavors Band: A Language for Specifying Musical Style." In *The Music Machine*. C. Roads, ed. Cambridge: MIT Press. 295-309.

Fux, J. J. 1965. *The Study of Counterpoint; from Johann Joseph Fux's Gradus ad Parnassum*. Translated by A. Mann. New York: W. W. Norton.

Gamma, E. and R. Helm, R. Johnson, J. Vlissides. 1994. *Design Patterns: Elements of Reusable Object-Oriented Software*. Boston: Addison Wesley.

Gardner, M. 1974. "Mathematical Games: The Arts as Combinatorial Mathematics, or, How to Compose Like Mozart with Dice." *Scientific American* 231(6): 132-136.

———. 1978. "Mathematical Games: White and Brown Music, Fractal Curves and One-Over-f Fluctuations." *Scientific American* 238(4): 16-32.

Gerhard, D. and D. H. Hepting. 2004. "Cross-Modal Parametric Composition." In *Proceedings of the International Computer Music Conference*. San Francisco: International Computer Music Association. 505-512.

Gill, S. 1963. "A Technique for the Composition of Music in a Computer." *The Computer Journal* 6(2): 129-133.

Giomi, F. and M. Ligabue. 1991. "Computational Generation and Study of Jazz Music." *Interface* 20(1): 47-63.

Goehr, L. 1992. *The Imaginary Museum of Musical Works: An Essay in the Philosophy of Music*. Oxford: Oxford University Press.

Good, M. D. 1979. *Scot: A Score Translator for Music 11*. B.S. Thesis, Massachusetts Institute of Technology.

Green, C. D. 2001. "Charles Babbage, the Analytical Engine, and the Possibility of a 19th-Century Cognitive Science." In *The Transformation of Psychology: Influences of 19th-Century Philosophy, Technology, and Natural Science*. C. D. Green, M. Shore and T. Teo, eds. Washington: American Psychological Association. 133-152.

Gross, R. and A. Brinkman, J. M. Croson. 2000. "Score-11 Reference Manual."

Guido of Arezzo. 1978. "Micrologus." In *Hucbald, Guido, and John on Music: Three Medieval Treatises*. C. V. Palisca, ed. Translated by W. Babb. New Haven: Yale University Press. 57-83.

Hamman, M. 2002. "From Technical to Technological: The Imperative of Technology in Experimental Music Composition." *Perspectives in New Music* 40(1): 92-120.

Harley, J. 1994. "Algorithms Adapted From Chaos Theory." In *Proceedings of the International Computer Music Conference*. San Francisco: International Computer Music Association. 209-212.

Harris, C. and A. Brinkman. 1986. "A Unified Set of Software Tools for Computer-Assisted Set-Theoretic and Serial Analysis of Contemporary Music." In *Proceedings of the International Computer Music Conference*. San Fracisco: International Computer Music Association. 331-336.

Havass, M. 1964. "A Simulation of Music Composition. Synthetically Composed Folkmusic." In *Computational Linguistics*. F. Kiefer, ed. Budapest: Computing Centre of the Hungarian Academy of Sciences. 3: 107-128.

Heilbroner, R. L. 1967. "Do Machines Make History?." *Technology and Culture* 8(3): 335-345.

Heinichen, J. D. 1728. *Der Generalbass in der Composition*. Dresden.

Hewlett, W. B. and E. Selfridge-Field. 1997. "MIDI." In *Beyond MIDI: the Handbook of Musical Codes*. E. Selfridge-Field, ed. Cambrdige: MIT Press. 41-72.

Hild, H. and J. Feulner, W. Menzel. 1992. "HARMONET: A Neural Net for Harmonizing Chorals in the Style of J.S. Bach." *Advances in Neural Information Processing 4* 267-274.

Hiller, L. 1956. "Abstracts: Some Structural Principles of Computer Music." *Journal of the American Musicological Society* 9(3): 247-248.

―――. 1959. "Computer Music." *Scientific American* 201(6): 109-120.

―――. 1967. "Programming a Computer for Music Composition." In *Computer Applications in Music*. G. Lefkoff, ed. Morgantown: West Virginia University Library. 65-88.

————. 1969. "Some Compositional Techniques Involving the Use of Computers." In *Music by Computers*. H. von Foerster and J. W. Beauchamp, eds. New York: John Wiley & Sons, Inc. 71-83.

————. 1970. "Music Composed with Computers: An Historical Survey." In *The Computer and Music*. H. B. Lincoln, ed. Ithaca: Cornell University Press. 42-96.

————. 1978. "Phrase Structure in Computer Music." In *Proceedings of the International Computer Music Conference*. San Francisco: International Computer Music Association. 192-213.

————. 1981. "Composing with Computers: A Progress Report." *Computer Music Journal* 5(4): 7-21.

Hiller, L. and R. Baker. 1964. "Computer Cantata: A Study in Compositional Method." *Perspectives of New Music* 3(1): 62-90.

Hiller, L. and L. Isaacson. 1958. "Musical Composition with a High-Speed Digital Computer." *Journal of the Audio Engineering Society* 6(3): 154-160.

————. 1959. *Experimental Music*. New York: McGraw-Hill.

Hoffman, P. 2000. "A New GENDYN Program." *Computer Music Journal* 24(2): 31-38.

————. 2002. "Towards an 'Automated Art': Algorithmic Processes in Xenakis' Compositions." *Contemporary Music Review* 21(2-3): 121-131.

————. 2004. "'Something rich and strange': Exploring the Pitch Structure of GENDY3." *Journal of New Music Research* 33(2): 137-144.

Holland, S. 2000. "Artificial Intelligence in Music Education: A Critical Review." In *Readings in Music and Artificial Intelligence*. E. R. Miranda, ed. Amsterdam: Harwood Academic Publishers. 239-274.

Holtzman, S. R. 1980. "A Generative Grammar Definition Language for Music." *Interface* 9: 1-47.

———. 1994. *Digital Mantras: The Languages of Abstract and Virtual Worlds*. Cambridge: MIT Press.

Honing, H. 1990. "POCO: An Environment for Analysing, Modifying, and Generating Expression in Music." In *Proceedings of the International Computer Music Conference*. San Francisco: International Computer Music Association. 364-368.

Huron, D. 1989. "Characterizing Musical Textures." In *Proceedings of the International Computer Music Conference*. San Francisco: International Computer Music Association. 131-134.

Jacob, B. 1996. "Algorithmic Composition as a Model of Creativity." *Organised Sound* 1(3): 157-165.

Johnson-Laird, P. 1991. "Jazz Improvisation: A Theory at the Computational Level." In *Representing Musical Structures*. P. Howell, R. West and I. Cross, eds. Academic Press. 291-325.

Jones, K. 1981. "Compositional Applications of Stochastic Processes." *Computer Music Journal* 5(2): 45-61.

———. 1995. "The Algorithmic Muse: New Listening Paradigms and the Harmonies of Chaos." In *Proceedings of the International Computer Music Conference*. San Francisco: International Computer Music Association. 19-22.

Kalay, V. E. 2004. *Architecture's New Media: Principles, Theories, and Methods of Computer-Aided Design*. Cambridge: The MIT Press.

Karplus, K. and A. Strong. 1983. "Digital Synthesis of Plucked-String and Drum Timbres." *Computer Music Journal* 7(2): 43-55.

Kippen, J. and B. Bel. 1989. "The Identification and Modelling of a Percussion 'language', and the Emergence of Musical Concepts in a Machine-Learning Experimental Set-Up." *Computers and the Humanities* 23: 199-214.

———. 1992. "Modeling Music with Grammars: Formal Language Representation in the Bol Processor." In *Computer Representations and Models in Music*. A. Marsden and A. Pople, eds. London: Academic Press. 367-400.

———. 1994. "Computers, Composition and the Challange of 'New Music' in Modern India." *Leonardo Music Journal* 4: 79-84.

Kirsch, J. L. and R. A. Kirsch. 1988. "The Anatomy of Painting Style: Description with Computer Rules." *Leonardo* 21(4): 437-444.

Klein, M. L. 1957. "Syncopation in Automation." *Radio-Electronics* 36.

Knight, T. W. 1989. "The generation of Hepplewhite-style chair back designs." *Environment and Planning B: Planning and Design* 7: 227-238.

Knowlton, K. C. 1968. "Computer-animated movies." In *Cybernetic Serendipity*. J. Reichardt, ed. London: Studio International, W. & J. Mackay. 67-68.

Koenig, G. M. 1970a. "Project One." In *Electronic Music Report*. Utrecht: Institute of Sonology. 2: 32-46.

———. 1970b. "Project Two - A Programme for Musical Composition." In *Electronic Music Report*. Utrecht: Institute of Sonology. 3.

———. 1971a. *Summary Observations on Compositional Theory*. Utrecht: Institute of Sonology.

———. 1971b. "The Use of Computer Programs in Creating Music." In *Music and Technology (Proceedings of the Stockholm Meeting organized by UNESCO)*. Paris: La Revue Musicale. 93-115.

———. 1979. *PROTOCOL: A Report of the 1974/75 Class in Programmed Music at the Institute of Sonology*. Utrecht: Institute of Sonology, University of Utrecht.

———. 1980a. "Composition Processes." In *UNESCO Computer Music: Report on an internationl project including the international workshop held at Aarhus, Denmark in 1978*. M. Battier and B. Truax, eds. Canadian Commission for UNESCO. 105-126.

———. 1980b. *PRIXM Manual*. Utrecht: Institute of Sonology, University of Utrecht.

———. 1983. "Aesthetic Integration of Computer-Composed Scores." *Computer Music Journal* 7(4): 27-32.

———. 1999. "PROJECT 1 Revisited: On the Analysis and Interpretation of PR1 Tables." In *Otto Laske: Navigating New Musical Horizons*. J. Tabor, ed. Westport: Greenwood Press. 53-72.

———. 2005a. Personal correspondence. 24 March 2005.

———. 2005b. Personal correspondence. 26 May 2005.

Koning, H. and J. Eizenburg. 1981. "The Language of the Prairie: Frank Lloyd Wright's Prairie Houses." *Environment and Planning B: Planning and Design* 8: 295-323.

Kornfeld, W. 1980. "Machine Tongues VII: LISP." *Computer Music Journal* 4(2): 6-12.

Kuehn, M. 2001. "The nGen Manual." Internet: http://mustec.bgsu.edu/~mkuehn/ngen/man/ngenman.htm.

Kugel, P. 1990. "Myhill's Thesis: There's More than Computing in Musical Thinking." *Computer Music Journal* 14(3): 12-25.

———. 1992. "Beyond Computational Musicology." In *Understanding Music with AI: Perspectives on Music Cognition*. M. Balaban, K. Ebcioglu and O. E. Laske, eds. Cambridge: AAAI Press / MIT Press. 31-48.

———. 2002. "Computers Can't Be Intelligent (...and Turing Said So)." *Minds and Machines* 12(4): 563-579.

König, H. G. 1992. "The Planar Architecture of Juan Gris." *Languages of Design* 1: 51-74.

Langston, P. S. 1991. "IMG/1: An incidental music generator." *Computer Music Journal* 15(1): 28-39.

Laske, O. 1973a. "In Search of a Generative Grammar for Music." *Perspectives of New Music* 12(1): 351-378.

———. 1973b. "Toward a Musical Intelligence System: OBSERVER." *Numus West* 4: 11-16.

———. 1981. "Composition Theory in Koenig's Project One and Project Two." *Computer Music Journal* 5(4).

———. 1988. "Introduction to Cognitive Musicology." *Computer Music Journal* 12(1): 43-57.

———. 1989. "Composition Theory: An Enrichment of Music Theory." *Interface* 18(1-2): 45-59.

———. 1990. "The Computer as the Artist's Alter Ego." *Leonardo* 23(1): 53-66.

———. 1991. "Toward an Epistemology of Composition." *Interface* 20(3-4): 235-269.

———. 1992a. "Artificial Intelligence and Music: A Cornerstone of Cognitive Musicology." In *Understanding Music with AI: Perspectives on Music Cognition*. M. Balaban, K. Ebcioglu and O. E. Laske, eds. Cambridge: AAAI Press / MIT Press. 3-28.

————. 1992b. "The OBSERVER Tradition of Knowledge Acquisition." In *Understanding Music with AI: Perspectives on Music Cognition*. M. Balaban, K. Ebcioglu and O. E. Laske, eds. Cambridge: AAAI Press / MIT Press. 259-289.

————. 1993. "What is Composition Theory?." In *Proceedings of the International Computer Music Conference*. San Francisco: International Computer Music Association. 28-30.

Laurson, M. and J. Duthen. 1989. "PatchWork, a Graphical Language in PreForm." In *Proceedings of the International Computer Music Conference*. San Francisco: International Computer Music Association. 172-173.

Laurson, M. 1996. *Patchwork*. Helsinki: Sibelius Academy.

Laurson, M. and M. Kuuskankare. 2002. "PWGL: A Novel Visual Language based on Common Lisp, CLOS, and OpenGL." In *Proceedings of the International Computer Music Conference*. San Francisco: International Computer Music Association. 142-145.

————. 2003. "Some Box Design Issues in PWGL." In *Proceedings of the International Computer Music Conference*. San Francisco: International Computer Music Association. 271-274.

Lauzanna, R. G. and L. Pocock-Williams. 1988. "A Rule System for Analysis in the Visual Arts." *Leonardo* 21(4): 445-452.

Leach, J. and J. Fitch. 1995. "Nature, Music, and Algorithmic Composition." *Computer Music Journal* 19(2): 23-33.

Lerdahl, F. and R. Jackendoff. 1983. *A Generative Theory of Tonal Music*. Cambridge: MIT Press.

Levitt, D. 1981. *A melody description system for jazz improvisation*. M.S. Thesis, MIT Department of Electrical Engineering and Computer Science, Cambridge.

Lewin, D. 1987. *Generalized Musical Intervals and Transformations*. New Haven: Yale University Press.

Lewis, J. P. 1989. "Algorithms for music composition by neural nets: Improved CBR paradigms." In *Proceedings of the International Computer Music Conference*. San Francisco: International Computer Music Association. 180-183.

———. 1991. "Creation by refinement and the problem of algorithmic music composition." In *Music and Connectionism*. P. Todd and D. G. Loy, eds. Cambridge: MIT Press. 212-228.

Little, D. 1993. "Composing with Chaos: Applications of a New Science for Music." *Interface* 22(1): 23-51.

Lovelace, Countess of. 1842. "Translator's notes to an article on Babbage's Analytical Engine." In *Scientific Memoirs*. R. Taylor, ed. 3: 691-731.

Loy, D. G. 1989. "Composing with Computers: a Survey of Some Compositional Formalisms and Music Programming Languages." In *Current Directions in Computer Music Research*. M. V. Mathews and J. R. Pierce, eds. Cambridge: MIT Press. 291-396.

———. 1991. "Connectionism and Musiconomy." In *Proceedings of the International Computer Music Conference*. San Francisco: International Computer Music Association. 364-374.

Loy, D. G. and C. Abbott. 1985. "Programming Languages for Computer Music Synthesis, Performance, and Composition." *ACM Computing Surveys* 17(2).

Luening, O. 1975. "Origins." In *The Development and Practice of Electronic Music*. J. H. Appleton and R. C. Perera, eds. Englewood Cliffs: Prentice-Hall. 1-21.

Lundbeck, R. J. 2005a. Personal correspondence. 25 April 2005.

———. 2005b. Personal correspondence. 30 April 2005.

MacGregor, B. 2002. "Cybernetic serendipity revisited." In *Proceedings of the 4th conference on creativity & cognition*. New York: ACM Press. 11-13.

Mandelbrot, B. 1982. *The Fractal Geometry of Nature*. New York: W. H. Freeman.

Marino, G. and M. Serra, J. Raczinski. 1993. "The UPIC System: Origins and Innovations." *Perspectives of New Music* 31(1): 258-269.

Marino, G. 1990. "The New UPIC System." In *Proceedings of the International Computer Music Conference*. San Francisco: International Computer Music Association. 249-252.

Mathews, M. V. 1963. "The Digital Computer as a Musical Instrument." *Science* 142(3592): 553-557.

———. 1969. *The Technology of Computer Music*. Cambridge: MIT Press.

———. 2005. Personal correspondence. 24 May 2005.

Mathews, M. V. and J. E. Miller. 1965. "Pitch Quantizing for Computer Music." *Journal of the Acoustical Society of America* 38.

Mathews, M. V. and L. Rosler. 1968. "Graphical Language for the Scores of Computer-Generated Sounds." *Perspectives of New Music* 6(2): 92-118.

Matossian, N. 1986. *Xenakis*. London: Kahn & Averill.

McAlpine, K. and E. Miranda, S. Hoggar. 1999. "Making Music with Algorithms: A Case-Study." *Computer Music Journal* 23(2): 19-30.

McCarthy, J. 1959. "LISP: a programming system for symbolic manipulations ." In *Preprints of papers presented at the 14th national meeting of the Association for Computing Machinery*. New York: ACM Press. 1-4.

———. 1960. "Recursive Functions of Symbolic Expressions and Their Computation by Machine." *Communications of the ACM* 3(4): 184-195.

McCartney, J. 1996. "SuperCollider: a New Real Time Synthesis Language." In *Proceedings of the International Computer Music Conference*. San Francisco: International Computer Music Association.

———. 2002. "Rethinking the Computer Music Language." *Computer Music Journal* 26(4): 61-68.

McCracken, D. 1955. "Monte Carlo Method." *Scientific American* 192(5): 90-96.

McIntyre, R. A. 1994. "Bach in a Box: The Evolution of Four-Part Baroque Harmony Using the Genetic Algorithm." *Proceedings of the IEEE Conference on Evolutionary Computation* 14(3).

MIDI Manufacturers Association. 1983. "Musical Instrument Digital Interface Version 1.0 Detailed Specification." *MIDI Manufacturers Association*.

Miranda, E. R. 1993. "Cellular Automata Music: An Interdisciplinary Project." *Interface* 22: 3-21.

———. 2000a. *Composing Music With Computers*. Burlington: Focal Press.

———. 2000b. "Regarding Music, Machines, Intelligence and the Brain: An Introduction to Music and AI." In *Readings in Music and Artificial Intelligence*. E. R. Miranda, ed. Amsterdam: Harwood Academic Publishers. 1-13.

Moore, F. R. 1980. "The Futures of Music." *Perspectives of New Music* 19(1-2): 212-226.

Moorer, J. 1972. "Music and Computer Composition." *Communications of the ACM* 15(2): 104-113.

Morris, R. 1987. *Composition with Pitch Classes: A Theory of Compositional Design*. New Haven: Yale University Press.

Myhill, J. 1952. "Some Philosophical Implications of Mathematical Logic: Three Classes of Ideas." *Review of Metaphysics* 6(2): 165-198.

———. 1978. "Some Simplifications and Improvements in the Stochastic Music Program." In *Proceedings of the International Computer Music Conference*. San Francisco: International Computer Music Association. 272-317.

Nake, F. 1968. "Notes on the programming of computer graphics." In *Cybernetic Serendipity*. J. Reichardt, ed. London: Studio International, W. & J. Mackay. 77-78.

Negroponte, N. 1970. *The Architecture Machine*. Cambridge: MIT Press.

Nelson, G. L. 1978. "Reflections on my Use of Computers in Composition." In *Proceedings of the International Computer Music Conference*. San Francisco: International Computer Music Association. 318-331.

Nettheim, N. 1992. "On the spectral Analysis of Melody." *Journal of New Music Research* 21: 135-148.

Noll, M. A. 1968. "A subjective comparison of Piet Mondrian's 'Composition with lines' 1917." In *Cybernetic Serendipity*. J. Reichardt, ed. London: Studio International, W. & J. Mackay. 74.

O'Beirne, T. H. 1968. "Music from paper tape." In *Cybernetic Serendipity*. J. Reichardt, ed. London: Studio International, W. & J. Mackay. 29-30.

Object Management Group. 2003. *OMG Unified Modeling Language Specification: Version 1.5*. Object Management Group.

Oliver Garfield Company. 1956. "New! A Machine that Composes Music." *Scientific American* 195(3): 262.

———. 1958. "Build 125 Computers at Home with GENIAC." *Astounding Science Fiction.*

Olson, H. F. and H. Belar. 1961. "Aid to Music Composition Employing a Random Probability System." *Journal of the Acoustical Society of America* 33(9): 1163-1170.

Oppenheim, D. V. 1986. "The Need for Essential Improvements in the Machine-Composer Interface used for the Composition of Electroacoustic Computer Music." In *Proceedings of the International Computer Music Conference.* San Francisco: International Computer Music Association. 443-445.

———. 1989. "Dmix: An Environment for Composition." In *Proceedings of the International Computer Music Conference.* San Francisco: International Computer Music Association. 226-233.

———. 1990. "QUILL: An interpreter for creating music-objects within the Dmix environment." In *Proceedings of the International Computer Music Association.* San Francisco: International Computer Music Association. 256-258.

———. 1991. "Towards a Better Software-Design for Supporting Creative Musical Activity (CMA)." In *Proceedings of the International Computer Music Conference.* San Francisco: International Computer Music Association. 380-387.

———. 1994. "Slappability: A New Metaphor for Human Computer Interaction." In *Music Education: An Artificial Intelligence Approach.* M. Smith, ed. London: Springer Verlag. 92-107.

Ord-Hume, A. W. J. G. 1983. "Coggs and Crochets: A View of Mechanical Music." *Early Music* 11(2): 167-171.

———. 1987. "Hydraulic Automatic Organs." *Music & Automata* 9: 2-13.

Pachet, F. 2000. "Computer Analysis of Jazz Chord Sequence: is Solar A Blues." In *Readings in Music and Artificial Intelligence*. E. R. Miranda, ed. Amsterdam: Harwood Academic Publishers. 85-113.

Padberg, M. H. A. 1964. *Computer-Composed Canon and Free Fugue*. Ph.D. Dissertation, St. Louis University.

Papadopoulos, G. and G. Wiggins. 1998. "A Genetic Algorithm for the Generation of Jazz Melodies." *STeP'98*.

Papworth, D. G. 1960. "Computers and change-ringing." *The Computer Journal* 3(1): 47-50.

Penneycook, B. and D. R. Stammen, D. Reynolds. 1993. "Toward a Computer Model of a Jazz Improviser." In *Proceedings of the International Computer Music Conference*. San Francisco: International Computer Music Association. 228-231.

Pennycook, B. W. 1985. "Computer Music Interfaces: A Survey." In *ACM Computing Surveys*. New York: ACM Press. 17(2): 267-289.

Pierce, J. R. 1950. "Science for Art's Sake." *Astounding Science Fiction*.

———. 1956. *Electrons, Waves and Messages*. Garden City, New York: Hanover House.

———. 1961. *Symbols, Signals and Noise: The Nature and Process of Communication*. New York: Harper.

Pinkerton, R. C. 1956. "Information Theory and Melody." *Scientific American* 194(2): 77-86.

Polansky, L. and P. Burk, D. Rosenboom. 1990. "HMSL (Hierarchical Music Specification Language): A Theoretical Overview." *Perspectives of New Music* 28(1-2): 136-178.

Polansky, L. and D. Rosenboom. 1985. "HMSL." In *Proceedings of the International Computer Music Conference*. San Francisco: International Computer Music Association. 243-250.

Pope, S. T. 1987. "A Smalltalk-80-based Music Toolkit." In *Proceedings of the International Computer Music Conference*. San Francisco: International Computer Music Association. 8.

————. 1989. "Modeling Musical Structures as EventGenerators." In *Proceedings of the International Computer Music Conference*. San Francisco: International Computer Music Association. 249-252.

————. 1991. "A Tool for Manipulating Expressive and Structural Hierarchies in Music (or: T-R Trees in the MODE: A Tree Editor Based Loosely on Fred's Theory)." In *Proceedings of the International Computer Music Conference*. International Computer Music Association. 324-327.

————. 1992. "The Smoke Music Representation, Description Language, and Interchange Format." In *Proceedings of the International Computer Music Conference*. San Francisco: International Computer Music Association.

————. 1993. "Music Composition and Editing by Computer." In *Music Processing*. G. Haus, ed. Oxford: Oxford University Press. 25-72.

————. 1995. "Fifteen Years of Computer Assisted Composition." *Proceedings of the Second Brazilian Symposium on Computer Music* 6.

————. 1996. "Object-oriented music representation." *Organised Sound* 1(1): 56-68.

Pressing, J. 1994. "Novelty, Progress and Research Method in Computer Music Composition." In *Proceedings of the International Computer Music Conference*. San Francisco: International Computer Music Association. 27-30.

Puckette, M. 1991. "Combining Event and Signal Processing in the MAX Graphical

    Programming Environment." *Computer Music Journal* 15(3): 68-77.

————. 1997. "Pure Data." In *Proceedings of the International Computer Music Conference*. San

    Francisco: International Computer Music Association. 224-227.

————. 2002. "Max at 17." *Computer Music Journal* 26(4): 31-43.

Putnam, H. 1965. "Trial-and-Error Predicates and the Solution to a Problem of Mostowski."

    Journal of Symbolic Logic 30(1): 49-57.

Quastler, H. 1955. "Discussion, following Mathematical theory of word formation, by W.

    Fucks." In *Information Theory: Third London Symposium*. E. C. Cherry, ed. New York:

    Academic Press. 168.

Rader, G. 1973. *An algorithm for the automatic composition of simple forms of music based on a variation*

    of formal grammars: Moore School of Electrical Engineering music report. Philadelphia: University

    of Pennsylvania.

Rahn, J. 1980. *Basic Atonal Theory*. NY: MacMillan.

————. 1990a. "The Lisp Kernel: A Portable Software Environment for Composition."

    Computer Music Journal 14(4): 42-64.

————. 1990b. "Processing Musical Abstraction: Remarks on LISP, the NeXT, and the

    Future of Musical Computing." *Perspectives of New Music* 28(1): 180-191.

Ramalho, G. and J. Ganascia. 1994. "Simulating Creativity in Jazz Performance." In *Proceeding*

    of the 12th AAAI Conference. 108-113.

Raymond, E. S. 2001. *The Cathedral & The Bazaar*. New York: O'Reilly.

Reichardt, J. 1968. *Cybernetic Serendipity: The computer and the arts*. London: Studio International, W. & J. Mackay.

Reitman, W. R. 1960. "Information Processing Languages and Heuristic Programming." In *Bionics Symposium (WADD Technical Report 60-600)*. Ohio: Wright-Patterson Air Force Base, Directorate of Advanced Systems Technology. 410.

Rittel, H. and M. Webber. 1984. "Planning Problems are Wicked Problems." In *Developments in Design Methodology*. N. Cross, ed. Chichester: Wiley.

Roads, C. 1977. "Composing Grammars." In *Proceedings of the International Computer Music Conference*. San Francisco: International Computer Music Association. 26-30.

———. 1984. "An Overview of Music Representations." In *Musical Grammars and Computer Analysis*. Firenze: Leo S. Olschki. 7-37.

———. 1985. "Research in music and artificial intelligence." In *ACM Computing Surveys*. New York: ACM Press. 17(2): 163-190.

———. 1996. *The Computer Music Tutorial*. Cambridge: MIT Press.

———. 2002. *Microsound*. Cambridge: MIT Press.

Rodet, X. and P. Cointe. 1984. "FORMES: Composition and Scheduling of Processes." *Computer Music Journal* 8(3): 32-48.

Rogers, J. E. 1975. "The Uses of Digital Computers in Electronic Music Generation." In *The Development and Practice of Electronic Music*. J. H. Appleton and R. C. Perera, eds. Englewood Cliffs: Prentice-Hall. 189-285.

Rollo, J. 1995. "Triangle and t-square: the windows of Frank Lloyd Wright." *Environment and Planning B: Planning and Design* 22: 75-92.

Rossum, G. van. 1996. "Foreward for 'Programming Python' (1st ed.)." In *Programming Python*. M. Lutz, ed. New York: O'Reilly.

Rothgeb, J. 1968. "Harmonizing the Unfigured Bass: A Computational Study." *Ph.D. dissertation, Yale University*.

———. 1980. "Simulating Musical Skills by Digital Computer." *Computer Music Journal* 4(2).

Rowe, R. 1992. "Machine Listening and Composing with Cypher." *Computer Music Journal* 16(1): 43-63.

———. 1993. *Interactive Music Systems: Machine Listening and Composing*. Cambridge: MIT Press.

———. 2000. "Interactive Music Systems in Ensemble Performance." In *Readings in Music and Artificial Intelligence*. E. R. Miranda, ed. Amsterdam: Harwood Academic Publishers. 145-161.

Russcol, H. 1972. *The Liberation of Sound: An Introduction to Electronic Music*. London: Prentice-Hall International.

Saint-Lambert, M. de. 1707. *Nouveau traité de l'accompagnement du Clavecin*. Paris.

Scaletti, C. 1987. "KYMA: An Object Orientated Language for Musical Composition." In *Proceedings of the International Computer Music Conference*. San Francisco: International Computer Music Association. 49-56.

———. 1989a. "Composing Sound Objects in KYMA." *Perspectives of New Music* 27(1): 42-69.

———. 1989b. "The Kyma/Platypus Computer Music Workstation." *Computer Music Journal* 13(2): 23-38.

———. 2002. "Computer Music Languages, Kyma, and the Future." *Computer Music Journal* 26(4): 69-82.

Scaletti, C. and R. E. Johnson. 1988. "An Interactive environment for object-oriented music composition and sound synthesis." In *Conference proceedings on Object-oriented programming systems, languages and applications.* New York: ACM Press. 222-233.

Schaeffer, P. 1970. "Music and Computers." In *Music and Technology (Proceedings of the Stockholm Meeting organized by UNESCO).* Paris: La Revue Musicale. 57-92.

Schillinger, J. 1941. *The Schillinger System of Musical Composition.* New York: Carl Fischer.

———. 1948. *The Mathematical Basis of the Arts.* New York: Carl Fischer.

Schottstaedt, W. 1983. "Pla: A Composer's Idea of a Language." *Computer Music Journal* 7(1): 11-20.

———. 1989a. "Automatic Counterpoint." In *Current Directions in Computer Music Research.* M. V. Mathews and J. R. Pierce, eds. Cambridge: MIT Press. 199-214.

———. 1989b. "A Computer Music Language." In *Current Directions in Computer Music Research.* M. V. Mathews and J. R. Pierce, eds. Cambridge: MIT Press. 215-224.

Schwartz, J. T. and R. Dewar, E. Dubinsky, E. Schonberg. 1986. *Programming with Sets: An Introduction to SETL.* New York: Springer Verlag.

Schweppe, J. 1989. *Research Aan Het Ij: LBPMA 1914 - KSLA 1989.* Baarn: Shell Research / Market Books.

Seirup, J. 1973. "TR4P4, A Fortran Program Dealing with the Computer Simulation of Traditional Four-Part Harmony." *Techniucal Reports from SUNY at Buffalo.*

Selfridge-Field, E. 1997a. "Beyond Codes: Issues in Musical Representation." In *Beyond MIDI: the Handbook of Musical Codes*. E. Selfridge-Field, ed. Cambrdige: MIT Press. 565-572.

———. 1997b. "Introduction: Describing Musical Information." In *Beyond MIDI: the Handbook of Musical Codes*. E. Selfridge-Field, ed. Cambrdige: MIT Press. 3-38.

Severo, R. 1982. "Composers Program Sense of Humanity into Computer Music." *New York Times* March 23: 22-C3.

Shannon, C. E. 1948. "A Mathematical Theory of Communication." *Bell Systems Technical Journal* 27: 379-423, 623-656.

Shannon, C. E. and W. Weaver. 1949. *A Mathematical Theory of Communication*. Urbana: University of Illinois Press.

Simoni, M. 2003. *Algorithmic Composition: A Gentle Introduction to Music Composition Using Common LISP and Common Music*. Ann Arbor: Scholarly Publishing Office, the University of Michigan University Library.

Skinner, R. J. 1976. "Technological Determinism: A Critique of Convergence Theory." *Comparative Studies in Society and History* 18(1): 2-27.

Smalley, D. 1986. "Spectro-Morphology and Structuring Processes." In *The Language of Electroacoustic Music*. S. Emmerson, ed. London: Macmillan Press. 61-93.

Smith, B. 2000. "Artificial Intelligence and Music Education." In *Readings in Music and Artificial Intelligence*. E. R. Miranda, ed. Amsterdam: Harwood Academic Publishers. 221-237.

Smith, L. 1972. "SCORE — A Musician's Approach to Computer Music." *Journal of the Audio Engineering Society* 20(1): 7-14.

Smoliar, S. 1967a. "Euterpe-Lisp: A Lisp System with Music Output." In *Artificial Intelligence Memo*. Cambridge: Artificial Intelligence Laboratory, Massachusetts Institute of Technology. 141.

———. 1967b. "Euterpe: A Computer Language for the Expression of Musical Ideas." In *Artificial Intelligence Memo*. Cambridge: Artificial Intelligence Laboratory, Massachusetts Institute of Technology. 129.

———. 1979. "Computer Aid for Schenkerian Analysis." In *Proceedings of the 1979 Annual Conference*. ACM Press. 110-115.

———. 1980. "A Computer Aide for Schenkerian Analysis." *Computer Music Journal* 4(2): 41-59.

Sowa, J. F. 1957. "A machine to compose music." In *Geniac Manual*. New York: Oliver Garfield Company.

———. 2005. Personal correspondence. 25 July 2005.

Spiegel, L. 1986. "Music Mouse — An Intelligent Instrument." Internet: http://retiary.org/ls/programs.html.

———. 1989. "Distinguishing Random, Algorithmic, and Intelligent Music." Internet: http://retiary.org/ls/writings/alg_comp_ltr_to_cem.html.

Steedman, M. J. 1984. "A Generative Grammar for Jazz Chord Sequences." *Music Perception* 2(1): 53-77.

Stiny, G. 1977. "Ice-ray: a note on Chinese lattice designs." *Environment and Planning B: Planning and Design* 4: 89-98.

Stiny, G. and J. Gips. 1972. "Shape Grammars and the Generative Specification of Painting and Sculpture." In *Information Processing 71*. C. V. Freiman, ed. Amsterdam: North Holland. 1460-1465.

———. 1978. *Algorithmic Aesthetics*. Berkeley: University of California Press.

Stone, K. 1980. *Music Notation in the Twentieth Century*. New York: W. W. Norton.

Strang, G. 1970. "Ethics and Esthetics of Computer Composition." In *The Computer and Music*. H. B. Lincoln, ed. Ithaca: Cornell University Press. 37-41.

Straus, J. N. 2003. "Uniformity, Balance, and Smoothness in Atonal Voice Leading." *Music Theory Spectrum* 25(2): 305-352.

Struycken, P. 1975. *LINARC*. Utrecht: Institute of Sonology.

Struycken, P. and R. H. Fuchs, S. Tempelaars. 1970. "Peter Struycken: Computer Structures 1969." In *Electronic Music Reports*. Utrecht: Institute of Sonology. 2: 45-60.

Supper, M. 2001. "A Few Remarks on Algorithmic Composition." *Computer Music Journal* 25(1): 48-53.

Swift, J. 2003. *Gulliver's Travels*. New York: Penguin Books.

Sychra, A. 1964. "Hudba a Kybernetika." *Nové Cesty Hudby* 1: 234.

Taube, H. 1989. "Common Music: A Compositional Language in Common Lisp and CLOS." In *Proceedings of the International Computer Music Conference*. San Francisco: International Computer Music Association. 316-319.

———. 1991. "Common Music: A Music Composition Language in Common Lisp and CLOS." *Computer Music Journal* 15(2): 21-32.

———. 1996. "Composing in Common Music and Stella." In *KlangArt-Kongreß 1993: Neue Musiktechnologie II*. B. Enders, ed. Mainz, Germany: Schott. 86-98.

———. 1997. "An Introduction to Common Music." *Computer Music Journal* 21(1): 29-34.

———. 2004. *Notes from the Metalevel: An Introduction to Computer Composition*. Amsterdam: Swets & Zeitlinger Publishing.

Tenney, J. 1963. "Sound Generation by Means of a Digital Computer." *Journal of Music Theory* 7(1): 24-70.

———. 1966. "Musical Composition with the Computer (Abstract from the 71st Meeting of the Acoustical Society of America)." *Journal of the Acoustical Society of America* 39(6): 1245.

———. 1969. "Computer Music Experiments." In *Electronic Music Report*. Utrecht: Institute of Sonology. 1: 23-60.

Thomas, M. T. 1985. "VIVACE: A Rule-Based AI System for Composition." In *Proceedings of the International Computer Music Conference*. San Francisco: International Computer Music Association. 267-274.

Tipei, S. 1975. "MP1 — a Computer Program for Music Composition." In *Proceedings of the Second Annual Music Computation Conference*. J. Beauchamp and J. Melby, eds. Urbana, Illinois: Office of Continuing Education and Public Service in Music. 68-82.

———. 1987. "Maiden Voyages: A Score Produced with MP1." *Computer Music Journal* 11(2): 49-64.

———. 1989. "Manifold Compositions: A (Super)Computer-Assisted Composition Experiment in Progress." In *Proceedings of the International Computer Music Conference*. San Francisco: International Computer Music Association. 324-327.

————. 1994. "MP1 Revisited - AGA MATTER, for Piano and Computer Generated
Tape." In *Proceedings of the International Computer Music Conference*. San Francisco:
International Computer Music Association. 3-6.

Toiviainen, P. 1995. "Modeling the target-note technique of bebop-style jazz improvisation:
An artificial neural network approach." *Music Perception* 12(4): 399-413.

Toop, D. 2002. "Humans, Are They Really Necessary? Sound Art, Automata and Musical
Sculpture." In *Undercurrents: The Hidden Wiring of Modern Music*. London: Continuum.
117-129.

Truax, B. 1973. "The Computer Composition — Sound Synthesis Programs POD4, POD5
and POD6." In *Sonological Reports*. Utrecht: Institute of Sonology. 2: 57.

————. 1976. "A Communicational Approach to Computer Sound Programs." *Journal of
Music Theory* 20(2): 227-300.

————. 1999. "Sonology: A Questionable Science Revisited." In *Otto Laske: Navigating New
Musical Horizons*. J. Tabor, ed. Westport: Greenwood Press. 21-36.

Tzara, T. 1981. *Seven Dada Manifestos and Lampisteries*. Translated by B. Wright. London:
Calder Publications.

Ulrich, W. 1977. "The analysis and synthesis of jazz by computer." In *Proceedings of the 5th
International Joint Conference on Artificial Intelligence*. Los Altos: Morgan Kaufman.

Vaggione, H. 2001. "Some Ontological Remarks about Music Composition Processes."
Computer Music Journal 25(1): 54-61.

Varèse, E. 2004. "The Liberation of Sound." In *Audio Culture: Readings in Modern Music*. C.
Cox and D. Warner, eds. New York: Continuum. 17-21.

Voss, R. F. and J. Clarke. 1975. "1/f Noise in Music and Speech." *Nature* 258: 317-318.

————. 1978. "1/f Noise in Music: Music from 1/f Noise." *Journal of the Acoustical Society of America* 63(1): 258-263.

Weeks, J. 1968. "Indeterminate dimensions in architecture." In *Cybernetic Serendipity*. J. Reichardt, ed. London: Studio International, W. & J. Mackay. 69.

West, B. J. and M. F. Schlesinger. 1990. "The Noise in Natural Phenomena." *American Scientist* 78: 40-45.

Wiener, N. 1948. *Cybernetics*. Cambridge: MIT Press.

Winkler, T. 1998. *Composing Interactive Music*. Cambridge: MIT Press.

Winograd, T. 1979. "Beyond Programming Languages." *Communications of the ACM* 22(7): 391-401.

Worthy, R. M. 1962. "A new American poet speaks: The works of A[uto] B[eatnik]." *Horizon* 4(3): 96-99.

Xenakis, I. 1955. "La crise de la musique sèrielle." *Gravesaner Blätter* 1.

————. 1965. "Free Stochastic Music from the Computer. Programme of Stochastic music in Fortran." *Gravesaner Blätter* 26.

————. 1966. "The Origins of Stochastic Music." *Tempo* 78: 9-12.

————. 1985. "Music Composition Treks." In *Composers and the Computer*. C. Roads, ed. Los Altos: William Kaufmann, Inc.

————. 1992. *Formalized Music: Thought and Mathematics in Music*. Indiana: Indiana University Press.

————. 1996. "Determinacy and Indeterminacy." *Organised Sound* 1(3): 143-155.

Yi, S. 2005. "blue: A Music Composition Environment for Csound." Internet: http://csounds.com/stevenyi/blue/blueDocs/index.html.

Youngblood, J. E. 1958. "Style as Information." *Journal of Music Theory* 2(24).

Zaripov, R. 1963. *Kibernetika i muzyka*. Moscow: Izd. Znanie.

———. 1969. "Cybernetics and Music." *Perspectives of New Music* 7(2): 115-154.

Zicarelli, D. 1987. "M and Jam Factory." *Computer Music Journal* 11(4): 13-29.

www.ingramcontent.com/pod-product-compliance
Lightning Source LLC
Chambersburg PA
CBHW060920060326
40690CB00041B/2809